MARION LANGHAM Ltd
Paperweights

http://www.ladyma...
http://www.ladymarion...

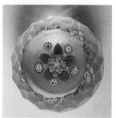

For further details contact Marion Langham
Claranagh, Tempo, Co Fermanagh BT94 3FJ. Tel: 028895 41247. Fax: 028895 41690
Email: paperweights@ladymarion.co.uk

Andrew Lineham Fine Glass
THE MALL, CAMDEN PASSAGE, LONDON N1 8ED

ALL GOOD CONTINENTAL AND ENGLISH COLOURED GLASS BOUGHT AND SOLD
VALUATIONS FOR INSURANCE, PROBATE OR DIVISION

Open: Wednesday 8am-3pm
Saturday 10.30am-4pm or by appointment
Website: http://www.AndrewLineham.co.uk

Tel/Fax: 01243 576241 anytime
0207 704 0195 Mobile: 07767 702 722
Email: Andrew@AndrewLineham.co.uk

MILLER'S glass

MILLER'S

glass

JEANETTE HAYHURST CONSULTANT

ART INSTITUTE OF ATLANTA LIBRARY
6600 PEACHTREE DUNWOODY RD.
100 EMBASSY ROW
ATLANTA, GA 30328

MILLER'S GLASS BUYER'S GUIDE

Created and designed by
Miller's
The Cellars, High Street
Tenterden, Kent, TN30 6BN
Tel: 01580 766411
Fax: 01580 766100

Consultant Editor: Jeanette Hayhurst
Project Editor: Carol Gillings
Production Co-ordinator: Kari Reeves
Editorial Assistants: Caroline Bugeja, Rosemary Cooke,
Lalage Johnstone
Production Assistants: Elaine Burrell, Gillian Charles
Advertising Executive: Jill Jackson
Advertising Assistants: Jo Hill, Melinda Williams
Designer: Philip Hannath
Advertisement Designer: Simon Cook
Production Controller: Catherine Lay
Jacket Design: Colin Goody
Indexer: Hilary Bird
Additional Photographers: Ian Booth, Robin Saker

First published in Great Britain in 2001
by Miller's, a division of Mitchell Beazley,
imprints of Octopus Publishing Group Ltd,
2–4 Heron Quays, London E14 4JP

© 2001 Octopus Publishing Group Ltd

A CIP catalogue record for this book is
available from the British Library

ISBN 1-84000-361-8

All rights reserved. No part of this work
may be produced or utilised in any form
or by any means, electronic or mechanical,
including photocopying, recording or by
any information storage and retrieval system,
without the prior written permission
of the Publishers

While every care has been exercised in the
compilation of this guide, neither the
authors nor publishers accept any liability
for any financial or other loss incurred
by reliance placed on the information
contained in
Miller's Glass Buyers Guide

Some images have appeared in previous editions of
Miller's Antiques Price Guide and *Miller's Collectables Price Guide*

Scanning and Film output: CK Litho Ltd, Whitstable, Kent
Colour origination: Pica Colour Separation Overseas Pte Ltd, Singapore
Printed and bound by Toppan Printing Co (HK) Ltd, China

Miller's is a registered trademark of
Octopus Publishing Group Ltd

Contents

SPECIAL FEATURES

Acknowledgements

The publishers would like to acknowledge the great assistance given by our consultants. We would also like to extend our thanks to all auction houses and their press offices, as well as dealers and collectors, who have assisted us in the production of this book.

Christine Bridge has run a successful antiques business for the past twenty-eight years. She specializes in 18th century English collectors' glass and 19th century coloured glass. She has a strong following amongst the trade, collectors and museums, and has exported her items all over the world. She regularly exhibits at the BADA and Olympia fairs and in Tokyo, USA, Belgium and Australia. Christine Bridge Antiques is a registered member of LAPADA, CINOA and BADA, the Associations of Art and Antique Dealers, all of whom have a strict code of practice regarding the integrity of their members, their experience and knowledge of their subject.

Lynda Brine was born and raised in Bath, where she still lives. She is a joint partner of the Assembly Antiques Centre, 5–8 Saville Row, Bath, BA1 2QP, where she specializes in buying and selling perfume bottles, *objects de virtue*, and also provides a valuation service. Clients range from beginners to enthusiasts with large collections. She is co-author of *Scent Bottles Through The Ages*, published in 1998, and consultant for Miller's *Perfume Bottles: A Collector's Guide* in 1999, and has appeared on television programmes about the subject. A supporter of the International Perfume Bottle Association (IPBA). She can be contacted on: Tel: 01225 448488 Fax: 01225 429661 Email: info@ukpbcc.co.uk Website: www.ukpbcc.co.uk

Peter Card's fascination for quality glass mascots began in the early 1970's, when quality items were easily found in the Portobello Road, and similar market places. Since then he has handled most variants of both glass and metal car mascots, and now uses that experience to write books about the early days of motoring, and has appeared on television with his collections. He has three daughters, and is employed by a major London-based auction house.

Margaret Crawley opened Chislehurst Antiques in 1979, dealing initially in Georgian and Victorian furniture. Some ten years ago she decided to specialize in lighting, and that has become a major feature of the business over the last decade. Chislehurst Antiques regularly exhibits at the LAPADA fairs and at Olympia, and Margaret is on the vetting committee for the NEC antiques fairs.

Jeanette Hayhurst started her career in antiques at Sotheby's where she worked as a photographer for eleven years. She began collecting glass in the 1970s and in 1980 became a glass dealer. Since 1986 she has owned a shop specializing in fine glass in Kensington Church Street, west London, a favourite haunt of antiques collectors.

Lin Holroyd has been dealing in glass for seventeen years. Her interest is largely Victorian decorative glass, from UK sources, and she has customers worldwide. Lin's stand can be found at many of the major fairs and exhibitions in the UK.

Joy McCall, after graduating with a Masters in British Art History and Critical Theory from the University of Sussex, began employment with Bonhams auctioneers in 1996. Within six months she joined the Decorative Arts Department, where she remains, specializing primarily in applied arts from 1860–1950, with a particular emphasis on Art Nouveau and Art Deco. Bonhams & Brooks, 65–69 Lots Road, Chelsea, London SW10 ORN.

Anne Metcalfe deals solely in glass paperweights, from her private gallery in Helsby, Cheshire. Sweetbriar Gallery Limited has a knowledgeable staff of four. They deal worldwide, by post and at the Paperweight Conventions in the USA. Anne has written a book for Miller's entitled *Paperweights of the 19th and 20th Centuries: A Collectors Guide* in 2000.

Tim Osborne is Managing Director of the internationally-renowned firm of Delomosne & Son Limited. After joining the firm in 1973 and serving his apprenticeship, Tim was made a Director of the Company. He now maintains the firm's traditional association with the best academic institutions and advises museums in Great Britain and the USA on conservation matters and purchases. He also advises collectors around the world on new acquisitions and how best to develop their collections. Tim Osborne serves on vetting committees for glass at leading British antiques fairs.

Alan Sedgwick's interest in Carnival glass arose as a result of his being given a piece by his grandmother, when setting up his first home. Some years later a second piece was added after finding a collection in the Reading Antique Centre. A third piece, given to him as a Christmas present the following year, set him off on the road to full-time collecting, and then dealing, in this beautiful glass.

Joscelyn Vereker has been in the antiques trade since 1983 when she started as a general dealer in Shrewsbury. A love of glass soon took over and she has specialized in glass since 1986, dealing mainly in table glass of the 18th and 19th centuries. Joscelyn now trades from the Arbras Gallery at 292 Westbourne Grove, Portobello.

Brian Watson started dealing in antique glass in 1991 having privately collected for about twenty years. He deals mainly in 18th and 19th century English drinking glasses, although he has other interesting glass objects. Apart from traditional collectors' glass, he has a particular interest in 19th century coloured drinking glasses, and has been researching with a view to classifying and dating patterns. He does not have a showroom, but deals from major antiques fairs including the London LAPADA Fair, the Chelsea Antiques Fair and Antiques for Everyone at the NEC in Birmingham. Despite being based in the United Kingdom he has customers from many other parts of the world including Europe, the USA and Australia.

General Information

The earliest date to which glass can be traced is around 3000 BC. Early glass vessels were either cast in moulds or carved from solid blocks, and it was not until about 50 BC that the technique of blowing glass was discovered. This discovery led to a huge increase in production and, instead of being purely a luxury product, more everyday articles became available.

With the break-up of the Roman Empire in the 5th century AD European glassmaking declined. Venice eventually became the glass-making metropolis, under strict government control, until 1292 when production moved to the nearby island of Murano and remained there for three centuries from 1400 to 1700.

The Romans introduced glassmaking into Britain, mainly in the forested areas of Sussex and Surrey where the raw materials of sand and potash, and fuel for their furnaces, were readily available. The early products were mainly window glass and simple vessels. It was not until the late 16th century that, with government encouragement, foreign glassmakers settled in England. During the 17th century British glassmaking radically changed course, following the ban by James I on the use of wood as fuel for glass furnaces, and glassmakers were forced to move north where coal was readily available.

With the rise of Venice in the 15th century and the establishment of glass-making on the island of Murano, it was there that glass makers developed the highly-prized and valuable complicated latticinio (lacework), ice glass and wing stem goblets that were sometimes enamelled or diamond-point engraved.

The next major change in the industry was in 1676 with the development of **lead glass**. Discovered by George Ravenscroft, lead glass was stronger than the previously used fragile Venetian *cristallo*, with a brilliance similar to natural rock crystal. This was known in some quarters as **flint glass** because of the flint content in the earlier pieces, which was subsequently replaced with sand. A similar formula is still used today by the crystal glass industry and full lead crystal must, by law, contain over thirty percent lead oxide. Such innovations brought English glass to the forefront and the style was admired and imitated in other countries.

During the 19th century the use of glass became more innovative and was increasingly used in architecture, the Crystal Palace in London being the finest example, built using the traditional blown cylinder method in 1851 to house the Great Exhibition. The range of colours increased considerably during this period, most research being carried out in France and Bohemia, and by the time of the Great Exhibition several Birmingham and Stourbridge factories were exhibiting an extensive colour range including oriental blue, rose, cornelian and pearl opal.

The Venetian glass industry was revived in the 1860s, making historically-inspired glass. In the mid-20th century they turned to designers such as Carlo Scarpa for Venini, who was one of the inspirations for the bright vibrant glass that is so highly collected today.

Towards the end of the century, both American and English factories invented shaded glass and **ruby glass**, or **cranberry** as it is known in the USA, became very popular. A wealth of decorative techniques emerged during this period including **cased glass**, consisting of two or more layers of differently coloured glass, the outer layer being cut or engraved to reveal a different colour beneath. The Bohemians capitalized on their development of decorative cased, coloured cut and engraved goblets and vases.

Acid etching was an important new technique which involved glass being coated with an acid-resistant wax through which the design was drawn with a pointed tool. The glass was immersed in hydrofluoric acid that would eat through the revealed glass. This technique could then be repeated with a weaker solution of acid to produce beautiful effects.

Probably the most spectacular event of the era was the revival by John Northwood of the art of cameo glass, originally produced by the Romans. His first piece, which took three years to complete, was a replica of the Roman Portland Vase, and thus began an industry in Stourbridge that was to flourish until the outbreak of World War I.

During the late 19th century, many artists and designers began to take an interest in the creative possibilities of glass, the foremost being in France Emile Gallé, and in America Louis Comfort Tiffany. Their imaginative and creative use of glass has inspired glassmakers to the present day – items created by them will always be a good investment and a joy to behold.

Until recently, 17th- and 18th- century German glass went through a difficult time as so much came onto the market with the opening of the borders in Germany, but now prices are beginning to rise again.

Glass-blowing techniques changed little with the advent of mechanization, with the exception of a technique invented in America known as press-moulding, whereby molten glass was pressed into a metal mould and extracted as a finished item. This process enabled a four-fold increase in production and meant that glass became available to even the most humble household.

THE INGREDIENTS

Glass is a cooled liquid, the basic ingredient being silica, usually in the form of a fine sand, with the addition of alkaline fluxes such as soda or potash. The mixture of raw materials is called the **batch** and, according to the type of glass being made, includes other ingredients such as lime or lead oxide. Cullet, or broken glass, is also added to aid fusion. The finished glass is called the **metal**. There are a number of ways of colouring glass. Metal oxide can be added, the resultant colour depending on the amount used and the quality.

COLD DECORATION

Many decorative glass techniques have evolved, although there are five main forms:

Painting: Glass can be painted with either lacquer or oil paints, or more usually enamel paint. Lacquer and oils are often applied to the reverse of an object as they cannot be fired and will easily rub off. Enamel paints are mixed from finely ground glass with the addition of metallic oxides in an oily base, that are painted onto the surface and fired at a low temperature.

Gilding: Sometimes combined with other decorative techniques. Honey gilding involves painting with a mixture of gold and honey and firing it at a low temperature. Cold gilding is less durable because the gold leaf is mixed with oil and applied to the surface but not fired. A variation of this, popular in 18th-century Bohemia, involved a layer of gold or silver leaf sandwiched between two layers of glass.

Cutting: A technique where sharp-edged patterns are cut with tools into the surface of the glass, reflecting the light and making the item more brilliant.

Engraving: Tools are used to cut patterns into the surface of the glass, where the surface of a piece comprising two or more layers of different coloured glass is engraved to reveal the colours underneath, cameo glass being an example.

Acid etching: This technique involves covering the surface of the glass with an acid-resistant coating and engraving a design through the coating onto the glass. The item is then dipped in acid giving the exposed areas a frosted effect.

HOT DECORATION

Various forms of decoration, both applied and impressed, take place while the glass is still hot:

Trailing and combing: One of the earliest forms of decoration, this involves the application of thin rods of molten glass around the outside of the piece in a spiral effect. The **trails** can be combed into patterns and then **marvered**.

Pincering: This is a method of squeezing or nipping trails or other decorations to create a frilled edge.

Prunts: These are blobs of molten glass that are applied to the piece, usually found on the stems of drinking glasses.

FRIGGERS

One of the many traditions in the glassmaking industry is friggering, the making of a one-off decorative piece by a glassmaker or apprentice for his own amusement. Friggers are made in a multitude of forms such as birds, animals, tobacco pipes, trumpets, books, hats, swords and walking sticks, and give the glassmaker an opportunity to experiment and demonstrate his skills.

CARE & RESTORATION

Of course, glass needs to be handled with care, particularly ancient glass. However, handling and feeling are the best ways to learn about the different types. Some glass should not be over-handled, particularly ancient glass and glass that has become oxidized or patinated following a long period of burial, giving an iridescent effect. Never lift items by a handle which, if damaged, could come away from the body.

Damaged glass can be repaired by an expert, although repairs will affect the value. Some chips can be removed, usually by grinding, without altering an item's value. Missing pieces can be replaced but the value may be drastically affected. Look for joins that may indicate that a clean break has been repaired. Repairs should not be attempted at home – amateur restoration is invariably a disaster.

- Cleaning should be carried out in warm soapy water using a cloth or soft sponge. Dry gently with a soft cloth to avoid damage, but thoroughly to avoid water stains.
- Liquids left in vessels over a long period may leave deposits, or cause cloudiness that cannot be removed.
- When a piece has become cloudy on the inside it is important to have it professionally cleaned. The surface may have to be repolished but if the item is simply dirty household bleach is usually sufficient.
- Do not use bleach on enamelled or gilded glass.
- Never put antique glass in the dishwasher.

Today glass is produced in a huge variety of colours and shapes with seemingly endless uses, from decorative to household, architectural to car windows. Toughened glass is strong enough to withstand a tremendous impact and extremely high temperatures, and is about four times as strong as ordinary glass. Laminated glass, made with a strong flexible plastic sheet sandwiched between two layers of glass, is the basis of bulletproof glass. Fibre glass is used to reinforce plastics and other materials in car bodies, boat hulls and furniture, and is widely used in the form of glass wool for insulating pipes, buildings etc. The versatility of glass is seemingly limitless, yet the appeal that it holds for the collector is unique.

Don't throw away a fortune!
Invest in
Miller's Buyer's Guides

All illustrated with over 2,000 examples, each with a price range, plus information on how to buy and sell, restoration and market trends

Contact: **Beagle Direct, Collets House, Crane Close, Denington Road, Wellingborough, Northamptonshire NN8 2QT**

or telephone the Credit Card Hotline
(quoting reference W261) on:

01933 443863

Lines open from 9:00am to 5:00pm

Registered office: 2-4 Heron Quays, Docklands, London E14 4JP.
Registered in England, No.3597451

9

How to use this book

It is our aim to make this book easy to use. In order to find a particular item, consult the contents list on page 5 to find the main heading – for example, Drinking Glasses. Having located your area of interest, you will find that larger sections have been sub-divided. If you are looking for a particular factory, designer or craftsman, consult the index which starts on page 311.

GOBLETS & WINE GLASSES

A Venetian enamelled goblet, with everted rim, painted in pale blue and white with a band of dots, with faint traces of red enamel and gilding, late 16thC, 4½in (11.5cm) high.
£3,500–4,000 S

A *façon de Venise* drinking vessel, with everted rim, on a short hollow stem with shoulder and basal knops, late 16thC, 4in (10cm) high.
£1,250–1,500 C

A Venetian wine glass, with wide cup-shaped bowl, on a hollow slender tapering stem between collars, on a wide conical foot with folded rim, late 16thC, 4¾in (12cm) high.
£1,500–1,800 S

A Venetian yellow-tinted wine glass, with ribbed lower section and trailed band above, on an incised twisted openwork stem with blue-tinted C-scroll wings, flanked by collars, on a wide conical foot with folded rim, late 16thC, 6¾in (17cm) high.
£12,500–15,000 S

Glass

- Early lead glass has a greenish tinge, while later techniques produced progressively more transparent glass.
- Lead glass should emit a clear ring when tapped with a fingernail – BE CAREFUL!
- Coloured glass was not popular until c1850, when it was used to produce bottles, decanters and tumblers.
- Look for the pontil mark on the base of glass – it could have been polished off, but the mark will still be visible.
- The presence of a pontil mark alone is no guarantee of age.

A part lead wine glass, with a large funnel bowl, on a hollow short double knop stem with a wide folded conical foot, c1680, 6in (15cm) high.
£1,800–2,000 S(S)

A Dutch *façon de Venise* grey-tinted goblet, on a knopped tapering stem with folded conical foot, 17thC, 7in (18cm) high.
£1,200–1,500 C

Further reading

Miller's Collecting Glass: The Facts at Your Fingertips, Miller's Publications, 2000

A Dutch *façon de Venise* winged goblet, the bowl with spiked gadroons to the lower part, the stem with a hollow knop between mereses above a hollow tapering section, on a folded conical foot, late 17thC, 8¼in (21cm) high.
£1,800–2,200 C
In a drinking glass, a merese is a flat disk of glass that links the bowl and stem, and sometimes the stem and foot.

A Dutch *façon de Venise* goblet, the wrythen-moulded coiled serpent stem with a central figure-of-eight and applied with opaque-white pincered decoration, on a basal knop and conical foot, 17thC, 7in 18cm) high.
£350–400 C

▶ An Anglo-Dutch armorial goblet, of crizzled lead glass, the bucket bowl engraved with the arms of William of Orange as Stadholder of the Netherlands flanked by military trophies, the reverse with a crowned lion of the Province of Holland, the base with 'nipt diamond waies' above a pair of hollow quatrefoil knops flanked by mereses, the wide conical folded foot engraved with a foliate band, c1685, 7½in (19cm) high.
£10,000–12,000 S

Price Guide
these are worked out by a team of trade and auction house experts, and are based on actual prices realised. Remember that Miller's is a price guide not a price list and prices are affected by many variables such as location, condition, desirability and so on. Don't forget that if you are selling it is quite likely you will be offered less than the price range. Price ranges for items sold at auction tend to include the buyer's premium and VAT if applicable.

Further Reading
directs the reader towards additional sources of information.

Information Box
covers relevant collecting information on factories, makers, care and restoration, fakes and alterations.

Caption
provides a brief description of the item including the maker's name, medium, year it was made and in some cases condition.

Source Code
refers to the Key to Illustrations on page 305 that lists the details of where the item was photographed.

Introduction

Glass is the most important metal in our lives today. Where would we be without it – no windows for the house, cars, cameras, telescopes, bottles and jars, televisions and computer screens, light bulbs and, lastly, the heat-resistant tiles on the space shuttle that were developed from glass technology. Glass can be clear or coloured, core-formed, free-blown, mould-blown to give an optic decoration, ribbed or trailed with coloured threads, or applied with decoration such as leaves and flowers or handles and feet. It can be mixed to give a malachite effect, press-moulded, cast in a similar way to bronzes, and cased in layers of different colours and blown into metal mounts. After it is cooled it can then be cut with all manner of designs, copper wheel engraved, intaglio cut or rock crystal engraved, acid-etched, enamelled, gilded and finally cameo carved.

The core-formed Egyptian glass is rare and expensive. However, glass from the Roman period is easily found and while large pieces can be expensive there are numerous small perfume phials at very reasonable prices.

Enamelling was introduced in the 13th century. Some of the most spectacular examples are the Islamic mosque lamps that became the inspiration for many late 19th-century enamelled lamps and vases.

Venetian glass, it was discovered, was too hard when, in the 17th century, tastes changed to include engraved and carved glass. Glassmakers in Silesia and Bohemia developed potash glass which was suitable for the new fashion. The British contribution was the development of lead crystal glass by George Ravenscroft at the end of the 17th century. It was much softer than other glass that lent itself to the new fashion for baluster glasses, and later for lustrous cutting. 18th-century British drinking glasses are as popular as ever. Early heavy balusters, engraved Newcastle light balusters, colour twists and Beilby enamelled glasses are quite expensive, but there are still plenty of interesting modestly-priced glasses. Buying a jelly glass is one of the best ways to add a rare shape to a collection without it being painful to the pocket, as hexagonal, honeycomb and panel-moulded bowls on stemware can be expensive.

The 19th century saw the rise of the French and Belgian glasshouses which, helped initially by the British, soon created their own styles of cut glass. The popularity of the paperweight in the 1840s saw the rise in importance of Baccarat, St Louis and Clichy.

Pressed glass was introduced from America in the early 19th century but it was in the 1870s and '80s that companies such as Sowerby and Davidson took pressing from imitating cut glass to an art form with the introduction of items inspired by Walter Crane's illustrations and aesthetic Japanese designs that highly influenced all decorated glass.

The Americans became captivated with their brilliant cut-glass, Tiffany iridescent vases and their wonderful lamps and, on a more commercial scale, there was a wide variety of colourful Carnival glass.

The period between the wars saw the influence of the Scandinavian countries with the introduction of beautiful simple shapes, the techniques of Arial and Graal, as well as engraved glass by a number of designers incuding Edward Hald, Simon Gate and Sven Palmquist.

A warning regarding Scandinavian glass – it is very difficult to understand the engraved date codes and, as with Venetian glass, designs have been re-issued or made for many years and the production date must be reflected in the price.

Scandinavian and Venetian Art glass were an inspiration to other countries, with Whitefriars introducing a range of Scandinavian styles in the 1950s and '60s. Whitefriars became a household name for inexpensive brightly-coloured textured vases designed by Geoffrey Baxter. These were featured by the Design Centre and are now avidly collected.

Where to buy? This is always a difficult question to answer without offending someone. I would recommend beginners to start by buying from someone who is willing to talk at length about your chosen field and point out the pitfalls as well as the pleasures. You should always ask if the condition is perfect, and insist on a written receipt that describes the item and its condition, then you are safe in the knowledge that you are covered by the Trades Description Act. Boot fairs are fine if you know what you are doing, or for just buying items that you like for small amounts of money. Auctions can be a little difficult for the beginner, as the condition is rarely mentioned and they do not guarantee the authenticity. The latest hype is buying on the Internet. This is fine if you know the seller but it is almost impossible to buy glass without handling it.

Only buy what you like and the best that you can afford; the pleasure of owning a cherished piece of glass soon outweighs the cost. In every type of glass there are vast differences in price but just because something is cheap it does not mean it is rubbish. There are items in all fields that are well designed and good value for money. It is fine to buy a rare damaged item at the right price – better to have a damaged item than no example at all.

Collecting glass can become addictive. We started with a glass-collecting habit that got out of control – now the same can be said for our shop! **Jeanette Hayhurst**

11

Animals

A pair of white pressed glass swans, c1890, 3¼in (8.5cm) high.
£55–65 ARE

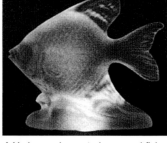

A Verlys opalescent glass angel fish, signed 'Verlys France', c1920, 4⅛in (11.5cm) high.
£180–200 BKK

An Edwardian iridescent green glass flower holder, in the form of a pig, c1910, 4⅛in (11.5cm) high.
£60–70 DA

A Lalique frosted glass sparrow, Moineau Hardi, after 1929, 2in (5cm) high.
£220–250 BKK

A Lalique frosted glass bird, Moineau Fier, after 1929, 5in (12.5cm) high.
£200–240 ASA

A glass inkwell, modelled as Bonzo dog, 1930s, 3½in (9cm) high.
£85–100 TMA

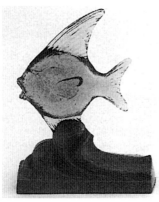

A Guy Underwood blue-tinted glass model of a fish, on a green-painted metal wave-scroll base, registration number, signed and dated '1934' on base, 7¼in (18.5cm) high.
£150–180 DN

► A set of four Italian handmade glass fish, 1950–60, largest 14in (35.5cm) wide.
£50–60 OCA

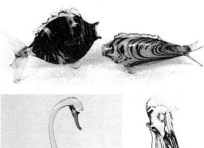

A glass Bambi, with blue and white spotted body, c1958, 3½in (9cm) high.
£10–12 PC

A clear glass swan, with yellow wings and beak, 1960s, 7½in (19cm) high.
£10–12 GIN

A Murano glass bird, with multi-coloured striped body, 1960s, 10in (25.5cm) high.
£18–20 RAC

A red glass swan ashtray, 1950s, 7in (18cm) wide.
£6–7 GIN

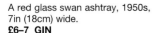

◄ A glass pheasant, with blue and yellow striped body, 1960s, 8in (20.5cm) long.
£12–14 GIN

► A Wedgwood glass long-tailed bird, Portland vase acid-etched mark, c1970, 9in (23cm) high.
£30–35 SWB

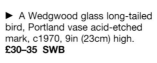

Baskets

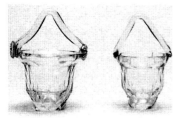

Two hanging glass baskets from a sweetmeat stand, c1750, largest 4in (10cm) high.
£300–350 MJW

A Sowerby pressed glass basket, c1880, 3in (7.5cm) high.
£65–80 MJW

A Davidson amber pressed glass basket, c1891, 7½in (19cm) wide.
£25–30 GLN

► A pair of Davidson blue pearline posy baskets, c1890, 7½in (19cm) long.
£85–100 CSA

A Victorian latticinio satin glass basket, with yellow air-twist stripes, mid-19thC, 6½in (16.5cm) high.
£85–100 AnS

► A pink glass hanging basket, with clear handle, the clear support in the form of a serpent, c1880, 9in (23cm) high.
£275–325 MJW

Bird Feeders

A selection of glass bird feeders, three with blue stoppers, c1800, largest 6½in (16.5cm) high.
£65–125 each MJW

► A glass bird feeder, with hollow and frilled knops, early 19thC, 7in (18cm) high.
£55–65 FD

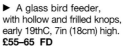

A glass bird feeder, mid-19thC, 6in (15cm) high.
£55–65 FD

A Victorian glass bird feeder, 6in (15cm) high.
£50–60 MRW

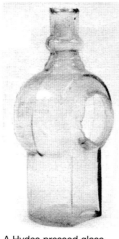

A Hydes pressed glass bird feeder, late 19thC, 4¼in (11cm) high.
£15–20 FD

► A Victorian blue glass bird feeder, with blue stopper, 5½in (14cm) high.
£50–60 CB

Bottles

A Roman glass bottle, 1st–2ndC AD, 4¾in (12cm) high.
£450–500 MJW
Many Roman glass items have been found on the sites of garrison towns and spas, particularly in the Middle East, and may have contained bath oils and perfumes.

A Roman glass bottle, 1st–2ndC AD, 5¾in (14.5cm) high.
£150–180 MJW

A Roman glass bottle, 1st–2ndC AD, 5½in (14cm) high.
£450–500 MJW

A Roman blue glass tear bottle, 1st–3rdC AD, 3in (7.5cm) high.
£150–180 JFG

A Roman glass bottle, 1st–3rdC AD, 6in (15cm) high.
£250–300 JFG

A Roman glass bottle, 1st–3rdC AD, 5¼in (13.5cm) high.
£375–450 JFG

A Roman glass bottle, 1st–3rdC AD, 5in (12.5cm) high.
£600–700 JFG

A Roman glass bottle, with strings around the neck, 1st–3rdC AD, 7in (18cm) high.
£650–750 JFG

Two glass miniature bottles, 2nd–3rdC AD, tallest 3in (7.5cm) high.
£150–300 each MJW

► An olive-green glass shaft-and-globe bottle, the long tapering neck with pronounced string rim, base pontil, some pitting, c1670, 9¼in (23.5cm) high.
£1,300–1,500 BBR

LOCATE THE SOURCE
The source of each illustration in Miller's can be found by checking the code letters below each caption with the Key to Illustrations, pages 305–307.

► A glass shaft-and-globe bottle, with evenly pitted surface, c1660, 9¼in (23.5cm) high.
£800–1,000 NWi

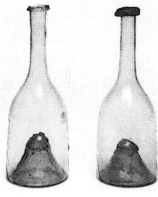

A pair of south German 'forest' glass cruet bottles, c1680, 5in (12.5cm) high.
£100–120 each MJW

An Indian green glass bottle, c1700, 11in (28cm) high.
£100–120 LIO

◄ An onion-shaped glass bottle, c1705, 6in (15cm) high.
£140–160 LIO

A Persian green glass bottle, c1700, 11½in (29cm) high.
£75–90 LIO

A mallet-shaped glass serving bottle, with slender tapering neck, the scroll handle with rolled-over terminal, c1720, 7¼in (18.5cm) high.
£1,800–2,000 S

◄ A north German mould-blown flat-sided glass bottle, c1720, 8in (20.5cm) high.
£220–250 NWi

An onion-shaped glass bottle, with overall body iridescence, base pontil and applied string rim, the seal with a fox surmounted by a coronet, c1700, 5¼in (13.5cm) high.
£1,400–1,600 BBR
Wine was not sold in bottles in the 17thC. The client would have his own glass bottles, which he would send to the wine merchant to be filled. Since these were costly items, they would be embossed with the owner's seal. These early onion-shaped bottles are very collectable today, and their seals can often be identified to provide an attractive and aristocratic provenance. This particular bottle is believed to be connected to the Pierpont family.

A blown bladder-shaped dark green glass bottle, c1730, 10½in (26.5cm) high.
£220–250 NWi

► A glass cylinder bottle, c1760, 14in (35.5cm) high.
£125–150 NWi

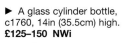

A half-size mallet-shaped glass bottle, with excavated character, c1740, 6½in (16.5cm) high.
£125–150 NWi

A Continental mallet-shaped olive/amber glass bottle, c1740, 7½in (19cm) high.
£170–200 NWi

Three French glass bottles:
l. c1760, 6in (15cm) high. **£100–125**
c. c1760, 7in (18cm) high. **£150–180**
r. c1740, 6½in (16.5cm) high.
£125–150 MJW

A glass wine
bottle, c1765,
12in (30.5cm) high.
£120–140 LIO

A glass double magnum
bottle, with seal for
'Edmd. Whiteway', c1776,
44in (112cm) high.
£420–500 NWi

A mallet-shaped glass
wine bottle, with string
neck fastening, c1780,
5¾in (14.5cm) high.
£65–80 OD

Two cruet bottles, with stoppers,
c1780, largest 7in (18cm) high.
£100–120 each MJW

An Irish glass
cruet bottle, c1780,
6in (15cm) high.
£110–130 MJW

A globular olive-green
glass serving bottle, with
opaque white decoration
in the Nailsea style, c1780,
12in (30.5cm) high.
£650–750 NWi

Cross Reference
See Colour Review

◀ A clear engraved glass vinegar bottle,
c1790, 7½in (19cm) high.
£150–170 CB

A Bristol blue glass cruet set, comprising three
gilt-labelled bottles in a papier mâché stand,
c1790, 6in (15cm) high.
£900–1,000 BELL

A pair of blue glass cruet bottles,
with gilt wine label cartouches,
'Soy' and 'Kyan', gilt facet-cut ball
stoppers, c1790, 4in (10cm) high.
£600–660 Som

Three blue glass spirit bottles, with bevelled
lozenge stoppers, c1790, 7in (18cm) high.
£200–230 Som

▶ A glass wine bottle, with applied seal with
'C' beneath a baronet's coronet, c1800,
10¾in (27.5cm) high.
£120–140 NWi

A set of four green glass spirit bottles, with canted edges and gilt labels for 'Rum', 'Brandy', 'Hollands' and 'Shrub', with gilt ball stoppers, in a fitted mahogany box, c1800, each bottle 7in (18cm) high.
£1,200–1,500 Som

l. A green glass sauce bottle, with gilt label inscribed 'Ketchup', gilt lozenge stopper, c1800, 3½in (9cm) high.
£210–230
r. A blue glass sauce bottle, with pouring lip and cut ball stopper, silver label inscribed 'Cayenne', c1800, 3½in (9cm) high.
£240–270 Som

Two Irish glass cruet bottles, for oil and vinegar, c1800, 6½in (16.5cm) high.
£100–120 WGT

An Irish glass spirit bottle, c1800, 9in (23cm) high.
£100–125 WGT

A Dutch square-tapered olive-green glass gin bottle, c1800, 9½in (24cm) high.
£80–90 NWi

A Hamilton aqua glass bottle, embossed 'N Paul & Burrow Real Soda Water 5 Bow Street Covent Garden 1802', 8½in (21.5cm) high.
£50–60 BBR

A set of three octagonal-sided glass spirit bottles, with a band of blaze cutting around the body tops, flute-cut necks, pouring lips and cut ball stoppers, in silver-plated stand, c1810, 6½in (16.5cm) high.
£470–550 Som

A pair of square glass spirit bottles, with flute-cutting and a band of diamond cutting, star-cut bases and cut mushroom stoppers, c1810, 6½in (16.5cm) high.
£220–250 Som

A green glass bottle, with a seal commemorating Halley's Comet, paper label inscribed 'Vieux Cognac', c1811, 14in (35.5cm) high.
£100–120 INC
The seal on this bottle commemorates Halley's comet and may be a mark of quality. 'Comet Wine' was a term given to wine made in years of great comets, which were believed to produce grapes of better flavour than other years.

◄ A French oil and vinegar bottle, with later engraving, c1825, 10in (25.5cm) high.
£135–155 JAS

An olive-green glass bottle, the seal inscribed 'Prytherect 1819', 10½in (26.5cm) high.
£200–220 NWi

Prices

The price ranges quoted in this book reflect the average price a purchaser might expect to pay for a similar item. The price will vary according to the condition, rarity, size, popularity, provenance, colour and restoration of the item. If you are selling it is quite likely that you will be offered less than the price range.

A glass cruet bottle, the body with prism and diamond cutting, stepped star-cut foot and silver lid, marked London 1830, 5½in (14cm) high.
£100–120 Som

A clear glass guest bottle, engraved 'I.W.', c1830, 5¼in (13.5cm) high.
£100–120 JAS
The bottle was placed by the guest's bed with a favourite nightcap.

A green glass serving bottle, with a silver mount, c1830, 14in (35.5cm) high.
£280–320 CB

► An amethyst glass spirit bottle, early 19thC, 14in (35.5cm) high.
£250–300 CB

l & r. A pair of green wrythen-moulded glass spirit bottles, c1830, 11½in (29cm) high.
£650–720
c. An amethyst spirit bottle, with plain body, c1830, 12½in (32cm) high.
£400–440 Som

Two wrythen-moulded glass spirit bottles, amber and blue, c1830, 10½in (26.5cm) high.
£220–250 each FD

Two blue wrythen-moulded glass spirit bottles, c1840, tallest 12¼in (31cm) high.
£220–250 each Som

An amethyst glass spirit bottle, with slice-cut base, c1830, 12in (30.5cm) high.
£230–260 BELL

A blue glass cylinder bottle with blob lip, front embossed 'Jas Mackie & Sons, Est 1835, Newcastle', some wear, 6¾in (17cm) high.
£50–60 BBR

► A round-bottomed aqua glass cylinder bottle, embossed in ribbon around shoulder 'Carrara Water Maughams Patent Registered 31 May 1845'.
£50–60 BBR

A green glass spirit bottle, the metal mount moulded with fruiting vine, c1840, 14in (35.5cm) high.
£175–200 CB

A French green-tinted glass olive oil bottle, with applied seal and pontilled base, c1840, 11in (28cm) high.
£100–125 NWi

An amethyst glass spirit bottle, with flute-cut body, cut pouring spout and cork/metal stopper, c1840, 13in (33cm) high.
£300–330 Som

A glass bottle, engraved 'Brandy', c1850, 4in (10cm) high.
£60–70 MJW

Coloured glass

The range of colours produced increased considerably during the 19th century. The best cranberry, or ruby glass, was derived from gold, though not, as popular tradition has it, from the gold sovereigns that factory managers would fling into the pots of molten glass. Other colours were achieved by the addition, to the molten glass, or metal, of various amounts of metallic oxides, blue being the easiest to achieve, and yellow and orange the most complex.

A cranberry glass bottle, with prism-cut neck and onion-shaped body, stopper missing, 19thC, 10in (25.5cm) high.
£110–130 PCh

Two French glass truffle bottles, mid-19thC, tallest 7¾in (19.5cm) high.
£10–16 each FD

▶ A Belgian glass 'cheat' bottle, with exaggerated kick-up to base, c1850, 10in (25.5cm) high.
£85–100 NWi

A cobalt blue glass bottle, engraved with vine leaves, c1860, 10in (25.5cm) high.
£220–250 Har

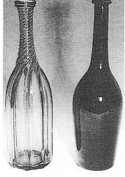

l. An amber glass wrythen-moulded spirit bottle, with annulated collar to neck, c1860, 11in (28cm) high.
r. A plain blue spirit bottle, c1840, 11½in (29cm) high.
£230–280 each Som

A wedge-shaped clear glass poison bottle, embossed 'Poison' to top, 'H. Gilbertson & Sons' to one side, 'Regd 30th Octr 1861' on the other, original paper labels, inscribed 'Laudanum-Poison, E. R. Ing Chemist, Swindon', slight damage, 3½in (9cm) long.
£350–400 BBR

Two embossed glass bottles, c1885, tallest 9½in (24cm) high.
l. £60–70 r. £12–15 BBR

▶ A pair of Bristol green glass bottles, the silver-mounted neck with vine-embossed decoration, 19thC, 13in (33cm) high.
£240–270 LF

A late Victorian amber glass bottle, c1885, 10¼in (26cm) high.
£50–60 BBR

An olive-green glass gin bottle, with embossed trademark, c1870, 10½in (26.5cm) high.
£80–100 NWi

An aqua glass poison bottle, the flat base with U-bend to the neck, curved end, embossed to one side 'The Martin Poison Bottle', 'Poison' to the other, 'Patented' to curved end, '8oz' under neck and 'S.S.A. Ltd, Manchester' to base, early 20thC, 7in (18cm) long.
£320–360 BBR
It is rare to find such a bottle this large.

A Gallé glass bottle and stopper, enamelled with small polychrome flowers on gilt stems, repeated on the button stopper, crack to neck, painted mark 'Emile Gallé', c1900, 4in (10cm) high.
£500–600 S(S)

Three green glass chemist's bottles, with glass labels, c1900, tallest 8in (20.5cm) high.
£65–80 JUN

▶ An Ally Sloper's glass Relish bottle, c1910, 11¾in (30cm) high.
£12–20 OD
This bottle was dug out of the old Potts Railway tip at the Welshpool/Shrewsbury Railway. The relish was very popular during WWI but went out of production around 1930. The bottles were factory-produced from 1900.

A glass bottle, inscribed 'Feeding Bottle For My Baby', c1910, 5½in (14cm) high.
£10–15 DOL

Three glass beer bottles, 1950s, tallest 3¼in (8.5cm) high.
£3–4 each MRW

A glass bottle, inscribed 'Mellin's Infant Food, London', 1910-20, 7in (18cm) high.
£4–6 HUX

◀ A Glaxo glass baby feeding bottle, with rubber teats, in original box, c1950s, 8in (20.5cm) long.
£14–18 MRW

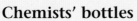

Chemists' bottles

Although Victorian chemists kept their stocks of liquids in carboys and large glass bottles, smaller amounts were dispensed from small bottles known as shop rounds.
Clear glass was used for most shop rounds, but syrup bottles could be cobalt blue, and poison actinic green. When moulded bottles became available, poison rounds often had fluting so that they could be distinguished by touch. Early bottles had engraved or painted labels, but later examples had moulded recesses into which curved glass labels were cemented.

A clear glass bottle, embossed 'The Property of O.T. Co, London', 1930s, 11½in (29cm) high.
£3–4 MAC

A Pyrex glass 8oz baby feeding bottle, in original box, 1960s, 6¾in (17cm) high.
£7–8 HUX

Bowls & Dishes

A Roman amber glass bowl, on a low flared foot, with a folded thickened rim, base restored, 3rd–4thC AD, 7in (18cm) diam.
£700–800 Bon

A Venetian grey-tinted glass bowl, marked 'nipt diamond waies' to underside, on spreading ribbed foot with folded rim, c1500, 12in (30.5cm) diam.
£3,400–4,000 S

A Venetian glass bowl with spiral gadrooning, the folded rim and ribbed foot with an applied translucent blue trail, c1500, 11½in (29cm) diam.
£3,400–4,000 S

A Venetian glass bowl, the sides applied with a blue trail above the ribs and under the folded rim, the spreading ribbed foot with thick applied blue trail around the rim, early 16thC, 10in (25.5cm) diam.
£3,400–4,000 S

An Irish boat-shaped glass fruit bowl, on a knopped stem with a moulded oval foot, c1700, 12in (30.5cm) diam.
£1,750–2,000 WGT

A glass bowl, engraved with a fruiting vine, c1740, 3½in (9cm) high.
£250–300 Del

A Liège Traforato glass fruit bowl and stand, c1760, 10in (25.5cm) diam.
£675–800 FD
Many heavy later copies of this design were called 'open work'.

A pair of flat cut-glass dishes, c1770, 6in (15cm) diam.
£250–300 Del

An Irish glass salad bowl, the everted rim with cross-cut diamonds, the faceted bowl on a domed fluted foot, c1790, 12in (30.5cm) diam.
£2,200–2,600 C(S)

A glass salad bowl, with turn-over rim cut with diamond pattern, a similar band below, on a knopped stem and domed circular foot with notched edge, c1790, 10in (25.5cm) high.
£1,500–1,800 Som

An Irish cut-glass fruit bowl, on a single-knopped stem with oval rib-moulded base, c1790, 13in (33cm) diam.
£1,700–2,000 MEA

◀ An Irish cut-glass bowl and cover, c1790, 11in (28cm) high.
£1,800–2,200 WGT

An Irish cut-glass preserve dish and cover, c1800, 7in (18cm) diam.
£200–240 WGT

A blue glass sugar basin, with cold-enamelled floral decoration, on a high conical folded foot, c1800, 4¾in (12cm) high.
£230–280 Som

An amethyst glass sugar basin, with moulded ogee body and everted rim, on small foot ring, c1800, 2½in (6.5cm) high.
£250–300 Som

A blue wrythen-moulded glass sugar basin, on a hollow conical folded foot, c1800, 3¼in (8.5cm) high.
£190–220 Som

A glass fruit bowl, with kettledrum body and turn-over rim, cut with diamonds and splits, on a bobbin knopped stem with square lemon squeezer foot, c1800, 9½in (24cm) diam.
£1,800–2,000 Som

Two canoe-shaped glass pedestal bowls, English or Irish, slight chips to both, c1800, 12½in (32cm) wide.
£1,500–1,800 CSK

An Irish cut-glass bowl, with turn-over rim, on square lemon squeezer foot, c1800, 10in (25.5cm) diam.
£1,250–1,400 CB

An Irish cut-glass bowl, with faceted sides beneath a waved bevelled rim, on a short stem and oval foot with facet-cut rim, c1800, 8½in (21.5cm) diam.
£1,000–1,200 C

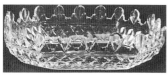

A hexagonal cut-glass dish, the diamond-cut body with crenellated rim and star-cut base, c1800, 8¾in (22cm) wide.
£250–300 Som

An Irish glass fruit bowl, with turn-over rim cut with geometric slices, the body cut with a band of alternate prisms, on a knopped stem with square domed lemon squeezer foot, c1800, 9¼in (23.5cm) diam.
£1,250–1,400 Som

An Irish cut-glass bowl, with herringbone design, c1800, 10in (25.5cm) diam.
£325–400 WGT

Miller's is a price GUIDE not a price LIST

A green over white cased glass finger bowl, c1800, 4⅛in (11cm) diam.
£125–150 WGT

◄ An oval cut-glass butter dish, cover and stand, all cut with bands of diamonds and prisms, with crenellated rim and ball finial, c1800, 6¼in (16cm) high.
£500–600 Som

An Irish cut-glass butter dish, the body and domed lid cut with small diamonds and prisms, c1810, 6½in (16.5cm) diam.
£300–350 Som

A glass patty pan, with folded rim, c1800, 3in (7.5cm) diam.
£40–45 BrW

A glass fruit bowl, the double ogee body with a band of vesica-cut decoration and notch cutting around the rim, a band of hollow facet chequer pattern below, on a knopped stem with a square domed lemon squeezer foot, c1810, 9in (23cm) high.
£1,200–1,450 Som

An oval cut-glass dish, the body with fluted and diamond cutting, with crenellated rim and star-cut base, c1810, 6½in (16.5cm) wide.
£240–280 Som
These dishes often had a rebate at the foot, as they came from ornate table centrepieces.

A pair of Continental strawberry diamond- and prism-cut bonbonnières, early 19thC, 11in (28cm) high.
£900–1,000 BELL

An Irish cut-glass butter dish and cover, with a band of husk decoration and flute cutting, cut ball finial, c1810, 5in (13cm) high.
£250–290 Som

Cut-glass

Lead glass is the most suitable type for cutting. Invented in England and Ireland it was most fashionable during the late 18th and early 19th centuries. Specialist craftsmen developed a variety of complex patterns during the Regency period, though simpler patterns became more fashionable during the 1820s. The object is held above an iron or stone wheel which cuts deep facets or grooves in the surface, which are then polished to create a brilliant sparkling surface.

A cut-glass sugar basin, with fan-cut rim, decorated with small diamonds flanked by alternate fans, star-cut base, c1810, 6¼in (16cm) diam.
£400–450 Som

An amethyst glass sugar bowl, the hollow conical foot with folded rim, c1810, 4in (10cm) high.
£240–290 Som

A cut-glass two-piece bowl, with step, diamond and flute cutting, c1820, 12in (30.5cm) diam.
£1,000–1,200 JHa
This type of bowl has to be made in two pieces, as it is impossible to cut the base of the bowl and the stem in one piece. Sometimes bases that have lost their bowls are called ham stands.

A blue glass finger bowl, with leaf band and looped gilt decoration, c1810, 3¾in (9.5cm) diam.
£430–500 Som

▶ An Irish glass butter dish and cover, with moulded and flute-cut body, the domed lid with mushroom finial, 1820, 7½in (19cm) high.
£420–490 Som

A cut-glass butter dish and cover, c1820, 7in (18cm) diam.
£450–550 CB

An Irish cut-glass footed bowl, c1825, 10in (25.5cm) diam.
£1,000–1,200 WGT
Sometimes this type of bowl is known as kettledrum shape.

A cut-glass cup-shaped fruit bowl, with cross-cut diamonds and circular bands of prisms, fan-cut rim, on plain foot star-cut underneath, c1825, 6in (15cm) high.
£425–500 Som

An Irish cut-glass bowl, the body cut with small diamonds between flute-cut pillars, fan-cut handles and notched rim, c1825, 5½in (14cm) diam.
£750–900 Som

A cut-glass butter dish, cover and stand, c1820, 7in (18cm) diam.
£550–650 CB

A cut-glass butter dish, cover and stand, with diamond, prism and blaze cutting, the domed cover with a mushroom finial, c1825, 5in (12.5cm) high.
£400–460 Som

An Irish two-piece cut-glass bowl and detachable stand, minor chips, c1825, 9½in (24cm) high.
£1,700–2,000 S

A two-piece cut-glass dish and stand, each with alternate panels of oval and arched prism cutting, the central boss with grid pattern diamond cutting, scalloped and pointed rim, c1820, 8½in (21.5cm) high.
£1,000–1,200 Som

A cut-glass sugar bowl, with diamond, flute and prism cutting, with a fan-cut rim, on a short knopped stem with circular foot star-cut underneath, c1825, 5in (12.5cm) high.
£400–480 Som

A glass comport and cover, cut with stylized leaves leaves between diamond panels, on a radial-cut foot, 1820–30, 6¼in (16cm) high.
£240–280 JHa

◀ A Scottish cut-glass bowl, c1830, 8in (20.5cm) high.
£450–550 BWA

◀ Three green glass finger bowls, c1830, largest 3¾in (9.5cm) high.
£85–100 Som

A glass bowl, cut with spirally fluted and diamond bands, early 19thC, 11in (28cm) diam.
£1,000–1,200 DN

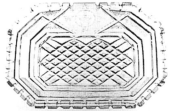

A William IV canted glass dish, with crenellated rim and diamond-cut base, the step-cut sides etched with a crown, national emblems, royal cipher and crest, rim chipped, 10¾in (27.5cm) wide.
£280–330 DN

An opaline glass sugar bowl, with cold-enamelled floral decoration, c1840, 4¼in (11cm) high.
£100–120 FD

A set of four amber-coloured glass finger bowls, flute-cut with flared rims and moulded bases, c1850, 3¼in (8.5cm) high.
£250–300 Som

A pair of Bohemian red glass dishes, with clear cut-glass centres, scalloped borders and gilt decoration, c1850, 5in (12.5cm) diam.
£240–280 MJW

A Victorian glass bowl and stand, with silver cover, by C T & G Fox, the bowl etched with trailing water lilies and lotus blossoms, the flat silver cover crested and with water lily finial, marked, London 1859, 6½in (16.5cm) diam, 9oz of silver.
£1,000–1,200 S(S)

A cranberry glass finger bowl stand, 1860, 6½in (16.5cm) diam.
£50–55 AMH

A cranberry glass bowl, c1860, 5½in (14cm) wide.
£110–130 AMH

▶ A Victorian glass sardine dish, with silver-plated stand, 8in (20.5cm) wide.
£125–150 TRU

A glass goblet-shaped sugar bowl, with blue hand-applied threading, on a baluster stem, c1860, 7¼in (18.5cm) high.
£300–350 MJW

A set of three Sowerby flint glass bowls, c1870, largest 8in (20.5cm) diam.
£55–65 GLN

A Sowerby Patent Ivory Queen's Ware pressed glass 'new bowl', moulded with a band of panels enclosing floral and foliate sprays, with two comb-shaped handles, 1879, 6in (15cm) wide.
£230–260 P(NE)

A purple slag glass two-handled bowl, marked 'Sowerby', c1880, 2½in (6.5cm) diam.
£50–60 GLN

A cranberry glass heart-shaped dish, c1880, 8in (20.5cm) wide.
£100–120 AMH

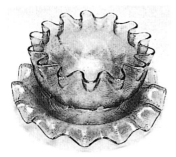

A wavy edged threaded glass bowl and stand, c1880, 3in (7.5cm) diam.
£100–120 CB

◄ A glass finger bowl, c1870, 5in (12.5cm) diam.
£60–70 DUN

Cross Reference
See Colour Review

► A pair of glass comports and covers, facet-cut, on square-shaped feet, the domed covers surmounted by shaped finials, c1880, 15¼in (38.5cm) high.
£2,200–2,600 S(Am)

A blue-threaded vaseline glass bowl, with a pincer work rim, c1880, 3½in (9cm) diam.
£85–100 CB

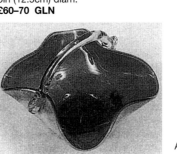

A purple slag malachite pressed glass bowl and cover, decorated with sprigs of holly, 1880, 5in (12.5cm) diam.
£60–70 GLN

An opalescent cranberry glass basket, c1880, 4in (10cm) wide.
£120–140 AMH

► Two Stourbridge cranberry glass bowls, with clear pincer feet and collars, c1880, largest 6½in (16.5cm) diam.
£120–140 each CB
The purpose of the collar was to support the bowl in a metal frame.

A cranberry glass dish, c1880, 6in (15cm) diam.
£100–110 AMH

A Sowerby caramel-coloured pressed glass two-handled bowl, c1880, 3½in (9cm) wide.
£65–80 MJW

A Victorian cranberry and opaline glass posy bowl, c1880, 5in (12.5cm) high.
£130–160 BELL

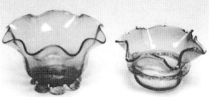

A glass sugar bowl, engraved with a fruiting vine, on a pedestal stem with star-cut foot, c1880, 5in (12.5cm) diam.
£140–160 CB

A cranberry glass powder bowl, c1880, 4in (10cm) diam.
£110–130 AMH

A threaded glass bowl, c1880, 5½in (14cm) diam.
£100–120 TS

A cut-glass fruit bowl, with silver rim, c1886, 8¼in (21cm) diam.
£250–300 CB

A pressed glass bowl, commemorating Queen Victoria's silver jubilee, 1887, 7in (18cm) diam.
£20–25 TS

A George Davidson pressed glass bowl, simulating cut-glass, registration No. 96945, c1888, 8in (20.5cm) diam.
£100–120 JHa
The use of registration marks in the form of diamonds ceased in February 1884. Five-figure numbers were used from 1884 to May 1888, and six-figure numbers thereafter.

◀ A Stevens & Williams rock crystal bowl, with yellow and green intaglio and cameo overlay, late 19thC, 9½in (24cm) diam.
£4,000–4,500 HAM

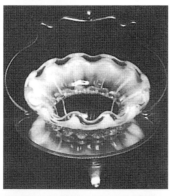

▶ A vaseline glass bonbon dish, with fluted edge and silver-plated holder, c1890, 6in (15cm) diam.
£125–150 ARE

A pair of Georgian-style cut-glass bowls, with crenellated rims over steep diamond-faceted sides, late 19thC, 9in (23cm) diam.
£425–500 S(S)

Just Glass

Antique Glass
Victorian Decorative Glass
including: Cranberry
Mary Gregory
Vaseline
North East Pressed Glass

M. J. GRAHAM
Cross House, Market Place, Alston, Cumbria
Telephone: 01434 381263
Shop/Mobile: 0783 399 4948

Open Wednesday, Thursday, Saturday & Sunday
OR BY APPOINTMENT

A set of six cut- and etched-glass finger bowls, c1890, 5in (12.5cm) diam.
£250–290 DUN

Prices

The price ranges quoted in this book reflect the average price a purchaser might expect to pay for a similar item. The price will vary according to the condition, rarity, size, popularity, provenance, colour and restoration of the item. If you are selling it is quite likely that you will be offered less than the price range.

A George Davidson yellow pearline glass dish, c1890, 7½in (19cm) diam.
£60–70 CSA

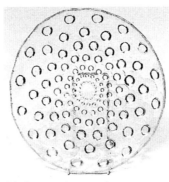

A Stevens & Williams swirl satin bowl, in lime green with brown spiral stripes, applied with *Mat-su-Noke* flowers and branches, with crimped rim, late 19thC, 8in (20.5cm) diam.
£420–500 P

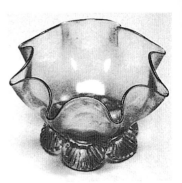

A Victorian amber glass bowl, 3½in (9cm) diam.
£75–90 CB

A sepia glass finger bowl, with etched decoration and star-cut base, c1890, 5in (12.5cm) diam.
£85–100 MJW

A glass butter dish and cover, c1900, 7in (18cm) high.
£20–25 AL

A Lalique opalescent glass peacock feather dish, c1900, 24in (61cm) diam.
£450–500 HEM

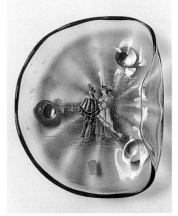

A Gallé green glass dish, with enamelled figures in the centre, on three ball-shaped feet, c1900, 6in (15cm) wide.
£1,000–1,200 ART

A set of six cut and engraved glass finger bowls, c1900, 4½in (11.5cm) diam.
£140–160 DUN

An Almaric Walter *pâte de verre* figural glass bowl, in pale lemon and amber streaked with blue, with twin-handles in the form of a cat and a dog, c1900, 5in (12.5cm) high.
£1,200–1,400 P

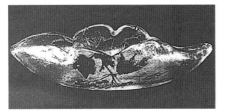

◄ A Gallé clear glass redcurrant coupe, overlaid with pink and etched with flowering redcurrants, the ground textured and fire-polished, cameo mark 'Gallé', c1900, 11½in (29cm) wide.
£1,200–1,500 S

A Continental opaque glass rose bowl, with green iridescent leaves, c1900, 6in (15cm) high.
£75–85 DKH

A cut-glass bowl and stand, each with Brunswick star and diamond cutting, c1900, 12½in (32cm) high.
£150–180 S(S)

An Art Nouveau Bohemian glass and copper bowl-on-stand, the green bowl with wavy rim, enhanced with iridescent blue webbing on four pierced foliate columns, early 20thC, 13¾in (35cm) high.
£400–500 P

Cross Reference
See Colour Review

A Venetian glass latticinio bowl and stand, c1910, stand 7in (18cm) diam.
Bowl £80–90
Stand £50–60 GRI

A rock crystal bowl and stand, cut with vertical bands and four panels engraved with shipping scenes, between swags and pendant ovals hung from ribbons, the silvered-metal stand with five feet in the form of diving dolphins, probably by Thomas Webb, c1900, 9in (23cm) high.
£1,300–1,500 S

A Stevens & Williams silver-mounted rock crystal glass rose bowl, engraved and dated '1904', 8in (20.5cm) diam.
£2,500–3,000 ALiN

A Verlys shallow pale amber-tinted opalescent glass bowl, moulded in relief with fish and kingfishers, signed, early 20thC, 13in (33cm) high.
£150–180 MCA

A green glass bowl, decorated with Native Americans, c1920, 7½in (19cm) diam.
£270–300 WeH

A pressed glass cheese dish and cover, c1900, 6½in (16.5cm) high.
£20–25 AL

Insurance values
Always insure your valuable antiques for the cost of replacing them with similar items, regardless of the original price paid. Both dealers and auctioneers will provide a valuation service for a fee.

A Daum internally-decorated glass dish, etched and painted in naturalistic colours with continuous bellflowers and gold borders, painted gold mark, c1905, 5in (12.5cm) wide.
£1,000–1,200 DORO

A Tiffany Favrile glass compote, with original label, c1905, 4in (10cm) high.
£650–750 ANO

A Continental glass powder bowl, painted with roses, 1920s, 6¼in (16cm) diam.
£35–40 SUS

A Lalique opalescent bowl, Anges, stencilled mark, after 1921, 14½in (37cm) diam.
£1,600–1,800 S

A Lalique opalescent glass fruit bowl, Ondines, moulded with six mermaids within swirling water and with blue stained finish, engraved 'R Lalique, France', numbered '381', after 1921, 8in (20.5cm) diam.
£700–800 CAG

A glass fruit bowl, c1925, 6½in (16.5cm) high.
£120–140 SUC

A Lalique clear and frosted glass bowl, Filix, No. 389, the exterior moulded in relief with spear-shaped foliage, wheelcut 'R Lalique, France', after 1927, 13in (33cm) diam.
£400–450 CSK

► An International Bottle Co pressed glass bowl, surmounted by the pink figure of a young girl, on a plinth, c1928, 13in (33cm) diam.
£40–50 BKK

► A Lalique glass bowl, Gui, moulded with mistletoe, the base with moulded signature and etched 'France', after 1921, 9¼in (23.5cm) diam.
£300–350 L&E

A Lalique opalescent glass bowl, Coquilles, engraved mark, after 1924, 5¼in (13.5cm) diam.
£140–160 HYD

A Lalique glass dish, Pissenlit, after 1921, 12in (30.5cm) diam.
£200–220 DAC

A Marcel Goupy Art Deco enamelled glass bowl, decorated in tones of blue with forget-me-nots and scrolls, signed in script, c1925, 11¾in (30cm) long.
£260–300 B&B

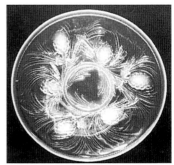

A Lalique opalescent glass bowl, decorated in deep relief with trailing vine and bunches of grapes, slight chips, signed, c1925, 7in (18cm) high.
£600–700 MCA

A Jobling opalescent glass dish, c1925, 10in (25.5cm) diam.
£60–70 CSA

A Lalique glass powder bowl, marked, c1925, 5in (12.5cm) diam.
£450–550 SHa

Condition

The condition is absolutely vital when assessing the value of an antique. Damaged pieces on the whole appreciate much less than perfect examples. However, a rare desirable piece may command a high price even when damaged.

An International Bottle Co pressed glass bowl, with etched decoration, surmounted by the figure of a young boy holding a fawn, on a plinth, c1928, 12½in (32cm) diam.
£35–45 BKK

An American Libbey Glass cut-glass bowl, marked, 1919–30, 8¾in (22cm) diam.
£300–330 BrW

An American glass bowl, with amethyst rim, c1930, 6in (15cm) diam.
£15–20 TS

A James Powell blue glass bowl, with thread design, 1930s, 9in (23cm) diam.
£90–110 JHa

A Bagley blue glass bowl, with painted decoration, 1930, 6¼in (16cm) diam.
£15–20 BKK

Bagley glass

Bagley, the glass company based in Knottingly, West Yorkshire, started making bottles in 1871, and in 1913 diversified into domestic and pub glassware under the name The Crystal Glass Co Ltd.

Queen's Choice, a design influenced by Chippendale, was introduced in 1922, soon to be followed by several other very successful patterns. The heyday of the company was the mid-1930s, when it was under the management of Dr Stanley Bagley and Mr Percy Bagley. A number of excellent Art Deco patterns were created, initially by designer Alexander Hardie Williamson, but later by in-house artists. Crystaltynt, a range of delicately-coloured glass, both clear and frosted, was introduced at the same time. This period of innovation ended with the outbreak of WWII. In 1947 an opaline glass, Crystopal, was produced, and many post-war designs were made from this material. Ten years later the company began to manufacture Jetique, a rich black glass that proved highly popular. Many articles were decorated, either by hand or by transfer, and often metal-mounted, but in general such decoration did little to enhance the beauty of the glass.

Both Stanley and Percy Bagley died in the late 1950s. Subsequently, the factory changed hands several times and recently has been modernized. It now produces high-quality glassware for the cosmetics industry. The period of interest for Bagley glass collectors runs from the early 1920s to the early 1960s.

A Bagley green pressed glass bowl and cover, 1929, 4in (10cm) high.
£8–10 BKK

A cut-glass powder bowl and cover, c1930, 5½in (14cm) diam.
£45–50 TAC

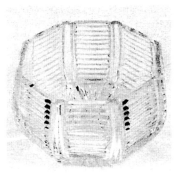

A Czechoslovakian amber pressed glass penguin bowl, on a plinth, c1929, 13in (33cm) diam.
£65–75 BKK

A Powell amethyst glass bowl, by Whitefriars, with wavy decoration, c1930, 6in (15cm) high.
£70–80 RUSK

A conical glass bowl, 1930s, 8in (20.5cm) high.
£45–50 HEM

◀ A lead crystal step-cut bowl, 1930s, 4¼in (11cm) high.
£70–80 PSA

A Lalique opalescent glass bowl, Lys, c1930, 9in (23cm) diam.
£600–650 RUSK

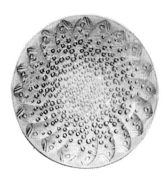

A Lalique opalescent bowl, Roscoff, signed 'R Lalique, France', after 1932, 16in (40.5cm) diam.
£450–550 MCA

René Lalique

René Lalique (1860–1945) was the foremost jeweller of the Art Nouveau period. He became the leading glass designer of the Art Deco period, making a wide range of objects, including car mascots, perfume bottles, vases, tableware and plates, clocks, jewellery, lighting and figurines. Some of his glass was incorporated into furniture. Most pieces were machine made for the mass market, although the perfume bottles were relatively expensive in their day, as they often held scent by top perfumiers.

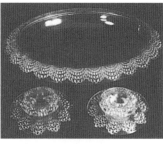

A Lalique clear glass oval fruit dish and four matching candlesticks, Saint Gall, with turn-over rim, the underside moulded in relief with swags of bubbles, candlesticks with detachable nozzles, acid-stamped 'R Lalique', after 1934, largest 12in (30.5cm) diam.
£700–800 CSK

A Lalique opalescent glass bowl, Perruches, No. 419, moulded in relief with a band of budgerigars perched on foliage, stencil-etched 'R Lalique', slight damage, after 1931, 9½in (24cm) diam.
£1,500–1,800 CSK

A green glass bowl, surmounted by a fish, on a plinth, c1932, 8½in (21.5cm) diam.
£45–50 BKK

A Powell pink glass bowl, 1930s, 13in (33cm) diam.
£100–120 TCG

A Bagley clear amber glass marine bowl, designed by Alexander H Williamson, pattern 3000, RD 798843, 1934, 12in (30.5cm) diam.
£50–60 PC

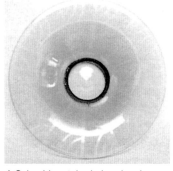

A Schneider etched glass bowl, c1939, 14in (35.5cm) diam.
£120–140 DAF

A Bagley 13 piece clear flint glass fruit set, Pendant 742, with intaglio bases, RD 742290, 1932, largest bowl 9in (23cm) diam.
£65–75 PC

A Bagley blue pressed glass bowl, Queen's Choice, 1933, 4¼in (11cm) diam.
£8–10 BKK

A Jobling green glass bowl, surmounted by the figure of a dancing girl, on a plinth, c1934, 9in (223cm) diam.
£35–45 BKK

A Venetian powdered gold glass bowl, 1930s, 12in (30.5cm) wide.
£60–70 PSA

A Sowerby amber pressed glass bowl, with holly leaf and berry design, on a black plinth, c1936, 15½in (39.5cm) diam.
£40–50 BKK

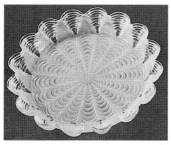

A Lalique shallow opalescent glass dish, Rosheim, decorated with stylized shell motif, c1935, 13in (33cm) diam.
£300–350 HYD

► A Bagley hand-decorated clear glass seven-piece fruit set, Adelphi 3162, 1946, largest bowl 8in (20.5cm) diam.
£35–40 PC

A Bagley clear blue glass sweet dish, Alexandra 3121/3, 1940, 11in (28cm) wide.
£15–20 PC

◄ A Bagley clear amber glass seven-piece fruit set, Carnival 3141, RD 849118, 1946, largest bowl 8½in (21.5cm) diam.
£25–30 PC

A Murano green glass dish, with gold leaf insert, 1950s, 5in (12.5cm) wide.
£20–25 FD

A James Powell footed glass bowl, with blue ribbon decoration, 1930–50, 3in (7.5cm) high.
£20–25 JHa

An American two-section red glass dish, with silver overlay, 1950s, 7in (18cm) wide.
£60–70 MON

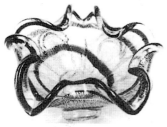

A Murano glass dish, with aubergine and gold decoration and curled edges, 1950s, 9½in (24cm) wide.
£30–35 FD

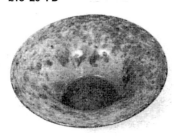

A Murano green glass dish, with silver leaf insert, 1950s, 5in (12.5cm) wide.
£15–20 FD

A Bagley clear flint glass sugar bowl, Katherine 3187, 1955, 5½in (14cm) high.
£15–20 PC

A Murano glass dish, with red, white and gold layers, 1950s, 3¾in (9.5cm) diam.
£25–30 FD

A Monart glass bowl, signed, 20thC, 9¼in (23.5cm) diam.
£70–80 BWA

A Vasart pink glass bowl, c1955, 7in (18cm) diam.
£40–50 CSA

◄ A Venetian blue glass dish, with gilt decoration, c1955, 7in (18cm) wide.
£25–30 CSA

Boxes

A glass box lid, with a sulphide depicting Louis Philippe, probably Baccarat, c1830, 2¼in (5.5cm) high.
£180–200 BrW

A French opaline glass hand-painted casket, c1870, 4in (10cm) high.
£850–950 CB

A Moser-style casket, enamelled with flowers and birds, with gilded mounts, c1880, 8in (20.5cm) wide.
£800–900 CB

A yellow and white swirl glass casket, with gilded brass mounts, c1890, 6in (15cm) wide.
£460–500 CB

A Lalique frosted glass powder box and cover, *Amour Assis*, the cover surmounted by a seated cherub, the sides with flowers and foliage, moulded 'R Lalique', c1920, 4½in (11.5cm) diam.
£1,700–2,000 CSK

A Lalique black glass circular box and cover, *Pommier du Japon*, the sides finely ribbed, moulded on the base 'R Lalique' and 'Arys', c1920, 3½in (9cm) diam.
£700–800 P

A heavy cut-glass box and cover, c1920, 7in (18cm) wide.
£120–140 DUN

A Lalique opalescent glass box and cover, Cyprins No. 42, the cover moulded with swimming fish, moulded 'R Lalique', c1922, 10½in (26.5cm) diam.
£1,000–1,200 S

A Lalique amber glass box and cover, Cleones No. 49, the cover moulded in relief on the underside with beetles, moulded 'R Lalique', c1922, 6½in (16.5cm) diam.
£650–800 CSK

A Lalique opalescent amber glass box cover, Cyprins No. 42, the underside moulded in relief with fan-tailed goldfish, moulded 'R Lalique', slight damage, c1922, 10in (25.5cm) diam.
£650–800 CSK
If perfect, this piece would be worth £1,200–1,400.

▶ A Lalique glass box and cover, Roger, moulded with long-tailed exotic birds perched in branches among clear glass discs, engraved 'Lalique, France', c1928, 5in (12.5cm) diam.
£300–350 S(S)

A Lalique frosted glass box and cover, Degas No. 66, the top with a finial moulded in the form of a ballerina, the tutu forming the cover, engraved 'R Lalique' and numbered, c1922, 3in (7.5cm) diam.
£500–550 CSK

A Powell yellow and amber glass powder box and cover, c1930, 3½in (9cm) high.
£80–100 TCG

A Lalique clear, frosted and blue-stained glass box and cover, Enfants, moulded with children, stencilled mark 'R Lalique, France', c1932, 3in (7.5cm) high.
£400–450 S(S)

Art Deco

Glass was one of the most distinctive products of the Art Deco period. While pieces by famous factories and designers such as Orrefors and René Lalique command high prices, much of the mass-produced ware from the 1920s and '30s remain comparatively inexpensive. These decorative domestic wares are made from pressed glass, often frosted, using muted colours. Works are geometrical in style and favourite motifs include nudes, fish and generalized aquatic forms.

A Lalique box and cover, Figurines et Voiles, moulded with a band of classically draped figures holding roses and swirling lengths of material, heightened in red, the lid with two similar figures, damaged, moulded mark 'R Lalique, made in France', c1930, 3in (7.5cm) high.
£200–250 S(S)

A Czechoslovakianπ malachite and green glass box, the cover decorated with a nude classical maiden in relief, 1930s, 6in (15cm) wide.
£130–150 P(B)

Candlesticks

A glass candlestick, with a square tapered stem and high ringed dome foot, c1740, 8in (20.5cm) high.
£1,800–2,000 C(S)

An air-twist candlestick, with a triple collar, the columnar stem enclosing an air-twist gauze spiral and terminating on an annulated knop, the domed foot moulded with radiating ribs, c1750, 8½in (21.5cm) high.
£2,000–2,500 C

An opaque white candlestick, with tall, waisted and collared stem, on a domed foot, Bristol or south Staffordshire, c1770, 10in (25.5cm) high.
£800–900 Som

An Irish glass library candlestick, with lemon squeezer square base, c1790, 5in (12.5cm) high.
£340–400 WGT

Sets/pairs

Unless otherwise stated, any description which refers to 'a set' or 'a pair' includes a guide price for the entire set or the pair, even though the illustration may show only a single item.

▶ A pair of George III cut-glass two-light candelabra, each with a star finial and petal-shaped canopy, the arms hung with prismatic crops, 21¾in (55.5cm) high.
£1,000–1,200 P

A pair of George III ormolu-mounted porcelain and cut-glass two-light candelabra, each centred by a facet spire with crescent and pagoda finial flanked by a pair of scrolled arms decorated with faceted drops, raised on a square stepped blue and gilt-decorated porcelain plinth, on bun feet, late 18thC, 23½in (59.5cm) high.
£4,500–5,000 (SNY)

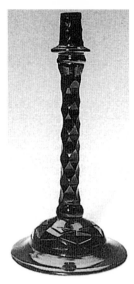

A blue glass faceted taper stick, the stem cut with diamond facets and terminating in a basal knop above a domed foot with geometric cutting, c1790, 10½in (26.5cm) high.
£1,200–1,500 Som

◀ A pair of glass candlesticks, the pan-top sconces on hollow sockets with circular neck rings, c1800, 6in (15cm) high.
£700–800 Som

▶ A pair of bronze and gilt-bronze candlesticks, each with leafy nozzle above a band of leaves hung with icicle pendants, the reeded stem on a square base, c1830, 12in (30.5cm) high.
£1,500–1,800 S

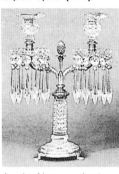

A pair of brass and cut-glass table lights, each of the candleholders with lustre drop-hung drip pans supported by leaf-cast arms and centred by a cone finial, the cut-glass tapered stem with a gilt-brass moulding and lions' paw feet, c1825, 13¾in (35cm) high.
£3,750–4,500 S

An American glass candlestick, c1840, 9in (23cm) high.
£240–280 MJW

An 'End of Day' candlestick, with colours overlaid on white glass, c1845, 9¼in (23.5cm) high.
£35–40 SER

A French *pâte-de-riz* agate and rose opaline glass candlestick, probably St Louis, 1850–70, 6½in (16.5cm) high.
£130–160 MJW

◀ A pair of mid-18thC-style crystal glass candlesticks, 1870, 8¾in (22cm) high.
£550–650 MJW

▶ A pair of Victorian cut-glass candelabra, with seven scrolling candle arms, each lacking one arm, late 19thC, 36½in (92.5cm) high.
£3,500–4,000 S(NY)

A pair of cut-glass candlesticks, c1880, 12in (30.5cm) high.
£420–500 DUN

A pressed glass candlestick, c1885, 7in (18cm) high.
£125–150 GLN

▶ A pair of Edwardian cut-glass candlesticks, the trumpet-shaped stems and bases cut with hobnail ornament, supporting thistle-shaped nozzles, 1901–10, 15in (38cm) high.
£1,000–1,200 CSK

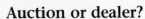

A pair of Bagley green pressed glass candlesticks, 1929, 5¼in (13.5cm) high.
£12–15 BKK

A pair of 18thC-style candlesticks, the cylindrical stems terminating in bell-shaped feet, all facet-cut, chipped, early 20thC, 10in (25.5cm) high.
£300–350 HSS
If perfect, these would have been worth as much as £800.

A pair of moulded glass candlesticks, c1920, 9in (23cm) high.
£75–90 DUN

Auction or dealer?

All the pictures in our price guides originate from auction houses and dealers. When buying at auction, prices can be lower than those of a dealer, but a buyer's premium and VAT will be added to the hammer price. Equally, when selling at auction, commission, tax and photography charges must be taken into account. Dealers will often restore pieces before putting them back on the market. Both dealers and auctioneers will provide professional advice, so it is worth researching both sources before buying or selling your antiques.

A pair of girandoles, with amethyst and smoked-glass drops and black metal candle holders, 1930s, 8in (20.5cm) high.
£450–550 JPr
The word 'girandole' derives from the Italian *girandola*, a kind of revolving firework. It was used in Britain from the 18thC to describe candelabra and sconces.

Cutting

The practice of cutting decorative facets into glass was developed in England, Ireland and northern Europe during the late 18th and early 19th centuries. Designs were created to reflect the light, making the glass object appear even more brilliant.

A Wedgwood green glass candleholder, with hollow stem, labelled and engraved, 1960–70, 11in (28cm) high.
£25–30 TCG

A pair of Czechoslovakian glass candlesticks, the bases with insect decoration, c1930, 8½in (21.5cm) high.
£60–70 BKK

Car Mascots

The most innovative mascots were produced by Lalique between 1925 and 1935. Their first commission was in 1925, to design a glass mascot for the Citroën 5CV. Following this success they went on to create 32 different designs, some with specially-ordered exotic colours.

Original Lalique mascots will be intaglio-moulded with 'R. Lalique' somewhere on, or near, the base. Tiny engraved catologue numbers can also be present and will usually indicate an early piece. It is important to remember, however, that Lalique still produce five of their original designs in modern lead crystal; Coq Nain, Tete de Coq, Eagle, Chrysis and Perch, the latter in various colours. These will only have a hand-engraved 'Lalique France' on the base, and should not be mistaken for originals. Remember, if the glass has a lead-clear, almost perfect depth then it may well be modern.

Another interesting company was H. G. Ascher Limited of Manchester who traded under the name of Red-Ashay. From the mid-1920s until the late 1930s, the company produced 30 or more different examples. Recent research indicates that, although the designs may have been British, they were manufactured in either Czechoslovakia or Bohemia and imported. Like their French equivalent, they were also famous for illuminated bases, often fitted with colour filters, illuminating the mascot at night, and making a bizarre and dazzling display. Although not sharing the same quality of finish, and consequently high value, some Red-Ashay mascots are, in fact, rarer than Lalique examples. A good collection of Red-Ashay can be created on a budget, with a probable high return.

Condition is of paramount importance, a minor chip will decrease the value by about 50 percent, and a crack or break by about 70 percent. When inspecting a glass mascot examine the base for signs of damage caused by the one-time fitting of an illuminated mount.

Corning Glass and Marius Sabino mascots have received little interest in the past. However, a number of interesting animal and allegorical designs were created. Recognizable by always having a light blue hue, they are a joy to own, and although they do not appear in the market very often, are not expensive at auction.

Some glass mascot types were never intended to be used as mascots. Various Red-Ashay, Etling and Hector Planchot varieties were sold as paperweights and ornaments, and some Lalique examples were mounted on black glass.

Undoubtedly, the most important thing to bear in mind when selecting a glass mascot, is it an original mascot in near-perfect condition? If not, then save your money for another opportunity to purchase. **Peter W. Card**

An H G Ascher satin finish glass car mascot, Butterfly Girl, by Red Ashay, in a square nickel-plated mount on an oak base, 1920s.
£1,800–2,000 BKS
Butterfly Girl was one of the most popular products of the H G Ascher company of Manchester, and one of the few mascots manufactured in the 1920s that did not copy a Lalique design. Sometimes called Dancing Girl, it was often colour-illuminated from below and wired so that the strength of the light increased with the speed of the car.

A Lalique clear glass car mascot, Five Horses, with original illuminated radiator mounting, intaglio-moulded 'R Lalique, France', engraved No. '1122' on base, August 1925.
£8,000–10,000 BKS
The only Lalique mascot produced especially for a particular car, Five Horses was created for use on the Citroën 5CV.

◀ A Lalique eagle's head glass car mascot, moulded 'R Lalique, France' on base, 1920s.
£800–900 BKS

A Model of France cockatoo glass car mascot, with original illuminated nickel-plated radiator mounting, c1922.
£250–300 BKS

▶ A Lalique clear and frosted glass car mascot, Falcon, its talons clasping a circular base, moulded 'R Lalique', after 1925, 6½in (16.5cm) high.
£1,000–1,200 P

A Lalique glass car mascot, The Archer, clear and light grey highlight recesses with stained finish, etched signature 'R Lalique, France', No. '1126' beneath base, 1926.
£1,500–1,800 BKS

An H G Ascher clear and satin finish glass car mascot, Charioteer, on a metal base, 1926.
£2,500–2,800 BKS
This mascot was developed to rival Lalique's first Cinq Chevaux; only a few were produced.

A Lalique clear and frosted glass car mascot, Swallow, No. 1143, moulded signature 'R Lalique', 1928.
£1,800–2,000 BKS

A Lalique clear and frosted glass car mascot, Ram's Head, intaglio-moulded signature 'R Lalique, France', 1928.
£2,000–2,300 BKS

A Lalique clear and frosted glass car mascot, Small Dragonfly, No. 1144, moulded signature 'Lalique' to lower section of wing, etched 'R Lalique' on side of base, 1928.
£2,700–3,000 BKS

▶ A Lalique dark grey and amber centre glass car mascot, *Coq Nain*, wheel-cut signature 'R Lalique' on rear of lower tail, etched No. '1135' on base, 1928.
£2,900–3,200 BKS

A lime-green glass car mascot, Eagle's Head, in the style of Lalique, intaglio-moulded 'Persons Worcester Mass', 1928.
£1,500–1,800 BKS

A Lalique amethyst-tinted and frosted glass car mascot, Victory, No. 1147, moulded signature 'R Lalique', 1928, 10in (25.5cm) long.
£17,500–20,000 BKS
The most famous of the Lalique mascots.

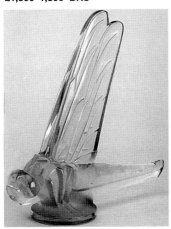

A Lalique frosted glass car mascot, *Grenouille*, on a circular base, chrome-mounted, signed 'R Lalique France', after 1928, 2½in (6.5cm) high.
£5,000–6,000 P

◀ A Lalique clear and frosted glass car mascot, Large Dragonfly, No. 1145, moulded signature 'R Lalique' on side section, etched 'R Lalique, France' to side of lower body, 1928.
£2,900–3,200 BKS

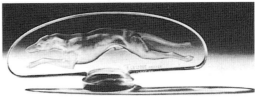

A Lalique oval glass car mascot, Greyhound, intaglio-moulded with a figure of a racing greyhound, moulded 'R Lalique France', after 1928, 7½in (19cm) wide.
£1,800–2,000 P

A Lalique clear and frosted glass car mascot, Victory, with Breves Galleries chrome base, moulded 'R Lalique France', reduced in length, after 1928, 9¾in (25cm) long.
£1,800–2,000 P

A Lalique dark grey glass car mascot, Grey Boar, intaglio signature 'R Lalique' between legs, stencilled 'R Lalique' under base, c1929.
£800–950 BKS

A glass car mascot, minor chips, unmarked, 1930s, 5½in (14cm) high.
£325–400 S(S)

A Walt Disney glass car mascot, Pinocchio, with original painted highlights, 1940–50s.
£425–475 S

A Lalique clear and frosted glass car mascot, *Coq Nain*, marked, after 1928, 8in (20.5cm) high.
£220–260 WL
René Jules Lalique was the major glass designer of the Art Deco Movement. Lalique signed his works, but after his death in 1945 the initial 'R' was omitted from items produced by the factory.

A Lalique glass car mascot, *Longchamps*, introduced by René Lalique on 12th June 1929.
£4,500–5,000 BKS
This example has the rare double mane which was withdrawn when the single-maned version was introduced on 10th September 1929.

A Lalique glass car mascot, Chrysis, etched 'R Lalique' under base, c1930, 5¾in (14.5cm) high.
£1,200–1,500 S

▶ A Sabino opalescent coloured glass fish car mascot, signed on base, slightly damaged, c1930, 2¼in (5.5cm) high.
£325–370 CSK
Marius Sabino (1878–1961) was a contemporary of Lalique, although very much in his shadow. Sabino's glass is instantly recognizable by its crystal blue and honey hue, which was obtained by using a six per cent solution of arsenic compared to Lalique's use of one per cent.

A Lalique clear and frosted glass car mascot, *Pintade*, modelled as a female guinea fowl, with chromed mount, on black glass base, slight damage, signed 'R Lalique France', after 1929, 5in (12.5cm) high.
£1,250–1,500 P

A Lalique wheel-cut and moulded opalescent glass car mascot, *Perche*, 1929–39, 6¼in (16cm) long.
£1,800–2,000 S

An Ernest Sabino glass car mascot, in the form of a mouse, signed and inscribed, c1930.
£1,200–1,400 BKS

MILLER'S

Essential Guides for the Collector

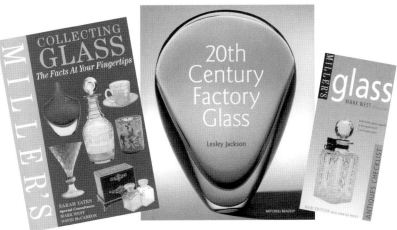

See our full range of books on antiques & collectables at
www.millers.uk.com
or call our credit card hotline for
UK telephone orders on **01933 443863**
free postage and packing

Carnival Glass

Carnival Glass is a form of press-moulded glass that has been iridized. Inspired by the success of the more costly Tiffany Glass, it quickly acquired the sobriquet 'Poor Man's Tiffany'. Its success damaged the market for Tiffany's glass. Originally, it was made in the USA from 1908 by the Fenton Art Glass Company, quickly followed by Dugan, Northwood and Imperial Glass. When introduced it was relatively cheap, Dugan items were advertised in the UK at between 5d and 9d. Its heyday in the USA was around 1910–20, after which it fell from fashion. However, interest continued in Europe, and from the late 1920s the European manufacturers started producing iridized pressed glass as one means of breaking out of recession. Called by an assortment of glamorous names by each maker, as the market declined the glass ended up as prizes at fairgrounds hence its current name came into being.

Over the past twenty years Carnival Glass has risen steadily in value, outpacing inflation. Some very rare and unique items have reached tens of thousands of dollars in the USA. The long-term prospects of holding a good market position are probably very sound. Its phenomena is uniquely American, and it therefore holds a very special place in the American collector market. Item prices are sometimes higher in the USA though not always.

The most important thing to consider when buying Carnival Glass is the quality of the iridescence; value can vary by three times between a poorly iridized example and one that dazzles. Minor damage, such as a chip to the collar, could devalue an item by 10–50 percent, serious damage such as cracks, by 70–90 percent.

Fakes are relatively rare in the UK. Three bowls of which to be wary, are Northwood's 'Peacocks on the Fence', 'Good Luck' and 'Grape and Cable'. Reproduction bowls usually feel heavy and are slightly smaller than the genuine item. There is also the risk of fraud with modern Carnival Glass which has had its trade mark ground off. The American Carnival Glass Societies in the 1950s and '60s pressured the manufacturers to put trademarks on their new items to distinguish them from the old.

The most collectable factory is probably Northwood. However, Swedish and Finnish items are currently attracting a good deal of interest. Probably the most popular patterns are those with animals, the least popular being those with grapes or cut patterns, though there are exceptions. There are, however, many books available to help the collector. **Alan Sedgwick**

A Northwood Carnival glass Peacock bowl, with amethyst base glass, 1908–15, 9in (23cm) diam
£100–125 ASe
The ruffling around the rim is known as a piecrust edge. This bowl is a reproduction, and the moulding is not as crisp as an original.

A Dugan Carnival glass Nautilus bowl, with marigold iridescence on opalescent glass, 1908–15, 6in (15cm) wide.
£220–250 ASe

A Northwood Carnival glass Spring Time butter dish, with amethyst base glass, 1908–15, 8½in (20.5cm) wide.
£250–300 ASe

A Fenton Carnival glass Stag and Holly footed bowl, with green base glass, 1908–25, 8in (20.5cm) diam.
£65–75 ASe

◄ A Fenton Carnival glass Peacock and Urn plate, with Bearded Berry exterior pattern, with blue base glass, 1908–25, 9½in (24cm) diam.
£180–200 ASe

A Fenton Carnival glass Vintage bowl, with green base glass, 1908–25, 8in (20.5cm) diam.
£45–55 ASe
Grape patterns were very popular in their day and are among the most available now.

◄ A Fenton Carnival glass Orange Tree hatpin holder, with blue base glass, 1908–25, 5½in (14cm) high.
£300–350 ASe

A Fenton Carnival glass Peacock Tail card tray, with amethyst base glass, 1908–25, 7in (18cm) wide.
£50–60 ASe
Card trays are distinct from bonbons in that they only have two sides turned up.

A Millersburg Carnival glass Seacoast pin tray, with satin-finished iridescence on amethyst base glass, 1909–11, 5in (12.5cm) wide.
£225–250 ASe
This is one of the smallest pieces of Carnival glass.

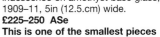

A Millersburg Carnival glass Peacock and Urn fruit bowl, with satin-finished iridescence on amethyst base glass, 1909–11, 6in (15cm) diam.
£150–175 ASe

A Fenton Carnival glass Peter Rabbit plate, with green base glass, 1909–15, 9½in (24cm) diam.
£1,000–1,200 ASe
This pattern can also be found on bowls.

Three Imperial Glass Carnival glass ripple vases, in lavender, purple and helios green, 1910–20, tallest 16in (40.5cm) high.
£30–90 each ASe
This pattern was very popular.

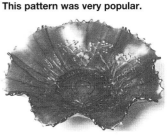

A Northwood Carnival glass amethyst comport, with basketweave exterior and plain Rainbow interior, 1910–20, 5in (12.5cm) high.
£60–70 TS

A Dugan Carnival glass Fish Scale and Beads bowl, with amethyst base glass, 1910–20, 6¼in (16cm) diam.
£45–50 TS

A Northwood Carnival glass green Good Luck bowl, 1910–20, 9in (23cm) diam.
£180–200 TS

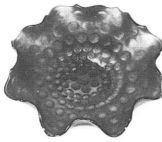

A Northwood Carnival glass Blackberry comport, with basketweave exterior, with amethyst base glass, 1910–20, 7in (18cm) high.
£60–70 TS

A Fenton Carnival glass amethyst glass bowl, decorated with coin spot pattern, 1910–20, 7½in (19cm) diam.
£35–40 WAC

An Imperial Glass Carnival glass Octagon wine set, with marigold iridescence, 1910–20, decanter 10½in (26.5cm) high.
£150–165 ASe

◄ A Fenton Carnival glass blue Peacock and Grape bowl, with Bearded Berry exterior, 1910–20, 8¾in (22cm) diam.
£65–75 TS

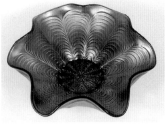

A Fenton Carnival glass Peacock Tail bowl, with amethyst base glass, 1910–15, 8¾in (22cm) diam.
£55–65 ASe

A pair of Imperial Glass Carnival glass Premium candlesticks, with marigold iridescence, 1910–25, 8½in (21.5cm) high.
£80–90 ASe

A pair of Imperial Glass Carnival glass Soda Gold candlesticks, with smoke iridescence, 1910–25, 3½in (9cm) high.
£70–£85 ASe

A Dugan Carnival glass Butterfly and Tulip footed bowl, with black amethyst base glass, 1910–31, 13in (33cm) wide.
£1,000–1,200 ASe

► An Imperial Glass Carnival glass Pansy sugar bowl and milk jug, with amber base glass, 1910–25, 3½in (9cm) high.
£120–135 ASe

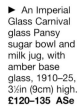

A Fenton Carnival glass Horses Medallion rosebowl, with blue base glass, 1910, 5½in (14cm) diam.
£250–300 ASe
The medallion of the three horses heads is based on a painting by John Frederick Herring. The studies of the head were of a horse Herring bought from Queen Victoria.

A Dugan Carnival glass scalloped Cherry bowl, with marigold iridescence, 1910–31, 8in (20.5cm) diam.
£20–25 MEG

An Imperial Fashion Glass Carnival glass punch set, with marigold iridescence, comprising a bowl base, six cups and six hooks, 1910–25, bowl 12in (30.5cm) diam.
£100–120 ASe

A Carnival glass Blackberry footed bowl, with marigold iridescence, c1920, 8¼in (21cm) diam.
£25–30 MAC

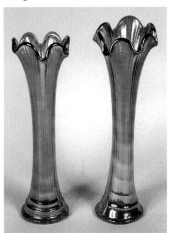

Two Imperial Glass Carnival glass ripple vases, with marigold iridescence, c1915, tallest 9¼in (23.5cm) high.
£18–20 TAC

A Northwood Carnival glass Peacocks on the Fence ruffled bowl, with marigold iridescence, c1915, 9in (23cm) diam.
£70–80 DBo

◄ An Eda Carnival glass Four Flowers Variant green glass bowl, c1920, 8½in (21.5cm) diam.
£65–75 WAC

A Fenton Carnival glass Stippled Rays bowl, with green base glass, 1920s, 6in (15cm) diam.
£30–35 DBo

A Sowerby Carnival glass Hen on the Nest butter dish, with marigold iridescence, 1925–35, 5½in (14cm) wide.
£35–45 ASe
This item was originally marketed as Chic, and some examples have very pale iridescence.

A Crown Crystal Carnival glass Butterfly and Waratah comport, with black amethyst base glass, c1925, 7in (18cm) high.
£175–200 TS

A Crown Crystal Carnival glass Kangaroo bowl, with black amethyst base glass, Australian, 1924–30, 9½in (24cm) diam.
£350–400 ASe
Two versions exist of this bowl: one with a small kangaroo and the other with a big kangaroo, probably to represent the Flying Grey and the Big Red kangaroos.

A Carnival glass Hobstar Reversed marigold glass rosebowl, c1930, 5¼in (13.5cm) diam.
£12–15 TS

A Sowerby Carnival glass Diving Dolphins footed bowl, in pale amethyst base glass, 1925–35, 8in (20.5cm) diam.
£150–175 ASe
This piece was made from an 1880s mould with a new plunger bearing the scroll-embossed pattern copied from Imperial Glass Co.

A Brockwitz Carnival glass May basket, c1930, 7in (18cm) diam.
£15–20 TS
This mould was used with a number of back patterns.

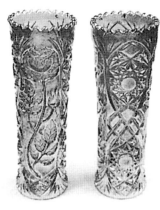

A pair of Brockwitz Rose Carnival glass Garden vases, with marigold iridescence, 1930–35, 9½in (24cm) high.
£180–200 ASe
Great use of intaglio patterns was made in Europe, whereas most US Carnival glass has embossed designs.

A pair of Finnish Riihimazi Carnival glass Kullervo candlesticks, with Rio pink base glass, c1939, 8½in (21.5cm) high.
£350–400 ASe

A Swedish Eda Carnival glass Amerika pattern rose or posy miniature bowl, with blue base glass, 1930s, 2½in (6.5cm) high.
£225–275 ASe

A Carnival glass commemorative plate, Independence Hall, 1970s, 8in (20.5cm) diam.
£25–30 TS

A Fenton red Carnival glass butter dish, modelled as a hen, c1975, 6¾in (17cm) high.
£25–30 MEG

Centrepieces

A cut-glass pineapple stand, the bowl cut with tapering panels within an everted scalloped rim, c1820, 6in (15cm) diam.
£275–300 P
Pineapple were very exotic and those people wealthy enough to own conservatories gave them pride of place on the sweet table.

A Stourbridge cut-glass centrepiece, possibly W H, B & J Richardson, the wide shallow bowl with shaped rim, cut with stylized leaves and hobnail diamonds, above a similarly cut detachable collar and flared pedestal, c1850, 17in (43cm) high.
£3,000–3,600 S

A Whitefriars/Powell iron-mounted table centrepiece, with wavy rim, c1880, 5in (12.5cm) high.
£240–280 JHa

A Bohemian amethyst flash and cut-glass three-tiered stand, chipped, c1860, 22⅞in (58cm) high.
£1,500–1,800 C

A Bohemian or Stourbridge cranberry-tinted épergne, the shallow bowl with crimped rim and high centre with gilt-metal mount, supporting a tall slender trumpet cased in clear glass, flanked by two similar trumpets and two pendant baskets, minor chips, c1880, 19¼in (49cm) high.
£750–850 S

A Victorian cranberry épergne bowl, with serpentine rim, centre trumpet vase and three similar trumpets with trefoil rims and applied clear crimped bands, 22in (56cm) high.
£500–550 WBH

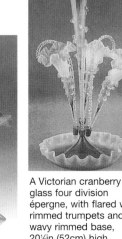

A Victorian cranberry glass four division épergne, with flared wavy rimmed trumpets and wavy rimmed base, 20½in (52cm) high.
£400–440 WL

Cross Reference
See Colour Review

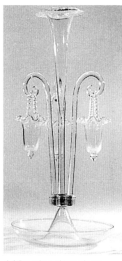

A Victorian clear glass épergne, the central tapered vase with crimped rim and with three scroll branches hung with baskets, on a plain circular base, 23½in (59.5cm) high.
£140–160 CAG

▶ A Victorian cranberry épergne, the central trumpet vase with applied crimped spiral band trefoil rim, with three smaller side vases, on a frilled circular base, 23in (58.5cm) high.
£300–330 WBH

A Victorian vaseline glass épergne, the central trumpet vase with applied trailing shell moulding, flanked by three smaller trumpets and three baskets with scrolled clear glass supports, on a scalloped circular base, 21¼in (54cm) high.
£550–600 TEN

◀ A centrepiece, on mirrored base, c1890, 6in (15cm) high. **£220–250 TER**

A five-trumpet green vaseline glass épergne, with one central and four radiating trumpets each with frilled rims and applied spiralling trails, above a dish with a frilled rim, slight damage and repairs, 19thC, 19¾in (50cm) high. **£350–450 CSK**

A cranberry glass épergne, with four trumpet vases and dish base, crinkled rims and pinched trailed decoration, c1890, 21in (53.5cm) high. **£550–650 RBB**

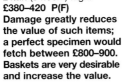

A Victorian glass centrepiece, engraved with holly leaves and berries, 16½in (42cm) high. **£250–350 CB**

A Victorian épergne, the central vase flanked by a matching pair of smaller vases and a pair of spiral stem branches suspending baskets, the opalescent borders applied with turquoise glass rims, some chips and cracks, 21½in (54.5cm) high. **£380–420 P(F) Damage greatly reduces the value of such items; a perfect specimen would fetch between £800–900. Baskets are very desirable and increase the value.**

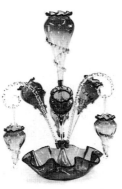

A Victorian cranberry glass épergne, with bulbous central vase and three smaller vases, three twisted cane arms supporting conforming baskets, all with crimped rims and with trailing ornaments, crimped circular base, central vase repaired, c1880, 22in (56cm) high. **£750–850 CAG**

A Victorian cranberry glass épergne, entwined with clear glass shell design, c1880, 22in (56cm) high. **£850–1,000 GAK**

A Bohemian ruby-tinted centrepiece, in two sections, comprising a shallow footed bowl, overlaid in opaque white and cut with circular panels painted with flowers, and tall stand with two large oval opaque white panels painted with flowers, on a flared foot with gilt leaf scroll reserve, late 19thC, 13in (33cm) high. **£2,000–2,500 S Although this was originally part of a suite, it is still desirable singly as a decorative substantial piece.**

A four-branch cranberry glass épergne, fitted with a central fluted trumpet vase, surrounded by three smaller trumpets above a crimped circular base, late 19thC, small chips, 21in (53.5cm) high. **£550–650 S(S)**

A cranberry glass épergne, the frilled bowl fitted with a tall trumpet vase flanked by two cranberry glass handkerchief vases, with clear glass spirals, late 19thC, 23in (58.5cm) high. **£500–600 S(S)**

A cranberry tinted glass épergne, with applied clear glass borders, fitted with a central trumpet-shaped vase and three smaller vases, flanked by scroll supports suspending three baskets, on dished round base, late 19thC, 15½in (39.5cm) high. **£950–1,100 DN**

Clocks & Garnitures

A René Lalique opalescent glass clock, Inseparables, after 1926, 4½in (11.5cm) high.
£1,000–1,200 S

Miller's is a price GUIDE not a price LIST

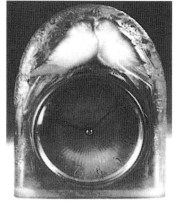

A Lalique opalescent glass clock, Deux Colombes, moulded in relief with a pair of doves among prunus blossom, moulded 'R Lalique', after 1926, 9in (23cm) high.
£1,500–1,800 P

A Lalique clock, Quatre Moineaux du Japon, the circular dial with black enamelled chapters, engraved 'R Lalique, France', with chrome base enclosing light fitting, after 1928, 7in (18cm) high.
£1,200–1,400 C(S)

A Bagley frosted green glass clock and two clear glass vases, Bamboo 3007, 1934, 5in (12.5cm) high.
£65–80 PC

A Bagley frostyed glass garniture, clock Wyndham 1333, posy vases Grantham 334, c1934, clock 5½in (14cm) high.
£65–80 PC

Custard Cups

An engraved custard cup, c1790, 2½in (6.5cm) high.
£125–145 MJW

Glass market

The market for glass is a steady one, underpinned by faithful collectors, and has remained constant even throughout the recession. Glass from the 18th century onwards is still relatively easy to find and value depends on the rarity of the decoration. Colourful glass of the 19th century is becoming increasingly popular with collectors and is also well-illustrated in this book.

A set of eight glass petal-moulded custard cups, c1850, 3½in (9cm) high.
£120–150 CB

A pink glass custard cup, on a clear base, c1890, 4in (10cm) high.
£35–50 CB

▶ Two Victorian custard cups, largest 3½in (9cm) high.
£10–15 Som

A pair of pressed glass lions, c1890, 5in (12.5cm) high.
£220–250 ARE

◀ A pair of Davidson pressed glass dogs, c1895, 5½in (14cm) long.
£225–250 GLN

Two Murano blown glass fish, 1930s, largest 11in (28cm) high.
£120–150 FD

A Sabino opalescent glass cockerel, c1930, 4½in (11.5cm) high.
£45–50 P(B)

A pair of opalescent glass book ends, modelled as stylized doves, marked 'Model, Paris', c1930, 6¾in (17cm) high.
£300–350 WTA

◀ A Sabino opalescent glass squirrel, c1930, 4½in (11.5cm) high.
£45–50 P(B)

▶ A set of four Italian handmade glass fish, c1955, 9in (23cm) high.
£70–80 OCA

Passion for Glass

UK and Europe's Premier Name for John Ditchfield Glass

Purveyors and buyers of quality French and European glass:
Sabino, Lalique, Daum, Sèvres, Baccarat, Verlys, Gallé, Loetz etc.

Telephone: +44 (0) 1253 354395
Mobile: +44 (0) 7790 515270
www.johnditchfield-glasform.com

A Venetian glass pine cone bottle, with a baluster stem on a conical foot, 17thC, 8½in (21.5cm) high.
£4,200–5,000 S

◀ A glass case bottle, with straight sides, c1750, 10½in (26.5cm) high.
£250–300 NWi

Miller's is a price GUIDE not a price LIST

▶ A green glass spirit decanter, gilded with Masonic symbols, stopper missing, c1790, 9in (23cm) high.
£650–750 NWi
Masonic pieces are uncommon, and the symbols on this piece are unusual.

A pair of glass spirit bottles, c1800, 8½in (21.5cm) high.
£500–550 Som

A set of six green glass condiment bottles, with gilded cartouche, in a papier mâché stand, c1800, 9in (23cm) high.
£1,600–2,000 CB

▶ A pair of Bristol blue glass chemists' bottles, c1800, 9in (23cm) high.
£120–140 FD

A pair of glass serving bottles, with metal mounts, and cork and metal stoppers, in silver-plated coasters, c1840, 14in (35.5cm) high.
£850–1,000 Som
Such bottles were used to serve wine and spirits, as it was considered ill-mannered to put manufacturers' bottles on the table.

▶ A glass bottle, by Ludwig Moser & Söhne, c1880, 3½in (9cm) high.
£170–200 MJW

A pair of amber glass spirit bottles, the bodies with slice, flute, diamond and printy cutting, and star-cut bases, possibly Irish, c1840, 11½in (29cm) high.
£720–800 Som

l & r. A pair of wrythen-moulded glass spirit bottles, c1840. **£500–600**
c. A glass spirit flagon.
£200–220 Som

A set of three spirit bottles, in a silver-plated stand, c1860.
£1,000–1,100 Som

◀ Two Victorian Aldridge & Co cod bottles, with original labels, 9in (23cm) high.
£10–12 TAR

JEANETTE HAYHURST
FINE GLASS

32a Kensington Church Street, London W8 4HA
Telephone/Fax: 020 7938 1539
Mon - Fri 10am - 5pm   Sat 12 - 5pm

A Venetian glass footed bowl, decorated with a band of gilt feathering, painted with green, blue and red dots, c1500, 6in (15cm) high.
£30,000–35,000 S

A wrythen-moulded glass sugar basin, c1800, 3½in (9cm) diam.
£160–200 Som

A glass bowl and cover, with slightly rubbed gilded decoration, c1800, 6in (15cm) high.
£550–650 CB

A glass sugar comport and cover, c1800, 5½in (14cm) high.
£600–650 Som

A blue glass finger bowl, decorated with a band of gilt anthemion within gilt panels, c1810, 3¼in (8.5cm) high.
£550–600 Som

A Bristol blue glass finger bowl, signed on base 'I. Jacobs, Bristol', c1810, 4¼in (11cm) diam.
£1,600–1,800 Som

An amethyst glass rib-moulded finger bowl, c1830, 3½in (9cm) high.
£150–180 MJW

A glass tea caddy bowl, c1830, 4¼in (11cm) high.
£180–220 MJW

A Bohemian Lithyalin glass bowl, by Buquoy Glasshouse, c1835, 7in (18cm) high.
£2,000–2,400 S

A green glass rib-moulded finger bowl, c1840, 4¾in (12cm) diam.
£130–160 CB

An amber cut-glass covered dish, c1840, 7½in (19cm) high.
£450–500 MJW

▶ A Bohemian glass bonbon dish, on a silver base, Vienna, c1844, 5¼in (13.5cm) high.
£700–800 MJW

◄ A Bohemian engraved blue-stained footed bowl, with scalloped rim, signed 'F. Zach', c1850, 11in (28cm) high.
£10,000–11,000 S
F Zach of F Steigerwald, Munich, Germany, c1855, was well-known for his fine engraving and subtle effects which made him a master engraver.

A Bohemian overlaid glass comport, 1860–70, 8¼in (21cm) high.
£380–450 P(B)

A cranberry glass bowl, with clear frill, in a silver-plated stand, c1880, 7in (18cm) high.
£120–150 CB

A Victorian cranberry glass bowl, with moulded swags and applied vaseline glass pinched feet, c1880, 6in (15cm) wide.
£100–120 BELL

A purple slag pressed glass lobed bowl, c1880, 5¾in (14.5cm) wide.
£30–35 GLN

A glass finger bowl, with green overlay, c1880, 5in (12.5cm) diam.
£120–140 MJW

A vaseline and opaline glass bonbon dish, with frilled edge, c1890, 4in (10cm) high.
£90–110 BELL

A cranberry glass bowl, on a clear baluster stem and conical foot, c1890, 5in (12.5cm) diam.
£140–170 CB

An orange glass coraline-decorated bowl, c1890, 9in (23cm) high.
£500–550 CB

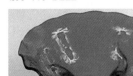

A Sowerby pressed glass bowl, moulded with flowers, on dolphin feet, c1890, 8½in (21.5cm) diam.
£100–120 JHa

A green glass bonbon dish, with a silver-plated stand, 1890–1910, 7in (18cm) high.
£120–150 CB

◄ A Stourbridge amethyst glass bowl, decorated with dragons and floral designs, c1900, 5in (12.5cm) high.
£750–900 MJW

A Victorian glass posy bowl, on a glass stand, c1900, 8in (20.5cm) high.
£240–280 CB

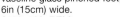

A Stevens & Williams reverse-cut cameo and intaglio glass dragon bowl, by Joshua Hodgetts, c1917, 9in (23cm) diam.
£1,500–1,800 ALiN

A John Walsh Walsh glass bowl, 1930s, 9in (23cm) diam.
£50–55 COL

An Argy-Rousseau *pâte-de-verre* coupe, Fers de Lance, moulded 'F Argy-Rousseau', c1930, 7in (18cm) diam.
£5,000–6,000 S(NY)

A Bagley frosted glass boat-shaped bowl, Salisbury 2832, c1932, 8¾in (22cm) diam.
£15–25 PC

A Sabino moulded opalescent and black enamel glass bowl, c1925, 7¾in (19.5cm) diam.
£450–550 SUC

A cloud glass footed bowl, 1930s, 6in (15cm) diam.
£20–25 BEV

A Sowerby pressed glass bowl, c1935, 8¼in (21cm) diam.
£40–50 BKK

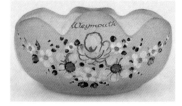

A Bagley glass bowl, 1940s, 12in (30.5cm) diam.
£20–25 COL

◄ An engraved glass bowl, The Warrior Dance, by Clare Henshaw, c1994, 11¼in (28.5cm) high.
£2,500–3,000 JHa

► A Glasform bowl, signed and numbered '4303', 1994, 6in (15cm) diam.
£65–80 GLA

An Art glass bowl, 1930s, 6½in (16.5cm) diam.
£40–50 JHa

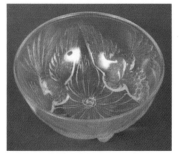

A Jobling glass bowl, decorated with birds, 1930s, 7½in (19cm) diam.
£80–90 BEV

A Sowerby pressed glass bowl, c1936, 7in (18cm) diam.
£40–50 BKK

A Bagley frosted glass bowl, Tulip Posy 3169, Rd No. 870054, c1953, 5½in (14cm) diam.
£20–25 PC
Bagley Glass was produced in a variety of colours, both decorated and undecorated.

An Imperial Glass Carnival glass
Twins pattern bowl, early 20thC,
6in (15cm) diam.
£15–20 PC

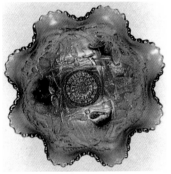

A Northwood Carnival glass
Wishbone pattern bowl, c1910,
7½in (19cm) diam.
£75–90 ASe

A Northwood Carnival glass Leaf
and Beads pattern rose bowl,
with blue base glass, c1910,
5½in (14cm) diam.
£65–85 ASe

A Fenton Carnival glass Orange Tree
glass bowl, with marigold iridescence,
1910–20, 8½in (21.5cm) diam.
£30–35 TS

An Imperial Glass Carnival glass
Lustre Rose pattern footed bowl,
with purple base glass, c1910,
7½in (19cm) diam.
£55–75 ASe

A Fenton Carnival glass Diamond
and Rib pattern vase, with green
base glass, c1910, 11in (28cm) high.
£22–24 ASe

A Northwood Carnival glass bonbon
dish, with green base glass, c1910,
7½in (19cm) wide.
£60–80 ASe

◄ An Imperial Glass Carnival glass
Diamond Lace pattern water set,
with purple base glass, c1915,
jug 9in (23cm) high.
£500–600 ASe

A Northwood Carnival glass Grape
and Cable pattern candle lamp,
c1910, 10½in (26.5cm) high.
£420–500 ASe

A Northwood Carnival glass Grape
and Cable pattern butter dish,
with green base glass, c1910,
6in (15cm) wide.
£175–250 ASe

A Northwood Carnival glass Grape
and Cable pattern plate, with green
base glass, c1910, 9in (23cm) diam.
£75–90 DKH

▶ An Imperial Glass Carnival glass
ripple pattern vase, c1920,
10in (25.5cm) high.
£65–70 TS

► A Sowerby Carnival glass Daisy Block rowboat, with pale amethyst base glass, made from an 1880s mould, 1925–35, 12in (30.5cm) long.
£150–175 ASe

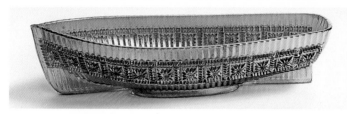

A Fenton Carnival glass bowl, with red base glass, c1925, 7in (18cm) diam.
£300–350 ASe

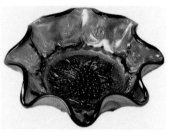

A Sowerby Carnival glass swan butter dish, with marigold iridescence, made from an 1880s mould, 1925–35, 6in (15cm) high.
£110–130 ASe

A Carnival glass bowl, c1930, 6½in (16.5cm) diam.
£3–5 MAC

A Brockwitz Carnival glass Curved Star pattern cheese dish, c1930, 8½in (21.5cm) diam.
£80–100 ASe

An Imperial Glass Carnival glass Heavy Grape pattern helios green fruit bowl, c1930, 7¼in (18.5cm) high.
£45–50 TS

A Carnival glass Grand Thistle pattern Art Deco-style water set, c1930, jug 11½in (29cm) high.
£1,000–1,200 ASe

A Victorian white opaque and ruby glass edged épergne, the four trumpet-shaped vases with clear trailed and crimped decoration, rims and base, 21½in (54.5cm) high.
£400–480 CAG
When buying these pieces, make sure that all parts belong and are not a marriage. Check they are securely plastered in, which should be with plaster of Paris for all mounts, and not any of the epoxy resins.

A three-trumpet cranberry glass épergne, c1880, 17¼in (44cm) high.
£600–700 MJW

A cranberry glass épergne, c1880, 21in (53.5cm) high.
£550–650 CB

A Victorian cranberry glass épergne, with baskets, c1880, 21in (53.5cm) high.
£750–850 CB

Cross Reference
See Vases

A René Lalique table decoration, Faisans, comprising two glass candelabra and a serving dish, dish with engraved mark, chips to dish, after 1942.
Candelabra £1,800–2,000
Dish £200–220 S

A Venetian enamelled glass flask and stopper, from the atelier of Osvaldo Brussa, c1730, 5½in (14cm) high.
£4,000–4,500 S

◄ Two opaque glass flasks, with enamelled floral decoration, c1790, 9in (23cm) high.
£650–680 each Som

► An opaque glass flask, decorated with flowers, insects and birds, c1760, 9½in (24cm) high.
£800–950 Som

A glass carafe, gilded in the atelier of James Giles, the slender neck with ogee upper part and dentil border, c1770, 8½in (21.5cm) high.
£1,500–1,800 C

A French cobalt blue cut and gilded glass decanter, with gilded stopper, c1775, 9in (23cm) high.
£3,000–3,500 CB

A mallet-shaped glass decanter, with two neck rings and lozenge stopper, engraved 'Brandy', c1780, 8¾in (22cm) high.
£400–450 Som

A glass spirit decanter with three neck rings and lozenge stopper, c1780, 8in (20.5cm) high.
£200–250 Som

Two club-shaped glass spirit decanters, with plain lozenge stoppers, c1790, 8in (20.5cm) high.
£250–300 each Som

A mallet-shaped glass spirit decanter, with lozenge stopper, gilt label 'Shrub', c1790, 7½in (19cm) high.
£270–320 Som

◄ A set of three club-shaped glass decanters, with gilt labels, lozenge stoppers with gilt initials, in an iron and leather-covered stand, c1790, 7½in (19cm) high.
£1,300–1,500 Som

Three glass spirit decanters, with gilt labels and stoppers, in a papier mâché and gilt stand, c1790, 8in (20.5cm) high.
£1,200–1,500 Som

A French glass magnum decanter, with enamel decoration, c1800, 13¼in (33.5cm) high.
£830–880 MJW

◄ A pair of glass decanters, inscribed in gilt 'R Wine', 'W Wine' and 'RH', c1790, 12in (30.5cm) high.
£2,250–2,500 BrW

A glass decanter and stopper, with three neck rings, c1815.
£250–300 Som

A pair of glass carafes, with diamond-moulded bodies, c1820, 9in (23cm) high.
£750–820 Som

A crackle glass decanter and stopper, with gilt rim and rings, c1820, 10in (25.5cm) high.
£220–260 MJW

A Nailsea red, blue and white glass flask, c1820, 8in (20.5cm) long.
£120–150 LIO

A Nailsea green, blue and white glass flask, c1820, 8in (20.5cm) long.
£120–150 LIO

Three compressed globular-shaped glass flagons, with loop handles, two with pewter mounts and one without, 1820–50, largest 8in (20.5cm) high.
£150–180 each Som

A pair of Bristol decanters, with lozenge stoppers, c1820, 11¾in (30cm) high.
£700–800 JHa

A glass decanter and stopper, c1820, 14in (35.5cm) high.
£200–250 CB

◄ An amethyst glass flagon, with metal mount, cork and metal stopper, c1825, 7¾in (19.5cm) high.
£350–400 Som

▶ Two glass flagons, with cork and metal stoppers, c1830, tallest 9in (23cm) high.
£130–160 each Som

◄ An onion-shaped glass carafe, with gilt label and cork and metal stopper, c1830, 8in (20.5cm) high.
£250–300 Som

CHRISTINE BRIDGE
ANTIQUES

LAPADA, BADA & CINOA member

Fine 18th century collectors' glass, 19th century coloured glass and small decorative antiques

Anytime, appointment only

Phone: 07000 4 GLASS (07000 4 45277)
Fax: 07000 FAX GLASS (07000 329 45277)
Mobile: 0831 126668

Email: christine@bridge-antiques.com

www.bridge-antiques.com
or www.antiqueglass.co.uk

Two glass flagons, with loop handles, metal mounts and cork and metal stoppers, c1830, 7¼in (18.5cm) high.
£150–180 each Som

A set of three wine bottles, with gilt-metal stoppers, in a papier mâché stand, c1820, 14in (35.5cm) high.
£700–800 BELL

Two onion-shaped glass carafes, with everted lips, c1830–50, largest 8¾in (22cm) high.
£130–160 each Som

l & r. A pair of wrythen-moulded glass wine bottles, c1840.
c. A glass wine bottle, with spire stopper, 12in (30.5cm) high.
£400–450 each Som

▶ A rib-moulded amethyst glass decanter and stopper, c1835, 13in (33cm) high.
£250–300 BELL

◀ An onion-shaped glass carafe, c1840, 8¼in (21.5cm) high.
£130–160 Som

Two onion-shaped glass carafes, c1840, largest 9in (23cm) high.
£130–160 each Som

◀ A pair of engraved glass carafes, with cork stoppers, c1840, 9in (23cm) high.
£400–450 CB

A glass decanter with step-cut neck, c1840, 12¾in (32.5cm) high.
£575–625 MJW

A glass ribbed spirit bottle, with ball stopper, c1840, 11¼in (28.5cm) high.
£320–350 Som

◀ A glass decanter with slice-cut neck and pillar-cut body, c1840, 11½in (29cm) high.
£400–450 MJW

A glass decanter, with red overlay, c1840, 12in (30.5cm) high.
£250–300 CB

A glass spirit bottle with looped moulded body, c1840, 14in (35.5cm) high.
£400–450 CB

An engraved blue-stained glass decanter and stopper, signed 'August Böhm', c1845, 15in (38cm) high.
£4,500–5,500 S

Three shaft-and-globe glass decanters, mid–19thC, largest 11in (28cm) high.
£150–180 each BELL

A glass decanter and stopper, c1850, 14in (35.5cm) high.
£600–700 MJW

A red glass carafe, with dimpled pattern, c1850, 9½in (24cm) high.
£325–375 MJW

A pair of glass decanters, in green with white overlay, c1860, 13½in (34.5cm) high.
£900–1,000 MJW

An amethyst glass globular decanter, engraved with a band of thistles and roses, c1860, 9½in (24cm) high.
£250–300 CB

A red glass decanter overlaid with white, decorated with gilt, c1850, 14½in (37cm) high.
£500–550 MJW

An amber glass decanter, with metal stopper, engraved with water lilies, c1850, 10in (25.5cm) high.
£250–300 MJW

An amber glass decanter, with metal stopper, engraved with water lilies, c1850, 10in (25.5cm) high.
£250–300 MJW

A pair of green glass decanters, with stoppers, c1850, 12in (30.5cm) high.
£420–500 CB

► A Nailsea glass hip flask, c1860, 7in (18cm) long.
£160–180 Som

A shaft-and-globe decanter,
c1860, 12in (30.5cm) high.
£400–450 MJW

A French pink glass decanter,
with white overlay, c1860,
12in (30.5cm) high.
£625–685 MJW

A Nailsea glass gimmel flask, with two compartments,
c1860, 10¾in (27.5cm) long.
£160–180 Som

A Bohemian ruby-flashed
glass decanter, engraved
with fruiting vines, c1880,
15¼in (38.5cm) high.
£150–175 CB

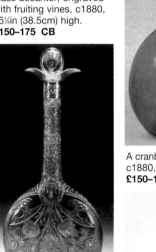

A Continental glass decanter,
with celery handle, c1880,
6½in (16.5cm) high.
£200–225 Har

A Victorian cranberry
glass decanter, c1900,
16in (40.5cm) high.
£170–200 OBS

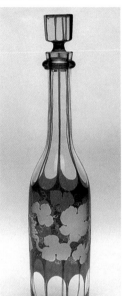

A Stourbridge glass decanter,
with blue overlay, c1870,
13½in (34.5cm) high.
£400–450 MJW

A cranberry glass decanter,
c1880, 9¾in (25cm) high.
£150–175 AMH

An Italian glass decanter,
with latticinio decoration,
Venice, late 19thC,
10¾in (27.5cm) high.
£320–360 DORO

A Bohemian glass decanter,
with blue dot decoration,
c1925, 10⅛in (26.5cm) high.
£150–180 DSG

A Stevens & Williams
silver-mounted intaglio-
cut glass decanter and
stopper, possibly cut by
Joshua Hodgetts, spout
inscribed 'JSC', c1896,
14½in (37cm) high.
£3,000–3,300 S

▶ A decanter, with gilt
spiral decoration, early
20thC, 11½in (29cm) high.
£185–220 JAS

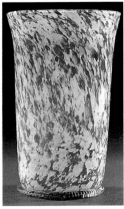

A cased *façon de Venise* glass beaker, with milled footrim, south Netherlands, c1600, 7in (18cm) high.
£14,000–16,000 S

A green-tinted glass roemer, applied with three rows of raspberry prunts, with a kick-in base and trailed everted foot, north German or Dutch, mid-17thC, 7in (18cm) high.
£1,800–2,200 S

A German enamelled glass tumbler, painted with a view of the Ochsenkopf mountain, dated '1662', 7in (18cm) high.
£15,000–16,500 S

An engraved glass roemer, c1680, 5½in (14cm) high.
£600–700 CB

A Viennese glass beaker, painted with Tarot cards, one inscribed 'N Hofman Wien 1806', 4¾in (12cm) high.
£6,000–6,500 S

A Viennese transparent enamelled glass beaker, painted with three Tarot cards, inscribed on reverse, on an amber-stained star-cut base, c1820, 4⅛in (11.5cm) high.
£7,000–7,500 S

A set of six glass roemers, with cup-shaped bowls, hollow stems and raspberry prunts, on trailed conical feet, c1825, 4in (10cm) high.
£450–500 Som

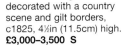

A glass roemer, with hollow strawberry-prunted stem, the domed foot with trailed decoration, c1825, 6in (15cm) high.
£130–150 Som

► A Viennese glass beaker, decorated with a country scene and gilt borders, c1825, 4⅛in (11.5cm) high.
£3,000–3,500 S

A Viennese transparent enamelled gilt-ground glass beaker, attributed to Anton Kothgasser, c1825, 5in (12.5cm) high.
£13,000–15,000 S

JASMIN CAMERON

Specialising in Drinking Glasses
and Decanters 1750 - 1910

*Early 20th Century
Art Deco Glass,
René Lalique and Monart*

ANTIQUARIUS, 131-141 KINGS ROAD
LONDON SW3 4PW
Fax/Shop: 020 7351 4154 Mobile 07774 871257
Home: 01494 774276

l & r. A pair of glass roemers, 1830, 4in (10cm) high.
£170–190
c. A single roemer, with heavy milled prunted knop and hollow ribbed foot, c1800, 5¼in (13.5cm) high.
£170–190 Som

A Bohemian Lithyalin glass beaker, each side cut with a leaf above a lozenge boss, c1830, 4¾in (12cm) high.
£3,500–3,800 S

A Bohemian Biedermeier enamelled and cut-glass beaker, c1830, 4in (10cm) high.
£1,200–1,400 S

A set of four glass rummers, with cup bowls on hollow stems, with raspberry prunts, c1830, 4in (10cm) high.
£300–350 Som

A turquoise opaline glass beaker, cold-enamelled and gilt with a floral band, c1860, 3¼in (8.5cm) high.
£100–120 Som

A pair of German glass rummers, made for the Islamic market, c1860, 5½in (14cm) high.
£250–285 MJW

A Bohemian clear glass beaker, with blue overlay and gilded rim, decorated with flowers, on a star-cut base, c1875, 5¾in (14.5cm) high.
£175–225 CB

▶ A Stourbridge engraved glass beaker, late 19thC, 5¼in (13.5cm) high.
£300–350 Hal

A pair of blue glass rummers, with barrel-shaped bowls, knopped stems and conical feet, c1830, 4½in (11.5cm) high.
£500–600 Som

An amethyst glass roemer, with hollow stem, prunts and trailed foot, c1880, 5in (12.5cm) high.
£85–95 CB

A set of six footed glass tumblers, with enamel decoration by Fritz Heckert, c1890, 3¾in (9.5cm) high.
£420–520 MJW

Three printed glasses, 1950–60, 5¼in (13.5cm) high.
50p–£1 each PC

Decanters & Flasks

A flask, 2nd–3rdC AD, 13in (33cm) long.
£250–280 MJW

▶ Two flasks,
2nd–3rdC AD,
longest 4½in
(11cm) long.
£165–180 MJW

A double flask, 1st–3rdC AD, 5in (12.5cm) long.
£400–450 MJW

◀ A flask,
2nd–3rdC AD,
5in (12.5cm) long.
£200–225 MJW

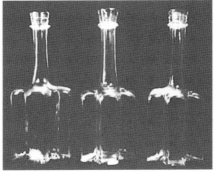

A set of three cruciform decanters, with bladed
string neck rings, c1730, 11½in (29cm) high.
£1,600–2,000 Som

◀ A shaft-and-globe decanter, inscribed in
diamond-point 'Wm Skelhorn, 10th June
1747', c1720, 8in (20.5cm) high.
£1,000–1,100 S

A moulded decanter,
with an annulated
string neck ring, c1730,
8in (20.5cm) high.
£450–500 Som

**Miller's is a price GUIDE
not a price LIST**

A central European
opaque white glass spirit
flask, painted in bright
colours with a half-length
portrait of a lady holding
a bloom, minor damage,
18thC, 5in (12.5cm) high.
£230–280 CSK

A central European spirit
flask, with canted corners,
enamelled in colours with
a milkmaid, sprays of
flowers to the reverse and
sides, slight damage,
18thC, 5in (12.5cm) high.
£300–330 CSK

▶ A mallet-shaped decanter, the neck with a triple-
ringed collar, slight damage, mid-18thC, 9in (23cm) high.
£170–200 P

A central European spirit
flask, with canted angles,
enamelled in colours,
the shoulder and sides with
bands of stylized foliage,
pewter cover replaced,
slight damage, mid-18thC,
7in (18cm) high.
£400–500 CSK

A port decanter and stopper, engraved with a label edged with berries, vines and leaves, inscribed 'Port', chip to rim, 1760–70, 11¼in (28.5cm) high.
£300–330 P

A French Bristol blue decanter, engraved with gilding and 'Noyeou', c1760, 9in (23cm) high.
£400–500 CB

Decanters

The original use for a decanter was to contain, in a more decorative item, liquid that had been poured from a storage vessel. This ensured that the wine served at the table was clear, as the sediment was left behind.

The first glass bottles appeared in Britain around 1650. They were dark green, squat, and stamped with glass seals that identified the owner of the bottle, and sometimes the date of manufacture. Decanters made in shapes with which we are familiar today first appeared at the beginning of the 18th century. Early decanters tended to be plain, but the rising popularity of wheel cutting and engraving in the 18th century led to decorated decanters becoming more common. By the late 18th century they had become heavily ornamented with elaborate cut decoration.

Examples produced in the 19th century used many of the innovative techniques developed by British glasshouses, and were displayed at the international exhibitions held during this period.

A club-shaped decanter, the quatrefoil simulated wine label inscribed 'Madeira', with a faceted lozenge stopper, c1770, 11½in (29cm) high.
£500–600 S

▶ A spirit decanter, with a flute-cut base and neck and slice-cut lozenge stopper, c1780, 8½in (21.5cm) high.
£250–300 Som

An electioneering decanter, inscribed 'Lowther and Upton Huzza', c1761, 10in (25.5cm) high.
£1,600–2,000 C
The toast celebrates the Westmorland Parliamentary division of 1761, when Sir James Lowther and John Upton were elected against a third candidate.

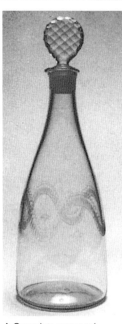

A Georgian engraved decanter and stopper, c1770, 11½in (29cm) high.
£400–450 MJW

A decanter and stopper, with three neck rings, c1780, 10½in (26.5cm) high.
£250–300 MJW

A mallet-shaped decanter, with a flute-cut base beneath a band of looped stars and egg and printy decoration, with scale-cut neck and round lunar-cut disc stopper, c1770, 9½in (24cm) high.
£350–400 Som

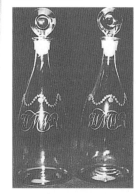

A pair of tapered decanters, with the monogram 'WMW' below a rose garland, c1780, 9½in (24cm) high.
£1,000–1,200 Som

A tapered decanter, the body engraved with leaf pattern and alternate birds and springs in between loops and bows, with a bevelled lozenge stopper, c1780, 9in (23cm) high.
£250–280 Som

A mallet-shaped decanter, engraved with swags, with a bull's-eye stopper, late 18thC, 11in (28cm) high.
£200–240 FD

A cut-glass armorial mallet-shaped decanter and stopper, engraved 'White Wine', slight wear, late 18thC, 12in (30.5cm) high.
£500–550 CSK

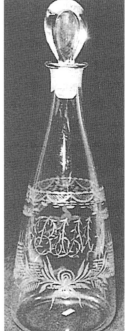

A tapered decanter, engraved with a band of hatched decoration, above the monogram 'RAM' within a floral cartouche, with a plain lozenge stopper, c1780, 9½in (24cm) high.
£280–320 Som

A Masonic decanter, the mallet-shaped body engraved with Masonic symbols within floral sprays and the monogram 'J.B.', with a bevelled lozenge stopper, c1780, 9in (23cm) high.
£800–1,000 Som

A tapered decanter, engraved 'W Wine', with a cartouche containing a hatched rose and fruiting vine, with a lozenge stopper, c1780, 9¾in (25cm) high.
£720–800 Som

A pair of tapered decanters, with a band of looped egg-and-tulip engraving and lunar-cut bevelled lozenge stoppers, c1780, 9in (23cm) high.
£1,000–1,200 Som

▶ A decanter, with three neck rings above wheel-cut swags and leaf sprays, with a fluted base, late 18thC, 10in (25.5cm) high.
£230–270 JAd

Cutting patterns

The type of cutting on glass varied according to the maker and the style in vogue at the time. Diamond cutting was generally the earliest type, and crosscut (often mistakenly called hobnail) was introduced in about 1830. These, and other commonly found types of glass cutting, are shown below:

DIAMOND | CROSS-CUT DIAMOND | STRAWBERRY DIAMOND | PRISM | BLAZES | PILLAR

Neck rings

Neck rings on 18th and early 19th century decanters were applied separately then moulded with a tool. The join in the neck ring was often carelessly made and could look like a crack.

The neck rings on many middle to late 19th century decanters are integral parts of the decanters. If a damaged neck has been replaced, it may be possible to feel a join on the inner surface.

Plain   Triangular   Triple   Milled   Cut   Square

A pair of Irish mallet-shaped decanters, engraved with a three-masted ship, late 18thC, 9½in (24cm) high.
£1,250–1,500 WW

► A pair of cut-glass decanters, with an engraved crest, c1780, 12½in (32cm) high.
£675–800 WGT

A mallet-shaped green decanter, with a gilt label, c1790, 9in (23cm) high.
£180–200 CB

An Irish decanter, with engraved anchor design, on a rib-moulded base, c1790, 12in (30.5cm) high.
£380–450 WGT

A decanter and stopper, engraved 'White Wine' within a cartouche and fruiting vines, c1790, 11½in (29cm) high.
£700–800 CB

A blue mallet-shaped brandy decanter, with gilt decoration and a lozenge stopper, c1790, 10in (25.5cm) high.
£180–200 CB

◄ A decanter, engraved with two bands of egg-and-tulip pattern, with lozenge stopper, c1790, 9½in (24cm) high.
£350–400 Som

A decanter, with three feathered double neck rings and moulded bull's-eye stopper, c1790, 10in (25.5cm) high.
£250–300 FD

A Bristol blue club-shaped rum decanter, with a lozenge stopper, c1790, 9¾in (25cm) high.
£200–275 JAS

An ale decanter, with three neck rings, engraved with hops and barley, with bull's-eye stopper, c1790, 10¼in (26cm) high.
£450–500 BrW

A wine urn, c1790, 13in (33cm) high.
£8,000–9,000 WGT

A central European Masonic flask, enamelled with instruments in a basket, the shoulders with dash decoration, slight wear, dated '1791', 4¼in (11cm) high.
£1,000–1,200 C

A pair of mallet-shaped decanters, with flute-cut bases and lozenge stoppers, c1800, 10in (25.5cm) high.
£320–400 BELL

A pair of serving carafes, with double neck rings, c1800, 6in (15cm) high.
£220–250 CB

Three decanters:
l. with three neck rings and a mushroom stopper, c1800, 9in (23cm) high.
£200–250
c. with straight-sided flute, diamond and prism cut body, two cut and one annulated neck rings, with a cut mushroom stopper, c1820, 9in (23cm) high.
£220–270
r. with tapered body, three bladed neck rings and a lozenge stopper, c1800, 9in (23cm) high.
£220–270 Som

▶ A decanter and stopper, c1800, 11½in (29cm) high.
£160–190 MJW

Miller's is a price GUIDE not a price LIST

A club-shaped blue miniature decanter, with a snake-trailed neck ring and a target stopper, c1800, 4in (10cm) high.
£160–180 Som

l. A tapered spirit decanter, engraved with a band of looped shamrocks and stars, with a lozenge stopper, c1800, 8½in (21.5cm) high.
£170–200
r. A spirit decanter, with flute cross-cut diamonds and three cut neck rings, with a cut mushroom stopper, c1825, 7in (18cm) high.
£160–180 Som

Three spirit decanters, with plain bodies and lozenge stoppers, c1800, tallest 7½in (19cm) high.
£120–140 each Som

A pair of Waterford decanters,
c1800, 10½in (26.5cm) high.
£550–650 FD

A set of three green spirit decanters,
the club-shaped bodies with gilt
simulated labels for 'Hollands', 'Rum'
and 'Brandy', gilt-decorated lozenge
stoppers, c1800, 7½in (19cm) high.
£650–800 Som

A pair of decanters, with three neck
rings and cut mushroom stoppers,
c1800, 8in (20.5cm) high.
£550–650 Som

Decanter shapes

| Cruciform 1730–50 | Shouldered 1760–70 | Tapered c1780 | Prussian 1790–1830 | Ship's c1820 | Fancy (Royal) 1830–50 |

◀ A pair of decanters, the bodies
with two raised bands, with three
neck rings and bull's-eye stoppers,
c1800, 10in (25.5cm) high.
£600–700 S(S)

A pair of mallet-shaped decanters,
engraved with the monogram 'RHA',
with three neck rings and target
stoppers, c1800, 8½in (21.5cm) high.
£650–750 Som

A pair of mallet-shaped decanters,
with three neck rings and target
stoppers, c1800, 8in (20.5cm) high.
£550–620 Som

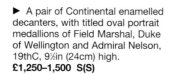

A pair of Bohemian amber-flashed
flask-shaped decanters, engraved
with continuous scenes of deer in
woodland, the ball stoppers with
a hound and game birds, slight
damage, 19thC, 11in (28cm) high.
£650–800 CSK

▶ A pair of Continental enamelled
decanters, with titled oval portrait
medallions of Field Marshal, Duke
of Wellington and Admiral Nelson,
19thC, 9½in (24cm) high.
£1,250–1,500 S(S)

A decanter, with three neck rings, and cut mushroom stopper, c1800, 10in (25.5cm) high.
£250–300 MJW

An Anglo-Irish mould-blown and cut-glass decanter, with three milled neck rings, c1800, 9¾in (25cm) high.
£330–365 BrW

A pair of French silver-mounted cut-glass liqueur decanters, with maker's mark 'JM', 19thC, 7in (18cm) high.
£500–550 FW&C

► A French blue glass liqueur decanter set, 19thC, 12in (30.5cm) high.
£425–500 WAG

Three opaque white decanters, decorated with scrolling panels of fruiting vines with 'Gin', 'Rum' and 'Brandy' in gilt, with cork stoppers and metal mounts, 19thC, 14in (35.5cm) high.
£425–500 CSK

A decanter, with three neck rings and a bull's-eye stopper, c1800, 10½in (26.5cm) high.
£170–200 JHa

Three semi-opaque decanters, in pale green, blue and pink, painted and gilded with trailing fruit and vines, with spire stoppers, on pierced metal stands, slight damage, 19thC, 16½in (42cm) high.
£700–800 CSK

Two toddy lifters, c1810, tallest 6½in (16.5cm) high.
£100–160 each Som

Three spirit decanters, c1810:
l. with a flute-cut base and three angular neck rings, with a mushroom stopper, 7in (18cm) high.
c. with three neck rings and a target stopper, 7in (18cm) high.
r. with a flute-cut base and three cut neck rings, with a mushroom stopper, 7½in (19cm) high.
£120–150 each Som

◄ An Irish Rodney decanter, the body engraved with vesica decoration, with three milled neck rings and a moulded target stopper, marked 'Cork Glass Co', c1810, 8½in (21.5cm) high.
£1,000–1,200 Som

Two deeply engraved bottle-shaped decanters, with faceted neck rings and silver-mounted stoppers, small chips, 19thC, 14in (35.5cm) high.
£600–700 C

A pair of decanters, the cylindrical bodies with prism, flute and small diamond cutting, diamond-cut neck rings and cut mushroom stoppers, c1810, 8½in (21.5cm) high.
£600–670 Som

An Irish cut-glass decanter, c1810, 8½in (21.5cm) high.
£340–400 WGT

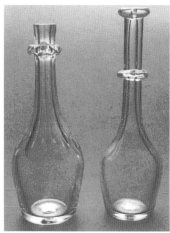

Two toddy lifters, c1810, tallest 6in (15cm) high.
£100–130 each Som

A pair of decanters, with flute and diamond cutting, with three diamond-cut neck rings and mushroom stoppers, c1810, 9in (23cm) high.
£600–700 Som

► Four spirit decanters, c1810, tallest 8in (20.5cm) high.
£120–140 each Som

◄ An Irish spirit decanter, with two bladed neck rings and moulded fluting at the base, engraved with three thistle sprays, with flat grid-moulded stopper, marked 'Edwards Belfast', c1810, 7in (18cm) high.
£650–800 Som

A pair of mallet-shaped decanters, cut with flutes and a band of small diamonds, with three neck rings and lunar-cut target stoppers, c1810, 9½in (24cm) high.
£750–900 Som

Two spirit decanters, with flute-cut bases and target stoppers, c1810:
l. 7¼in (18.5cm) high.
£70–80
r. 7¾in (19.5cm) high.
£110–130 Som

► A mallet-shaped magnum decanter, with bands of flute, prism and diamond cutting, with a cut mushroom stopper, c1810, 11in (28cm) high.
£700–800 Som

A pair of spirit decanters, with triple neck rings and target stoppers, c1810, 9½in (24cm) high.
£340–400 BELL

l. An Irish decanter, with three annulated neck rings and a moulded mushroom stopper, probably Cork Glass Co, c1810, 8in (20.5cm) high.
£300–350
r. A Waterford decanter, with moulded fluting at the base and a disc lozenge stopper, indistinctly marked, 9in (23cm) high.
£1,000–1,200 Som

A pair of cut-glass club-shaped decanters and stoppers, with three neck rings above prism-cut bands, the lower sections cut with a checked pattern, on star-cut bases, slight wear, 19thC, 9½in (24cm) high.
£360–420 CSK

◄ Three decanters, c1810:
l & r. with fluted bases and neck and mushroom stoppers, 8½in (21.5cm) high.
c. with a target stopper, 9in (23cm) high.
£200–300 each Som

A pair of decanters, with fluted bases, a band of small cut diamonds and flute-cut necks, with three annulated neck rings and target stoppers, c1810, 9in (23cm) high.
£550–650 Som

l. An Irish decanter, with diamond-cut arched panels enclosing cut stars and flute-cut base and shoulder, with three annulated neck rings and mushroom stopper, c1810, 8in (20.5cm) high.
£200–220
r. A flute-cut decanter, with one cut neck ring and a mushroom stopper, c1830, 8½in (21.5cm) high.
£65–80 Som

A toddy lifter, with diamond-and prism-cut body, flute-cut stem and diamond-cut neck ring, c1810, 6in (15cm) high.
£250–300 Som

Toddy lifters were used for transferring punch from the bowl to the glass.

A flute-cut mallet-shaped decanter, with three neck rings, engraved with the monogram 'JB', damaged, early 19thC, 12in (30.5cm) high.
£370–450 CSK

A carafe, with flute, prism and diamond cutting, cut neck rings, star-cut base and cut mushroom stopper, c1810, 10½in (26.5cm) high.
£850–1,000 Som

▶ A pair of toddy lifters, with flute-cut necks, c1810, 5¼in (13.5cm) high.
£230–260 Som

l & r. A pair of Prussian-shaped decanters, with flute-cut bases and mushroom stoppers, c1810, 8½in (21.5cm) high.
£500–550
c. A flute-cut spirit decanter, with a target stopper, c1810, 7½in (19cm) high.
£100–125 Som

A Cork Glass Co engraved decanter, decorated with hatch pattern and stars within a band of loops, the lower part and base with hammered flutes, with a moulded bull's-eye stopper, chips to stopper, marked, early 19thC, 10¼in (26cm) high.
£520–580 C

A mallet-shaped ice decanter, with notched lens stopper, the base with a metal-mounted cork stopper, slight chips to stopper, early 19thC, 13in (33cm) high.
£2,000–2,500 C

▶ An Irish flute-cut decanter, engraved with fruiting vine, a rose spray and a thistle, with two milled neck rings and a moulded grid-patterned disc stopper, c1810, 9in (23cm) high.
£340–380 Som

An Irish cut-glass decanter, c1820, 9½in (24cm) high.
£280–350 WGT

▶ A pair of ship's decanters, decorated with gadroons above a band of sunray medallions and stylized foliage, with three neck rings and gadrooned cut ball stoppers, on a star-cut base, damaged, possibly Perrin Geddes and Co, Warington, c1820, 11in (28cm) high.
£3,200–4,000 S

l. An Irish decanter, with deep flute-moulded base, engraved with hatched rose sprays and a bird in flight, the reverse with an empty star cartouche, with two bladed neck rings, probably Belfast, c1810, 9in (23cm) high.
£350–450
r. An Irish decanter, with flute-moulded base and engraved vesica decoration, with three annulated neck rings, marked 'Cork Glass Co', c1810, 9in (23cm) high.
£1,000–1,200 Som

Two cut-glass spirit decanters, c1820, 7½in (19cm) high.
£100–125 each Som

A set of three barrel-shaped decanters, moulded with diamond and vertical bands, with pinched necks and flattened stoppers, on a black papier mâché stand with brass handle, mounts and feet, early 19thC, 10¼in (26cm) high.
£250–280 DN

A pair of diamond- and flute-cut decanters, with prism-cut necks and cut cushion stoppers, c1820, 10¼in (26cm) high.
£600–700 GS

A pair of decanters, with broad flute-cut bodies, three neck rings and target stoppers, c1820, 8½in (21.5cm) high.
£550–650 Som

A pair of Irish decanters, cut with flutes, prisms and panels of small diamonds, with three annulated neck rings and cut mushroom stoppers, c1820, 9½in (24cm) high.
£600–670 Som

A toddy lifter, with flute- and printy-cut bowl, facet-cut neck and diamond-cut neck ring and lip, c1820, 6¼in (16cm) high.
£140–160 Som

Auction or dealer?

All the pictures in our price guides originate from auction houses and dealers. Prices, when buying at auction, can be lower than those of a dealer, but a buyer's premium and VAT will be added to the hammer price. Equally, when selling at auction, commission, tax and photography charges must be taken into account. Dealers will often restore pieces before putting them back on the market. Both dealers and auctioneers will provide professional advice, so it is worth researching both sources before buying or selling your antiques.

Three decanters, with diamond, strawberry diamond, fluted and prism cutting, with mushroom stoppers, c1825, largest 8½in (21.5cm) high.
£220–240 each Som

Two toddy lifters, c1820, tallest 7½in (19cm) high.
£95–120 Som

Three Bristol blue spirit decanters and stoppers, engraved in gilt 'Hollands', 'Brandy' and 'Rum', within gilt labels, on a silver-plated stand, with reeded leaf-chased frame and central loop handle, early 19thC, 11in (28cm) high.
£1,700–2,000 DN

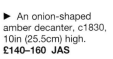

▶ An onion-shaped amber decanter, c1830, 10in (25.5cm) high.
£140–160 JAS

A pair of spirit decanters, with cut mushroom stoppers, c1825, 7½in (19cm) high.
£340–400 Som

◀ A cut-glass liqueur decanter, with triple neck ring, c1830, 14in (35.5cm) high.
£250–300 CB

An American blown glass three-mould decanter, c1830, 11in (28cm) high.
£200–240 A&A

Two large green glass decanters, with stoppers, and a slender decanter with cut decoration, 19thC, 13½in (34.5cm) high.
£85–100 LF

l & r. A pair of green flagons, with metal mounts and cork and metal stoppers, c1830, 7¾in (19.5cm) high.
£150–180
c. An amber flagon, with loop handle, 7½in (19cm) high.
£125–150 Som

Flagons

Defined as a vessel with a handle, spout and narrow neck, flagons were devised to carry wine, cider, etc. Usually with metal tops, they can be found in a variety of colours.

Two blue flagons, with loop handles, metal mounts and cork and metal stoppers, c1830, 7½in (19cm) high.
£300–360 Som

Three flagons, with compressed sides and loop handles, c1830.
£160–200 Som

A cut-glass port decanter and stopper, c1830, 14in (35.5cm) high.
£140–165 CS

A pair of mallet-shaped decanters, cut with large diamond facets beneath a waisted hexagonal neck, with faceted club stoppers and star-cut bases, c1840, 13½in (34.5cm) high.
£340–400 S(S)

A Bristol blue decanter, with silver neck, c1838, 16½in (42cm) high.
£400–480 MJW

A green decanter, with single neck ring and spire stopper, c1840, 13¼in (33.5cm) high.
£260–300 BrW

An amber decanter, with a single neck ring and spire stopper, c1840, 14½in (37cm) high.
£475–525 MJW

LOCATE THE SOURCE

The source of each illustration in Miller's can be found by checking the code letters below each caption with the Key to Illustrations, pages 305–307.

A decanter and stopper, with trailing decoration to the neck, c1840, 11in (28cm) high.
£150–180 MJW

◄ A facet-cut decanter, c1840, 13¾in (35cm) high.
£125–150 MJW

A Baccarat flask, cut with arches beneath a faceted neck and string rim, enclosing a double sulphide portrait of Helen of Troy and Aeneas and another of Madame de Sévigné, slight damage, c1840, 8¼in (21cm) high.
£320–380 C

Two green onion-shaped carafes, each engraved with a band of thistles and roses, c1840, largest 9in (23cm) high.
£200–230 each Som

A decanter, c1840, 13in (33cm) high.
£120–150 MJW

A square decanter and stopper, c1840, 10¼in (26cm) high.
£140–170 MJW

A decanter and stopper, with single neck ring, c1840, 13in (33cm) high.
£140–170 MJW

A pair of amethyst decanters and stoppers, c1840, 15½in (39.5cm) high.
£1,000–1,100 AMH

► An amber-flashed glass decanter, etched with fruiting vines, c1840, 13in (33cm) high.
£180–200 BELL

A Victorian decanter, with star-cut base, flute-cut neck and cut ball stopper, c1850, 8¼in (21cm) high.
£100–120 Som

l. A cylindrical decanter, with three neck rings and a hexagon-cut stopper, c1840, 9in (23cm) high.
£150–180
c. A spirit-sized diamond- and flute-cut decanter, with plain flat neck rings and a mushroom stopper, c1810, 8in (20.5cm) high.
£100–120
r. A cylindrical decanter, with three neck rings and a cut hexagonal stopper, c1840, 8¼in (21.5cm) high.
£150–180 Som

Three cylindrical decanters, with panel-cut bodies, three neck rings and spire stoppers, c1850, on earlier Sheffield plate stand, with central posted scroll handle and pierced foliate shell feet, c1835.
£280–335 N

A red carafe, c1850, 9½in (24cm) high.
£325–375 MJW

▶ A pair of decanters, each with three slat-cut neck rings and faceted and star-cut cushion stoppers, on star-cut bases, one rim chipped, mid-19thC, 13¼in (34.5cm) high.
£470–520 S(S)

Stoppers

It is difficult to guarantee that a stopper is original except on Victorian clear glass decanters, which often have matching numbers etched on the stopper and decanter neck. Coloured glass decanters may have the number painted on the stopper and underside of the decanter. Generally a stopper is acceptable when it is the same cut and colour as the decanter, and of the right style and period. Decanters often become damaged by the careless replacement of the stopper or by being knocked over. Chipped surfaces or edges can be restored, which may alter the proportions of the lip, but will not greatly affect the value. Broken stopper pegs can be replaced by glueing on a replacement, then grinding and polishing the whole peg. A very thin radial line will indicate where this has been done.

A carafe and tumbler, engraved with vines, c1850, carafe 6¼in (16cm) high.
£150–180 MJW

A decanter and stopper, c1850, 12in (30.5cm) high.
£200–225 MJW

A green rum decanter and stopper, c1850, 10in (25.5cm) high.
£130–160 WGT

A blue claret decanter and stopper, c1850, 10in (25.5cm) high.
£130–160 WGT

A green whiskey decanter and stopper, c1850, 10in (25.5cm) high.
£130–160 WGT

A pair of pear-shaped decanters, with flute-cut bases, scale-cut necks and a band of engraving, with cut spire stoppers, on solid square domed feet, c1850, 14in (35.5cm) high.
£725–825 Som

A Nailsea carafe and stopper, with opaque white pull-up decoration, c1860, 8¾in (22cm) high.
£350–400 Som

◄ A pair of Victorian decanters, with diamond-cut bodies, flute-cut necks and cut ball stoppers, c1860, 9½in (24cm) high.
£180–220 Som

An engraved sherry decanter, with a spire stopper, c1860, 15¼in (38.5cm) high.
£235–265 MJW

A spirit decanter, engraved with hops and barley, with a foot ring and engraved ball stopper, c1860, 8in (20.5cm) high.
£200–250 Som

A pair of miniature carafes, with two neck rings, c1870, 1¾in (4.5cm) high.
£60–70 BrW

A decanter and stopper, with applied cranberry prunts, c1870, 10½in (26.5cm) high.
£580–650 ARE

A pair of cut-glass Greek key pattern decanters, c1870, 12½in (32cm) high.
£250–300 DUN

A Gothic revival cut-glass rosewater decanter and stopper, in an ormolu mount, c1870.
£340–400 AHL

► A Max Greger decanter and stopper, inscribed 'By Special Appointment to Her Majesty', c1880, 11¼in (28.5cm) high.
£400–450 MJW

A blue jug decanter, with a clear glass stopper and handle, c1880, 9½in (24cm) high.
£220–250 MJW

An amber shaft-and-globe miniature decanter, with four champagne glasses, c1870, decanter 1¾in (4.5cm) high.
£80–90 BrW

A pair of vase-shaped decanters, with diamond slice-cut bodies and star-cut foot rings, with pouring lips and spire stoppers, c1880, 10½in (26.5cm) high.
£200–250 Som

A pair of Victorian decanters, with printy-cut bodies, flute-cut necks and diamond-cut ball stoppers, c1880, 23in (58.5cm) high.
£160–200 Som

A set of two decanters and a claret jug, with diamond- and printy-cut bodies, facet-cut necks and diamond-cut ball stoppers, c1880, 9½in (24cm) high.
£550–650 Som

A shaft-and-globe decanter, the neck cut with facets, the body and stopper with cut printies, 1880–1910, 10in (25.5cm) high.
£35–45 JHa

A decorated spirit barrel, c1880, 10¼in (26.5cm) high.
£120–140 DUN

▶ A pair of liqueur decanters, decorated in gilt, with pouring lips and stopper, c1880, 10in (25.5cm) high.
£350–400 MJW

A green jug decanter, with clear glass handle and stopper, c1880, 9in (23cm) high.
£75–90 MJW

A pair of Stourbridge engraved decanters and stoppers, engraved in the manner of Joseph Keller with dragonflies and other insects among foliage, the feet with dot ornament, possibly Stevens & Williams, slight damage, c1880, 12¼in (31cm) high.
£650–750 C

A Victorian three-bottle oak tantalus, the decanters with ball stoppers, 14in (35.5cm) high.
£250–280 Doc

◀ A Victorian decanter, with clear glass handle and stopper, 11in (28cm) high.
£160–200 FMN

A silver-mounted cut-glass decanter, c1884, 8in (20.5cm) high.
£180–200 DUN

◀ A pair of late Victorian amber decanters, the necks applied with prunts and ribbon moulding, the beaded silver collars and stoppers surmounted by Chinese ivory finials carved with a reclining sage holding a spray of flowers and a child grinding rice, the mounts by John Aldwinckle and Thomas Slater, London 1885, 8in (20.5cm) high.
£1,000–1,200 DN

A Gallé enamelled glass liqueur set, inscribed 'E Gallé', c1890, decanter 8½in (21.5cm) high.
£10,000–12,000 S(NY)

◀ An emerald green decanter, with lily-of-the-valley pattern in white, c1885, 13in (33cm) high.
£100–120 TS

Three late Victorian club-shaped decanters, engraved with festoons, with stoppers, in a trefoil frame on caryatid feet, with carrying handle, 13¾in (35cm) high.
£375–425 WL

A decanter and stopper, c1890, 12¾in (32.5cm) high.
£120–140 MJW

Three claret jugs, one with a stopper, 19thC, tallest 12in (30.5cm) high.
£450–650 each P(S)

▶ A decanter and spire stopper, c1890, 14in (35.5cm) high.
£200–240 MJW

A pair of decanters and stoppers, with silver mounts by William Comyns, London 1896, 10in (25.5cm) high.
£1,100–1,300 THOM
The value of these decanters is enhanced by the identifiable silver mounts and original stoppers.

A Dutch silver-mounted claret decanter, the plain glass octagonal body with loop handle in a repoussé silver coaster embossed with landscapes, the silver-mounted stopper applied with a figural finial, late 19thC, 11in (28cm) high.
£130–150 CGC

A cut-glass swirl decanter and stopper, c1890, 11½in (29cm) high.
£95–110 DUN

A shaft-and-globe decanter, with slice-cut neck and printies to body, late 19thC, 13in (33cm) high.
£75–90 JHa

A Victorian green decanter, with concave sides, floral engraving, silver mounts and a stopper, Chester 1898, 9½in (24cm) high.
£300–350 L

A WMF metal-mounted green glass decanter, with metal stopper, the metal mounts with female figures bathing in a river at the base, c1900, 15⅛in (39.5cm) high.
£700–800 Mit

An American crystal cut-glass decanter and stopper, by Thomas Hawkes & Co, New York, c1900, 14in (35.5cm) high.
£250–300 CB

A Gallé enamelled decanter, with gold inclusions, c1900, 9½in (24cm) high.
£4,000–4,500 ART

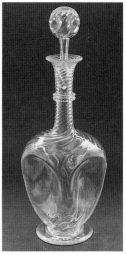

A wrythen dimpled decanter and stopper, c1900, 12in (30.5cm) high.
£100–120 JHa
Although the original wrythen dimpled service was designed by Harry Powell for James Powell, (Whitefriars), c1880, it became so popular that many factories, including Walsh Birmingham, Webb's and Webb Corbett made their own variations.

A waisted cylindrical decanter, the silver mount with a tricorn spout, London 1909, 13in (33cm) high.
£320–360 WeH

A silver-mounted claret jug, by William Hutton & Sons, Birmingham, with flared clear cut-glass body below a plain collar, with flat cover having a chair back thumbpiece, 1910, 10¾in (27.5cm) high.
£180–200 CGC

A French decanter, with enamelled flower decoration, c1920, 10in (25.5cm) high.
£160–200 MJW

A cut-glass duck decanter, c1920, 7in (18cm) high.
£180–200 DUN

A set of four Lobmeyr blown and facet-cut drinking glasses and a decanter, designed by Otto Prutscher, c1920, decanter 12in (30.5cm) high.
£1,800–2,000 C
This design was manufactured and sold by Lobmeyr until c1935.

A Lalique amber glass carafe and stopper, Marienthal, the stopper moulded with fruit and foliage, etched 'R Lalique' and 'No. 5126', after 1927, 8½in (21.5cm) high.
£200–240 CSK

A Whitefriars decanter, with cut mushroom stopper, 1930–50s, 9in (23cm) high.
£40–50 JHa

A pair of Georg Jensen decanters, with ball stoppers, c1930, 10¼in (26cm) high.
£1,500–1,700 SFL

An Art Deco cocktail set, comprising decanter and six glasses, with anchor motifs, silver overlay rims and top, 1930s, decanter 7in (18cm) high.
£150–170 BEV

Further reading
Miller's Glass of the '20s & '30s: A Collector's Guide, Miller's Publications, 1999

An Art Deco silver-plated tantalus, the two glass bottles with decorative designs, plated mounts, hinged lids and locking device, c1930, 9½in (24cm) high.
£180–200 GAK

A Lalique clear and frosted glass decanter, Saint Cyr, etched 'R Lalique', after 1930, and four white wine glasses, Riquewhir, etched and numbered, after 1925, decanter 11in (28cm) high.
Decanter £200–220
Glasses £180–200 CSK

◀ An Art Deco cocktail set, comprising decanter and six glasses, black-enamelled with geometric design, 1930s, decanter 10in ((25.5cm) high.
£400–450 ASA

Dressing Table Sets

A Czechoslovakian blue pressed glass dressing table set, Mermaid, comprising ten pieces, c1928, tray 10½in (26.5cm) wide.
£85–100 BKK

A Bagley pink pressed glass part dressing table set, c1932.
£45–50 BKK

Cross Reference
See Colour Review

A Bagley amber glass dressing table set, c1933.
£40–45 BKK

A Bagley frosted glass trinket set, Wyndham 1333, comprising seven pieces, c1933, tray 11in (28cm) wide.
£90–100 PC

A Bagley green glass trinket set, pattern No. 3008, comprising four pieces, 1934, tray 13in (33cm) wide.
£90–100 PC

A Bagley frosted green glass trinket set, pattern No. 3002, comprising seven pieces, 1934, tray 15in (38cm) wide.
£70–80 PC

Drinking Glasses

In 1700 the world was very different from the one in which we live today. There were fewer people and, indeed, some countries were unknown to us. Wealth was restricted to a minority, for the majority were more concerned with survival than beautiful objects, particularly fragile objects such as drinking glasses.

By 1900 the Industrial Revolution had changed manufacturing methods to such an extent that glass drinking vessels were available to all but the very poor on both sides of the Atlantic. They were cheap and expendable in a way that would have been incomprehensible two hundred years before.

Styles changed as techniques developed, as the following pages clearly show. However, each change was merely a refinement of a process which has remained essentially unchanged for two thousand years – the metamorphosis of silica into an attractive object from which liquor could be drunk. It is what men have been able to do with glass that makes the building of a collection interesting, and it is the building of collections that causes some people to invest large sums of money in such fragile objects.

Early Venetian goblets have long been collectable, but 18th century drinking glasses were of little interest until the very end of the 19th century. Only then did certain collectors begin to appreciate the limpid quality of the fabric of which English glasses, particularly, were made. The infinite variety of their stems: balusters, air twists, opaque twists, plain, hollow, colour twists and facet cut, together with a range of bowl shapes and decoration, could produce a display that would be at least as satisfactory as silver or porcelain.

Much 19th century glass is still affordable. It was produced in large quantities and there is a lot to be found at prices that compare favourably with modern glass. It is, therefore, both collectable and potentially useful, and many people now choose to use Victorian glass because, as they say, it makes the wine taste better!

During the last five years coloured drinking glasses have become much more collectable as the quality of the glass and the relationship between colour and cutting on pieces from the 1840s and 1850s has been recognized. Unfortunately, from the collectors' point of view, the price has increased accordingly.

Certainly, as more people have discovered the pleasure of collecting glass it has become a more expensive pastime than a few years ago. However, it is still much cheaper than some other collecting fields. The availability of drinking glasses is such that there is no difficulty in finding a niche to suit one's own pocket. The following pieces should serve as a useful checklist, particularly for those who are starting to collect.

Brian Watson

BEAKERS & RUMMERS

A Continental beaker, possibly Murano, the brown tint enamelled in white with stylized fleur-de-lys, applied foot ring, repaired, 14thC, 6½in (16.5cm) high.
£850–950 C

▶ An armorial beaker, possibly Bohemian or Brandenburg, enamelled in ochre, blue, pale blue, brown and white with a coat-of-arms surmounted by a crest, the lower part and the base gadrooned, restored, dated '1696', 3¼in (8.5cm) high.
£120–140 C

A set of four north German or Dutch pale green-tinted roemers, each stem applied with raspberry prunts beneath a milled band, 17thC, 4¾in (12cm) high.
£1,300–1,500 S(Am)

A German diamond-point engraved green-tinted humpen, probably Bohemian, inscribed, with applied foot ring and kick-in base, cracked, dated '1617', 10½in (26.5cm) high.
£7,000–7,700 S

A Bohemian engraved heavy-walled beaker, with three cartouches within scrollwork, engraved with monograms 'IL', 'EL', 'CL' and 'TL' within polished circlets, the base with a stylized flower, c1690, 4½in (11.5cm) high.
£1,700–2,000 S

◀ A Bohemian beaker, each panel engraved with an allegorical figure of the Continents between line banding, c1700, 4½in (11.5cm) high.
£950–1,100 S
The engraving of the four allegorical figures of Europe, Asia, Africa and America contributes to the value of this piece.

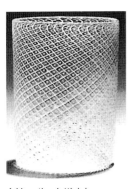

A Venetian latticinio tumbler, in *vetro a reticello*, late 17th/18thC, 3½in (9cm) high.
£1,000–1,100 C
The term *vetro a reticello* means criss-cross or network pattern.

A Bohemian engraved beaker, with three panels engraved with religious symbols, divided by columns and panels of concave lenses, mid-18thC, 5in (12.5cm) high.
£500–600 P

A Bohemian enamelled beaker, painted with a couple and a dog within a gilt border, Riesengebirge, regilt, minor damage, c1760, 3¾in (9.5cm) high.
£500–600 S

A Bohemian engraved flared beaker, decorated with figures of ladies and groups emblematic of Faith, Hope, Love and Charity below inscriptions, the rim with loose sprays of fruit between scrolling leaves, slight wear, early 18thC, 4½in (11.5cm) high.
£1,250–1,500 CSK

◄ A wine and water glass, engraved with fruiting vine, c1740, 3¼in (8.5cm) high.
£250–300 BrW

A water glass, the bellied bowl engraved with a Jacobite rose, sunflower and daffodil, c1750.
£900–1,100 Som

A barrel-shaped tumbler, with Lynn rings, c1770, 3½in (9cm) high.
£200–225 BrW
Lynn glass was made during the late 18th and early 19thC, and is recognized by horizontal grooved rings around the bowls or bodies of vessels. Every type of vessel was made, from wine glasses and tumblers to jugs, decanters and bowls. Lynn glass was believed to have been made at King's Lynn, although many examples have been found in other parts of Norfolk.

A German or Dutch, rummer, with a cup-shaped bowl merging into a hollow cylindrical stem applied with two rows of raspberry prunts beneath a milled band, and with kick-in base, on a spreading folded foot, base cracked, 17th/18thC, 8½in (21.5cm) high.
£1,450–1,700 S

A German engraved beaker, the thick flared sides cut with facets and polished circlets around the base, engraved on one side in polished *tiefschnitt* with Eve offering the apple to Adam, after Dürer, the reverse inscribed, early 18thC, 5¼in (13.5cm) high.
£1,400–1,600 S

Three bonnet glasses, on plain conical feet, c1750, 3in (7.5cm) high.
£50–60 each Som

BRIAN WATSON
ANTIQUE GLASS

Foxwarren Cottage
High Street, Marsham
Norwich NR10 5QA
Tel & Fax: 01263 732519

A flute-moulded rummer, engraved 'The Queen Forever', c1780, 5in (12.5cm) high.
£180–220 FD

A Georgian cut-glass tumbler, 3½in (9cm) high.
£70–90 CB

A tankard with baluster body, folded rim, and gadrooned base, on a plain conical foot, with reeded handle, c1790, 6in (15cm) high.
£450–500 Som

A pair of conical beakers, engraved with naval inscriptions, c1800, 5in (12.5cm) high.
£580–650 Som

A tapered beaker, engraved with 'ICA' within a floral cartouche, the reverse with a bird in flight, c1780, 4¼in (11cm) high.
£140–160 Som

An Irish rummer, c1790, 6in (15cm) high.
£90–110 WGT

A German or Dutch rummer, the cup-shaped bowl engraved with scrolling flowers and foliage, merging into a hollow cylindrical stem applied with two rows of raspberry prunts beneath a milled band and with kick-in base, on a spreading folded foot, 18thC, 8½in (21.5cm) high.
£2,000–2,500 S

A set of engraved rummers, c1790, 4½in (11.5cm) high.
£700–800 FD

A tumbler, engraved with a rose and a bird, c1790, 4½in (11.5cm) high.
£160–200 BELL

A Bohemian tumbler, engraved with the four Continents, 'Europa', 'Asia', 'Africa' 'America', late 18thC, 4½in (11.5cm) high.
£800–900 CB

▶ A clear boot glass or stirrup cup, with band of etched decoration and monogram 'T.E.S.', c1800, 3¾in (9.5cm) high.
£70–80 Som

A blue boot glass, c1790, 4½in (11.5cm) high.
£250–280 Som

A tumbler, engraved 'Ford for Ever', c1790, 4in (10cm) high.
£350–400 BrW
The initials on this tumbler appear to relate to Sir Francis Ford, who became Member of Parliament for Newcastle-under-Lyme in 1792.

Prunts & Printies

Prunts: are blobs of glass applied to the surface of a vessel as decoration.
Printies: are decorative patterns of shallow concave, rounded shapes made on cut glass.

A rummer, the ovoid bowl on a collared stem with domed moulded lemon squeezer base, c1800, 5½in (14cm) high.
£90–110 Som

A pair of commemorative naval tumblers, each engraved with four anchors and inscribed 'Howe 1st June 1794, St Vincent 14th February 1797, Duncan 11th October 1797' and 'Nelson 1st August 1798', the lower section cut with flutes, slight wear, c1800, 4½in (11.5cm) high.
£1,000–1,200 C

A glass rummer, with lemon squeezer base, c1800, 6in (15cm) high.
£95–110 CB

A Sunderland Bridge rummer, with bucket bowl, on a blade knop stem, c1800, 6in (15cm) high.
£340–380 FD

A conical beaker, the body engraved with Masonic symbols and initials 'JW' on the reverse, c1800, 5in (12.5cm) high.
£400–440 Som

A set of six diamond- and panel-cut rummers, on blade knop stems, c1805, 5in (12.5cm) high.
£650–750 FD

◀ A rummer, the ovoid body engraved with Nelson's funeral car, the reverse with 'Jan'y 9, 1806', 5½in (14cm) high.
£850–1,000 Som

A Lowlands or north German green-tinted rummer, the ovoid bowl merging into a cylindrical stem, with trailed collar above three rows of applied raspberry prunts, on a high conical spun foot, c1800, 7in (18cm) high.
£1,500–1,800 S

A rummer, the ovoid bowl engraved with a band of vesica and star decoration, on a plain conical foot, c1800, 5in (12.5cm) high.
£120–140 Som

◀ A rummer, possibly Irish, c1800, 4½in (11.5cm) high.
£80–100 WGT

A rummer, the ovoid bowl engraved with a plough and 'Speed the Plough', the reverse with initials 'IEB' between barley ears, on a square base, c1800, 5½in (14cm) high.
£370–420 Som

A Sunderland Bridge rummer, the bowl engraved with sailing ships passing beneath the Iron Bridge, with a commemorative inscription, the reverse with a crest below the motto 'I Mean Well', on a short spreading stem with square lemon squeezer base, chipped, c1800, 8½in (21.5cm) high.
£2,000–2,500 C

A commemorative rummer, the ovoid bowl engraved with Admiral Lord Nelson's catafalque, the reverse engraved 'Lord Nelson, Jan'y 9, 1806', 5½in (14cm) high.
£850–1,000 Som

A rummer, with petal-moulded base to the bowl and sharp pontil, c1810, 5½in (14cm) high.
£45–55 CaL

A rummer, the ovoid body finely engraved with Masonic symbols, the initial 'G' on the reverse, on a capstan stem with a plain conical foot, c1810, 6in (15cm) high.
£370–420 Som

An Irish rummer, the ovoid bowl cut with alternate panels of small diamonds and sunbursts, bands of prisms and slanting blazes, on a cushion knopped stem, on plain conical foot star-cut beneath, c1810, 5in (12.5cm) high.
£90–110 Som

A commemorative rummer, the cup bowl engraved with Nelson's catafalque, on a plain stem with plain conical foot, c1806, 5in (12.5cm) high.
£675–800 Som

► A pair of Georgian panel-cut rummers, with bucket bowls, c1810, 5¼in (13.5cm) high.
£110–130 FD

Sets/pairs

Unless otherwise stated, any description which refers to 'a set' or 'a pair' includes a guide price for the entire set or the pair, even though the illustration may show only a single item.

l. & r. A pair of ovoid rummers, c1810, 5in (12.5cm) high.
£200–225

c. A rummer, with curtain and star looped engraving, c1810, 4in (10cm) high.
£100–120 Som

Two rummers, engraved with bands of stiff leaves and tied ribbons, c1810, 5½in (14cm) high.
£100–120 each Som

Three panel-moulded rummers, the ovoid bodies each with a band of floral and leaf decoration, c1810, tallest 5in (12.5cm) high.
£85–100 each Som

A rummer, with engraved bowl, c1810, 5¾in (14.5cm) high.
£200–220 Som

► A tumbler, engraved 'M. Parkin' within a floral cartouche, c1810, 4¼in (11cm) high.
£90–100 BrW

LOCATE THE SOURCE

The source of each illustration in Miller's can be found by checking the code letters below each caption with the Key to Illustrations, pages 305–307.

A rummer, the large bucket bowl with flute-cut base, engraved with Masonic symbols and the initials 'J.E.D.' on the reverse, on a ball-knopped stem with plain conical foot, c1810, 7in (18cm) high.
£500–600 Som

A rummer, engraved with Masonic symbols, on a capstan stem with plain foot, c1810, 6in (15cm) high.
£300–350 Som

l. & r. A pair of rummers, with petal-moulded bowls and engraved floral decoration, c1810, 4½in (11.5cm) high.
£180–200
c. A rummer, with petal-moulded bowl and engraved decoration, c1810, 4in (10cm) high.
£75–90 Som

Three rummers, with petal-moulded ovoid bowls, on drawn stems with plain feet, c1810, 5in (12.5cm) high.
£110–135 each Som

Three Masonic engraved drinking glasses, c1810, tallest 7in (18cm) high.
£400–500 each Som

A pair of rummers, on lemon squeezer feet, c1810, 7½in (19cm) high.
£200–250 Som

l. A rummer, with ovoid bowl, short stem and conical foot, c1810, 4½in (11.5cm) high.
£65–80
r. A rummer, the ovoid bowl engraved 'S. Marrion', with floral decoration and a bird in flight, c1820, 5in (12.5cm) high.
£150–180 Som

A rummer, the petal-moulded body engraved with 'God Speed the Farmer' and a band of stars, on a rudimentary stem with plain conical foot, c1810, 5in (12.5cm) high.
£300–340 Som

◄ Three rummers, with plain bucket bowls, on knopped stems with plain conical feet, 1810–15, tallest 6½in (16.5cm) high.
£60–100 each Som

An engraved rummer, attributed to William Absolon, inscribed 'May Farming Flourish', the reverse inscribed 'A Trifle From Yarmouth' above the initials 'R.S.', on a short stem, spreading stepped foot and square base, slight damage, early 19thC, 6in (15cm) high.
£600–700 C

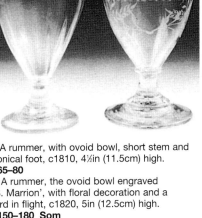

A rummer, with bucket bowl, the hollow knop containing a silver coin dated 1810, 6in (15cm) high.
£250–300 Som

A rummer, the bowl with petal-moulded base c1810, 5¾in (14.5cm) high.
£45–55 CaL

> **Cross Reference**
> See Colour Review

An Irish lipped mixing rummer, with panel-cut bowl below a band of fine diamonds, on a knopped stem, 1810–20, 6½in (16.5cm) high.
£100–120 FD

► A rummer, the ovoid bowl engraved with a floral spray and the initials 'F.C.P.', the reverse with a bird in flight, with hatched rim, on a square domed lemon squeezer foot, c1810, 5½in (14cm) high.
£250–290 Som

► A rummer, the cup bowl engraved with St George slaying the dragon, the reverse with 'T.E.B.' and date '1818', on a plain stem with square domed lemon squeezer foot, 6½in (16.5cm) high.
£1,200–1,400 Som

An engraved tumbler, c1820, 4in (10cm) high.
£85–100 CB

A conical beaker, engraved with a three-masted sailing ship, the reverse with monogram 'W.E.R.', c1820, 4in (10cm) high.
£250–300 Som

Two rummers, one with engraved bowl, c1820.
l. **£120–150**
r. **£65–80 Som**

A set of four tumblers, the conical bodies with flute, prism and small diamond cutting, c1820, 4in (10cm) high.
£300–350 Som

A rummer, the petal-moulded bowl with engraved border, early 19thC, 5in (12.5cm) high.
£70–80 CaL

A pair of rummers, the bucket bowls engraved with the Sunderland Bridge motif, the reverse sides with a rectangular cartouche and the initials 'RA' surrounded by a basket of flowers and floral sprays, on knopped stems with plain feet, c1820, 5½in (14cm) high.
£360–450 each Som

A pair of rummers, engraved with the Sunderland Bridge motif, the reverse with initials 'RMH' within a rectangular floral cartouche, c1820, 5½in (14cm) high.
£750–850 Som

► A rummer, engraved with a monogram, c1820, 8½in (21.5cm) high.
£175–200
A toddy lifter, with neck ring, c1820, 5in (12.5cm) long.
£85–100 CB

A rummer, the ovoid bowl engraved 'Queen Caroline 1820' surrounded by birds, the reverse with a crown and initials, on a short stem with circular foot, 6in (15cm) high.
£400–450 P
Caroline of Brunswick was married to the Prince Regent. He became King in 1820, but at his Coronation in 1821, he refused Caroline entry to the Abbey. She died in the same year.

A pair of rummers, with double ogee bowls, on capstan stems and plain feet, c1825, 6in (15cm) high.
£100–120 Som

◄ A Bohemian beaker and cover, possibly by Anton Simm, engraved with The Last Supper, after Leonardo da Vinci, inscribed, the lower section cut with panels of fine diamonds, the domed cover cut with raised diamonds, c1825, 7½in (19cm) high.
£3,200–3,600 S
This subject was very popular in the Biedermeier period and was used by a number of different glass engravers.

A pair of rummers, the bucket bowls engraved with monogram 'WB' within a leaf cartouche, on knopped stems with plain conical feet, c1825, 6½in (16.5cm) high.
£175–200 Som

Two blue glass naval rummers, the bowls inscribed in gilt, below a gilt rim line, gilt worn, early 19thC, 5in (12.5cm) high.
£800–900 CSK

Four rummers, with double ogee bowls, on capstan stems with plain conical feet, c1825, 5in (12.5cm) high.
£65–75 each Som

A north Bohemian beaker, with four cut panels, one engraved with Jesus Christ within an oval medallion, rosette-cut base, c1830, 5in (12.5cm) high.
£850–1,000 S

A loving cup, engraved with a rose and thistle, the reverse with the initials 'JD' within a shamrock spray, on a knopped stem with conical foot, c1825, 7¾in (19.5cm) high.
£540–600 Som

A pair of Bohemian engraved glasses, 19thC, 5in (12.5cm) high.
£55–65 PSA

◄ A pair of rummers, the incurved bowls with a band of moulded blaze decoration, on cushion knopped stems with plain conical feet, c1830, 5in (12.5cm) high.
£110–130 Som

A Bohemian commemorative transparent beaker, engraved with a train, engine driver and carriage on a red ground, c1830, 5¼in (13.5cm) high.
£250–300 DORO

A Sunderland Bridge tumbler, c1825, 4in (10cm) high.
£280–350 BELL

◄ Two rummers, the bucket bowls with engraved initials, c1825, 5½in (14cm) high.
£150–200 each Som

Three rummers, with bucket bowls, on short stems with plain conical feet, c1830, tallest 5½in (14cm) high.
£140–160 each Som

◄ A petal-moulded rummer, c1830, 5¼in (13.5cm) high.
£70–80 CB

► A pair of heavy rummers, with flute-cut bucket bowls, on knopped stems with plain feet, c1830, 6in (15cm) high.
£120–140 Som

A rummer, the bucket bowl engraved with a coursing scene, on a short stem with ball knop and plain conical foot, c1830, 6in (15cm) high.
£600–700 Som

A pair of rummers, with bucket bowls, on bladed knopped stems with plain feet, c1830, 5½in (14cm) high.
£100–120 Som

A pair of rummers, the double ogee bowls with blazes and flute cutting, on ball knopped stems, c1835, 5in (12.5cm) high.
£180–220 GS

A pair of rummers, c1830, 5in (12.5cm) high.
£85–100 DUN

A pair of amberina glasses, with diamond quilted pattern, c1840, 4in (10cm) high.
£70–80 A&A

A rummer, with bucket bowl, on bladed knop stem, c1830, 6¼in (16cm) high.
£65–75 CaL

A rummer, with heavy ogee bowl, c1840, 5in (12.5cm) high.
£38–45 CB

◀ A blue tumbler, possibly Continental, enamelled 'Remember Me', c1840, 4in (10cm) high.
£110–125 CB

A French heavy facet-cut and engraved tumbler, c1840, 3¾in (9.5cm) high.
£100–120 CB

A Bohemian light blue marbled glass beaker, decorated with gilded foliage, slight rubbing, c1840, 4½in (11.5cm) high.
£1,400–1,600 DORO

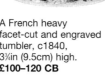

A French or Bohemian sulphide clear glass tumbler, the foot with scalloped fringe, dated '1840', 4⅛in (11.5cm) high.
£375–450 P

A Viennese enamelled beaker, painted in sepia with classical figures, the foot rim with a dentil-cut above a star-cut base, worn, 19thC, 4in (10cm) high.
£250–300 CSK

> Items in the Drinking Glasses section have been arranged in date order.

▶ A Bohemian flared tumbler, enamelled in transparent colours, inscribed in gilt on an amber flash cartouche, with cut base, slight wear, c1845, 4½in (11.5cm) high.
£1,000–1,200 C

A Hale Thomson patent silver and green engraved mercury glass, c1850, 4in (10cm) high.
£200–220 JHa

Three whisky tumblers, with flute-cut conical bowls, c1850, 4in (10cm) high.
£60–70 Som

A Baccarat cut-glass tumbler, enamelled in colours on gilt foil with the crowned Badge of the *Légion d'Honneur*, the centre with a portrait of Henri IV, slight damage, mid-19thC, 3¾in (9.5cm) high.
£350–400 C

A Baccarat cut-glass tumbler, enamelled in colours on gilt foil with a loose bouquet of flowers, mid-19thC, 3¾in (9.5cm) high.
£900–1,000 C

A Bohemian beaker, transfer-printed and painted in transparent colours with a portrait of the Archduke Charles of Austria, the reverse with a map, beneath a border of red lozenge, amber-flash and gilt decoration, the cogwheel foot and star-cut base stained in amethyst, gilding rubbed, mid-19thC, 4¼in (11cm) high.
£750–850 C

► A Baccarat cut-glass tumbler, enamelled in colours on gilt foil with a pansy on a raised oval panel and cut with diamonds on a wide band, minor chips, mid-19thC, 3¼in (8.5cm) high.
£650–720 C

A Baccarat cut-glass tumbler, enamelled in colours on gilt foil with flower spray on an oval red ground medallion within a shield-shaped cartouche, chips to rim, mid-19thC, 3½in (9cm) high.
£550–610 C

A rummer, with decorative cutting to bowl, on a bladed knop stem, c1860, 6¼in (16cm) high.
£65–75 CaL

A Bohemian transparent enamelled beaker, attributed to Carl von Scheidt, the faceted bell shape with leaf panels around the middle and painted with eight Chinese figures, on a heavily cut scalloped foot, slight wear, mid-19thC, 5¾in (14.5cm) high.
£650–720 P

◄ A Viennese transparent enamelled and gilt beaker, with a diamond-cut base, painted in the Kothgasser style with a view of Vienna, some damage, mid-19thC, 4¼in (11cm) high.
£950–1,100 P

THE **ORIGINAL** NATIONAL
G L A S S
COLLECTORS FAIRS

13 May and 4 November 2001

11.00am - 4.00pm
(Early entry 9.30am)

THE NATIONAL MOTORCYCLE MUSEUM

Birmingham **M42**
Junction **6 (A45)**

Over 100 Quality dealers offering glass from throughout the ages:
Ancient; 18th C. Drinking glasses; Victorian; Pressed; Paperweights; Studio; Art Nouveau/Deco

Specialist Glass Fairs Ltd

**Tel/Fax: 01260 271975
e-mail: dil.hier@talk21.com**

A rummer, with bladed and rounded knops, c1860, 6¼in (16cm) high.
£65–75 CaL

A pair of Bohemian amber schnapps glasses, with fine engraving, 19thC, 2¼in (5.5cm) high.
£65–75 JAS

A Davidson pearline pressed glass beaker, c1890, 5½in (14cm) high.
£25–30 CSA

▶ A blue-flash waisted beaker, engraved with a topographical view entitled 'Ludwigs Kirche' within a rectangular panel, the reverse cut with lenses between cut bands of arches, late 19thC, 5½in (14cm) high.
£250–300 CSK

A pair of Bohemian clear-glass footed beakers, with transparent cobalt blue overlay and engraved decoration, minor rim chips, c1860, 5in (12.5cm) high.
£150–175 DORO

A Lobmeyr tumbler, engraved and gilt-filled, 1880, 4in (10cm) high.
£120–145 MJW

A Bohemian beaker, with enamelled coat-of-arms of the Holy Roman Empire, 19thC, 8in (20.5cm) high.
£180–220 McC

A tumbler, engraved with flora, fauna and the initials 'J. M.', c1890, 4⅛in (11.5cm) high.
£35–40 JHa

An engraved beaker, with a half length portrait of 'Caroline Auguste Kaiserin von Oesterreich' on a matt ground, damaged, 19thC, 5½in (14cm) high.
£700–800 C

A German or Bohemian Historismus beaker, enamelled with a coat-of-arms, c1880, 4in (10cm) high.
£150–170 MJW
In the second half of the 19thC, there was great interest in the Renaissance, which led to a demand for reproduction items. In consequence, Venetian styles of the past were copied across Europe. In Germany and Bohemia, glassmakers also produced their versions of 17th and 18thC German glasses. It can often be difficult to tell Historismus glasses, as they are known, from the originals.

A Bohemian amber beaker, engraved 'Anne Pertina' and with cameo views of buildings, on a petal foot, late 19thC, 4¾in (12cm) high.
£85–100 P(O)

Glass facts
- Early lead glass has a greenish tinge, while later techniques produced progressively more transparent glass.
- Lead glass should emit a clear ring when tapped gently with a fingernail.
- Coloured glass was not popular until c1850, when it was used to produce bottles, decanters and tumblers.
- Look for the pontil mark on the base of glass – it could have been polished off, but the mark will still be visible.
- The presence of a pontil mark alone is no guarantee of age.

A footed tumbler, engraved with birds on branches and fencing, c1890, 5¼in (13.5cm) high.
£80–90 JHa

A tumbler, engraved with a Masonic symbol within a floral cartouche, c1900, 4¼in (11cm) high.
£60–75 BrW

A green Pony glass, late 19thC, 4in (10cm) high.
£15–20 CB

A Bohemian tumbler, the red overlay cut through to clear glass, late 19thC, 5in (12.5cm) high.
£140–160 CB

Further reading

Miller's Collecting Glass: The Facts at Your Fingertips, Miller's Publications, 2000

A German beaker, enamelled in colours with the King of Sweden on horseback, with the inscription 'Gustavus Adolphus Konig in Schweden, Cum deo ef Victoribus Armis, Anno Domini 1631', late 19thC, 6in (15cm) high.
£380–450 C(S)

A Weiner Werkstätte hand-painted beaker, c1908, 6in (15cm) high.
£250–300 ABS

Two Lobmeyr engraved tumblers, after designs by Michael Powolny, engraved and acid-etched, with a scalloped border to rim and an elf playing the mandolin within a similar cartouche and scattered flower sprays, c1914, 3½in (9cm) high.
£1,750–2,000 C

Auction or dealer?

All the pictures in our price guides originate from auction houses and dealers. When buying at auction, prices can be lower than those of a dealer, but a buyer's premium and VAT will be added to the hammer price. Equally, when selling at auction, commission, tax and photography charges must be taken into account. Dealers will often restore pieces before putting them back on the market.

Both dealers and auctioneers will provide professional advice, so it is worth researching both sources before buying or selling your antiques. (See source codes for each picture.)

A tumbler, decorated with a smiley face, c1970, 4½in (11.5cm) high.
£5–6 RCh

◄ A shaded cranberry glass beaker, in silver holder, marked, 1928, 4in (10cm) high.
£38–45 AA

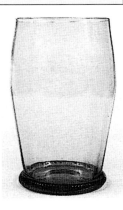

◄ A James Powell tumbler, 1930s, 6in (15cm) high,
£70–80 JHa

GOBLETS & WINE GLASSES

A Venetian enamelled goblet, with everted rim, painted in pale blue and white with a band of dots, with faint traces of red enamel and gilding, late 16thC, 4½in (11.5cm) high.
£3,500–4,000 S

A Venetian yellow-tinted wine glass, with ribbed lower section and trailed band above, on an incised twisted openwork stem with blue-tinted C-scroll wings, flanked by collars, on a wide conical foot with folded rim, late 16thC, 6¾in (17cm) high.
£12,500–15,000 S

A Venetian wine glass, the bell-shaped bowl with a light blue trail around the rim, on a collar above a hollow inverted baluster stem with wide conical foot, 16th/early 17thC, 6in (15cm) high.
£1,800–2,000 S

A Dutch *façon de Venise* winged goblet, the bowl with spiked gadroons to the lower part, the stem with a hollow knop between mereses above a hollow tapering section, on a folded conical foot, late 17thC, 8¼in (21cm) high.
£1,800–2,200 C
In a drinking glass, a merese is a flat disk of glass that links the bowl and stem, and sometimes the stem and foot.

► A part lead wine glass, with a large funnel bowl, on a hollow short double knop stem with a wide folded conical foot, c1680, 6in (15cm) high.
£1,800–2,000 S(S)

A Dutch *façon de Venise* grey-tinted goblet, on a knopped tapering stem with folded conical foot, 17thC, 7in (18cm) high.
£1,200–1,500 C

A *façon de Venise* drinking vessel, with everted rim, supported on a short hollow stem with shoulder and basal knops, late 16thC, 4in (10cm) high.
£1,250–1,500 C

A Dutch *façon de Venise* goblet, the wrythen-moulded coiled serpent stem with a central figure-of-eight and applied with opaque-white pincered decoration, on a basal knop and conical foot, 17thC, 7in 18cm) high.
£350–400 C

A Venetian wine glass, with wide cup-shaped bowl, on a hollow slender tapering stem between collars, on a wide conical foot with folded rim, late 16thC, 4¾in (12cm) high.
£1,500–1,800 S

The Withens goblet, inscribed 'Francis Withens' and '10 Maie 1590', set on a merese, the stem with coiled tubing enclosing white and brick-red threads, on a folded conical foot, 17thC, 10in (25.5cm) high.
£10,000–12,000 S
The inscription possibly records the birth of Francis Withens on 10th May 1590. The aristocratic family of Withens is recorded in Leiden, near Amsterdam. Coincidentally, Sir Francis Withens – or Wythens – (1634–1704) was an English High Court Judge who lived at Eltham, London. The form of this glass is typical of the production of the Low Countries in the second half of the 17thC. It is interesting to note the combination of foliate scroll with spiral threads between double line borders. However, it is probable that this piece was made as an anniversary goblet and the style of engraving copies that of the 16thC.

A Venetian winged glass goblet, the stem applied with opposing turquoise scrolls edged with clear pincered ornament, on a conical foot, late 17thC, 5¼in (13.5cm) high.
£2,500–3,000 C

A coin goblet, the round funnel bowl with central band of chain trailing, the base with 'nipt diamond ways', set on a teared ball knop above a hollow knop, enclosing a silver shilling dated '1686' and applied with raspberry prunts, with basal knop and folded conical foot, 10in (25.5cm) high.
£7,300–8,200 Som
This goblet is probably from the Savoy Glasshouse.

An Anglo-Venetian ale glass, the bowl with spirally-moulded decoration, on a stem with a merese and propeller knop, c1690, 6in (15cm) high.
£1,350–1,500 Som

> 'nipt diamond ways' is an expression used to describe the diamond-shaped pattern on the base of the bowl.

A Bohemian double goblet and cover, gadrooned and engraved, the smaller domed cover with floral finial, c1690, 14⅝in (37cm) high.
£3,700–4,200 S

◀ A diamond-engraved ale glass, on a merese above a short shoulder-knopped stem with pincered propeller ornament and folded conical foot, c1695, 5in (12.5cm) high.
£2,300–2,700 C

An Anglo-Dutch armorial goblet, of crizzled lead glass, the bucket bowl engraved with the arms of William of Orange as Stadholder of the Netherlands flanked by military trophies, the reverse with a crowned lion of the Province of Holland, the base with 'nipt diamond ways' above a pair of hollow quatrefoil knops flanked by mereses, the wide conical folded foot engraved with a foliate band, c1685, 7½in (19cm) high.
£10,000–12,000 S

A Bohemian engraved armorial goblet, the bowl engraved with a coat-of-arms and the initials 'CM' and 'VF', set on a tall slender multi-knopped stem and wide folded conical foot engraved with crossed leaf fronds, c1690, 9½in (24cm) high.
£1,000–1,200 S
The arms are those of von Frankenberg of Silesia.

▶ A goblet, the bowl with gadrooned lower part, on an almost hollow stem with a cushion knop, above an inverted baluster section terminating in a basal knop, on a folded conical foot, late 17thC, 12in (30.5cm) high.
£4,000–4,800 C

An Anglo-Venetian wine glass, the flared funnel bowl with spiked gadrooning to the lower part, on a merese, four-bladed propeller stem and base knop, on a folded conical foot, c1685, 5½in (14cm) high.
£2,600–2,900 Som

A Dutch *façon de Venise* goblet and cover, the stem with two hollow quatrefoil knops set between pairs of mereses, c1690, 16in (40.5cm) high.
£2,300–2,600 C

A lead green-tinted wine glass, possibly Duke of Buckingham glasshouse, on a four-sided pedestal stem with folded conical foot, late 17thC, 6½in (16.5cm) high.
£1,500–1,650 S

A Bohemian goblet, on a wide conical folded foot, c1700, 10½in (26.5cm) high.
£1,800–2,200 S

An ale glass, the stem with inverted baluster and ball knops, on a domed folded foot, c1700, 7½in (19cm) high.
£1,700–2,000 Som

► A baluster cordial glass, the stem moulded with lugs and stars at the angles, with a melon basal knop enclosing a large elongated tear, on a folded conical foot, c1705, 6in (15cm) high.
£5,500–6,500 C

A heavy baluster goblet, with deep round funnel bowl, on a stem with an inverted baluster and base knops containing air tears, on a folded conical foot, c1700, 10¼in (26cm) high.
£2,300–2,600 Som

An Anglo-Venetian ale glass, the deep round funnel bowl with wrythen and pincered decoration, on a short knopped stem with folded conical foot, c1700, 5in (12.5cm) high.
£850–950 Som

A Bohemian engraved goblet, on a triple hollow knopped stem flanked by mereses, on a wide conical folded foot, c1700, 9in (23cm) high.
£1,200–1,500 S

A goblet, with a solid base section enclosing a tear, on a folded conical foot, c1700, 6½in (16.5cm) high.
£1,500–1,700 Som

A Bohemian armorial marriage goblet, engraved with a coat-of-arms and inscribed below 'Heinrich von Brombsem' and 'Magdalena von Kirchering', very small blown bubble to inside of rim, early 18thC, 11¼in (28.5cm) high.
£1,400–1,700 C

A goblet, on a stem with inverted baluster knop, enclosing a tear, on a folded conical foot, c1700, 6in (15cm) high.
£900–1,100 Som

A toastmaster's glass, with a thick conical bowl, on a short stem with an inverted baluster knop and folded conical foot, c1700, 4½in (11.5cm) high.
£950–1,100 Som

A heavy baluster goblet, with a teared wide angular knop and basal knop, bowl scratched, c1710, 8½in (21.5cm) high.
£1,800–2,200 S

A baluster wine glass, the stem with a triple annulated waist knop and basal knop, enclosing a tear above a domed and folded foot, early 18thC, 6in (15cm) high.
£700–850 C

A baluster wine glass, the conical bowl with a solid section enclosing a tear, on a stem with a collar and large ball knop with tear, small base knop, on a domed folded foot, c1710, 6in (15cm) high.
£1,250–1,500 Som

◀ A baluster wine glass, on a collar above a wide angular knop and swelling knop enclosing a tear, on a folded conical foot, c1710, 5½in (14cm) high.
£1,250–1,500 C

Bohemian glass

Traditionally the making of engraved glass has been a Bohemian speciality, with vessels sculpturally cut in relief or engraved in intaglio, or a richly-wrought combination of both.

A baluster wine glass, with bell bowl, on a stem with annulated and base knops enclosing tears, on a domed folded foot, c1710, 6in (15cm) high.
£850–1,000 Som

A baluster goblet, the bell bowl with solid base enclosing a tear, on a teared inverted baluster stem with base knop and folded foot, c1710, 6¾in (17cm) high.
£800–900 JHa

A goblet, with round funnel bowl, the stem with base knops and enclosing a tear, on a folded conical foot, c1710, 8in (20.5cm) high.
£2,000–2,200 Som

A baluster wine glass, the conical body with solid section, on a stem with inverted baluster and base knops enclosing a tear, on a domed folded foot, c1710, 7½in (19cm) high.
£1,700–2,000 Som

A baluster wine glass, with bell bowl, on a plain stem with large base annulated knop, on a domed folded foot, c1710, 6in (15cm) high.
£750–900 Som

A baluster toastmaster's glass, the deceptive straight-sided funnel bowl on an inverted baluster stem enclosing an elongated tear, on a folded conical foot, c1710, 4½in (11.5cm) high.
£950–1,100 C

A baluster toastmaster's glass, the deceptive straight-sided funnel bowl on a teared ball knop, above a short plain section, on a folded conical foot, c1710, 4½in (11.5cm) high.
£950–1,100 C

A soda glass wine glass, on a six-sided pedestal stem enclosing a tear and on a folded foot, early 18thC, 4in (10cm) high.
£90–100 FD

Williamite glasses

Williamite glasses commemorated the victory of King William III over James II at the Battle of the Boyne in Ireland in 1690.

A George I Royal commemorative goblet, the funnel bowl with teared solid base and engraved with a crown and cypher 'GR' direct and indirect, on a teared inverted baluster stem with folded domed foot, c1715, 10in (25.5cm) high.
£5,000–6,000 S
The cypher is that of King George I (reigned 1714–27).

A baluster goblet, on a stem with shoulder ball and central cushion knops, on a folded conical foot, c1720, 8in (20.5cm) high.
£650–750 Som

A Williamite wine glass, the trumpet bowl finely engraved with King William and ribbon tribute above 'To the Glorious Memory of King William', with diaper-type engraved border around rim, on a cylinder knop stem and ball knop, on a folded conical foot, c1710, 6in (15cm) high.
£2,300–2,600 Som

A toastmaster's glass, with solid base, on an octagonal moulded stem with diamonds on the shoulder and central tear, on a folded conical foot, c1715, 4½in (11.5cm) high.
£850–1,000 S

A wine glass with cylinder knop, on a folded foot, c1720, 7in (18cm) high.
£2,500–3,000 CB

A baluster goblet, the stem with angular and base ball knop and elongated tear, on a folded conical foot, c1720, 7½in (19cm) high.
£2,000–2,200 Som

A Bohemian engraved goblet, the multi-knopped stem incorporating a faceted baluster inset with spiralling gold and cobalt blue threads, the wide folded foot engraved with a scroll, c1720, 8in (20.5cm) high.
£1,400–1,700 S

A Bohemian engraved goblet, with inscriptions, on a wrythen knop and baluster stem enclosing translucent red threads and flanked by collars, the conical foot with scroll ornament and stylized stiff leaf border, c1720, 10in (25.5cm) high.
£1,300–1,600 S

► A Dutch engraved ship goblet, on an annulated knop and octagonal pedestal moulded stem, the shoulder studded with diamonds, with basal collar and folded domed foot, c1720, 8in (20.5cm) high.
£2,000–2,500 S

A baluster goblet, the bell bowl with a tear, on a stem with annulated shoulder knop and base ball knop, on a folded conical foot, c1720, 7in (18cm) high.
£600–700 Som

A Silesian engraved goblet, on a faceted inverted baluster, with collar, the conical foot with hound's tooth rim, c1720, 8½in (21.5cm) high.
£7,500–9,000 S

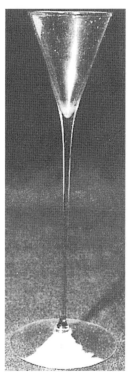

A soda glass toasting glass, possibly Continental, on a slender stem with conical foot, c1720, 9¾in (25cm) high.
£670–750 Som

An ale glass, the funnel bowl with flammiform edged wrythen-moulding, set on a wrythen knop above a plain section and basal knop, on a folded conical foot, early 18thC, 5in (12.5cm) high.
£500–600 C

► A drawn wine glass, the stem enclosing a tear, on a domed and folded foot, c1720, 9in (23cm) high.
£280–350 WW

A wine glass, on a six-sided Silesian stem with domed folded foot, c1720, 6in (15cm) high.
£730–820 Som

A gin glass, the baluster stem with shoulder, inverted baluster and base knops, on a folded conical foot, c1720, 5in (12.5cm) high.
£250–300 Som

A baluster wine glass, with bell bowl, on a stem with central cushion knop, on a plain domed foot, c1720, 6½in (16.5cm) high.
£320–380 Som

► A baluster cordial glass, the stem with cushion drop and true baluster knops, on a domed folded foot, c1720, 5½in (14cm) high.
£1,300–1,500 Som

A baluster wine glass, on an inverted baluster and base knopped stem, on a plain domed foot, c1720, 6in (15cm) high.
£630–700 Som

Somervale Antiques

Wing Cdr. R. G. Thomas M.B.E. R.A.F. (Ret'd).
6 Radstock Road (A362)
Midsomer Norton, Bath BA3 2AJ
Tel & Fax: 01761 412686 Mobile: 07885 088022
Email: ronthomas@somervaleantiquesglass.co.uk
Internet: http://www.somervaleantiquesglass.co.uk

**Shop open only by appointment.
Resident on premises. 24 hour telephone service.
Trains to Bath met by arrangement.**

Specialist in 18th and early 19th century English drinking glasses, decanters, cut and coloured, "Bristol" and "Nailsea", glass, etc. Also bijouterie, scent bottles, etc.

LAPADA
MEMBER

We wish to buy examples of the above glass, but only Good Quality items.
Member of British Antique Dealers' Association
Member of the Association of Art and Antique Dealers (LAPADA)

Three baluster wine glasses, two with bell bowls and domed folded feet, one of Kit-Kat type with trumpet bowl and plain conical foot, c1720, largest 6½in (16.5cm) high.
£300–750 each Som

Three baluster wine glasses:
l. with inverted baluster knopped stem and folded conical foot, c1720, 5½in (14cm) high.
£350–400
c. with multi-knopped stem and plain conical foot, c1740, 7in (18cm) high.
£400–450
r. with hollow inverted baluster knop stem and folded conical foot, c1720, 6½in (16.5cm) high.
£310–350 Som

Three baluster wine glasses:
l. with swelling knop, the stem enclosing a tear, on a plain conical foot, c1720, 6½in (16.5cm) high.
£360–450
c. the stem with annulated and base knops, on a folded conical foot, c1720, 6in (15cm) high.
£550–650
r. the stem with central ball knop, on a plain conical foot, c1725, 6½in (16.5cm) high.
£380–420 Som

◄ Two baluster wine glasses, the bowls with solid sections enclosing a tear, on knopped stems with folded conical feet, c1720, largest 6in (15cm) high.
£1,500–1,800 each Som

A baluster wine glass, with trumpet bowl, the stem with tear and knop, on a domed foot, small chip to foot, c1720, 6½in (16.5cm) high.
£450–500 WW

A baluster wine glass, with conical bowl, on a stem with a cylinder knop enclosing a tear, on a folded conical foot, c1720, 5½in (14cm) high.
£2,800–3,400 Som

An engraved balustroid goblet, the stem with central ball knop between plain sections above a domed foot, 1720, 7in (18cm) high.
£400–500 C

A baluster wine glass, the trumpet bowl with solid base enclosing a tear, on a stem with a double collar, above a true baluster knop with tear and folded conical foot, c1720 7in (18cm) high.
£700–775 Som

A wine glass, with a bell bowl, on an annular knopped baluster stem with conical folded foot, c1720, 7in (18cm) high.
£800–900 S(S)

◄ A baluster wine glass, with conical bowl, on a mushroom and base knopped stem, on a domed folded foot, c1720, 6in (15cm) high.
£2,000–2,400 Som

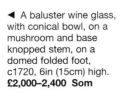

◄ A toastmaster's glass, with an inverted baluster knop enclosing a tear, on a folded conical foot, c1720, 4in (10cm) high.
£1,000–1,200 Som

A wine glass, with trumpet bowl, on a long drawn composite stem with short air-beaded inverted baluster section, on a domed plain foot, c1720, 7in (18cm) high.
£580–640 Som

Two Kit-Kat-type wine glasses, c1720: **l.** the trumpet bowl solid section with inverted baluster knop and plain domed foot, 7in (18cm) high. **r.** with folded conical foot, 7½in (19cm) high.
£460–520 each Som

Further reading
Miller's Glass Antiques Checklist, Miller's Publications, 2000

A baluster wine glass, the base of the bowl enclosing a tear, on a folded foot, c1720, 6in (15cm) high.
£650–750 FD

A baluster wine glass, with cushion knop above a beaded knop, flattened knop and drop knop terminating in a basal knop, on a domed foot, c1720, 6½in (16.5cm) high.
£1,000–1,200 C

A baluster wine glass, the stem with a slender plain section terminating in a spreading knop above a cushion knop, on a folded conical foot, c1720, 7in (18cm) high.
£380–450 C

A baluster wine glass, the bell bowl with a tear in the base, on a stem with an annulated shoulder knop and folded domed foot, c1720, 6in (15cm) high.
£400–460 Som

A baluster wine glass, with bell bowl, on a stem with inverted baluster and base knops enclosing tears, on a folded conical foot, c1720, 6½in (16.5cm) high.
£850–1,000 Som

A baluster wine glass, with trumpet bowl, on a drawn stem enclosing a tear, with swelling and base knops, on a domed terraced foot, c1720, 6in (15cm) high.
£700–800 Som

Types of drinking glass

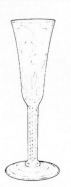

Dram glass 4in (10cm)

Wine glass 6in (15cm)

Rummer 5in (12.5cm)

Dwarf ale glass 5in (12.5cm)

Ratafia glass 7in (18cm)

Ale glass 8in (20.5cm)

A baluster wine glass, the stem with a seven-ringed annular knop and base knop, on a domed folded foot, c1720, 6¼in (16cm) high.
£1,500–1,800 Som

A Kit-Kat-type baluster wine glass, the trumpet bowl with solid shank enclosing a tear, with inverted baluster and ball knops, on a plain domed foot, c1720, 7in (18cm) high.
£625–700 Som

A baluster wine glass, with bell bowl, on a triple-annulated knop above an inverted baluster section and basal knop, on a folded conical foot, c1720, 6in (15cm) high.
£600–700 C

A cordial glass, the conical bowl with solid section enclosing a tear, on a baluster stem with inverted baluster knop and base knop, on a folded conical foot, c1720, 5½in (14cm) high.
£550–620 Som

A Saxon engraved armorial goblet, Berlin or Dresden, the reverse inscribed, on a faceted knop and teared inverted baluster, on a wide conical folded foot, c1725, 10½in (26.5cm) high.
£2,000–2,500 S

A Jacobite goblet and cover, on an eight-pointed pedestal stem with a domed and folded foot also with eight moulded panels, the cover similarly engraved and with an octagonal spire finial, early 18thC, 12in (30.5cm) high.
£2,400–2,800 P

A drawn trumpet Kit-Kat-type baluster glass, on a folded foot, c1725, 5¾in (14.5cm) high.
£420–500 GS

A baluster wine glass, with a bell bowl, the base enclosing a tear, on a stem with annulated and base knop with central tear, on a folded conical foot, c1725, 6in (15cm) high.
£730–820 Som

◄ A baluster wine glass, with a bell bowl, the stem with a triple annulated knop above a plain section and enclosing a tear, terminating in a basal knop, on a folded conical foot, c1725, 6½in (16.5cm) high.
£340–400 C

◄ A wine glass, the thistle bowl engraved with a band of foliate decoration and with solid base, on a four-sided pedestal stem, on a folded conical foot, c1725, 6½in (16.5cm) high.
£900–1,100 Som

Three gin glasses, with trumpet bowls, on knopped baluster stems with folded conical feet, c1725.
l & r. £150–170 each
c. £640–720 Som

► An engraved armorial goblet, probably Bohemian, on a faceted cushion knop and inverted baluster with basal knop, the conical foot with leaf band, c1730, 8½in (21.5cm) high.
£3,000–3,500 S

A baluster goblet, the bell bowl on a triple annulated knop, on an inverted baluster stem terminating on a basal knop, on a conical foot, c1730, 6½in (16.5cm) high.
£600–700 C

An armorial goblet, possibly Saxon, engraved with a coat-of-arms above tied laurel branches, on a folded conical foot, 18thC, 9in (23cm) high.
£850–950 CSK

A Silesian engraved goblet, by Warmbrunn, inscribed 'Vivat Negotium', on a conical foot, c1730, 6½in (16.5cm) high.
£4,000–5,000 S

A Kit-Kat-type glass, with drawn trumpet bowl engraved with fruiting vine, on a plain stem terminating in a knop and domed foot, c1730, 6¾in (17cm) high.
£600–700 P

Kit-Kat refers to a painting by Keller depicting members of the Kit-Kat Club drinking from glasses of similar shape.

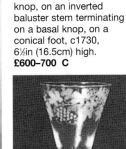

A baluster wine glass, the round funnel bowl engraved with a band of fruiting vine, on a stem with shoulder, angular inverted baluster and base knops, on a domed folded foot, c1730, 7in (18cm) high.
£720–800 Som

A wine glass, the moulded pedestal stem enclosing an elongated tear, on a folded conical foot, c1730, 6in (15cm) high.
£650–750 C

► A Dutch engraved light baluster goblet, inscribed 'T. Groeÿen en Bloeÿen van Oranie Meer', on a multi-knopped stem with a conical foot, chipped, c1740, 8½in (21.5cm) high.
£2,800–3,500 C

A goblet, with an air-beaded cushion knop and inverted baluster knop, c1730, 10in (25.5cm) high.
£650–750 Som

A baluster champagne glass, with a double ogee bowl, the stem with a beaded knop between two plain sections, on a domed foot, minor chip, c1730, 5in (12.5cm) high.
£340–400 C

Two baluster wine glasses, with trumpet bowls, the drawn stems enclosing tears and with ball knops, on plain domed feet, c1730, tallest 7½in (19cm) high.
£675–800 Som

Goblets & Wine Glasses • DRINKING GLASSES 105

A Newcastle light baluster goblet, with deep bell bowl, on an air-beaded ball knop between two angular knops, above an inverted baluster enclosing a tear, with basal knop and conical foot, c1740, 8½in (21.5cm) high.
£1,000–1,200 P
Newcastle light baluster glasses were made in the north-east of England between c1730 and 1755. They are distinctive for the lightness of the glass of which they were made. These glasses often had knops with tears in them to create the impression of light within the stem.

A Dutch Newcastle baluster wine glass, inscribed 'S Lands Welvaren', on a multi-knopped stem with a slender inverted baluster and basal knop, on a conical foot, c1740, 7in (18cm) high.
£4,750–5,500 S

A Dutch engraved armorial light baluster wine glass, the funnel bowl engraved with the arms of Holland, c1740, 7in (18cm) high.
£800–950 S

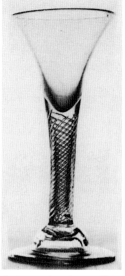

A drawn wine glass, with trumpet bowl, on an air-twist stem with domed partially-folded foot, c1740, 6½in (16.5cm) high.
£350–400 WW

A Saxon engraved goblet and cover, with inscription, on a faceted teared inverted baluster stem with folded conical foot, the domed cover with faceted spire finial and engraved with leaf fronds, c1740, 11in (28cm) high.
£2,700–3,200 S

A baluster wine glass, with bell bowl, on a stem with base ball knop, on a plain folded foot, c1740, 6½in (16.5cm) high.
£320–360 Som

◄ A wine glass, the trumpet bowl engraved with fruiting vine, on a plain drawn stem with folded conical foot, c1740, 7in (18cm) high.
£250–300 Som

► A Dutch Newcastle baluster wine glass, inscribed 'Het.Aanstaande.Huwelyk', on a beaded cushion knop and baluster knop, on a conical foot, c1740, 7in (18cm) high.
£1,700–2,000 S

A Jacobite 'Boscobel oak' wine glass, the drawn trumpet bowl engraved with an oak tree, the branches enclosing three crowns and a face in diamond point, the stem enclosing a tear, on a conical foot, c1740, 6½in (16.5cm) high.
£12,500–14,000 S
The tree probably represents the so called 'Boscobel oak' in which Charles II hid from the Parliamentarians after the Battle of Worcester on 3rd September 1651. The trunk of the oak may represent the Church as the foundation of the state, supported by three crowns representing the kingdoms of England, Scotland and Ireland. The oak tree, and in particular the oak leaf, remained a popular symbol of the Stuart cause. It has been suggested that glasses of this type may be centenary glass, and that the crowns could represent James, the Old Pretender, and his two sons, Prince Charles Edward and Henry, later Cardinal of York.

A baluster wine glass, the trumpet bowl engraved with a band of fruiting vine, inverted baluster and base knop stem, on a plain domed foot, c1740, 7in (18cm) high.
£640–720 Som

A cordial glass, the drawn stem with a pair of medium air-twist corkscrews, on a plain conical foot, c1740, 7½in (19cm) high.
£700–800 Som

A toasting glass, the bowl spirally wrythen, continuing on the slender stem and forming spiral ribs on the conical foot, c1740, 8in (20.5cm) high.
£650–720 P

A Kit-Kat-type baluster wine glass, the trumpet bowl on a long drawn section enclosing a tear, with inverted baluster knop, on a folded conical foot, c1740, 7in (18cm) high.
£600–675 Som

A Newcastle wine glass, with rounded funnel bowl, on a multi-knopped stem with flattened central knop, rim chip, c1740, 7in (18cm) high.
£375–450 DN
The damage to this glass affected its price quite considerably when sold at auction.

A wine glass, the pointed round funnel bowl with solid base section, on an eight-sided moulded Silesian stem with folded conical foot, c1740, 5½in (14cm) high.
£850–1,000 Som

A Privateer wine glass, the funnel bowl inscribed 'Prosperity to the London' in a ribbon above a spray of fruiting vine, the reverse with an insect, on a spiral air-twist cable stem with conical foot, 6in (15cm) high.
£1,800–2,000 S
The *London*, a galley of 170 tons, 18 guns and 60 men, was declared on 16th December 1742 with John Mitchell as the commander and John Noble as sole owner.

A wine glass, with bell bowl and drop knop, on a folded foot, c1740, 6in (15cm) high.
£1,500–1,800 CB

Cross Reference
See Colour Review

▶ A Jacobite wine glass, the bell-shaped bowl engraved with a rose and one bud, the baluster stem with a cushion, air-beaded cushion, inverted baluster and base cushion knops, on a domed folded foot, c1740, 6¾in (17cm) high.
£1,800–2,000 Som

▶ A baluster wine glass, with bell bowl, on a stem with basal ball knop, on a folded conical foot, c1740, 6½in (16.5cm) high.
£300–350 Som

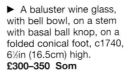

A flammiform ale glass, c1740, 4½in (11.5cm) high.
£275–325 FD

A Dutch goblet, possibly by Jacob Sang, the funnel bowl engraved and part-polished, on a multi-knopped stem with a teared inverted baluster below two beaded cushion knops, the rim of the bowl and the conical foot engraved with a narrow ovolo band, the pontil area finished as a daisy, c1745, 9in (23cm) high.
£7,000–8,000 S

A pair of Dutch engraved wine glasses, each with funnel bowl inscribed 'De Negotie' and 'De Zee-haart' within a scroll cartouche, on a knopped baluster stem with conical foot, 1740–50, 7in (18cm) high.
£1,800–2,000 S

A Dutch stipple-engraved armorial goblet, attributed to Alius, the round funnel bowl decorated in both diamond-point and stipple techniques with the crowned arms of Princess Frederika Sophia Wilhelmina, c1745, 7½in (19cm) high.
£3,300–4,000 S

◄ A Jacobite goblet, engraved with a heraldic rose flanked by open and closed buds, on a double knopped air-twist stem with conical foot, c1745, 9½in (24cm) high.
£2,200–2,500 S

A Newcastle light baluster wine glass, engraved with tthe arms of the Dutch Count van der Stragen of Brabant, c1740.
£1,800–2,200 CB

A Dutch engraved whale-hunting goblet, the funnel bowl inscribed 'T Welvaaren van de Groenlansche Vissery', c1745, 7½in (19cm) high.
£4,500–5,500 S

◄ A gin glass, on a shoulder and base knopped stem, on a folded foot, c1745, 4¾in (12cm) high.
£180–220 GS

The Gregson of Tilliefour Old Pretender goblet, of Jacobite significance, the waisted bell-shaped bowl with solid base enclosing a small tear, engraved in diamond point with a crown surmounting the cypher 'JR' direct and reversed, intertwined with the figure '8', inscribed on each side 'Send Him soon home To Holyruood Houfe And that no Sooner Than I do Wifh', and inscribed below 'Vive La Roy', on a plain stem with conical folded foot, c1745, 9½in (24cm) high.
£25,000–30,000 S
This important glass belongs to the same series as the Amen Glasses and is engraved in similar style. It will be noticed that Holyrood has a superfluous 'u' (erased). While the majority of the 40 known Amen glasses have trumpet bowls, only three examples are known with bell-shaped bowls. One, the Steuart Amen, can be found in the collection of the National Museums of Scotland; the other, the Ferguson Amen, is in the Cinzano Collection. They are listed 36 and 38 respectively, by Charleston and Seddon.

Two wine glasses, on air-twist stems, c1745, 6in (15cm) high.
l. £340–390
r. £440–490 Som

A pair of wine glasses, on stems with multiple-spiral air-twists and swelling shoulder knops, on folded conical feet, c1745, 6½in (16.5cm) high.
£750–900 Som

Three wine glasses, the trumpet bowls engraved with fruiting vine, on double knopped stems with multiple-spiral air-twists, on domed conical feet, c1745, 7in (18cm) high.
£1,600–2,000 Som

◄ A toasting glass, on a teared stem, mid-18thC, 7in (18cm) high.
£200–230 FD

A gilded green wine glass, 18thC, 5in (12.5cm) high.
£180–200 CB

A Jacobite dram glass, the reverse with the motto 'Fiat' beneath a star, on a cushion knop enclosing a tear, c1745, 4in (10cm) high.
£1,500–1,800 C

A baluster wine glass, on a stem with central knop and tear, c1745, 5¾in (14.5cm) high.
£180–220 FD

ANTIQUE GLASS

Margaret Hopkins at Frank Dux Antiques
33 Belvedere, BATH BA1 5HR
Tel & Fax 01225 312367

www.antique-glass.co.uk
e-mail: antique.glass@which.net

A composite stem wine glass, on a multiple-spiral air-twist section and inverted baluster air-beaded knop, on a plain domed foot, c1745, 7in (18cm) high.
£700–800 Som

l. A firing glass, with trumpet bowl, on a drawn stem with multiple spiral air-twists, on a thick flat foot, c1745, 4½in (11.5cm) high.
£300–350
r. A wine glass, with similar bowl and stem, on a plain conical foot, c1745, 6½in (16.5cm) high.
£320–370 Som

A Dutch engraved wine glass, with the name 'D Vrindschap', on a dumbbell knop above an inverted baluster stem, the shoulders enclosing two rows of beads, on a plain conical foot, c1745, 8in (20.5cm) high.
£1,450–1,700 S(S)

A cordial glass, with trumpet bowl, on a drawn stem with multiple-spiral air-twist, on a plain conical foot, c1745, 4½in (11.5cm) high.
£450–500 Som

▶ A goblet and two wine glasses, with trumpet bowls, on plain drawn stems enclosing tears, c1745, largest 7½in (19cm) high.
£150–180 each Som

A wine glass, with trumpet bowl, on a composite stem with multiple-spiral air-twist section above a plain section with inverted baluster air-beaded knop, c1745, 7in (18cm) high.
£700–800 Som

A Jacobite wine glass, engraved with 'Redeat' beneath the rim, on an air-twist stem with a domed foot, c1745, 6in (15cm) high.
£1,500–1,800 WW

An ale glass, with a deep funnel bowl engraved with barley ears and vines, on an air-twist stem, c1745, 8in (20.5cm) high.
£550–620 Som

A wine glass, with trumpet bowl, on an air-twist stem with folded conical foot, c1745, 8in (20.5cm) high.
£350–400 WW

◀ Two wine glasses, on plain conical feet, c1745, 7½in (19cm) high:
l. with bell bowl and cable air-twist stem,
r. with pan-top bowl and double air-twist stem.
£360–400 each Som

▶ A Dutch Friendship goblet, the bell bowl finely engraved in the style of Jacob Sang and part-polished with a three-masted ship with 'The Plough' forward, inscribed within two bands, one with a snake biting its tail, 'Dusleyde ons Vriendschap', c1748, 7½in (19cm) high.
£1,800–2,200 S

LOCATE THE SOURCE
The source of each illustration in Miller's can be found by checking the code letters below each caption with the Key to Illustrations, pages 305–307.

▶ A moulded baluster wine glass, the bowl with all-over honeycomb moulding, on a stem with two cushion knops above a plain section, on a conical foot, c1745, 6½in (16.5cm) high.
£420–480 C

A German goblet and cover, engraved with a female figure below the title 'Unico', with matched cover, 18thC, 11¼in (28.5cm) high.
£420–500 CSK

► A Dutch armorial goblet, the funnel bowl engraved with the arms of Anne, daughter of George II, c1750, 7⅛in (19cm) high.
£2,300–2,600 S

A Dutch Kraamvrouw goblet, attributed to Jacob Sang, the reverse with inscription, on a beaded knop flanked by an angular knop and plain section with basal knop, on a conical foot, c1750, 7½in (19cm) high.
£4,000–4,500 S

A wine glass, the funnel bowl engraved with a building flanked by a fruit tree and row of hops, on an air-twist stem with a gauze core and two spiral threads, on a conical foot, mid-18thC, 5½in (14cm) high.
£800–1,000 C

A goblet, the ogee bowl engraved with a sunflower and a moth, on a plain stem, c1750, 6¼in (16cm) high.
£300–350 BrW

A Silesian engraved Friendship goblet and cover, the domed cover with faceted finial, c1750, 10in (25.5cm) high.
£1,700–2,000 S

◄ A Lauenstein armorial goblet, the bowl with solid base, engraved with a coat-of-arms and inscribed 'J'aime, qui m'aime', on a blue-tinted inverted baluster stem encasing silver foil, on a folded domed foot, c1750, 8½in (21.5cm) high.
£900–1,100 S

A Jacobite portrait goblet, the bowl with a bust portrait of Prince Charles Edward, inscribed above 'Audentior ibo', on a double knopped air-twist stem filled with spiral threads, on a conical foot, c1750, 6½in (16.5cm) high.
£4,700–5,200 C

A Dutch armorial light baluster goblet, possibly Jacob Sang, the funnel bowl engraved with the arms of Princess Frederika Sophia Wilhelmina of Prussia, on a beaded knop flanked by an angular knop and plain section with basal knop, on a conical foot, c1750, 7in (18cm) high.
£1,700–2,000 S

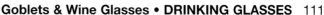

A goblet, with bucket bowl, on a multiple-spiral air-twist stem, c1750, 7in (18cm) high.
£450–500 Som

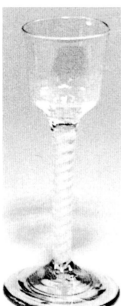

A Dutch armorial goblet, the funnel bowl engraved with the arms of Saxony and Württemberg *accolé*, signed 'V. Baker' on the upper knop, c1750, 7½in (19cm) high.
£2,500–3,000 S

◄ An opaque-twist glass, with faint fluted bowl, on a multi-strand stem with conical foot, mid-18thC, 5¾in (14.5cm) high.
£200–250 Hal

A wine glass, the funnel bowl engraved with two carnations and a bee, on a shoulder knopped multiple-series air-twist stem, c1750, 5¾in (14.5cm) high.
£500–600 JHa

An ale glass, engraved with hops and barley, the stem with multiple-spiral air-twist and swelling knop, on a plain conical foot, c1750, 7¼in (18.5cm) high.
£600–700 Som

A double dram glass, mid-18thC, 5in (12.5cm) high.
£250–280 FD

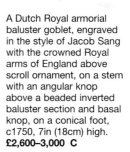

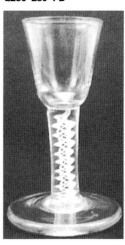

A double dram glass, with bell bowls, c1750, 3½in (9cm) high.
£250–280 FD

A pair of Jacobite baluster wine glasses, the flared funnel bowls engraved with a rose and bud, on a cushion knop above a beaded knop, the swelling stems terminating on a basal knop, on domed and folded feet, one bowl stained, c1750, 7in (18cm) high.
£750–900 C

A Dutch Royal armorial baluster goblet, engraved in the style of Jacob Sang with the crowned Royal arms of England above scroll ornament, on a stem with an angular knop above a beaded inverted baluster section and basal knop, on a conical foot, c1750, 7in (18cm) high.
£2,600–3,000 C

► A miniature dram glass, with funnel bowl, on a double-series opaque-twist stem with heavy foot, c1750, 3¾in (9.5cm) high.
£400–450 BrW

A Venetian enamelled armorial goblet, base of bowl cracked, c1500, 5in (12.5cm) high.
£15,500–17,000 S

An engraved wine glass, with inscription 'De Goed Negootie', mid-18thC, 8in (20.5cm) high.
£1,300–1,500 Bon

A light green export-type wine glass, with double ogee bowl, c1760, 7in (18cm) high.
£900–1,000 Som

► A green wine glass, with shoulder and base knops, the incised stem over a plain foot, c1760, 4½in (11.5cm) high.
£1,000–1,200 JHa

A ceremonial goblet and domed cover, with flared funnel bowl, crown finial, the stem formed as four wrythen-moulded loops, late 17thC, 18in (45.5cm) high
£65,000–72,000 C

l. A wine glass, with opaque spiral thread stem, c1765, 7in (18cm) high.
£3,500–4,000
r. An air-twist stem wine glass, c1760, 7½in (19cm) high.
£2,500–3,000 C

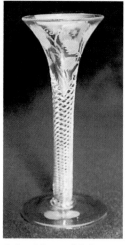

A Potsdam-Zechlin engraved and gilt armorial goblet, the beaded faceted knopped stem heightened with gilding, the foot cut with radiating petals, c1740, 8½in (21.5cm) high.
£10,500–12,000 S

A wine glass, with bell bowl on a plain stem and plain folded conical foot, c1750, 7in (18cm) high.
£320–350 Som

A wine glass, with incised twist stem, c1760, 5¼in (13.5cm) high.
£370–450 Som

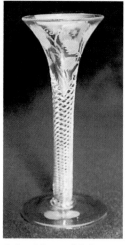

A Jacobite cordial glass, the small trumpet bowl engraved with a Jacobite rose, on a drawn multiple spiral air-twist stem and plain conical foot, c1745, 5½in (14cm) high.
£1,700–2,000 Som

A Potsdam-Zechlin goblet, engraved and gilt-decorated, c1750, 7in (18cm) high.
£3,800–4,500 S

An export-type wine glass, c1760, 5½in (14cm) high.
£320–400 Som

A Beilby armorial wine glass, attributed to William Beilby, on a double-series opaque twist stem and conical foot, gilding rubbed, c1765, 6in (15cm) high.
£10,000–11,000 S

A triple twist wine glass, the round funnel bowl on a stem with a canary-coloured central cable, an inner spiralling opaque white thread and an outer laminated ply, c1770, 6in (15cm) high.
£8,000–8,800 Som

A green export-type wine glass, c1780, 6in (15cm) high.
£450–500 Som

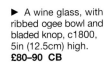

► A wine glass, with ribbed ogee bowl and bladed knop, c1800, 5in (12.5cm) high.
£80–90 CB

A tulip-shaped wine glass, with plain foot, 1780–1820, 5¼in (13.5cm) high.
£50–60 JHa

A Bristol wine glass, with ribbed cup bowl, c1790, 5in (12.5cm) high.
£250–300 CB

A set of six wine glasses, with conical bowls, plain drawn stems and plain conical feet, c1790, 5¼in (13.5cm) high.
£400–480 Som

A wine glass, with cup bowl and knopped incised twist stem, c1800, 5½in (14cm) high.
£450–500 CB

◄ A set of seven wine glasses, each with conical bowls on stems with bladed knops, c1800, 5in (12.5cm) high.
£475–550 Som

A Continental green faceted wine glass, with gilded decoration, early 19thC, 5¾in (14.5cm) high.
£85–100 CB

► A pair of panel-cut green wine glasses, with conical bowls, blade and collar knop stems, c1820, 5in (12.5cm) high.
£130–150 FD

Four green wine glasses, c1830, largest 5¼in (13.5cm) high.
£60–85 each Som

Two cup-shaped wine glasses, c1830, 4¾in (12cm) high:
l. with knopped stem.
r. with ribbed bowl and plain drawn stem.
£70–80 each Som

l & r. Two peacock blue wine glasses, with knopped stems, 1830–40, 5in (12.5cm) high.
c. A green wine glass, with part-fluted bowl and knopped stem, c1840, 5½in (14cm) high.
£70–75 each Som

A set of eight Bristol trumpet-shaped green wine glasses, c1840, 5¼in (13.5cm) high.
£500–550 MJW

Two wine glasses:
l. with ogee fluted bowl.
£85–100
r. with cup-shaped bowl, 1840, 5in (12.5cm) high.
£170–200 Som

► A set of eight amber wine glasses, the cup-shaped bowls with engraved fruiting vine decoration, on plain drawn stems and conical feet, c1840, 4½in (11.5cm) high.
£340–380 Som

◄ Four turquoise wine glasses, with conical bowls on stems with ball knops, c1830, 4½in (11.5cm) high.
£250–300 Som

l & r. A pair of green wine glasses, with tulip bowls, plain stems and feet, c1840.
£100–125
c. A wine glass with conical bowl and knopped stem, c1830, 5½in (14cm) high.
£65–80 Som

◄ A Bohemian amber-stained goblet and cover, attributed to Franz Hansel, minute repairs, c1840, 18in (45.5cm) high.
£9,500–10,500 S

A petal-moulded wine goblet, c1840, 6in (15cm) high.
£170–200 CB

A set of eight wine glasses, the trumpet bowls with base collars, on stems with shoulder ball knops and plain conical feet, c1840, 5in (12.5cm) high.
£700–800 Som

A Bohemian goblet, c1840, 9½in (24cm) high.
£800–1,200 MJW

A set of five wine glasses, with ovoid bowls and flute-cut stems, c1840, 5in (12.5cm) high.
£300–350 Som

► A pair of wine glasses, with wide ovoid bowls and flat-cut stems, c1840–50, 5in (12.5cm) high.
£40–50 each BrW

An electric blue wine glass, with slice-cut bowl and cut stem, c1850, 5¾in (14.5cm) high.
£100–120 JHa

Three mercury glass goblets, c1850:
l. Varnish & Co, 9¾in (25cm) high.
£350–400
c. Hale & Thompson, 5in (12.5cm) high.
£175–200
r. Varnish & Co, 8in (20.5cm) high.
£500–600 ARE

A pair of wine glasses, c1850, 5in (12.5cm) high.
£85–100 JAS

A pair of wine glasses, c1860, 5in (12.5cm) high.
£100–120 JAS

◄ A set of four wine glasses, with flute-cut bowls, on cut knopped stems and plain conical feet, c1850, 5½in (14cm) high.
£250–300 Som

A Stourbridge overlay goblet, c1850, 5in (12.5cm) high.
£225–265 MJW

A pair of red overlay wine glasses, c1870, 5in (12.5cm) high.
£150–170 MJW

A Bohemian cameo and intaglio-engraved goblet, signed 'F. Zach', c1860, 6¼in (16cm) high.
£2,000–2,500 ALiN

A Bohemian engraved goblet, attributed to Franz Zach, depicting a pair of fighting stags in a woodland scene, the flared-cut foot with a band of flutes, the reverse cut with a lens, c1860, 6in (15cm) high.
£3,200–3,500 S

A Bohemian engraved amber glass goblet, c1870, 6¾in (17cm) high.
£130–150 MJW

Items in the Drinking Glasses section have been arranged in date order within each sub-section.

◄ A pair of amethyst wine glasses, with engraved decoration, c1870, 5½in (14cm) high.
£200–245 MJW

A pair of wine glasses, with gilt rims, c1890, 5½in (14cm) high.
£60–70 MJW

A Venetian wine glass, c1890, 4½in (11.5cm) high.
£150–170 MJW

A set of nine Webb amber wine glasses, c1930, 8in (20.5cm) high
£300–350 ARE

A goblet, with green overlay, c1870, 5¾in (14.5cm) high.
£245–265 MJW

A pair of Bohemian goblets and covers, early 20thC, 21in (53.5cm) high.
£2,000–2,500 C

◄ A Lobmeyer goblet, c1890, 7¼in (18.5cm) high.
£425–465 MJW

► A set of six Webb blue cocktail glasses, with clear glass stems, signed, 1930s, 6¼in (16cm) high.
£220–240 MON

A Bohemian glass ruby-flashed goblet and scalloped cover, engraved with four vignettes depicting stags, late 19thC, 11½in (29cm) high.
£500–550 WL

A Bohemian etched goblet, 1920–30, 4½in (11.5cm) high.
£75–85 FMN

A limited edition RMS *Elizabeth* souvenir goblet, 1940–68, 8¼in (21cm) high.
£140–160 OBS

Two Nailsea-type water jugs, c1800.
l. 4½in (11.5cm) high.
r. Wrockwardine, 4in (10cm) high.
£250–450 each Som

◄ Three North Country blue glass cream jugs, c1800, tallest 5in (12.5cm) high.
£100–150 each Som

A wine jug, c1800, 8in (20.5cm) high.
£750–850 Som

A Nailsea jug, with applied loop handle, c1810, 4¾in (12cm) high.
£350–380 Som

A Wrockwardine glass jug, with marvered decoration, c1810, 8½in (21.5cm) high.
£550–650 Som

A pair of glass ewers, with crenellated rims and applied clear glass handles, decorated with enamel arabesques, 19thC, 10½in (26.5cm) high.
£85–100 HBC

◄ A cranberry glass jug, with amber trailed neck, c1820, 5½in (14cm) high.
£175–220 ARE

A blue glass claret jug, with barley-twist clear handle and facet-cut stopper, c1820, 6in (15cm) high.
£125–150 CB

A uranium glass jug, c1840, 10in (25.5cm) high.
£375–450 MJW

A jug and two goblets, by Richardsons of Stourbridge, lozenge mark for 1845.
£1,200–1,500 Som

A Bohemian glass 'alabaster' jug and cover, made for the Turkish market, cut with facets and stylized leaves, with applied scroll handle and octagonal knop, c1850, 8¾in (22cm) high.
£2,000–2,200 S

A Bohemian glass jug, engraved with vines and cupids, c1860, 10¾in (27.5cm) high.
£330–400 MJW

◄ A glass cream jug, decorated with white stripes, with a clear handle and foot, c1860, 4in (10cm) high.
£175–200 CB

An amberina glass jug, c1870, 11in (28cm) high.
£300–350 MJW

An amber glass claret jug, engraved with flowers and ferns, with a clear glass handle and stopper, c1870, 9in (23cm) high.
£150–170 CB

A glass decanter/claret jug, with barley-twist handle, c1880, 10in (25.5cm) high.
£120–150 CB

A cranberry glass jug, with white trailed decoration, c1880, 9in (23cm) high.
£250–300 MJW

A Northwood intaglio jug, c1880, 5½in (14cm) high.
£550–650 MJW

A Continental glass jug and two tumblers, with enamel decoration, c1890, jug 5½in (14cm) high.
£85–100 DKH

A cranberry ice-glass jug, with moulded handle, c1890, 9in (23cm) high.
£180–200 CB

A Stourbridge Webb glass claret jug, c1897, 11in (28cm) high.
£950–1,150 CB

A glass jug, with purple overlay, c1900, 8in (20.5cm) high.
£320–350 MJW

A Stevens & Williams silver-mounted white wine jug, 1900, 12¾in (32.5cm) high.
£1,000–1,200 MJW

◄ An E Bakalowits & Söhne glass sherry jug, by Koloman Moser, in dimpled glass with silver-plated mounts, c1900, 10in (25.5cm) high.
£3,200–3,850 S

A vaseline glass jug, with white spiral decoration and plain loop handle, c1900, 7¾in (19.5cm) high.
£150–170 ARE

► An Arts & Crafts glass claret jug, c1900, 11¼in (28.5cm) high.
£350–400 MJW

A bronze hall lantern, with glass smoke deflector and pierced decoration, c1820, 33in (84cm) high.
£22,000–25,000 S

A French glass hanging lamp, modelled as a bunch of grapes, c1910, 8½in (21.5cm) high.
£120–140 ML

A crackle glass globe ceiling light, with chrome fitting, 1930s, 8½in (21.5cm) high.
£65–80 ML

▶ A painted and marbled glass ceiling bowl hanging light, 1930s, 12½in (32cm) diam.
£35–40 TWa

A brass gas lantern, with vaseline glass shade, converted to electricity, 1890s, 25in (63.5cm) high.
£700–800 CHA

A brass six-sided lantern, with six green glass panels, c1920, 14in (35.5cm) high.
£120–140 RUL

◀ A stained glass lantern, 1930s, 9in (23cm) high.
£90–110 LIB

A French brass hanging oil lamp, with matching glass shade, fount and smoke bell, c1910, 24in (61cm) high.
£400–450 LIB

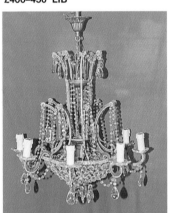

A French gilt-brass and crystal chandelier, 1920s, 35in (89cm) high.
£1,250–1,500 JPr

A Victorian glass oil lamp, the shade etched with flowers, burner stamped 'Hink's Duples Patent', 29in (73.5cm) high.
£1,000–1,200 P

Buyer beware

Many copies of original designs are being made today. Modern Corinthian column oil lamps are to be found in large numbers, as are lanterns and plafonniers (shallow flush-fitting ceiling lights), with little reference being available to the buyer to check authenticity.

Buying hints

• Most antique lights are obviously bought for use rather than as pure collectables. When considering such a purchase for your home, the following points should be borne in mind. If the fitting is not wired to current standards, rewiring may be difficult, in the case of unconverted gas pieces or some early electric lights this may even be impossible without using surface wiring.
• The interest in all forms of antique lighting continues to grow and prices have risen accordingly, especially for the best quality and for named designers, this trend is likely to continue for the forseeable future.

Two green glass oil lamps, 1920s, 4½in (11.5cm) high.
£8–10 each ML

A French electric lamp, in the form of a copper-gilt bowl, with glass fruit, c1890, 15in (38cm) high.
£1,000–1,200 PC

◄ An Emile Gallé cameo glass table lamp, marked, c1900, 13in (33cm) high.
£24,000–27,000 C

A Müller Frères cameo glass and wrought-iron lamp, signed, c1900, 19in (48.5cm) high.
£17,000–20,000 S(NY)

A Venetian glass millefiori boudoir lamp, c1890, 11in (28cm) high.
£1,250–1,500 PC

A Jugendstil metal table lamp, on marble base, c1900, 14¼in (36cm) high.
£220–260 P

A Daum Nancy cameo glass table lamp, the shade with quatrefoil rim, the base applied with two carved glass snails, marked, c1900, 18½in (47cm) high.
£40,000–45,000 C

A lamp modelled as a basket of fruit, the basket of silver-plate with glass fruit, c1900, 15in (38cm) high.
£700–800 ARE

► An Emile Gallé double-overlaid, wheel-carved and etched glass table lamp, c1901, 26in (66cm) high.
£31,000–35,000 CNY

A Delatte Nancy cameo glass table lamp and shade, acid-etched with vines and polished, signed, 1900, 13¼in (33.5cm) high.
£1,200–1,400 P

A French gilt-bronze and alabaster three-light lily lamp, after a model by Albert Cheuret, inscribed, early 20thC, 15in (38cm) high.
£4,250–4,750 B&B

An American leaded glass and patinated-metal table lamp, slight damage, early 20thC, 27½in (70cm) high.
£2,800–3,200 B&B

A Duffner & Kimberly leaded glass and gilt-bronze lamp, shade with impressed mark, c1910, 29in (73.5cm) high.
£13,5000–15,000 S(NY)

A Emile Gallé cameo glass table lamp, signed, c1910, 22in (56cm) high.
£11,000–12,500 ART

◄ A Pairpoint reverse-painted glass and silver-metal butterfly and roses lamp, c1915, 20½in (52cm) high.
£5,000–6,000 S(NY)

A Pairpoint reverse-painted glass and gilt-metal lamp, c1910, 23in (58.5cm) high.
£9,000–10,000 S(NY)

► A Handel reverse-painted glass and patinated-metal lamp, model No. 6688, signed, c1915, 23in (58.5cm) high.
£10,000–12,000 S(NY)

A Handel reverse-painted glass and patinated-metal lamp, c1915.
£3,750–4,500 S(NY)

► A Handel reverse-painted glass and patinated-metal lamp, c1920.
£9,000–10,000 S(NY)

A Pairpoint reverse-painted glass scenic seagull lamp, c1915, 25in (63.5cm) high.
£4,250–5,000 S(NY)

A Handel reverse-painted glass and cold-painted metal lamp, c1920.
£9,500–11,000 S(NY)

▶ A Handel cameo-cut and reverse-painted glass and metal lamp, enamelled and gilded with peacocks, designed by George Palme, c1924, 23½in (59.5cm) high.
£7,000–8,000 S(NY)

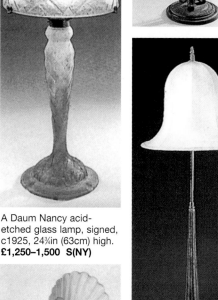

A Daum Nancy cameo glass table lamp, acid-etched with tobacco flowers, wheel-carved details, c1920, 13in (33cm) high.
£6,000–7,000 ART

A bronze and glass floor lamp, La Tentation, the bronze by Edgar Brandt, the glass by Daum, c1924, 64½in (164cm) high.
£34,000–38,000 CNY

A Daum Nancy acid-etched glass lamp, signed, c1925, 24¾in (63cm) high.
£1,250–1,500 S(NY)

◀ A Sabino opalescent glass lamp, Suzanne Au Bain, chipped, c1930, 10in (25.5cm) high.
£1,500–1,700 S

▶ A Bagley glass lamp, 1930s, 8in (20.5cm) high.
£95–100 BEV

A Süe et Mare gilt-bronze floor lamp, with a waisted domed silk shade, c1925, 64in (162.5cm) high.
£20,000–22,000 CNY

◀ A brass swan-neck wall lamp, with glass shade, c1930, 15in (38cm) wide.
£100–120 LIB

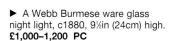

A pair of Greene and Greene inlaid mahogany and leaded-glass wall sconces, with square lanterns, mounted on mahogany wall brackets, c1907, 19in (48.5cm) high.
£28,000–32,000 CNY

▶ A Webb Burmese ware glass night light, c1880, 9½in (24cm) high.
£1,000–1,200 PC

A Victorian glass night light, 7in (18cm) high.
£100–120 ML

A Tiffany Favrile glass and silvered wirework chandelier, c1890, 48in (122cm) high.
£5,000–6,000 S(NY)

A Tiffany Favrile glass and bronze turtle-back tile Moorish chandelier, slight damage, inscribed 'L.C.T.', c1899, 38in (96.5cm) high.
£45,000–50,000 S(NY)

A Tiffany Favrile and bronze lamp, c1900, 25in (63.5cm) high.
£7,000–8,000 S

▶ A Tiffany Favrile glass and bronze lamp, c1900, 27in (68.5cm) high.
£12,000–14,000 S(NY)

A Tiffany Favrile glass and bronze blown-out lamp, c1895, 19¾in (50cm) high.
£15,000–18,000 S(NY)

A Tiffany floral lamp, c1900, 24in (61cm) high.
£17,000–19,000 S

A Tiffany Favrile glass and bronze counter-balanced desk lamp, c1900, 14½in (37cm) high.
£5,500–6,500 CNY

A Tiffany leaded glass and bronze tulip table lamp, c1900, 31in (78.5cm) high.
£17,000–19,000 FBG

A Tiffany Favrile glass and bronze filigree ball lamp, c1899, 21¾in (55.5cm) high.
£18,000–22,000 S(NY)

A Tiffany Favrile glass and bronze chandelier, mounted with a pierced bronze frame, c1900, 12in (30.5cm) diam.
£14,000–16,000 S(NY)

A Tiffany Favrile glass and gilt-bronze Venetian lamp, impressed marks, c1899, 19¾in (50cm) diam.
£20,000–24,000 S(NY)

A Tiffany bronze and iridescent glass lamp, c1900, 16in (40.5cm) high.
£5,000–6,000 C

A Tiffany glass and bronze table lamp, c1900, 15in (38cm) high.
£4,200–5,000 CNY

A Tiffany leaded glass and bronze Zodiac table lamp, stamped 'Tiffany Studios New York 507a', c1910, 30in (76cm) high.
£35,000–40,000 CNY

E-mail: subscriptions@antiquesbulletin.com

Antiques
MAGAZINE

The indispensable weekly guide
to buying & selling antiques

The full-colour weekly magazine
offering a combination of News,
Views and Specialist Articles for
lovers of antiques, including
Exhibitions coverage, up-to-date
Auction Reports, the unique Art
Prices Index and comprehensive
Fairs and Auction Calendars.

1 year's subscription is £52 UK
(45 issues), Europe £72.00,
USA/Canada £92.00,
Australia/New Zealand £132.00

To Subscribe please contact:
The Subscriptions Department,
Antiques Magazine,
2 Hampton Court Road,
Harborne,
Birmingham B17 9AE

Telephone: 0121 681 8017
or Fax: 0121 681 8005

**Subscribe NOW
and receive The
Antiques Fairs &
Centres Guide
absolutely FREE, a
publication that no
serious fair goer
can afford to miss**

Website: http://www.antiquesbulletin.com

0121 681 8017

A Tiffany Favrile glass and bronze grape trellis chandelier, the crown pierced with geometric devices, c1910, 31in (78.5cm) diam.
£50,000–60,000 S(NY)

A Tiffany Favrile glass and bronze peony floor lamp, shade impressed 'Tiffany Studios New York 1505', base 'Tiffany Studios New York/381', c1910, 65in (165cm) high.
£60,000–70,000 S(NY)

A Tiffany Favrile glass and bronze dogwood ball lamp, c1910, 33in (84cm) high.
£11,500–13,000 S(NY)

Miller's is a price GUIDE not a price LIST

A Tiffany Favrile glass and bronze dragonfly lamp, c1910, impressed marks, 21in (53.5cm) high.
£20,000–22,000 S(NY)

A Tiffany Favrile glass and bronze begonia lamp, the shade impressed '350–6', the base '7805', c1910, 16½in (42cm) high.
£30,000–35,000 S(NY)

A Tiffany Favrile glass and bronze reticulated lamp, c1910, 24in (61cm) high.
£15,000–17,000 S(NY)

A Tiffany Favrile glass and bronze dogwood lamp, impressed marks, c1910, c1910, 25½in (65cm high.
£12,000–14,000 S(NY)

A Tiffany Favrile glass and bronze hydrangea chandelier, c1910, 29in (73.5cm) diam.
£20,000–24,000 S(NY)

A Tiffany Favrile glass and bronze apple blossom lamp, c1910, 23in (58.5cm) high.
£10,500–12,000 S(NY)

A Tiffany Favrile glass and bronze filigree poppy lamp, c1910, 25in (63.5cm) high.
£25,000–30,000 S(NY)

A Tiffany Favrile glass and bronze poinsettia border lamp, c1910, 18½in (47cm) high.
£15,000–17,000 S(NY)

A Tiffany Favrile glass and bronze woodbine lamp, c1910, 19in (48.5cm) high.
£9,000–11,000 S(NY)

A Tiffany Favrile glass and bronze cyclamen lamp, c1910, 10½in (26.5cm) high.
£17,000–19,000 S(NY)

A Tiffany Favrile glass and bronze 'jewelled' feather lamp, damaged, impressed marks, c1910, 22in (56cm) high.
£3,500–4,000 S(NY)

A Tiffany Favrile glass and enamelled copper daffodil lamp, c1910, 18½in (47cm) high.
£7,200–8,500 S(NY)

A Tiffany Favrile glass and bronze poinsettia border lamp, c1910, 20in (51cm) high.
£16,500–18,000 S(NY)

A Tiffany Favrile glass and bronze clematis lamp, impressed marks, c1910, 22in (56cm) high.
£21,000–24,000 S(NY)

◄ A Tiffany Favrile glass and bronze dogwood border lamp, c1910, 23½in (59.5cm) high.
£12,000–14,000 S(NY)

A Tiffany Favrile glass and bronze miniature wisteria lamp, base impressed, c1910, 17in (43cm) high.
£36,000–40,000 S(NY)

Miller's is a price GUIDE not a price LIST

A Tiffany Favrile glass and bronze counter-balance bridge lamp, c1910, 52in (132cm) high.
£5,500–6,500 S(NY)

A Tiffany Favrile glass and gilt-bronze dragonfly lamp, impressed marks, c1910, 20¼in (52.5cm) high.
£15,500–17,000 S(NY)

A Tiffany Favrile glass and bronze peony lamp, c1910, 23in (58.5cm) high.
£40,000–45,000 S(NY)

► A Tiffany Favrile glass and bronze lamp, c1910, 24in (61cm) high.
£16,000–18,000 S(NY)

A Tiffany Favrile glass and bronze prism lamp, base impressed, c1910, 20¼in (51.5cm) high.
£4,200–4,600 S(NY)

A Tiffany Favrile glass and gilt-bronze Lily lamp, c1910, 21¼in (54cm) high.
£25,500–28,000 S(NY)

A Tiffany Favrile glass and bronze poinsettia border lamp shade and base, c1910, 19in (48.5cm) high.
£15,000–17,000 S(NY)

A Tiffany Favrile glass and bronze lotus bell lamp, c1910, 20in (51cm) high.
£15,500–17,000 S(NY)

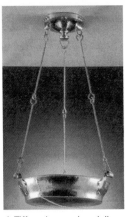

A Tiffany brass chandelier, supported by three linked arms, c1914, 36in (91.5cm) high.
£5,000–6,000 CNY

A Tiffany Favrile glass lantern, c1914, 13in (33cm) high.
£7,500–9,000 S(NY)

A Tiffany leaded glass and bronze rose table lamp, stamped 'Tiffany Studios New York 1915', 32in (81.5cm) high.
£30,000–32,000 CNY

A Tiffany Favrile glass and bronze turtle-back tile standard lamp, c1915, 67½in (171.5cm) high.
£16,000–18,000 S(NY)

◄ A Tiffany Favrile glass and bronze turtle-back tile geometric chandelier, shade impressed 'Tiffany Studios New York', c1915, 20in (51cm) high.
£10,000–12,000 S(NY)

A Tiffany Favrile glass and bronze lotus lamp, c1915, 25in (63.5cm) high.
£23,000–25,000 S(NY)

A Tiffany Favrile glass and gilt-bronze turtle-back tile geometric lamp, c1915, 26in (66cm) high.
£10,000–12,000 S(NY)

A Tiffany Favrile glass and bronze lily lamp, c1915, 19½in (49.5cm) high.
£11,000–13,000 S(NY)

A Tiffany Favrile glass and bronze daffodil lamp, base impressed, c1919, 27in (68.5cm) high.
£25,000–28,000 S(NY)

◄ A Tiffany Favrile glass and gilt-bronze lily lamp, c1925, inscribed and impressed marks, 23in (58.5cm) high.
£30,000–35,000 S(NY)

A Tiffany Favrile glass and bronze wisteria lamp, on a tree trunk base, base impressed 'Tiffany Studios New York 26854', c1915, 26in (66cm) high.
£110,000–120,000 S(NY)

A Tiffany Favrile glass and gilt-bronze poppy filigree lamp, c1920, 20in (51cm) high.
£25,000–27,000 S(NY)

► A Tiffany Favrile glass and bronze grape trellis chandelier, replaced ceiling cap and fittings, impressed, c1920, 26½in (67.5cm) diam.
£13,000–15,000 S(NY)

A firing glass, mid-18thC, 3½in (9cm) high.
£70–80 FD

A wine glass, with trumpet bowl, on a drawn multiple-spiral air-twist stem, on a plain conical foot, c1750, 6½in (16.5cm) high.
£340–400 Som

A wine glass, engraved with a fruiting vine, on a stem with multiple-spiral air-twist and shoulder knop, on a plain conical foot, c1750, 6½in (16.5cm) high.
£425–475 Som

▶ A Newcastle baluster goblet, the round funnel bowl engraved with a border of floral swags pendant from tied tassels, on a multi-knopped inverted baluster air-beaded knopped stem, on a plain conical foot, c1750, 7in (18cm) high.
£1,700–2,000 Som

A wine glass, on a spiral colour-twist stem, 18thC.
£2,000–2,500 N(A)

A Newcastle-type goblet, engraved with the Royal coat-of-arms, on a knopped air-beaded stem, c1750, 7½in (19cm) high.
£1,500–1,800 Som

A Newcastle baluster goblet, on a multi-knopped stem with a plain conical foot, c1750, 7in (18cm) high.
£1,000–1,200 Som

A baluster wine glass, on a folded conical foot, c1750, 6in (15cm) high.
£300–350 Som

A Newcastle engraved goblet, on a stem with angular and inverted baluster air-beaded knops, on a plain conical foot, c1750, 7½in (19cm) high.
£1,200–1,400 Som

A Newcastle-type goblet, the round funnel bowl engraved with a fine band of scrolling and floral decoration, on a knopped and air-beaded stem, on a plain conical foot, c1750, 7in (18cm) high.
£1,400–1,650 Som

Cross Reference
See Colour Review

◀ A Newcastle-type wine glass, engraved with a floral band with perched parrots, on a baluster stem with shoulder ball and inverted baluster knops, on a plain domed foot, c1750, 7in (18cm) high.
£1,100–1,300 Som

A baluster goblet, engraved with a band of scrolling foliage and exotic birds, on a multi-knopped stem with a plain domed foot, 1750, 7½in (19cm) high.
£1,200–1,500 Som

A Newcastle baluster goblet, on a plain domed foot, c1750, 7in (18cm) high.
£1,200–1,500 Som

A Dutch engraved armorial baluster wine glass, on a stem with a swollen section flanked by two cushion knops and a basal knop, all enclosing tears, on a conical foot, c1750, 7in (18cm) high.
£750–900 S

An ale glass, the deep round funnel bowl engraved with hops and barley motif, on a plain stem with folded conical foot, c1750.
£250–300 Som

A set of six wine glasses, with round funnel bowls, on stems with multiple-spiral air-twists and shoulder and centre knops, on plain conical feet, c1750, 6in (15cm) high.
£2,000–2,400 Som

Three wine glasses, on multiple-spiral air-twist stems with plain conical feet, c1750, largest 7½in (19cm) high.
£380–570 each Som

Two wine glasses, on multiple-spiral air-twist stems with plain conical feet, c1750, largest 7½in (19cm) high.
£400–450 each Som

A Dutch Newcastle baluster wine glass, inscribed 'S Lands Welvaren', on a teared slender stem with central swelling flanked by cushion knops and basal knop, on a conical foot, c1750, 7½in (19cm) high.
£1,200–1,400 S

l. An ale glass, the deep round funnel bowl engraved with a barley motif, on a plain drawn stem with plain conical foot, c1750.
£220–250
r. A wine glass, with ogee bowl, on a plain stem with folded conical foot, c1750.
£150–170 Som

A Jacobite wine glass, the trumpet bowl engraved with a Jacobite rose, two buds and a star, on a plain drawn stem with air tear, on a plain conical foot, c1750, 6½in (16.5cm) high.
£1,200–1,500 Som

A wine glass, with pan-top bowl, on a multiple-spiral, air-twist stem with shoulder and central knops, on a plain conical foot, c1750, 6in (15cm) high.
£450–550 Som

A Silesian goblet, the straight-sided quatrefoil bowl engraved with the monogram 'J. A.' beneath a coronet and above the motto 'Fructis Laboris', on a faceted inverted baluster stem with a double basal knop, the spreading foot etched to the rim and flute-cut to the underside, mid-18thC, 7in (18cm) high.
£500–600 CSK

A Dutch engraved goblet, inscribed 'T' Welvaren Van Land en Kerk', on a ball knop above a tapering hexagonal stem, set into a baluster knop on a conical foot, engraved in diamond point with the initial 'F', c1750, 8½in (21.5cm) high.
£900–1,100 C

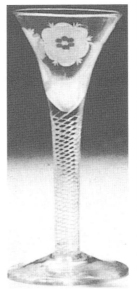

A Jacobite wine glass, the drawn trumpet bowl engraved with a rose, a bud and a half-opened bud, the reverse with the motto 'Fiat', on an air-twist stem filled with spiral threads above a conical foot, engraved with an oak branch, its foliage flanking the motto 'Redi', c1750, 6½in (16.5cm) high.
£1,700–2,000 C

A Jacobite wine glass, the trumpet bowl engraved with a Jacobite rose, two buds and an oak leaf, on a plain drawn stem with plain conical foot, c1750, 6in (15cm) high.
£1,300–1,500 Som

A Jacobite wine glass, the funnel bowl engraved with a six-petalled rose and bud, on a multiple-spiral air-twist stem with a plain conical foot, c1750, 6in (15cm) high.
£1,300–1,500 Som

▶ A Jacobite wine glass, the trumpet bowl engraved with oak leaves and acorns, the reverse with 'I.S', mid-18thC, 6½in (16.5cm) high.
£1,200–1,400 C
The initials are regarded as a memorial to James Stuart.

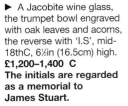

Jacobite glasses

Jacobite glasses were used by secret societies who supported the claim to the throne of the descendants of the Roman Catholic Stuart King, James II of England, who abdicated in 1688 in favour of the Protestants, William and Mary. The glasses were engraved with a variety of Stuart mottoes and emblems. The most frequently found Jacobite symbol is the rose, representing the English crown. One or two buds beside the rose stand for the Pretenders – James II's son, James Francis Edward Stuart, known as the Old Pretender, and his son, Charles Edward Stuart (Bonnie Prince Charlie), the Young Pretender.

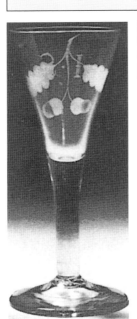

A Silesian goblet and cover, the double ogee bowl engraved with a continuous scene, the conical foot with faceted bud finial, engraved with scrolling between gilt line border, c1750, 9in (23cm) high.
£3,200–3,800 S

◀ A Jacobite wine glass, the trumpet bowl engraved with a Jacobite rose, two buds and a star, c1750, 6½in (16.5cm) high.
£1,100–1,300 Som

Two wine glasses, on multiple-spiral air-twist stems with plain conical feet, c1750, largest 6½in (16.5cm) high.
£450–500 each Som

A pair of wine glasses, the trumpet bowls engraved with fruiting vine, on plain drawn stems with plain conical feet, c1750, 7in (18cm) high.
£500–600 Som

Two balustroid wine glasses, with ogee bowls, on stems with central ball knops, c1750:
l. plain conical foot, 5in (12.5cm) high.
£260–290
r. folded conical foot, 5½in (14cm) high.
£200–220 Som

A wine glass, with round funnel bowl, on a double knopped multiple-spiral air-twist stem with plain conical foot, c1750, 6¾in (17cm) high.
£300–350 Som

A wine glass, with funnel bowl, on a mercury air-twist stem with spiralling threads, on a plain conical foot, c1750, 6in (15cm) high.
£320–390 Som

▶ An ale glass, with deep funnel bowl, on a multiple-spiral double knopped air-twist stem, on a plain conical foot, c1750, 7¾in (19.5cm) high.
£800–900 Som

An ale glass, the bucket bowl engraved 'Welcome' over a punchbowl surrounded by hops and barley, on a double-series air-twist stem, c1750, 7½in (19cm) high.
£750–850 JHa

A dram glass, with round funnel bowl, on a plain stem with heavy foot, c1750, 4in (10cm) high.
£200–220 BrW

◀ A wine glass, on a composite air-twist stem set into an inverted baluster knop, on a domed foot, c1750, 6in (15cm) high.
£750–900 C

A wine glass, with bell bowl, on a multiple air-twist stem with plain conical foot, c1750, 6½in (16.5cm) high.
£250–300 Som

An ale glass, the trumpet bowl engraved with hops and barley, on a multiple-spiral air-twist stem, c1750, 8in (20.5cm) high.
£675–750 Som

Twists

Air-twist stems took many forms, ranging from 12 even filaments in a multiple spiral to a more complex arrangement of two series of twists, one inside the other. The incised twist was a less expensive method of producing an air-twist effect. Some twist stems incorporate opaque white glass. Colour twists, sometimes combined with air or opaque twists, are rare.

| Multiple spiral | Single series | Double series |

l. A wine glass, with trumpet-bowl, on a multiple-spiral air-twist stem, on a plain conical foot, c1750, 6½in (16.5cm) high.
£340–380
r. A wine glass, with round funnel bowl, on a stem with a single-series corkscrew mercury twist, on a plain conical foot, c1750, 6¼in (16.5cm) high.
£430–480 Som

Two wine glasses, with trumpet bowls, on drawn plain mercury air-twist stems, on plain conical feet, c1750, largest 7in (18cm) high.
£380–450 each Som

◄ A pair of Jacobite wine glasses, on multi-spiral air-twist stems with conical feet, c1750, 6in (15cm) high.
£800–900 S

A Jacobite wine glass, the trumpet bowl engraved with a Jacobite rose, two buds and 'Fiat', on a multiple-spiral air-twist stem, on a folded conical foot, c1750, 7in (18cm) high.
£1,600–1,800 Som

An engraved wine glass, with pan-topped bowl, on an air-twist stem with swelling waist knop, on a conical foot, c1750, 6in (15cm) high.
£550–650 C

A Dutch engraved baluster wine glass, on a multi-knopped stem comprising an angular knop, a teared ball knop above a teared inverted baluster and basal knop, on a conical foot, c1750, 8in (20.5cm) high.
£1,000–1,200 S

Cross Reference
See Colour Review

An incised twist wine glass, the large round funnel bowl with honeycomb-moulded base and band of floral engraving, coarse incised-twist stem, on plain conical foot, c1750, 6in (15cm) high.
£780–820 Som

► A Jacobite wine glass, on a double knopped air-twist stem filled with spiral threads, on a conical foot, c1750, 7in (18cm) high.
£900–1,100 C

A Jacobite wine glass, with trumpet bowl, on a stem with entwined mercury corkscrew spirals, on a conical foot, small chips, c1750, 6in (15cm) high.
£650–750 C

A firing glass, with bell bowl, on an air-twist stem filled with spiral threads, on a thick foot, c1750, 4in (10cm) high.
£350–400 C

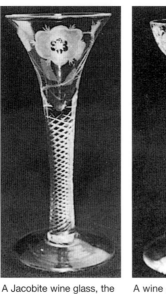

A Jacobite wine glass, the trumpet bowl engraved with a Jacobite rose, a bud and a star, on a multiple-spiral air-twist stem, on a plain conical foot, c1750, 6½in (16.5cm) high.
£1,300–1,500 Som

A wine glass, the pan-top bowl engraved with honeysuckle, rose and carnation, on a multiple-spiral air-twist stem with swelling knop, on a plain conical foot, c1750, 7½in (19cm) high.
£460–520 Som

A wine glass, with pan-top bowl, on a multiple-spiral air-twist stem, on a folded conical foot, c1750, 6in (15cm) high.
£460–520 Som

◄ A wine glass, the trumpet bowl with base ribbing, on a multiple-spiral air-twist stem with plain conical foot, c1750, 6½in (16.5cm) high.
£400–450 Som

A dwarf ale glass, the conical bowl with flammiform wrythen-moulded decoration, on a knopped stem with plain conical foot, c1750, 6½in (16.5cm) high.
£170–200 Som

A wine glass, with pan-top bowl, on a multiple-spiral air-twist stem with a central swelling knop, c1750, 7in (18cm) high.
£380–450 GS

A wine glass, with drawn trumpet bowl, on a multiple-spiral air-twist stem, c1750, 6¾in (17cm) high.
£200–250 DN

A wine glass, with bell bowl, on a multiple-spiral air-twist stem with vermicular collar, on a conical foot, c1750, 6¼in (16cm) high.
£450–500 GS

▶ A cider glass, on a double knopped air-twist stem, on a conical foot, c1750, 7½in (19cm) high.
£3,200–3,800 C

A Saxon Royal portrait goblet and cover, the bowl with Dutch engraving of Princess Anne of Hanover beneath tasselled drapery, damaged, restored, c1755, 15in (38cm) high.
£2,500–3,000 C

A Dutch light baluster goblet, probably Jacob Sang, the funnel bowl engraved with a prancing horse below the inscription 'Aurea Libertas', on an inverted baluster with beaded shoulder flanked by an angular knop and basal knop, on a conical foot, c1755, 7½in (19cm) high.
£2,000–2,500 S

A Jacobite glass, engraved with a rose and carnation, c1755, 7in (18cm) high.
£700–800 JAS

A wine glass, with trumpet bowl, on a double knopped air-twist stem, c1755, 6in (15cm) high.
£310–350 FD

A wine glass, with bell bowl, on a composite multiple-spiral air-twist stem with a beaded basal knop over a short plain section, c1755, 6¾in (17cm) high.
£480–550 GS

> A composite stem is one that incorporates all the elements of all the popular stem types made between 1745 and 1775. Opaque twists in composite stems are rare.

A Dutch engraved Friendship light baluster goblet, with funnel bowl, on a beaded knopped and inverted baluster stem with basal knop, on a conical foot, restored, chipped, signed and dated on the foot 'Jacob Sang, inv=et Fec: Amsterdam, 1759' 7½in (19cm) high.
£3,000–3,500 C

A wine glass, the wide round funnel bowl engraved with fruiting vine, on a double-series opaque-twist stem, on a plain conical foot, c1760, 5½in (14cm) high.
£280–320 Som

► A wine glass, with pan-top bowl, on a multiple-spiral air-twist stem with swelling knop, on a conical foot, c1755, 5¾in (14.5cm) high.
£320–380 GS

A wine glass, with a hammered rounded funnel bowl, on a centre-knopped incised-twist stem with conical foot, c1755, 6¼in (16cm) high.
£800–900 P
Incised-twist stems incorporating knops are rare.

Three ale glasses, with deep funnel bowls, on double-series opaque-twist stems, on plain conical feet, c1760, largest 8in (20.5cm) high.
£280–320 each Som

A set of six goblets, with ogee bowls, on double-series opaque-twist stems, on plain conical feet, c1760, 6½in (16.5cm) high.
£3,400–4,000 Som

The Confederate Hunt goblet, of Jacobite significance, the bucket bowl engraved with a rose, bud and thistle, on the remains of an opaque twist stem replaced by a turned wooden foot with a metal band, inscribed, c1760, 9½in (24cm) high, together with a card disc listing the names of the Cycle Club, dated '1825'.
£6,800–8,000 S
In the guise of a hunting goblet honouring the lady patronesses, this goblet commemorates the election of Lady Williams Wynne as Lady Parramount and of the cycles held by the well-known Jacobite families of Mytton, Owen, Shakerley and Williams. Wenman and Dashwood were well-known supporters of the Jacobite cause, and Sir Watkin Williams Wynn, MP for Denbigh, was known as 'father' of the Cycle Club. Ladies of these families were elected Lady Patronesses in the middle of the century because some 30 years later, when the club jewel was instituted in 1780, there was no Lady Parramount, but the then Lady Williams Wynn was elected Lady Patroness and held that office for some years.

A Dutch engraved Royal armorial light baluster goblet, with the crowned arms of Willem V of Orange and Nassau within the Garter, flanked by crowned lion supporters above the motto 'Je Maintiendrai', on a ribbon cartouche, on a slender multi-knopped stem with a conical foot, c1760, 9in (23cm) high.
£2,000–2,500 C

A goblet, on a double-series opaque white twist stem, on a plain conical foot, c1760, 5½in (14cm) high.
£400–450 Som

An armorial light baluster goblet, the funnel bowl Dutch engraved and polished in the style of Jacob Sang with the arms of Willem V of Orange and Nassau within the mottoed Garter, c1760, 8¾in (22cm) high.
£2,500–3,000 C

A Dutch armorial goblet, probably by Jacob Sang, the funnel-shaped bowl finely engraved and part-polished, on a teared angular knop above a teared inverted baluster flanked by ball and basal knops, on a conical foot, c1760, 8¼in (21cm) high.
£4,200–5,000 S

◄ A green glass goblet, with ovoid bowl, on a drawn plain stem with plain conical foot, c1760, 6½in (16.5cm) high.
£370–420 Som

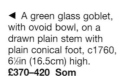

◄ A Dutch light baluster goblet, the funnel bowl engraved with Noah's Ark on a continuous band of water, on a composite stem, c1760, 7in (18cm) high.
£1,500–1,800 C

A Lynn wine glass, the bowl moulded with horizontal rings, on an opaque-twist stem with a pair of intertwined solid corkscrews encircled by a multi-series spiral strand, on a conical foot, 1760–70, 5¼in (13.5cm) high.
£550–650 P

A wine glass, with bell bowl, on a multiple-spiral air-twist stem with shoulder knop, on a conical foot, c1760, 6¼in (16cm) high.
£300–350 FD

A wine glass, with hammered funnel bowl, on a mercury-twist stem with two spirals around a single cable, c1760, 6in (15cm) high.
£280–320 FD

A wine glass, the flared funnel bowl with moulded basal flutes, on a single-series air-twist stem, c1760, 6¼in (16cm) high.
£340–380 BrW

A Masonic firing glass, on a double-series opaque-twist stem, c1760, 4in (10cm) high,
£550–650 Som

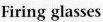

A firing glass, with ogee bowl, on a short double-series opaque-twist stem, on a thick terraced firing foot, c1760, 3½in (9cm) high.
£400–450 Som

Firing glasses

Firing glasses are always short stemmed. They are dram glasses or small wines made with a specially strong, thick foot. They were used at meetings where the members would strike the table simultaneously with their glasses when a toast was offered; the noise was said to resemble the firing of a musket.

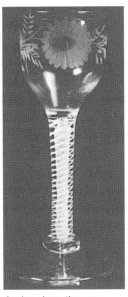

A wine glass, the ogee bowl engraved with a sunflower and sprig, on a double-series opaque-twist stem with plain conical foot, c1760, 5in (12.5cm) high.
£200–250 Som

A Silesian Friendship goblet and cover, with engraved double ogee bowl, on a faceted inverted baluster stem with basal knop, the conical foot engraved with leaf scrolls, the domed cover with faceted finial, c1760, 8½in (21.5cm) high.
£1,500–1,800 S

◄ **l.** A flute, with flared trumpet bowl, on a slender drawn stem with double-series opaque-twist, on a plain conical foot, c1760, 7½in (19cm) high.
£300–350
r. A dwarf ale glass, with wrythen conical bowl, on a short stem with cushion knop, on a plain conical foot, c1800, 5in (12.5cm) high.
£50–60 Som

Three wine glasses, on opaque-twist stems, c1760, 5½in (14cm) high.
£250–280 each Som

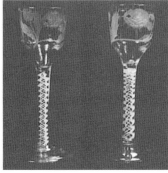

Three glasses, on double-series opaque-twist stems with plain conical feet, c1760:
l. with bell bowl, 6½in (16.5cm) high.
c. with ale bowl engraved with hops and barley, 7½in (19cm) high.
r. with ogee bowl, 6in (15cm) high.
£320–380 each Som

Two wine glasses, the ogee bowls engraved with a Jacobite rose, bud, and thistle, on double-series opaque-twist stems with plain conical feet, c1760, 6in (15cm) high.
£450–500 each Som

Three wine glasses, on double-series opaque-twist stems with plain conical feet, c1760, largest 6in (15cm) high.
£240–280 each Som

Cross Reference
See Colour Review

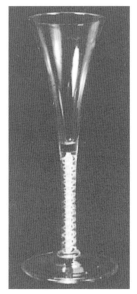

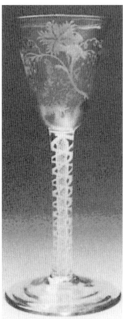

A Beilby wine glass, the funnel bowl enamelled in white with grapes and vine leaves, on a double-series opaque-twist stem, on a spreading foot, foot chipped, c1760, 6in (15cm) high.
£550–610 C

A flute, with slender trumpet bowl, on a mixed-twist stem with central opaque white gauze and outer pair of spiralling air-twist threads, on a plain conical foot, c1760, 7½in (19cm) high.
£550–650 Som

A wine glass, the round funnel bowl engraved with fruiting vine motif, on a double-series opaque-twist stem with plain conical foot, c1760, 6in (15cm) high.
£300–350 Som

▶ A Lynn wine glass, with horizontally ribbed round funnel bowl, on a double-series opaque-twist stem, on a plain conical foot, c1760, 5½in (14cm) high.
£800–900 Som

A glass, on a multiple-series opaque-twist stem with a thick foot, c1760, 4½in (11.5cm) high.
£250–280 FD

A pair of wine glasses, the round funnel bowls engraved and polished with a floral band, on double-series opaque-twist stems with plain conical feet, c1760, 6in (15cm) high.
£670–750 Som

A dram firing glass, with ogee bowl, on a double-series opaque-twist stem with heavy disc firing foot, c1760, 4in (10cm) high.
£280–320 Som

Air-twist stemmed glasses

Air-twists were formed by denting a gather of molten glass and placing another gather on top, thereby creating air bubbles. The pattern made by the air was elongated and twisted by drawing and rotating the molten glass until it assumed the length and breadth needed for a stem.

Air-twist stemmed glasses proliferated between 1750 and 1760 as craftsmen sought to find a way to produce drinking glasses that were both light in weight and sufficiently decorative to have consumer appeal. Early air-twists were made in two pieces, the twist extending into the bowl.

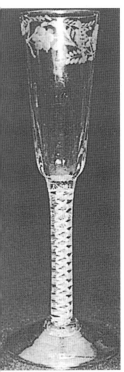

An export-type wine glass, with cup bowl, on a hollow knopped stem with plain domed foot, c1760, 6¼in (16cm) high.
£500–550 Som

A cordial glass, the small funnel bowl engraved with a drapery border, on a double-series opaque-twist stem with domed foot, c1760, 6¾in (17cm) high.
£800–900 Som

A flute, with trumpet bowl, on a mixed air-twist stem, c1760, 7½in (19cm) high.
£700–800 Som

A ratafia glass, the narrow deep round funnel bowl rib-moulded on the lower half, with a band of wild roses under the rim, on a double-series opaque-twist stem with plain conical foot, c1760, 7in (18cm) high.
£800–880 Som

▶ A wine glass, with pan-topped bowl, on a stem with opaque central gauze cable encircled by two solid spiralling strands, c1760, 6½in (16.5cm) high.
£300–350 P

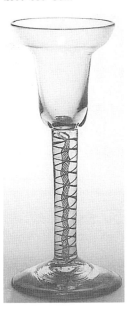

A cordial glass, with fluted bucket bowl, on a double-series opaque-twist stem with central gauze, c1760, 6¾in (17cm) high.
£600–700 DN

A wine glass, the trumpet bowl engraved with fruiting vine and a bird in flight, on a double-series opaque-twist stem with a plain conical foot, c1760, 7½in (19cm) high.
£450–500 Som

A wine glass, with ogee bowl, on a single-series opaque-twist stem, c1760, 6¼in (16cm) high.
£225–250 GS

A pair of ale glasses, the deep conical bowls finely gilded with hops and barley, the reverse showing two dragonflies, on double-series opaque-twist stems with plain conical feet, c1760, 7in (18cm) high.
£1,400–1,600 each Som

▶ A wine glass, on a diamond facet cut stem with centre knop, on a conical foot, c1760, 5¼in (13.5cm) high.
£160–180 JHa

A cordial glass, the fluted round funnel bowl engraved with a band of roses, on a double-series opaque-twist stem, on a plain conical foot, c1760, 6in (15cm) high.
£510–570 Som

A wine glass, with honeycomb-moulded ogee bowl and foot, on a double-series opaque-twist stem, c1760, 6in (15cm) high.
£500–600 Som

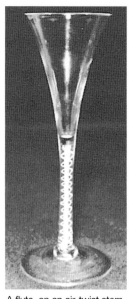

A flute, on an air-twist stem, c1760, 7½in (19cm) high.
£350–400 Som

A green wine glass, with cup bowl, on a stem with coarse incised twist and swelling knop, on a plain conical foot, c1760, 5in (12.5cm) high.
£450–500 Som

A wine glass, the ogee bowl engraved with a basket of flowers and two birds in flight, on a double-series opaque-twist stem with plain conical foot, c1760, 6in (15cm) high.
£400–450 Som

▶ A Dutch engraved wine glass, by Jacob Sang, the bowl engraved with a three-masted ship, the reverse inscribed 'Het Land's Welvaaren', on a beaded inverted baluster flanked by an angular knop and a basal knop, on a conical foot, the pontil engraved in diamond point 'J: Sang Fec: 1762', 7½in (19cm) high.
£10,000–12,000 S

Two wine glasses, with round funnel bowls, on double-series opaque-twist stems with plain conical feet, c1760, 6½in (16cm) high.
£240–270 each Som

A set of nine wine glasses, with ovoid bowls, on double-series opaque-twist stems with plain conical feet, c1760, 6½in (16cm) high.
£2,300–2,600 Som

A wine glass, with bell bowl, the stem with an air-twist gauze spiral entwined with a single brick-red thread, on a conical foot, c1765, 6¾in (17.5cm) high.
£2,200–2,600 C

An ale flute, the bowl engraved with two ears of barley and a hop spray, on a colour-twist stem, c1765, 6½in (16.5cm) high.
£3,200–3,800 C

A cordial glass, with a thick funnel bowl, the opaque-twist stem with a laminated corkscrew core, on a conical foot, c1765, 7in (18cm) high.
£700–800 C

A Beilby wine glass, the funnel bowl enamelled in white with fruiting vine motif, on a double-series opaque-twist stem, on a plain conical foot, c1765, 6in (16.5cm) high.
£1,700–2,000 Som

A wine glass, the colour-twist stem with an opaque laminated twisted core entwined by two opaque ribbons and two translucent blue threads, on a conical foot, c1765, 6½in (16.5cm) high.
£2,000–2,500 C

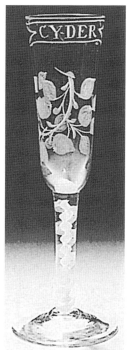

A glass, the bowl engraved 'Cyder', on a stem with an opaque corkscrew core within a multi-ply spiral, on a conical foot, c1765, 8in (20.5cm) high.
£4,000–4,500 C

◄ A firing glass, the deceptive bowl with a band of diagonal tool marks, on a double-series opaque-twist stem with a gauze core, on a terraced foot, c1765, 4in (10cm) high.
£600–700 C

A wine glass, with cobalt blue ogee bowl, on a clear stem with swelling waist knop and filled with spiral opaque threads, on a cobalt blue foot, c1765, 6½in (16.5cm) high.
£12,000–14,000 C
Although wine glasses of this type that combine green and clear glass are known, this one appears to be the only recorded example in blue and clear glass.

A Captain glass, with a funnel bowl, the opaque-twist stem with a laminated corkscrew core within an eight-ply spiral, on a terraced foot, c1765, 10in (25.5cm) high.
£5,000–6,000 C

▶ An engraved wine glass, the colour-twist stem with an opaque laminated corkscrew core edged with chocolate brown and translucent green threads, on a conical foot, c1765, 6½in (16.5cm) high.
£1,800–2,000 C

A wine glass, with an ogee bowl, the stem with an opaque gauze corkscrew core entwined by two translucent dark red spirals, on a conical foot, c1765, 6in (15cm) high.
£2,500–2,800 C

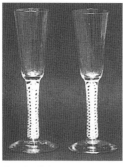

A pair of ale glasses, with hammered bowls, the double-series opaque-twist stems with spiral gauzes outside a central columnar gauze, c1765, 7in (18cm) high.
£450–500 FD

A wine glass, with ogee bowl, the stem with a twisted opaque ribbon core within two corkscrew spirals with translucent red inner edges, on a conical foot, c1765, 6in (15cm) high.
£2,300–2,700 C

▶ A firing glass, with engraved ogee bowl, on a single-series opaque-twist stem, on a terraced foot, c1765, 4in (10cm) high.
£350–400 FD

A Masonic firing glass, with engraved ogee bowl, on a double series opaque-twist stem, on a terraced firing foot, c1765, 3¾in (9.5cm) high.
£500–600 JHa

A Beilby enamelled wine glass, the funnel bowl painted with opaque white fruiting vine, traces of gilding, on a double-series opaque-twist stem with conical foot, chipped, c1765, 6in (15cm) high.
£1,800–2,000 S
The Beilby family, notably William and his sister Mary, were renowned glass enamellers in Newcastle-upon-Tyne from c1762 to 1778.

A Lynn wine glass, with six-band ogee bowl, on a double-series opaque-twist stem, c1765, 5½in (14cm) high.
£800–900 GS

A wine glass, with bell bowl, on a double-series opaque-twist stem, c1765, 6¼in (16cm) high.
£180–200 JHa

A cordial glass, with ogee bowl, on a single-series opaque-twist stem, c1765, 7in (18cm) high.
£900–1,100 BELL

▶ A German goblet and cover, possibly Saxon or Hesse, engraved with a crest with the initials 'SGF', inscribed, on a faceted knop and hollow inverted baluster, the faceted domed foot with floral garland, domed cover with faceted finial, 1768, 16in (40.5cm) high.
£2,100–2,500 S

A Dutch facet-stemmed goblet, attributed to Jacob Sang, engraved with monogram 'MAH', flanked by a boy and a girl above the date '1769', within an elaborate scrolling cartouche, the reverse inscribed 'Welvaar T Huys. Daar't Arme Kind Met Noot Druft. Hulp En Bystand Vindt', 8in (20.5cm) high.
£3,000–3,500 S

An ale glass, the deep round funnel bowl engraved with hops and barley motif, on a diamond-faceted stem with plain conical foot, c1770, 7½in (19cm) high.
£170–190 Som

A wine glass, engraved with a single rose bud and a jay in flight, the rim with swags, the stem cut with diamond facets, c1770, 5¼in (13.5cm) high.
£220–250 GS

A pair of cordial glasses, the ovoid bowls with a band of hatched decoration, on hexagon facet-cut stems with plain conical feet, c1770, 5in (12.5cm) high.
£420–490 Som

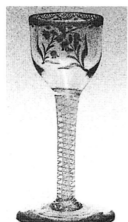

A wine glass, with engraved bowl, on a double-series opaque-twist stem, c1770, 5½in (14cm) high.
£200–250 FD

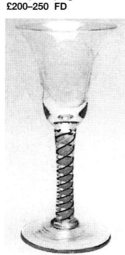

A Jacobite wine glass, with bell bowl, on an opaque green and blue twist stem, c1770, 6½in (16.5cm) high.
£2,000–2,400 CB

◄ A Beilby wine glass, the bell bowl enamelled in white with a border of fruiting vine beneath a gilt rim, the opaque-twist stem with a gauze corkscrew core entwined by two spiral threads, on a conical foot, c1770, 7in (18cm) high.
£2,200–2,500 C

A set of four wine glasses, the round funnel bowls engraved with looped stars and printies, on hexagon-faceted stems with plain conical feet, c1770, 5½in (14cm) high.
£500–600 Som

A set of four Georgian wine glasses, with rounded funnel bowls, on opaque-twist stems with plain feet, 6in (15cm) high.
£850–1,000 Sim

► Two facet-cut wine glasses, with round funnel bowls, on diamond-cut facet stems with plain conical feet, c1770, largest 5½in (14cm) high.
£150–180 each Som

l. A wine glass, on a diamond-knopped stem, c1770, 6in (15cm) high.
£150–180
c. An ale glass, engraved with a band of stars and printies, on a diamond-cut stem, c1770, 7in (18cm) high.
£200–230
r. A wine glass, with pan-top bowl, on a drawn hexagon-cut stem, c1770, 5½in (14cm) high.
£450–500 Som

A Beilby enamelled wine glass, on an opaque-twist stem with a gauze core within four spiral threads, on a conical foot, c1770, 6in (15cm) high.
£1,800–2,000 C

Goblets & Wine Glasses • DRINKING GLASSES 143

A wine glass, the deceptive bowl engraved with fruiting vine, on a drawn stem with diamond facet cutting and swelling centre knop, on a heavy disc firing foot, c1770, 5½in (14cm) high.
£640–720 Som

A Beilby wine glass, the funnel bowl enamelled in white, the rim with traces of gilding, on an opaque-twist stem with a gauze corkscrew core within two spiral threads, on a conical foot, c1770, 6in (15cm) high.
£1,800–2,000 C

Two ale glasses, one engraved with hops and barley, with hatched border around rim, on drawn facet-cut stems with plain conical feet, c1770, largest 7½in (19cm) high.
£280–320 each Som

A wine glass, by James Giles, the ogee bowl gilt-decorated with a continuous branch of fruiting vine below a gilt rim line, on an opaque-twist stem of four gauze spirals, on a conical foot, gilding rubbed, c1770, 5½in (14cm) high.
£1,000–1,200 P
James Giles (1718–80) had a workshop in Berwick Street, London, producing high quality gilding and enamelling. The slight rubbing to the gilding on this glass reduced the value by about 25 per cent.

A firing glass, the colour-twist stem with an opaque gauze core entwined by a pair of translucent green and a pair of orange spiral threads, on a thick foot, c1770, 4½in (11.5cm) high.
£3,000–3,500 C

A flute, with trumpet bowl, on a slender mixed-twist stem with annulated collar, central opaque white gauze and a pair of spiralling outer air threads, on a plain conical foot, c1770, 7½in (19cm) high.
£650–750 Som

A wrythen ale glass, on a folded foot, c1770, 5in (12.5cm) high.
£60–70 JHa

A dwarf ale glass, the bowl engraved with hops and barley, on a plain stem with a folded foot, c1770, 6in (15cm) high.
£85–100 CB

A glass, the bell bowl engraved with a vine and grapes, on a drawn stem with a tear and folded foot, c1770, 6in (15cm) high.
£170–200 CB

A wine glass, engraved with grapes and vines, on a plain stem with a folded conical foot, c1770, 6in (15cm) high.
£170–200 CB

◄ A Beilby goblet, the bucket bowl enamelled in white with fruiting vine, the rim with traces of gilding, on an opaque-twist stem with a gauze corkscrew core within two spiral threads, on a conical foot, footrim chipped, c1770, 7in (18cm) high.
£2,200–2,600 C

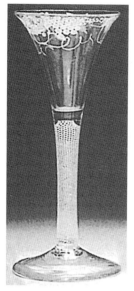

A ratafia glass, the deep round funnel bowl engraved with a band of stars and printies, on a diamond facet-cut stem with plain conical foot, c1770, 7in (18cm) high.
£640–720 Som

A wine glass, the drawn trumpet bowl enamelled in white, with opaque-twist stem filled with spiral threads, on a conical foot, c1770, 7in (18cm) high.
£1,800–2,000 C

A Beilby Gothick wine glass, the funnel bowl enamelled in opaque white with a ruined Gothic cloister flanked by three cypresses and a tree, on a double-series opaque-twist stem with conical foot, c1770, 6in (15cm) high.
£7,200–8,000 S
This would appear to be the only known example of a Beilby wine glass in the Gothick style.

A wine glass, with pan-top bowl, on a stem with a central air-twist gauze and outer pair of opaque spiralling threads, c1770, 7½in (19cm) high.
£750–850 Som

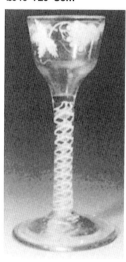

A Beilby wine glass, the ogee bowl decorated in white enamel with fruiting vine, on a double-series opaque-twist stem with plain conical foot, c1775, 5½in (14cm) high.
£1,800–2,200 Som

A Beilby wine glass, the gilt-rimmed ogee bowl with opaque white band of fruiting vine, on a double-series opaque-twist stem with a plain conical foot, c1775, 6in (15cm) high.
£1,800–2,000 Som

A Masonic dram firing glass, inscribed 'Lodge of Harmony, No. 559', c1780, 3⅛in (9cm) high.
£300–350 Som

A wine glass, the bowl engraved with a continuous horse-racing scene, the stem cut with diamond facets, on a conical foot, c1780, 6in (15cm) high.
£850–1,000 C

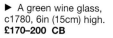

▶ A green wine glass, c1780, 6in (15cm) high.
£170–200 CB

◀ A dram firing glass, with a conical bowl, on a short stem enclosing a tear, with heavy flanged firing foot, c1780, 4⅛in (11.5cm) high.
£90–110 Som

An engraved wine glass, on a facet-cut stem, c1780, 6in (15cm) high.
£750–850 C

A set of four wine glasses, with round funnel slice-cut everted rim bowls, on hexagon-facet centre knop cut stems with scalloped feet, c1780, 6in (15cm) high.
£1,000–1,200 Som

A pair of ale glasses, the bowls engraved with hops and barley, on single-knopped stems with circular feet, 18thC, 5½in (14cm) high.
£220–250 E

A wine glass, the funnel bowl engraved with a bird in flight flanked by trees and foliage issuing from a tree stump, on a facet-cut stem, c1780, 6in (15cm) high.
£525–625 C

A pair of ale glasses, on diamond facet-cut stems, c1780, 7in (18cm) high.
£350–400 Som

A firing glass, with deep conical bowl, on a flanged firing foot, c1780, 4½in (11.5cm) high.
£100–120 Som

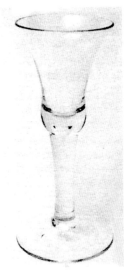

A wine glass, with bell bowl, on a plain stem, 18thC, 6¾in (17cm) high.
£180–200 OBS

A wine glass, with pan-top bowl, on a hexagon-cut facet stem, the facets extending into the bowl base, c1780, 5½in (14cm) high.
£280–330 GS

▶ A Lauenstein engraved and gilt armorial goblet and cover, inscribed 'CEC.G.U H.Z.L.' highlighted in gilding, on a knopped stem with domed foot, engraved with a band of stiff leaves, the later domed cover with bud finial, late 18thC, 14in (35.5cm) high.
£9,000–11,000 S
The arms and initials are those of Carl Ernst Casimir Graf und Edler Herr zu Lippe, Lieutenant-Colonel and Adjutant-General in the service of Württemberg.

A light green double-bowl wine glass, the bowls with moulded strawberry prunts, on a short stem, c1780, 5¾in (14.5cm) high.
£500–600 Som

A wine glass, the funnel bowl engraved with swags, on a facet-cut stem, c1780, 5in (12.5cm) high.
£150–180 FD

A Dutch armorial Newcastle baluster wine glass, the funnel bowl finely engraved 'FTR' within an elaborate coroneted cartouche, in the style of Jacob Sang, the reverse with a building and garden and 'Floreat Pastoratus 1786', set on a multi-knopped stem including two beaded knops, with conical foot, 7½in (19cm) high.
£5,000–6,000 S

A set of six hock glasses, on decorative hollow stems, late 18thC, 4½in (11.5cm) high.
£250–300 JAS

▶ A Dutch diamond-engraved goblet, the funnel bowl engraved with the figures of Justice and Liberty within an oval panel flanked by drapery and an inscription, the reverse also inscribed and dated '1795', set on a faceted baluster stem and conical foot with scallop rim, 7in (18cm) high.
£2,200–2,700 S
The inscription refers to the French occupation of Holland in 1795 and translates as 'French wine makes men happy but the French people give freedom to slaves'.

A Continental cut-glass goblet and cover, with stylized leaf decoration beneath a gilt rim, on a faceted double-knopped stem and domed foot, the faceted spire finial with gilding, slight rubbing, late 18thC, 12¾in (32.5cm) high.
£575–635 C

A pair of green wine glasses, with cup bowls, c1790, 4½in (11.5cm) high.
£120–140 FD

▶ A wrythen ale glass, c1800, 5½in (14cm) high.
£45–55 CaL

A Russian glass goblet, engraved with the crowned monogram 'EAII' for Catherine II flanked by martial trophies, late 18thC, 8½in (21.5cm) high.
£900–1,000 C

A Williamite portrait wine glass, the funnel bowl engraved with a portrait of William III in profile to the right within the inscription 'The Immortal Memory', the reverse with a crowned Irish harp flanked by fruiting vine, on a double-series opaque-twist stem with conical foot, chipped, late 18thC, 6in (15cm) high.
£2,500–3,000 C

A green wine glass, late 18thC, 5in (12.5cm) high.
£65–80 CB

A Volunteer wine glass, the trumpet bowl inscribed 'Succefs to Sir William Parsons and the Birr Volunteers', the stem filled with spiral threads, on a conical foot, small chips, late 18thC, 7in (18cm) high.
£2,500–3,000 C

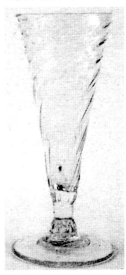

An ale glass, engraved
with hops and barley,
c1800, 4¾in (12cm) high.
£45–55 CaL

A pair of Davenport
goblets, each with etched
straight-sided bowl, on a
knopped stem with conical
foot, one with minor foot
rim chip, inscribed 'Patent'
on the base, c1805,
6in (15cm) high.
£3,000–3,500 S

A glass goblet, the ogee
bowl with an engraved
floral band to the rim
and a circular cartouche
with inset initials 'E.S.'
surrounded by floral
sprays and central bow,
the reverse with hops and
barley motif, on a capstan
stem, with plain foot,
c1810, 7in (18cm) high.
£200–250 Som

An ale glass, engraved
with hops and barley, on
a slice-cut stem, c1810,
6in (15cm) high.
£45–55 JHa

◄ Three dwarf
ale glasses, the
conical bowls
engraved with
hops and
barley, on short
knopped stems,
c1810, tallest
5in (12.5cm) high.
£60–70 each Som

A pair of green wine
glasses, early 19thC,
5in (12.5cm) high.
£100–120 JAS

A blue moulded goblet,
c1810, 6in (15cm) high.
£150–180 CB

A green honeycomb-
moulded wine glass, with
trumpet bowl, 1810–30,
5¼in (13.5cm) high.
£85–95 FD

A Davenport port glass,
with flared bucket bowl,
the rim etched with leaf
and ovolo band within
line borders and hatching,
on a graduated triple-
knopped stem with solid
domed foot, c1810,
4in (10cm) high.
£250–300 S

Four dwarf ale glasses, with wrythen-moulded conical
bowls, on plain conical feet, c1810, tallest 5in (12.5cm) high.
£60–70 each Som

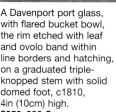

◄ A dwarf ale glass, the
conical bowl engraved with
monogram 'JM' within a
garter cartouche and floral
sprays, on a short knopped
stem with plain foot, c1810,
5in (12.5cm) high.
£60–75 Som

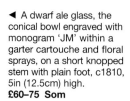

► Three wrythen-moulded
ale glasses, on rudimentary
knopped stems with plain
conical feet, c1810.
£120–150 Som

A set of six dwarf ale glasses, engraved with hops and barley motifs, on capstan stems with plain conical feet, c1810, 5in (12.5cm) high.
£450–500 Som

A goblet, the bucket bowl engraved with various Masonic symbols and monogram 'TB', on a stem with a bladed knop and plain conical foot, c1820, 7½in (19cm) high.
£540–600 Som

A cut-glass cock-fighting trophy goblet, with engraved etched panels in the Regency style, the surrounding panels depicting the four stages of cock fighting, on a heavy pedestal base, early 19thC, 10in (25.5cm) high.
£850–1,000 B

A goblet, with flared rim and annulated band around the bowl, on a knopped stem, with loop handle, c1820, 5½in (14cm) high.
£190–220 Som

An ale flute, the conical bucket bowl cut with flutes, c1820, 5¼in (13.5cm) high.
£40–45 GS

▶ A set of 11 port glasses, c1820, 3½in (9cm) high.
£580–650 Som

A pair of flutes, on bladed knop stems, c1820, 6in (15cm) high.
£60–70 Som

An ale glass, with petal-moulded bowl, c1820, 5in (12.5cm) high.
£35–40 CaL

A green wine glass, probably Continental, on a faceted stem, with gilding, c1820, 6in (15cm) high.
£85–100 CB

A port or sherry glass, cut with arch and feather design, on a slice- and step-cut stem, c1820, 4in (10cm) high.
£25–30 JHa

A green wine glass, early 19thC, 5in (12.5cm) high.
£50–60 DUN

A set of seven wine glasses, c1825, 4in (10cm) high.
£250–300 Som

◀ Four turquoise wine glasses, c1825, tallest 5¼in (13.5cm) high.
£50–90 each Som

A set of 19 port glasses, the shallow cup bowls with fine flute cutting, on knopped stems, c1830, 3in (7.5cm) high.
£680–760 Som

A set of six hock glasses, two green overlaid and slice-cut, two ruby and two blue, 19thC, 8in (20.5cm) high.
£70–85 LF

An Irish dark glass goblet, the round bowl with overall star pattern and engraved with a band of stars within a wrigglework border with flute-cut base, on a facet-cut stem with plain conical foot, c1830, 8¾in (22cm) high.
£340–380 Som

A set of four green wine glasses, with cup bowls, on plain stems with plain conical feet, c1830, 4¾in (12cm) high.
£200–240 Som

◄ Three green wine glasses, with conical bowls, on plain stems with shoulder collars, c1830, 5¼in (13.5cm) high.
£40–60 each Som

A set of eight green wine glasses, with panel-cut tulip bowls, c1830, 5in (12.5cm) high.
£350–400 FD

A pair of green wine glasses, with cup bowls, on knopped stems with plain conical feet, c1830, 5in (12.5cm) high.
£110–130 Som

An amber wine glass, the conical bowl with milled collar, on a hollow stem with raspberry prunts and trailed foot, c1830, 4in (10cm) high.
£120–140 Som

A glass, the bell bowl engraved with a horse and rider, c1830, 7in (18cm) high.
£200–240 BWA

A set of ten green cut-glass wine glasses, c1830, 5½in (14cm) high.
£330–400 CB

l. A set of four jelly glasses, c1830, 4½in (11.5cm) high.
£120–140
r. Two wine glasses, on ball knopped stems, c1830, 5in (12.5cm) high.
£65–80 Som

► A set of eight wine glasses, with prism-cut bowls, on short knopped stems, c1830.
£290–330 Som

A set of four pale green wine flutes, engraved with fruiting vines, on drawn slice-cut stems, c1830, 4½in (11.5cm) high.
£240–280 FD

A set of six wine flutes, with flute-cut flared trumpet bowls, on bladed knop stems with plain feet, c1830, tallest 7in (18cm) high.
£250–300 Som

A set of five port glasses, the double ogee bowls cut with arches and fans, c1835, 3¾in (9.5cm) high.
£120–135 GS

A blue drinking glass, c1840, 4¾in (12cm) high.
£85–100 CB

A green glass, with facet-cut funnel bowl, on a bladed knop stem, c1840, 4½in (11.5cm) high.
£45–50 CB

An amethyst cut-glass wine glass, c1840, 5½in (14cm) high.
£65–80 CB

A set of six green wine glasses, c1840, 5in (12.5cm) high.
£280–320 BELL

A set of five liqueur glasses, c1840, 3in (7.5cm) high.
£120–140 Som

A green cut-glass wine glass, c1840, 4½in (11.5cm) high.
£40–50 CB

A pair of panel-cut champagne flutes, with everted lips and faceted knops, c1840, 8in (20.5cm) high.
£110–130 FD

An amethyst-tinted wrythen dwarf ale glass, with trumpet bowl, the stem with two ball knops, on a plain foot, 1840–60, 5in (12.5cm) high.
£250–280 Som

A set of six Victorian panel-cut champagne flutes, 1840–60, 8in (20.5cm) high.
£300–360 DUN

◀ A Bohemian spa goblet, engraved with a topographical view, on a square-section star-cut foot, chipped, 19thC, 6in (15cm) high.
£300–350 C

◄ A set of four glass goblets, the round funnel bowls cut with printies, on cut baluster stems with plain conical feet, c1850, 6¼in (16cm) high.
£120–150 Som

A Victorian blue enamelled and gilt goblet, 5¼in (13.5cm) high.
£45–55 TAC

A goblet, engraved with stylized acanthus, on a hollow-cut pedestal stem, mid-19thC, 6¼in (16cm) high.
£65–75 JHa

A Victorian green glass panel-cut goblet, c1850, 5in (12.5cm) high.
£60–70 DUN

A white opaline glass, with blue and white cane rim, c1850, 7in (18cm) high.
£430–480 MJW

A pair of hock glasses, with green panels, c1850, 5in (12.5cm) high.
£125–150 JAS

A pair of flutes, with trumpet bowls, on flute-cut knopped stems with plain feet, c1850, 6½in (16.5cm) high.
£120–150 Som

A Bohemian amber-stained goblet, on an octagonal stem, the flared octagonal foot with scalloped rim and a star- and diamond-cut base, c1850, 8½in (21.5cm) high.
£600–700 S

A Richardson's of Stourbridge enamelled goblet, stencilled in black 'Richardson's Vitrified Enamel Colours', c1850, 6½in (16.5cm) high.
£700–770 S

l & r. A pair of amethyst wine glasses, with conical bowls, on plain stems and feet, c1850, 5¼in (13.5cm) high.
£200–240 Som
c. A pair of amber wine glasses, with flute-cut trumpet bowls, on baluster stems with plain feet, c1850, 4¾in (12cm) high.
£100–120 Som

An amber glass goblet, c1860, 9½in (24cm) high.
£140–170 DUN

◄ A drawn wine glass, with trumpet bowl, on an air-twist and basal knopped stem with domed foot, mid-19thC, 7in (18cm) high.
£600–700 CSK

► A Bohemian goblet, with red flashing, one side engraved with three deer in a woodland scene, the other with a circle of six lenses surrounded by baroque scrolling, on cogwheel foot, c1860, 5½in (14cm) high.
£340–400 Som

A blue-cased glass goblet, enamelled with gold, on a plain facet stem, c1860, 6¼in (16cm) high.
£165–225 CB

A set of six Victorian panel-cut champagne flutes, c1860, 7in (18cm) high.
£210–250 DUN

A set of six wine glasses, with orange bowls, on clear stems and feet, c1870, 5in (12.5cm) high.
£240–270 MJW

A Bohemian glass two-handled goblet, engraved with vines, c1860, 5¼in (13.5cm) high.
£140–170 MJW

A Victorian champagne flute, with bladed knop, 6¼in (16cm) high.
£40–50 CaL

A champagne glass, engraved with fruiting vine, on a cut baluster stem, c1870, 5in (12.5cm) high.
£35–40 BrW

l. A set of six wine glasses, with cup bowls, on plain stems, c1860, 5¼in (13.5cm) high.
£230–260
r. A set of eight wine glasses, with ovoid bowls on drawn flute-cut stems, c1850, 5in (12.5cm) high.
£360–400 Som

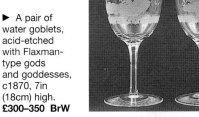

A set of four pale green wine glasses, with flute-cut trumpet bowls, on facet-cut knopped stems with plain feet, c1860, 5in (12.5cm) high.
£210–250 Som

► A pair of water goblets, acid-etched with Flaxman-type gods and goddesses, c1870, 7in (18cm) high.
£300–350 BrW

A Powell glass goblet, designed by T G Jackson for William Morris, c1870, 5¾in (14.5cm) high.
£100–120 JHa

A pair of goblets, engraved with passion flowers, c1870, 6¾in (17cm) high.
£200–220 JHa

◄ A pressed glass ale glass, late 19thC, 7¼in (18.5cm) high.
£75–85 JAS
This decoration was an imitation of the earlier thumb-print design.

A pair of goblets, with acid-etched and engraved floral decoration, c1875, 7in (18cm) high.
£225–250 JHa

A Historismus *façon de Venise*, by C H F Müller, Hamburg, c1875, 9in (23cm) high.
£600–700 S

A Bohemian ruby-flash goblet and cover, engraved with a stag in a continuous sparsely-wooded landscape, c1875, 10¾in (27.5cm) high.
£700–800 C

A set of six Victorian panel-cut open-bowl goblets, c1880, 5in (12.5cm) high.
£150–180 DUN

Two green sherry glasses and a wine glass, c1880, tallest 5½in (14cm) high.
£30–55 each JAS

A set of six Victorian panel-cut goblets, c1880.
£180–220 DUN

A champagne glass, engraved with a geometric pattern and stars, c1880, 4¾in (12cm) high.
£20–25 BrW

A set of six Bohemian blue glass goblets, c1880, 6½in (16.5cm) high.
£130–160 MON

A pair of glass goblets, cut with printies and engraved with Greek key design, c1880, 6¼in (16cm) high.
£80–90 BrW

▶ A pair of James Powell wine glasses, designed by T G Jackson, c1880, 5in (12.5cm) high.
£130–145 RUSK

A set of seven clear wine glasses, with cut cranberry flashing, late 19thC, 5in (12.5cm) high.
£350–400 DQ

Three pressed-glass goblets, with Nova Scotia Gothic, Kenlee, raspberry and shield patterns, c1890, 6in (15cm) high.
£250–300 RIT

A Lobmeyr enamelled decorative glass, c1890, 7½in (19cm) high.
£400–450 MJW

Two goblets, each with ovoid bowl, on a single blade knop, short stem and circular foot, one engraved with two panels of figures and animals, the other inscribed 'I & M Wilson' within a laurel wreath, the reverse with a flower-spray, 19thC, 6½in (16.5cm) high.
£500–600 S(S)

A glass champagne flute, c1900, 6in (15cm) high.
£30–35 DUN

▶ A pair of cut-glass and engraved goblets, c1900, 6in (15cm) high.
£40–50 DUN

A set of six cut-glass goblets, c1890, 5½in (14cm) high.
£280–300 DUN

A Stevens & Williams green and clear hock glass, intaglio-engraved with thistles, c1895, 8in (20.5cm) high.
£1,000–1,200 ALiN
Ex-Stevens & Williams Collection, Honeybourne Museum.

A Victorian flake-cut goblet, 5in (12.5cm) high.
£45–50 OBS

A Bohemian wine glass, engraved with a continuous encircling band of coats-of-arms, c1900, 7in (18cm) high.
£175–200 CSK

A set of six cut and etched hock glasses, on amber stems, c1900, 7in (18cm) high.
£185–220 DUN

A Lobmeyr opaline glass, decorated with polychrome enamelling, c1890, 5¾in (14.5cm) high.
£800–880 MJW

A pair of cut glasses, engraved with fighting cocks, c1900, 5in (12.5cm) high.
£40–45 DUN

Three engraved goblets, with fluted lower sections below Imperial Russian eagles holding an orb and sceptre below Romanov crowns flanked by sprays of flowers, the reverse with oval panels inscribed 'N I', on faceted stems with conical feet, c1900, 6in (15cm) high.
£850–950 CSK

Cutting facets

Cutting decorative facets into glass was developed in England, Ireland and northern Europe in the late 18th and early 19th centuries. Designs were created to reflect the light, making the glass object appear even more brilliant.

◄ A Lobmeyr set of 48 clear glasses, designed by Josef Hoffmann, comprising 12 each of claret, hock, champagne, and port glasses, c1908, tallest 6in (15cm) high.
£1,000–1,200 S

An American champagne glass, made for the Shriner Convention, Pittsburgh, the bowl inscribed 'Syria', the stem in the form of tobacco leaves, 1909, 4½in (11.5cm) high.
£80–90 ASe

A cut-glass goblet, depicting footballers in action, c1920, 10in (25.5cm) high.
£300–350 MSh

A set of 12 hock glasses, with facet-cut amethyst rims, c1900, 7¼in (18.5cm) high.
£700–800 MJW

A Le Verre Français cameo glass goblet, in yellow glass overlaid with orange and green and etched with fruits, on a purple veined stem and flared foot, with applied millefiori cane, c1920, 13½in (34.5cm) high.
£300–360 S(S)

A James Powell goblet, M54 service, 1930s, 6in (15cm) high.
£25–35 JHa

An Austrian double champagne flute and saucer, c1930, 8in (20.5cm) high.
£60–70 JHa

A Bohemian red glass goblet, c1940, 7¾in (19.5cm) high.
£45–55 MON

A Bohemian green glass goblet, c1945, 7¾in (19.5cm) high.
£40–50 MON

A Bohemian green hock glass, with engraved bowl, on a clear glass stem, c1950, 8¼in (21cm) high.
£60–70 MON

◄ A souvenir goblet of the RMS *Mary*, 1967, 6½in (16.5cm) high, with box.
£140–160 OBS

A Bohemian amber hock glass, with engraved bowl, on a clear glass stem, c1965, 7¼in (18.5cm) high.
£35–40 MON

Gray-Stan

In 1922, Elizabeth Graydon-Stannus, an antique dealer whose speciality was Irish glass, set up Graydon Studios to make reproductions of Irish table glass. A move to better equipped premises, in Battersea, followed in 1925, and in 1926 the small glassworks introduced a range of hand-made art glass under the Gray-Stan label.

Although both colourless and coloured glass wares were made, Gray-Stan is notable for its coloured-and-cased glass, no doubt inspired by the success of the contemporary Monart range from the Moncrieff Glassworks in Scotland. This was made by rolling molten clear glass in white enamel, then adding coloured enamel powders, which formed mottled, swirling and sometimes multi-coloured patterns over the white ground. These were sealed (cased) by another layer of clear glass.

A characteristic of Gray-Stan coloured-and-cased glass is the variety of striking colours that can be found, ranging from delicate pastel shades to quite intense, almost fiery, tones. In general, all of them have a distinct powdery appearance, more so than the comparable Monart wares.

The colourless and coloured glasses were used to make many different products, including vases, bowls, drinking glasses and dessert services, which could be plain or incorporate ribbed or wrythen decorative effects. Applied tears and coloured threading were other common decorative features. However, no doubt because of their eye-catching colours and swirling patterns, coloured-and-cased vessels tended to be much simpler in form.

Much of the output of the Gray-Stan works was sold through Elizabeth Graydon-Stannus' own antique shop, although the wares were also exhibited at various international trade fairs, leading to their export to countries such as Canada and the USA.

Despite the success of Gray-Stan art glass, it remained in production for only ten years, the works finally closing in 1936. Although many pieces are unsigned, they may be identified from known examples that bear signatures. Not surprisingly, the latter fetch the highest prices.

A Gray-Stan glass vase, decorated with green swirls, 1930s, 10in (25.5cm) high.
£250–280 CMO

A Gray-Stan glass vase, decorated with white and turquoise swirls, 1930s, 7¼in (18.5cm) high.
£280–320 CMO

A Gray-Stan brown glass vase, 1920–30, 7½in (19cm) high.
£100–120 TCG

A Gray-Stan yellow mottled-effect glass candlestick, c1930, 5in (12.5cm) high.
£70–80 TCG

A Gray-Stan glass vase, decorated with red swirls over white, cased in clear glass, engraved signature, 1930s, 9in (23cm) high.
£380–450 CMO

A Gray-Stan glass candlestick, decorated with a green, lilac and white spiral pattern, c1930, 3in (7.5cm) high.
£55–65 TCG

A Gray-Stan dimpled red glass vase, 1930s, 10in (25.5cm) high.
£280–350 JHa

A Gray-Stan glass vase, decorated with green swirls over white, cased in clear glass, engraved signature, 1930s, 9¾in (25cm) high.
£280–350 CMO

> Items in the Gray-Stan section have been arranged in date order.

A Gray-Stan baluster-shaped glass candlestick, the top and stem with spiral green glass threading, the domed foot edged with green, engraved signature, c1930, 11¼in (28.5cm) high.
£260–300 CMO

A Gray-Stan green glass vase, decorated with pulled-up swags, on a disc foot, engraved signature, c1930, 8½in (21.5cm) high.
£300–350 CMO

A Gray-Stan glass bowl, decorated with mauve over white, cased in clear glass, engraved signature, c1930, 10in (25.5cm) diam.
£220–250 CMO

◀ A Gray-Stan glass vase, decorated with brown swirls on white, cased in clear glass, engraved signature, c1930, 7¼in (18.5cm) high.
£180–220 CMO

A Gray-Stan blue marble-effect glass vase, c1920, 7in (18cm) high.
£280–320 MJW

A Gray-Stan glass vase, decorated with green swirls on a white ground, cased in clear glass, engraved signature, c1930, 11½in (29cm) high.
£300–350 CMO

A Gray-Stan glass vase, decorated with pink festoons over white, cased in clear glass, on clear disc foot, engraved signature, c1930, 10½in (26.5cm) high.
£350–400 CMO

A Gray-Stan blue glass vase, c1930, 12in (30.5cm) high.
£300–350 MJW

A Gray-Stan vaseline glass goblet, applied with amber trails, ribbed stem and ribbed folded foot, engraved signature, c1930, 10½in (26.5cm) high.
£300–350 CMO

A Gray-Stan glass vase, decorated with mauve swirls on white, cased in clear glass, engraved signature, c1930, 6in (15cm) high.
£300–350 CMO

A Gray-Stan glass conical vase, decorated with blue threads pulled into loops on a clear body, knopped base, on a ribbed foot, engraved signature, c1930, 13½in (34.5cm) high.
£200–220 CMO

A Gray-Stan glass goblet, the ovoid body decorated with blue swirls on white, cased in clear glass, on rudimentary knopped stem and folded foot, engraved signature, c1930, 7¾in (19.5cm) high.
£200–240 CMO

A Gray-Stan dimpled glass vase, decorated with blue swirls pulled down into yellow at the base over white, cased in clear glass, engraved signature, c1930, 9¼in (23.5cm) high.
£400–450 CMO

Jars

A pair of George III glass urn-shaped jars and covers, cut with diamond and spiral bands, 12in (30.5cm) high.
£2,500–2,800 DN

A pair of cut-glass jars and covers, possibly Irish, cut with bands of diamonds and flutes, set on a collared faceted stem, with square pedestal foot and star-cut base, the domed cover similarly cut, c1800, 13½in (34.5cm) high.
£2,300–2,600 S

◄ A cut-glass preserve pot, with cover, c1810, 4¼in (11cm) high.
£220–260 BrW

A pair of cut-glass pickle jars, with covers, on lemon squeezer feet, c1810, 6in (15cm) high.
£600–700 Som

Two glass jars, with covers, c1820, largest 11in (28cm) high.
£120–150 each DUN

A Nailsea glass snuff jar, with olive-green crown and turned-over rim, c1820, 11in (28cm) high.
£175–200 Som

A cut-glass pickle jar and cover, c1825, 5½in (14cm) high.
£250–300 Som

A pair of glass confitures, with slice-cut rims, raised on stepped circular bases with slice- and star-cut feet, mid-19thC, 8½in (21.5cm) high.
£500–600 HSS

A Steuben Aurene glass jar and cover, inscribed, c1910, 14in (35.5cm) high.
£1,800–2,000 S(NY)

► A Sowerby pressed glass jar and cover, decorated with ferns, c1885, 8½in (21.5cm) high.
£30–35 GLN

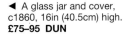

◄ A glass jar and cover, c1860, 16in (40.5cm) high.
£75–95 DUN

Jugs & Ewers

A marble *milchglas* jug, with slender neck and everted trefoil rim with spout, on a pincered circular foot and with applied scroll handle, the pale cream glass marbled with cobalt blue, iron red and white, possibly north Italian or south German, 17thC, 5in (12.5cm) high.
£1,700–2,000 S

A glass decanter jug, the gadrooned lower part below a band of applied chain ornament, with applied scroll handle, later silver mount to foot rim, damaged, c1680, 9¼in (23.5cm) high.
£1,100–1,300 C

Milchglas

Milchglas – milk glass (or *lattimo* in Italian) – is an opaque white glass made with oxide of tin. Invented in Italy in the 15th century, it was used to make drinking vessels and bottles in an attempt to imitate porcelain wares imported from the East. In the 18th century, *milchglas* was made at the Bristol glasshouses as well as in Germany, Bohemia and Holland.

A glass decanter jug and cover, the lower part moulded with gadroons beneath a trailed triple-ply chain band, the ribbed loop handle with thumb-rest and scrolling terminal, the cover with knob finial, some damage, c1685, 11½in (29cm) high.
£2,800–3,400 C

▶ A glass ale or beer jug, the baluster body engraved with hops and barley and 'R.I.T', applied foot ring and plain handle, c1780, 7in (18cm) high.
£750–850 Som

A glass baluster cream jug, the flared funnel bowl with pouring lip, on a cushion knop above a teared inverted stem, with applied scroll handle, c1710, 6in (15cm) high.
£4,200–5,000 S

Three blue glass cream jugs, c1780, 3½in (9cm) high.
£280–350 each Som

Three blue glass cream jugs:
l. faintly wrythen-moulded, c1780, 4in (10cm) high.
£220–250
c. plain body, c1860, 4in (10cm) high.
£200–220
r. pear-shaped body, c1800, 4½in (11.5cm) high.
£200–220 Som

A blue glass cream jug, with angular diamond-moulded body, with loop handle, on a solid conical foot, c1790, 4in (10cm) high.
£300–350 Som

A green glass seal bottle, converted to a Perrier water jug, with silver-plated handle and mount, glass 18thC, top 1890–1910, 10in (25.5cm) high.
£340–375 INC

A rib-moulded glass jug, north of England, c1790, 3¼in (8.5cm) high.
£250–300 MJW

An Irish glass jug, c1790, 6in (15cm) high.
£440–500 WGT

A cut-glass magnum claret jug, c1790, 10½in (26.5cm) high.
£1,800–2,200 WGT

A Bristol blue glass cream jug, c1800, 4½in (11.5cm) high.
£180–200 CB

A cut-glass jug, with bands of prisms and small diamonds, heavy strap handle, on a pedestal foot star-cut underneath, c1810, 7½in (19cm) high.
£400–450 Som

► Three blue glass cream jugs, c1800, largest 5in (12.5cm) high.
£200–250 each Som

A Georgian cut-glass footed jug, with applied handle, c1800, 10in (25.5cm) high.
£850–1,100 CB

A glass cream jug, the baluster body with flute and relief diamond cutting, on a heavy cogwheel foot, c1810, 5in (12.5cm) high.
£250–300 Som

◄ A cut-glass cream jug, on a scalloped cut foot, with cut strap handle, on a star-cut base, c1810, 4½in (11.5cm) high.
£220–260 Som

A North Country clear soda glass jug, with wrythen-moulded body and translucent blue rim, with applied handle, c1800, 5in (12.5cm) high.
£250–280 Som

A wrythen-moulded glass cream jug, of bellied shape, with folded rim and loop handle, c1800, 2¾in (7cm) high.
£80–90 Som

◄ A Bristol blue cream jug, c1800.
£180–200 CB

A comb-, panel- and diamond-cut glass claret jug, with a faceted three-ring neck and mushroom stopper, c1810, 8½in (21.5cm) high.
£450–500 FD

A glass ewer or claret jug, the ovoid body cut with prism bands and vertical fluting, with notched rim, on a knopped stem with terraced foot star-cut underneath, applied strap handle, c1810, 11in (28cm) high.
£1,000–1,200 Som

A glass water jug, the ovoid body with flute-cut base and a band of diamonds, with notched rim and cut strap handle, c1810, 8in (20.5cm) high.
£300–350 Som

A cut-glass jug, early 19thC, 6½in (16.5cm) high.
£180–200 DUN

A Nailsea olive-green bottle glass jug and pitcher, decorated with opaque white marvered inclusions, with loop handles, c1810, largest 7½in (19cm) high.
£340–380 each Som

A glass water jug, cut with small diamonds below a deep band of flute cutting, with notched rim and cut strap handle, c1810, 6¼in (16cm) high.
£300–350 Som

An Irish glass water jug, the body with panels of cut raised diamonds, flute and prism cutting, with deep scalloped rim and cut strap handle, c1810, 7in (18cm) high.
£420–500 Som

A Nailsea-type light green glass cream jug, the vertically-ribbed baluster body with white splash decoration and folded rim, with loop handle and applied foot ring, c1810, 4½in (11.5cm) high.
£320–360 Som

A glass cream jug, with cut strawberry diamonds, prism-cut bands, with notched rim and star-cut base, c1815, 4in (10cm) high.
£300–350 Som

◄ A Nailsea-type bottle glass footed pitcher, with opaque white decoration, c1810, 9½in (24cm) high.
£325–375 NWi

A cut-glass water jug, the body with panels of small cut diamonds, prism and blaze cutting, notched rim, with heavy strap handle and plain foot rim, c1820, 6in (15cm) high.
£280–320 Som

◄ An amethyst glass cream jug, the body cold-enamelled with the inscription 'Be Canny with the Cream', c1820, 4¾in (12cm) high.
£270–300 Som

► A Bohemian cranberry glass ewer, with painted blue enamel forget-me-nots, crimped clear handle and stopper, late 19thC.
£85–100 RBB

A cut-glass claret jug, with notched cut spout and strap handle, c1820, 8½in (21.5cm) high.
£450–500 Som

A glass cream jug, engraved with roses, thistles and shamrocks, c1820, 4½in (11.5cm) high.
£100–120 JHa

A blue wrythen-moulded glass cream jug, with waisted body, folded rim and loop handle, c1820, 3in (7.5cm) high.
£150–180 Som

A glass water jug, the body with leaf- and fan-cut decoration, bridge flute-cut above and below, prism-cut neck and notched rim, with a plain strap handle, c1825, 7½in (19cm) high.
£280–320 Som

A glass water jug, the cut body with base fluting, a band of strawberry diamonds, printy-cut neck and a scalloped rim, with strap handle, c1825, 7in (18cm) high.
£300–350 Som

◄ An inverted pear-shaped glass jug, with a panel-cut neck, on a ball knop stem, 19thC, 8in (20.5cm) high.
£60–70 FD

► A cut-glass claret jug and stopper, the body cut with strawberry diamonds, ovals and prisms, with a heavy strap handle, c1825, 8½in (21.5cm) high.
£500–550 Som

A glass jug, the bowl engraved with a barrel and coopers' tools, with the inscription 'Mr N. Player, P.O.K.H.S.' and date 'July 1st 1828', with a heavy strap handle, 8½in (21.5cm) high.
£850–950 Som

A pair of glass claret jugs, with ovoid flute-cut bodies and strap handles, marked 'Sherry' and 'Claret', c1830, 6¾in (17cm) high.
£500–600 Som

A claret jug, with flute-cut neck and base, bevelled lip and strap handle, with a cut mushroom stopper, c1830, 9½in (24cm) high.
£450–500 Som

► A glass claret jug, flute-cut and with a single neck ring and cut spout, with a strap handle, the base star-cut underneath, c1830, 9¾in (25cm) high.
£280–350 Som

◄ A glass claret jug, the body with broad cut flutes and two annulated neck rings, with notched rim and heavy strap handle, with a cut mushroom stopper, c1830, 11½in (29cm) high.
£340–380 Som

A glass claret jug, flute- and prism-cut and with notched and prism-cut lip, with a heavy strap handle, the base star-cut underneath, c1830, 9½in (24cm) high.
£250–300 Som

◄ A cut-glass jug, c1830, 13in (33cm) high.
£720–820 MJW

A pillar-moulded glass jug, c1830, 7in (18cm) high.
£110–130 FD

A glass water jug, with pillar-moulded decoration, with a prism-cut neck, serrated rim and star-cut base, with applied strap handle, c1830, 7in (18cm) high.
£150–180 Som

Prices

The price ranges quoted in this book reflect the average price a purchaser might expect to pay for a similar item. The price will vary according to the condition, rarity, size, popularity, provenance, colour and restoration of the item. If you are selling it is quite likely that you will be offered less than the price range.

A glass water jug, the body cut overall with small diamonds, flutes and prisms, with notched rim, applied strap handle and star-cut foot, c1830, 6½in (16.5cm) high.
£340–400 Som

A Biedermeier white alabaster and old rose pink glass jug, with gilt decoration and beading, c1835, 4in (10cm) high.
£300–330 DORO

◄ A pair of glass claret jugs, with flute-cut ovoid bodies, three annulated half neck rings and strap handles, c1840, 9½in (24cm) high.
£850–1,000 Som

An American amber blown pattern-moulded glass pitcher, with threaded neck, ribbed sides and strap handle, small crack, c1840, 6in (15cm) high.
£1,800–2,000 S(NY)

A glass baluster jug, with slice-cut neck and leaf-cut body, stick-down handle, c1850, 9in (23cm) high.
£120–140 JHa
This jug can be dated from the way the handle has been applied. The gather of glass was attached at the top, then pulled over and down.

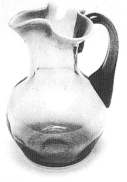

A blue opalescent glass jug, c1860, 6in (15cm) high.
£35–40 CB

► A pale turquoise glass claret jug, with star-cut base, amber barley-sugar twist handle and faceted stopper, c1860, 8in (20.5cm) high.
£120–150 CB

A pair of Dobson & Pearce glass claret jugs, the globular bodies with stepped shoulders and flared rims, engraved with a boar's head crest above the monogram 'HGT', between star and dot borders, with applied angular handles, 1860–70, 13in (33cm) high.
£1,800–2,000 S

Cross Reference
See Colour Review

A glass jug, engraved with a classical design, c1860, 11in (28cm) high.
£300–350 MJW

An engraved glass claret ewer, possibly Stourbridge for Dobson and Pearce, the scroll handle engraved in the form of a snake with a cherub mask terminal, c1860, 10½in (26.5cm) high.
£2,200–2,500 S

A Victorian glass wine jug and stopper, c1860, 14in (35.5cm) high.
£250–300 MJW

A glass jug, with vine engraving, c1860, 10in (25.5cm) high.
£280–350 MJW

A Creswick & Co mid-Victorian silver-mounted glass shaft-and-globe claret jug, Sheffield 1861, 10½in (26.5cm) high.
£1,600–1,900 HSS

▶ A pair of Victorian frosted glass and silver-mounted claret jugs, on circular feet, inscribed on the feet 'Green & Co Fecit London 1867', 13½in (34.5cm) high.
£6,500–7,500 P(O)

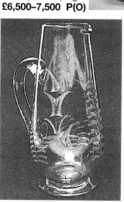

A classical-shaped engraved clear glass jug, c1870, 9½in (24cm) high.
£100–120 CB

A frosted glass water jug, with clear loop handle, c1870, 11¾in (30cm) high.
£200–220 BrW

A Victorian glass ewer, engraved with ferns, c1870, 9½in (24cm) high.
£80–95 DUN

A glass jug, engraved with a swan and cygnet, 1870–80, 9½in (24cm) high.
£580–650 MJW

A Victorian vaseline glass cream jug, 3¾in (9.5cm) high.
£50–60 AnS

◀ A glass miniature water jug, c1870, 1¼in (3cm) high.
£40–50 BrW

▶ A glass jug, engraved with a decorative tree, c1870, 10½in (26.5cm) high.
£400–440 MJW

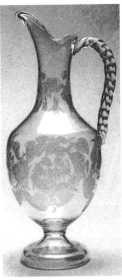

A glass jug, acid-etched with fuchsia, c1870, 12in (30.5cm) high.
£350–400 MJW

A glass jug, engraved with foliage, c1870, 11½in (29cm) high.
£760–840 MJW

A pair of French glass jugs, with torsaded filigree decoration, c1870, 12¾in (32.5cm) high.
£3,000–3,300 MJW

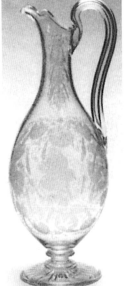

A glass jug, etched with convolvulus, c1870, 12½in (32cm) high.
£220–260 MJW

An engraved glass claret jug, probably Philip Pargeter, Stourbridge, engraved on one side with a pair of classical figures, probably by James O'Fallon, the reverse with the monogram 'RAH' within a circular cartouche, with applied scroll handle and drip ring, rim repaired, c1875, 9in (23cm) high.
£1,800–2,000 S

A late Victorian silver-mounted glass claret jug, decorated with a satyr mask, vines and bunches of grapes and with a star-cut base, the hinged cover with a heraldic lion and shield finial, with wrythen-decorated handle, maker's mark 'CB', London 1876, 11in (28cm) high.
£600–700 GC

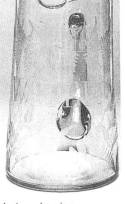

A clear glass jug, engraved with ferns and inscribed 'Water', c1880, 7in (18cm) high.
£65–80 CB

A pillar-mounted glass claret jug, with French silver rococo mounts, c1880, 9in (23cm) high.
£1,200–1,400 CB

A Victorian crackle glass jug, 12¼in (31cm) high.
£85–100 OBS

◄ A glass jug, engraved with flower design, c1880, 10½in (26.5cm) high.
£500–600 MJW

A glass claret jug and stopper, with engraved crest, c1880, 18in (45.5cm) high.
£1,800–2,200 MJW

A glass claret jug, with an etched band of diamonds, notched neck, applied handle and notched spire stopper, c1880, 10in (25.5cm) high.
£170–190 Som

Two Victorian crackle glass jugs:
l. 6in (15cm) high.
£25–30
r. 3¾in (9.5cm) high.
£12–15 FMN

Two Victorian green glass jugs, with lily of the valley pattern and gilt rims, 5½in (14cm) high.
£45–50 each TS

A Victorian cranberry glass jug, c1880, 6¼in (16cm) high.
£80–90 AnS

A Stourbridge cased glass jug, c1880, 6in (15cm) high.
£55–65 WAC

A glass jug, engraved with flowers, c1880, 10in (25.5cm) high.
£300–350 MJW

A glass claret jug, c1880, 13½in (34.5cm) high.
£220–270 MJW

A shaded cranberry glass water jug, c1880, 9in (23cm) high.
£150–180 DUN
If this jug was entirely cranberry, rather than shaded, it would rise in value.

A late Victorian diamond-, hobnail- and panel-cut glass claret jug, with silver mounts to the rim, the hinged cover with baluster finial, with acanthus-capped inverted S-scroll handle, maker's mark 'H & T', Birmingham 1889, 10½in (26.5cm) high.
£500–600 HSS

◄ A cut-glass baluster jug, with panels of diamonds between fan cutting, with stick-up handle, c1890, 11in (28cm) high.
£180–200 JHa
From 1860 to 1870, the application of the handles changed from stick-down to the apparently stronger stick-up type.

A pair of silver and crystal glass claret jugs, c1889, 11¾in (30cm) high.
£7,500–8,500 MJW

A pair of enamelled Continental glass claret jugs and stoppers, each painted with clusters of vine and holly between pincered ribs, late 19thC, 9in (23cm) high.
£350–420 S(S)

◄ A Davidson blue pearline glass jug, c1890, 2in (5cm) high.
£25–30 CSA

A cut-glass lemonade jug, with silver mount, Birmingham 1890, 9½in (24cm) high.
£500–600 TC

A glass jug, with twisted handle, c1890, 7½in (19cm) high.
£250–290 ARE

A cranberry glass jug, with clear handle, c1890, 6¼in (16cm) high.
£100–120 DKH

A Stevens & Williams Rockingham glass claret jug, with brown, green and clear glass overlay, with silver top, c1893, 9¼in (23.5cm) high.
£3,800–4,200 MJW

A late Victorian William Hutton & Sons cut-glass claret jug, engraved with flowers and scrolls in a rock crystal effect, with embossed silver top and hinged gadrooned-edge cover with a chased finial, London 1894, 11in (28cm) high.
£1,000–1,200 WW

A Nailsea-style glass jug, late 19thC, 3½in (9cm) high.
£35–40 AA

A green glass and silver-mounted claret jug, with silver collar and lid with thumb rest, marked for 1894, maker 'N & W', late 19thC, 8¾in (22cm) high.
£500–600 P(B)

A Daum fleur-de-lys pitcher, the clear glass with martelé effect, heightened with gilding, the underside with gilt mark 'Daum Nancy', c1895, 7½in (19cm) high.
£420–500 S

A cranberry glass jug, slight flaw in handle, late 19thC, 9in (23cm) high.
£100–120 DQ

A Gallé glass ewer, decorated with enamelled thistle design and gilded details, signed, c1895, 8¼in (21cm) high.
£1,800–2,000 PSG

Cranberry glass

Cranberry glass was probably produced originally in the early 18th century in Bohemia, although its heyday was in the late 19th/early 20th centuries, when it reached Britain, France, Belgium, Bavaria and the USA. Known originally as a type of ruby glass, cranberry glass derives its name from New England, USA, where cranberries are grown. The colour is produced with a thin layer of ruby over an inner layer of clear glass. Early pieces were comparatively simple in style, but later wares were often decorated with trailing, enamelling or overlay, in which the outer layer of glass is cut through to reveal the colour beneath. Some of the most collectable pieces today are British (notably Stourbridge).

A William Comyns & Sons glass claret jug, London 1898, 10¾in (27.5cm) high.
£750–825 WIL

Two late Victorian silver-mounted green glass overlay jugs, in the form of griffins, by J T Heath and J H Middleton, slight damage, Birmingham 1894 and 1899, 7½in (19cm) high.
£700–800 DN

◄ A Bohemian glass claret jug, with emerald green colouring tapering to clear glass, decorated with gilded enamel, foliate scrolls and flowerheads, late 19thC, 15¾in (40cm) high.
£200–220 P(E)

A glass jug, with green stripe decoration and silver rim, c1900, 11in (28cm) high.
£200–220 ARE

Cross Reference
See Colour Review

An Edwardian glass claret jug, with cut floral and hobnail decoration, silver- plated rim, mask spout, shaped handle and hinged dome cover, on a star-cut base, 11in (28cm) high.
£150–180 Gam

A Stourbridge green flash slender oviform glass ewer, with hinged silver cover, engraved with lilies and stylized foliage, with a clear notched handle, on a circular foot, early 20thC, 12½in (32cm) high.
£600–700 CSK

A Gallé grey-green carved and applied glass pitcher, carved mark on the handle 'Gallé', c1905, 9in (23cm) high.
£45,000–55,000 C

A glass water jug, c1910, 5in (12.5cm) high.
£38–45 DUN

► A Bagley frosted amber glass flower jug, Sunburst 3072, 1939, 9½in (24cm) high.
£32–40 PC

Jug Sets

A jug and glass set, engraved with a leaf design, possibly Richardson, c1860, 5in (12.5cm) high.
£600–800 MJW

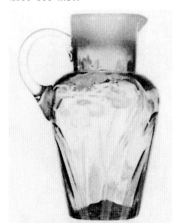

A cranberry and opaque cider set, moulded with irises, comprising a jug with applied loop handle and six cylindrical tumblers, late 19thC.
£650–750 CSK

A Lalique clear and frosted glass set, Chinon, the glass stems moulded in relief with bands of spirals, stained pink, comprising a jug, six water and six white wine glasses, etched 'R Lalique', after 1930, jug 7in (18cm) high.
£700–800 CSK

A Lalique clear and frosted glass lemonade set, Jaffa, intaglio-moulded with vertical serrated foliage, comprising a lemonade jug, six beakers and a circular tray, etched 'Lalique France', slight damage, after 1931, jug 9in (23cm) high.
£600–700 CSK

A Stourbridge ewer and two goblets, probably Richardson, each piece engraved with stars and triple-feather crest, the motto of the Prince of Wales on one side and that of the City of London on the other, c1860, ewer 10¾in (27.5cm) high.
£1,800–2,000 S

▶ A Fenton's Carnival glass lemonade set, 1930, jug 9in (23cm) high.
£300–350 BEV

A Lalique amber glass orangeade set, Blidah, moulded in relief with fruit and foliage, comprising an oviform jug, six large beakers and a circular tray, etched 'R Lalique', after 1931, jug 8in (20.5cm) high.
£850–1,000 CSK

Insurance values

Always insure your valuable antiques for the cost of replacing them with similar items, regardless of the original price paid. Both dealers and auctioneers will provide a valuation service for a fee.

A claret jug and two glasses, possibly Stevens & Williams, each piece finely engraved with oval panels of flowers, reserved on a muslin ground, c1870, jug 12in (30.5cm) high.
£850–1,000 S(S)

A Lalique amber-tinted water jug and four glasses, Isétubal, after 1931, jug 7in (18cm) high.
£1,000–1,200 ANO

A Lalique clear and frosted glass lemonade set, Hespérides, intaglio-moulded with spiralling foliage, comprising a jug, six beakers and a circular tray, etched 'R Lalique', slight damage, after 1931, jug 8½in (21.5cm) high.
£1,000–1,200 CSK

Legras

Auguste Légras was one of several French art glass makers working around the turn of the 20th century, whose work eschewed the complex cutting of their predecessors, moving away from the traditional Renaissance and Venetian styles that had been prevalent and embracing the Art Nouveau movement. To them, the sculptural and surface possibilities of the material were all important. They preferred naturalistic decoration, and the sculptural forms of the Nancy school had a great influence on their work.

Together with the likes of Emile Gallé, the Daum brothers, Desirée Christian and the Muller brothers, Légras led a revival of interest in cameo decoration and helped to popularize enamelled glass.

Combining the skills of chemists, master glass blowers and imaginative designers, these glass makers created innovative and exciting forms. Moreover, improvements in mass production techniques meant that the style of hitherto expensive studio pieces could be reproduced at more affordable prices.

Légras produced enamelled cameo vases and commercial glassware, tending to prefer floral and landscape decoration. Other common features were internally mottled and streaked glass. He also made perfume bottles designed by René Lalique.

Although Légras' work bears a strong resemblance to that of his contemporaries, Gallé and the Daum and Muller brothers, in general it fetches lower prices. Most Légras pieces are signed 'LÉGRAS'.

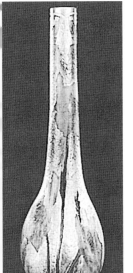

A Legras flame red glass vase, Indiana, with foil inclusions, overlaid with clear glass with large poppy heads in low relief, on an acid-finished verdigris-coloured ground, the neck with a geometric-design gilt collar, the underside with gilded maker's monogram and 'Indiana', chips to collar and base, c1900, 24in (61cm) high.
£1,800–2,000 S

A Legras glass vase, enamelled with blackberry clusters with large orange leaves and tendrils against a yellow and orange ground, signed, c1900, 9½in (24cm) high.
£300–350 P

A Legras acid-etched glass vase, decorated with leafy boughs in purple-coloured glass against a frosted ground, signed, c1900, 12in (30.5cm) high.
£420–500 P

A pair of Legras green glass vases, decorated with enamelled flowers in red, yellow and green, c1910, 13in (33cm) high.
£420–500 ANO

A Legras cameo glass landscape vase, early 20thC, 5in (12.5cm) high.
£700–800 ASA

A Legras glass vase, decorated internally with red and orange feathering, with yellow tendril-like bands to the exterior, signed, early 20thC, 13in (33cm) high.
£180–200 P

A Legras orange and yellow glass vase, End of Day, over-painted with poppies, signed, c1910, 18in (45.5cm) high.
£300–350 AAV

A Legras enamelled glass vase, decorated in brown, white and mauve on a frosted ground, signed, early 20thC, 10in (25.5cm) high.
£300–350 P

Lighting

Glass manufacture has had an important and integral role in the development of domestic lighting over the past three hundred years. Initially clear glass was used in early candle chandeliers and lacemaker's lamps in the eighteenth century. During the following century the advent of oil lamps produced a great surge in the variety of designs for shades and the colours available. With the rapid growth of gas lighting towards the middle of the nineteenth century the glassmakers could extend their range of shades with etched decoration and even more colours.

The next major innovation in the history of domestic lighting was, of course, the advent of electrical fittings. The period 1890 to 1910 was to see a great competition between gas and electricity as sources for domestic lighting. The introduction of the Welsbach inverted mantle for gas fittings (eliminating the shadow problems that plagued the earlier designs) did, for a while, halt the progress of electricity, but the introduction of the tungsten filament bulb by Swan in the UK and Edison in the USA sealed the fate of gas.

These changes in technology were to be reflected in necessary changes in the glass shades made over this period. The earlier up-lighting gas shades with their characteristic wide throat had a straight rim, while shades for the later inverted mantles necessarily had a lip which enabled them to be retained securely in the mounting gallery. The shades for electrical use could now be produced with much narrower throats because of the lesser heating effect; in many cases the bulbholder could now retain the shades.

The introduction of electrical lighting coincided with the Art Nouveau period and many early electric lights are of this design, usually made in brass with the customer choosing either a natural or plated finish but some being made in oxidized copper. Customers also had the choice of fabric or glass for their shades, cranberry and vaseline shades being very popular at this time.

In America, at around this time, the producers of Tiffany lamps generated wonderful stained-glass shades in jewel-like colours, this was an expensive process for that time and is the reason for the very high prices these pieces fetch today. In Europe Emile Gallé and Daum of Nancy produced cameo glass for use in lampshades and examples of their work also command high prices today. The mass production of fittings during the twenties and later led to the widespread use of moulded glass for both hanging and wall lights, and the amount of brass used in these designs was very much reduced.

Margaret Crawley

HANGING & CEILING LIGHTS

A pair of glass hanging lights, the tulip-shaped bodies with cut-trellis pattern, supported on chains from a brass rim, with birds' head hooks and a glass smoke shade, chains later, early 19thC, 24in (61cm) high.
£3,500–4,000 S

A Genoese cast and embossed brass twelve-light chandelier, of inverted trumpet shape, the circlet with bands of Greek key pattern and stiff-leaf ornament, hung with chains of graduated and faceted glass beads and silvered glass spheres, 19thC, 50in (127cm) high.
£650–750 CSK

A French gilt-bronze hanging Colza lamp, the foliate-cast girdle hung with drops, one reservoir stamped 'Miller & Sons, 179 Piccadilly London', 19thC, 25½in (65cm) high.
£1,400–1,600 P

An L G Zimmermann hall lantern, with cast-metal scrollwork frame, the four sides set with lithophane opaque glass panels depicting girls with doves and soldiers after a battle, set with blue glass panes, Austrian, 19thC, 12¼in (32cm) high.
£750–825 DD

Items in the Lighting section have been arranged in date order within each sub-section.

▶ A Victorian lamp, the cranberry glass shade on a polished brass frame with peacock medallions, with cranberry glass font, Venus burner and clear-cut crystal prisms, 18in (45.5cm) high.
£700–800 JAA

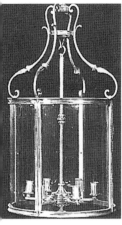

A Victorian brass hanging lantern, the brass-moulded and glazed sides with double scroll supports, centred by a later six-arm light fitment, c1850, 16½in (42cm) high.
£3,200–3,500 S

A brass hanging lantern, with the original glass, c1860, 32in (81.5cm) high.
£3,800–4,500 LEN

A French parcel-gilt and iron hexagonal hall lantern, the glazed facets surmounted by a cresting pierced with quatrefoils and scrollwork, applied with flowers and scrolling acanthus leaves, c1870, 68½in (174cm) high.
£7,000–8,000 S

A Continental three-branch gasolier, with cranberry glass shades, fitted for electricity, c1870, 34in (86.5cm) high.
£950–1,100 CHA

A Victorian brass hanging lantern, with leaf-capped wrythen stem, foliate finials, bevelled glass panels and turned feet, 32in (81.5cm) high.
£1,400–1,600 AH

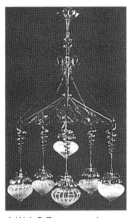

A W A S Benson and James Powell brass ceiling light, with six onion-shaped opalescent glass shades, c1880, 51in (129.5cm) high.
£13,000–14,000 S
W A S Benson set up a metal workshop in 1880 and opened a Bond Street shop in 1887. He retired in 1920. His lighting is highly collectable.

A set of four hanging lights, stamped 'Benson' on the upper leaf and shade supports, c1890, 4½in (11.5cm) diam.
£1,500–1,700 CHA

A Continental gilt-metal-banded centre light, the central stem entwined with metal flowerheads, hung with graduated facets of cut-glass drops and with central cut ball finial, late 19thC, 26¾in (68cm) high.
£2,000–2,200 HOK

An opal and iridescent glass and twisted-wire ornamental hanging shade, attributed to Tiffany, late 19thC, 18in (45.5cm) high.
£1,800–2,000 SK

A ten-branch cut-glass chandelier, each scroll arm with drop-hung drip pans, united by swags of drops and with swags rising to ten drop-hung scrolled arms with spires, restored, late 19thC, 63in (160cm) high.
£10,500–11,500 S

A Viennese cut-glass eight-light chandelier, with glass shaft and glass ball top, fitted for electricity, late 19thC, 35½in (90cm) high.
£1,250–1,500 DORO

A gilt-bronze and cut-glass hanging lamp, the tapering shade below a pierced anthemion-cast corona, late 19thC, 19¼in (49cm) high.
£200–250 P

Safety regulations

Following changes to electrical safety regulations, the most important message from the Department of Trade and Industry is that all electric lighting supplied for sale must be safe, and anyone supplying unsafe products is liable to prosecution. Antique and secondhand lighting does not need to be CE marked (the European safety regulation mark), but suppliers must guarantee and confirm its safety. The most effective way to ensure this is to have it independently tested by a qualified electrician.

- Table and floor lamps must be wired and have a 3 amp fused and sleeved plug.
- Wiring must be effectively insulated and capable of carrying the correct voltage.
- Metal lights or lights with metal fittings must be earthed.
- There must be no exposed wires or access to live parts.
- Porcelain insulation lamp holders should not be chipped or broken.
- It is not sufficient that the lamp is in working order as it may still be unsafe.

A Victorian bronze and glass gas lantern, the corona issuing six brackets with acanthus clasp, the bevelled glass surmounted by female masks, traces of original gilding, late 19thC, 28½in (72.5cm) high.
£1,200–1,400 Bon(C)

A French cut-glass and gilt-bronze lantern, the corona modelled with fleur-de-lys decoration, the terminal with a fruiting finial, late 19thC, 24in (61cm) high.
£1,100–1,300 CSK

A centre light fitting, the glass bowl formed with diamond-cut radiating bands, secured by a gilt-bronze and brass ring, the centre with a pomegranate, c1900, 29¼in (74.5cm) high.
£5,800–6,500 P(S)

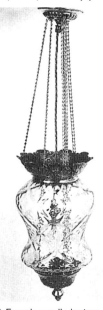

A French candle lantern, with cranberry glass shade, fitted for electricity, c1900, 16in (40.5cm) high.
£500–600 CHA

A forged-steel gas lantern, with cranberry glass shade, fitted for electricity, c1900, 35in (89cm) high.
£800–900 CHA

An extending rod hanging light, originally gas, c1900, 32in (81.5cm) high.
£150–185 LIB

A French ormolu hall lantern, after the Alhambra model, with a pierced Moorish foliate design, supporting four candle branches, the lower part supporting the moulded glass shade, fitted for electricity, c1900, 26¾in (68cm) high.
£3,000–3,500 C

A French gilt-bronze and cut-glass ceiling light, the inverted dome with hobnail and starburst decoration, the frame cast with lattice decoration and applied with scallop shell mounts, c1900, 12¾in (32.5cm) high.
£2,800–3,200 CSK

A Müller Frères mottled glass ceiling light, 1900–33, 12in (30.5cm) high.
£300–350 P(B)

► An Edwardian cut- and moulded-crystal chandelier, the central baluster column with fluted decoration and scalloped canopy suspending pendants and swags linking eight curved branches, 34¼in (87cm) high.
£420–500 P(S)

An Edwardian cast-brass three-branch electrolier, with cranberry glass shades, 18in (45.5cm) high.
£850–950 CHA

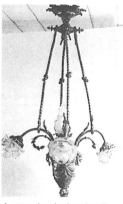

A neo-classical-style gilt-brass five-light electrolier, the urn-shaped centre cast with swags and female masks, flambeau pattern glass centre shade and four branches with frosted-glass flowerhead pattern shades, early 20thC, 31in (78.5cm) high.
£700–800 CAG

A glass and metal light, in the shape of a star, early 20thC, 12in (30.5cm) diam.
£150–180 ASM

An Edwardian brass three-light electrolier, with etched glass shades, 32in (81.5cm) high.
£1,200–1,450 CHA

A Hector Guimard gilt-bronze and glass ceiling light, the central support with four curved arms joining a square framework with pierced organic motif suspending alternating glass and bronze rods, c1908, 21½in (54.5cm) high.
£3,500–4,200 CNY

A ceiling light, with decorative brass gallery and cut-glass shade, c1910, 9in (23cm) diam.
£190–225 LIB

An Arts and Crafts beaten copper lantern, with vaseline glass and turquoise inserts, c1910, 19in (48.5cm) high.
£600–700 CHA

An Art Nouveau three-light electrolier, with green frosted glass shades, c1910, 20in (51cm) high.
£650–750 CHA

An Edwardian brass three-branch light, with vaseline glass shades, c1910, 48in (122cm) high.
£950–1,100 CHA

An Edwardian brass ceiling light, the domed shade with fluted glazing bars, a pierced circlet hung with beaded chains, surmounted by outspreading acanthus leaves, with open scrolling corona above a stiff-leaf-wrapped terminal, c1910, 21in (53.5cm) high.
£800–900 CSK

► An Edwardian brass centre light, with five holophane glass shades, c1910, 30in (76cm) diam.
£950–1,100 CHA

Art Nouveau and Art Deco

Art Nouveau and Art Deco lighting is not only functional and highly decorative, it is frequently of fine quality, and likely to have been executed by a leading glass designer.
Ceiling lights form the perfect solution for the nervous glass enthusiast. They can be viewed from their best vantage point and their secure location limits vulnerability.

A brass ceiling light, with a glass holophane bowl, c1910, 13in (33cm) diam.
£400–500 CHA

An Edwardian cut-glass ceiling light, with brass fittings, c1910, 16in (40.5cm) high.
£400–500 CHA

An Edwardian brass and copper lantern, with bevelled-glass panels, each centred with a sunburst motif below a scrolling corona, c1910, 30in (76cm) high.
£700–800 CSK

A René Lalique frosted-glass hanging lamp, moulded with leaves, engraved mark, after 1914, 18¼in (46.5cm) diam.
£4,000–4,500 S

A vaseline glass hanging ceiling light, 1910–20, 12in (30.5cm) high.
£350–400 RUL

A Lalique frosted-glass plafonnier, Charmes, with moulded leaves, signed, c1920, 15in (38cm) diam.
£1,500–1,800 ASA

A Handel leaded-glass and filigree-bronze oasis chandelier, the shade with panels of striated and swirled glass in shades of red, white, amber and green overlaid with an elaborate bronze filigree, No. 5381, c1915, 13½in (34.5cm) diam.
£5,000–5,500 S(NY)

► A German five-arm crystal chandelier, with coloured beads, c1920, 20in (51cm) high.
£400–500 ML

◄ A hanging glass ceiling light, with hand-painted decoration and silver-plated fittings, c1920, 17½in (44.5cm) diam.
£150–180 CHA

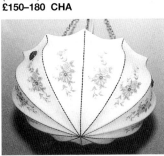

A Gallé cameo glass ceiling light, the shade with a design of applied blossoms cut in deep amber over a frosted ground, original brass hanger, signed, c1920, 14in (35.5cm) diam.
£2,750–3,000 JAA

A French Art Deco light fitting, enclosing multiple light sockets, contained within silver-plated mounts, c1920, 20in (51cm) high.
£1,000–1,200 ASA

A hanging glass ceiling light, with transfer-printed design, 1920s, 16in (40.5cm) diam.
£100–120 CHA

A Sabino frosted-glass ceiling light, moulded with graduated roundels and cloud-like scrollwork, moulded 'Sabino Paris Déposé', c1920, 10in (25.5cm) diam.
£200–300 P

► A pair of leaded glass ceiling lights, c1920, 22in (56cm) wide.
£350–400 GAZ

A pair of French iron and glass ceiling lights, with transfer-printed milk-glass shades, c1920, 9½in (24cm) high.
£80–100 ML

A Lalique glass plafonnier, Dahlias, heightened with brown staining, with hanging chains, wheel-cut mark 'R Lalique France', after 1921, 12in (30.5cm) diam.
£800–1,000 S

► An Edgar Brandt and Daum chandelier, the shade marked 'Daum Nancy' with a Cross of Lorraine, ceiling rose stamped 'E Brandt', c1925, 26in (66cm) diam.
£2,200–2,600 S

An Art Deco chrome four-branch ceiling light, with frosted-glass shades, 1920–30, 19¾in (50cm) wide.
£120–150 OOLA

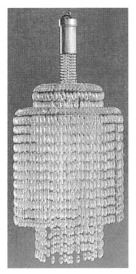

A pair of glass chandeliers, in the style of Emile-Jacques Ruhlmann, each with fluted silvered-bronze standard conjoining strings of pendant glass beads, c1925, 32in (81.5cm) high.
£6,000–7,000 S(NY)

A black iron-framed chandelier, with two-dimensional lyre-shaped pendant amethyst, smoke and crystal cut-glass drops, 1920–30, 21in (53.5cm) high.
£450–550 JPr

A Lalique glass lampshade, Dahlia, signed, 1920–30, 12in (30.5cm) high.
£350–450 MARK

A turquoise blue holophane glass ceiling light, 1920s, 9in (23cm) high.
£100–120 RUL

► A Lalique amber-tinted glass ceiling light, Rinceaux, moulded in bold relief with fan-shaped panels, etched mark, 1920s, 14¾in (37.5cm) diam.
£950–1,100 DN

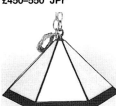

An Art Deco green and white glass hanging light, 1920s, 9½in (24cm) high.
£85–95 LIB

An Art Deco holophane glass hanging lamp, with brass gallery and frosted glass shade, 1920s, 16in (40.5cm) long.
£150–175 LIB

A hanging lamp, with pink holophane glass shade, 1920s, 6½in (16.5cm) high.
£80–90 LIB

An Art Deco ceiling light, with copper gallery and frosted glass shade, 1920s, 10in (25.5cm) high.
£100–120 LIB

A W H Gispen nickel-plated and opaque and frosted-glass ceiling light, c1927, 23½in (59.5cm) diam.
£550–650 S

Items in the Lighting section have been arranged in date order within each sub-section.

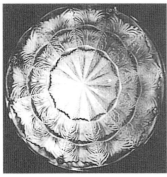

A Lalique colourless frosted-glass ceiling light, Gaillon Marcilhac, No. 2474, moulded with concentric acanthus leaves, wheel-cut mark 'R Lalique, France', after 1927, 17½in (44.5cm) diam.
£1,000–1,200 S

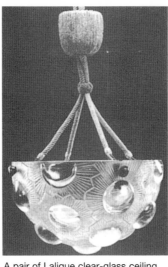

A pair of Lalique clear-glass ceiling lights, Soleil, with brown staining and silk hanging cords, wheel-cut mark 'R Lalique France', after 1928, 12in (30.5cm) diam.
£1,000–1,200 S

A Löys Lucha domed octagonal hanging ceiling shade, decorated with pink and blue hydrangeas on green foliage, with triple silk suspension cords, c1929, 23in (58.5cm) diam.
£900–1,000 RID

A pair of Art Deco bronze-metal and glass light fittings, c1930, 18in (45.5cm) wide.
£1,000–1,200 ASA

An Art Deco glass and chrome hexagonal hanging lamp, c1930, 14½in (37cm) wide.
£120–140 ML

An Art Deco set of three silver-plated bronze and frosted-glass ceiling lights, c1930, 12in (30.5cm) diam.
£800–900 DAF

A multi-coloured glass ceiling bowl, 1930s, 12in (30.5cm) diam.
£30–40 TWa

A pair of Italian clear glass ceiling lights, each of dual undulating handkerchief shape, with green glass piping to the rims, c1960, 19¾in (50cm) diam.
£600–700 P

A brass ceiling light, with four etched-glass panels, foliate chains and motifs, c1930, 35½in (90cm) high.
£400–450 LRG

▶ A French gilt-brass chandelier, with crystal glass drops, 1930s, 20in (51cm) high.
£350–400 JPr

A white opaque-glass ceiling light, with brass fitting, 1930s, 11in (28cm) diam.
£140–160 RUL

Miller's is a price GUIDE not a price LIST

A ceiling light, the five glass shades with pierced chrome fittings and orange linings, 1960s, 26in (66cm) high.
£70–80 TWa

OIL LAMPS

An oil lamp, with three wick orifices, on a plain stem with folded conical foot, c1750, 6in (15cm) high.
£950–1,100 Som

An English coral satin glass oil lamp, c1880, 20in (51cm) high.
£420–500 CR

An oil lamp, with cast-iron base, c1880, 18½in (47cm) high.
£150–175 LIB

▶ A Victorian oil lamp, with brass base, the shade etched shade with fuchsia design, and a circular wick, 25in (63.5cm) high.
£200–250 JMC

A Victorian brass oil lamp, with chinoiserie-painted reservoir, glass chimney and shade, c1870, 26in (66cm) high.
£325–375 S(S)

A heavy cut-glass oil lamp, c1880, 17in (43cm) high.
£750–850 DUN

An ormolu-mounted opaque-glass oil lamp, with embossed band and two lions' mask ring handles, 19thC, 27in (68.5cm) high.
£350–400 PCh

An oil lamp, with double burner, green glass reservoir and enamel base, c1880, 22in (56cm) high.
£250–275 LIB

A brass peg lamp, with Burmese glass shade and cranberry font, 19thC, 18in (45.5cm) high.
£170–200 GAK
Peg lamps are oil lamps with a peg designed to fit a candle base.

A Victorian brass Corinthian column oil lamp, with chimney, etched-glass shade and moulded yellow glass reservoir, c1880, 34in (86.5cm) high.
£500–600 S(S)

Oil lamp checklist

- Good oil lamps are often marked on the burner and the discovery of a maker's name is an indication of quality.
- A large number of reproduction oil lamps have been manufactured and the brass tends to be both lighter and brighter.
- When buying ensure that the vendor demonstrates how the lamp works.
- The vendor should state if a lamp is original or a marriage between an early base and later shade.
- The buyer should always request a fully documented receipt.

A Victorian brass base oil lamp, with cranberry font and etched cranberry shade, c1890, 22in (56cm) high.
£650–700 CHA

A Prince & Symmons Lion Lamp Works adjustable reading lamp, with ruby glass reservoir, late 19thC, 21in (53.5cm) high.
£270–300 DD

A Victorian oil lamp, with cranberry glass shade, telescopic action, on three scroll supports and triangular base, 72in (183cm) high.
£250–300 WBH

A Victorian brass oil lamp, with floral-decorated font and etched amber glass shade, c1890, 33in (84cm) high.
£850–900 CHA

A Victorian brass oil lamp, with gadrooned vase-shaped reservoir supporting an etched-glass shade, c1890, 17in (43cm) high.
£350–400 S(S)

A Victorian oil lamp, in the form of a snowy owl, slight damage, 29in (73.5cm) high.
£290–320 LT

A Victorian oil lamp with cut-glass reservoir and marble stand, 29in (73.5cm) high.
£200–300 ASA

► A Victorian brass and glass oil lamp, with shade and chimney, the green glass reservoir painted with flowers, c1890, 27in (68.5cm) high.
£450–500 S(S)

A Victorian oil lamp, with double burner, decorated glass reservoir and cast-iron base, 22in (56cm) high.
£185–200 LIB

A Regency-style glass oil lamp, with hobnail-cut and fluted hemispherical glass reservoir, conforming domed base, tapered octagonal-faceted pillar, on gilt brass paw feet, late 19thC, 20in (51cm) high.
£450–550 N

The birth of oil lamps

In 1850 James Young, a Scotsman, patented a refining process for producing paraffin. The fuel burned efficiently without any danger of spontaneous combustion, and its discovery lead to the massive production of oil lamps. Cheap, safe and reliable, these lamps began to replace candles as a major source of domestic lighting.

Many different designs were produced worldwide and lamps were imported to Britain from Germany and the USA. On these 19th and early 20th century examples the brass tends to be weighty whilst the glass shades can often be very light and finely made - hence the reason why many period shades no longer survive.

A silver-plated oil lamp, with cranberry glass tinted shade, in original working condition, c1890, 32in (81.5cm) high.
£1,000–1,100 CHA

A late Victorian oil lamp, with cranberry glass shade, on fluted brass support, with black slag socle, 23in (58.5cm) high.
£450–500 GAK

A French oil lamp, with onyx column and base and green enamelled glass bowl, c1900, 27½in (70cm) high.
£230–260 TWa

A Duplex double-burner oil lamp, with blue glass reservoir, c1900, 22½in (57cm) high.
£150–175 LIB

A Doulton oil lamp, c1900, 22½in (57cm) high.
£550–650 MEG

A wall-mounted oil lamp, c1900, 15in (38cm) high.
£30–35 AL

An Edwardian brass oil lamp, with corinthian column base, with cut-glass font and amber cranberry glass shade, c1900, 34in (86.5cm) high.
£750–850 CHA

◄ A clear-glass oil lamp, with handle, c1900, 15in (38cm) high.
£38–45 HEM

► A brass pressure oil lamp, by Aladdin Industries Ltd, Model No. 12, c1905, 23¼in (59cm) high.
£65–75 HEM

An oil lamp, with alabaster and brass base and moulded green glass font, c1910, 22in (56cm) high.
£80–95 TWa

An Edwardian brass oil lamp, with original shade, c1910, 17in (43cm) high.
£70–80 JMC

A Rozenburg lamp, globe replaced, c1910, 17¾in (45cm) high.
£420–500 OO

An original Famos nickel-plated oil lamp, with fluted shade, c1920, 26in (66cm) high.
£70–80 JMC

► Two Continental nursery bedside oil lamps, one with Ostende crest, 1920s, 5½in (14cm) high.
£10–15 each TAC

A lighthouse night light, c1930, 6in (15cm) high.
£35–40 TER

An oil lamp, with pink-painted metal base, 1920s, 10¼in (26cm) high.
£8–10 TAC

► A French opaline glass oil lamp, decorated with flowers, 1930s, 8in (20.5cm) high.
£15–20 LIB

A pair of French enamel and brass oil lamps, 1920s, 10in (25.5cm) high.
£40–48 LIB

► A brass chamberstick oil lamp, 1930s, 7¼in (18.5cm) high.
£20–22 ML

Buying oil lamps

Oil lamps have, for some time, been a rich field for collectors, many of whom being interested in the various patents produced during the 19th century. Some of the best of Victorian glass was made for oil lampshades, and this explains the high prices these make today. It is important that oil lamps have genuine shades for oil lamps and not gas shades. The inexperienced buyer must be aware of reproductions, and here, as in all aspects of buying antiques, the best advice is to buy from a reputable source and obtain a detailed receipt.

LACEMAKER'S LAMPS

Two lacemaker's lamps, mid-18thC, tallest 9in (23cm) high:
l. with hollow baluster stem, on conical folded foot, with drip pan and handle.
£300–350
r. with incised twist stem.
£170–220 FD

A lacemaker's lamp, c1760, 3in (7.5cm) high.
£250–300 MJW

A lacemaker's condensing globe, on pedestal foot, late 18thC, 10in (25.5cm) high.
£280–310 FD

A pair of lacemaker's lamps, with globular reservoirs, knopped stems and applied loop handles, each on dished folded foot, 19thC, 5in (12.5cm) high.
£200–250 DN

◄ A Bristol blue glass lacemaker's lamp, c1790, 10½in (26.5cm) high.
£750–850 FD

► A French moulded-glass lacemaker's lamp, 1890, 11in (28cm) high.
£100–120 CB

STORM LAMPS

A pair of Wedgwood gilt-brass and glass storm lamps, the engraved shades on bead-moulded and leaf-cast pierced supports, the drum bases depicting classical scenes, on bead-moulded feet, re-gilded, c1775, 19¼in (49cm) high.
£3,500–4,000 S

A mahogany and brass storm lamp, the tulip-shaped glass shade with moulded brass support, on an anthemion-carved stem and turned base, c1790, 23in (58.5cm) high.
£2,000–2,400 S

A storm shade candlestick, on an ormolu-mounted blue drum base, c1790, 18½in (47cm) high.
£600–700 WGT

A pair of Regency glass storm lanterns, in the style of William Bullock, each glass shade engraved with scrolling convolvulus flowers and foliage, on a bronze base with gilt-bronze mounts, 14in (35.5cm) high.
£2,400–2,800 HYD

LOCATE THE SOURCE
The source of each illustration in Miller's can be found by checking the code letters below each caption with the Key to Illustrations, pages 305–307.

TABLE & STANDARD LAMPS

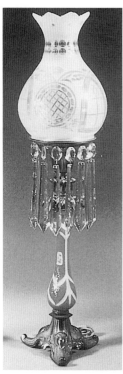

A Sandwich glass astral lamp, the wheel-cut and acid-etched shade with Gothic arches, damaged, 19thC, 33in (84cm) high.
£2,200–2,500 SK(B)
This lamp was originally owned by Deming Jarvis, owner of Boston Sandwich Glass Company.

A pair of glass and gilt-bronze lamp stands, the blue glass vases cast with bacchic masks linked by vined garlands, on reeded bases with flower garlands, 19thC, 29in (73.5cm) high.
£3,000–3,500 P

A crystal glass table lamp, late 19th/early 20thC, 15in (38cm) high.
£75–90 ASA

◄ An American astral lamp, the standard of opalescent and blue glass with gilt highlights, the shade wheel-cut with shield, lyres and foliate devices, on a brass and marble base, late 19thC, 30in (76cm) high.
£2,200–2,500 SK(B)

▶ A French glass and silver-plated electric lamp, modelled as a basket of fruit, c1890, 7½in (19cm) high.
£1,100–1,300 PC

A Gallé cameo glass lamp, Trees at Sunset, the domed top with butterflies hovering over blossoms, signed, c1895, 14in (35.5cm) high.
£7,500–8,250 NOA

A Gallé cameo glass lamp base, the yellow glass overlaid with deep blue and etched with flowering chrysanthemums, light wheel-cut finishing, the rim with metal mount, cameo marks 'Gallé', c1900, 21½in (55.5cm) high.
£5,000–6,000 C

An A Hart lamp, Wisteria, with light and dark blue wisteria blossoms cascading from an openwork branch upper section, on patinated bronze tree trunk-shaped base, minor losses, c1900, 21½in (54.5cm) high.
£1,100–1,300 S(NY)

An American table lamp, the blue, mauve and white glass enclosed within a pierced gilt-metal mount cast with flora radiating from swan-neck vases and birds perched amid foliage, c1900, 21¾in (55.5cm) high.
£750–900 P

▶ A pewter table lamp, attributed to Orivit, with two stems, on a black marble base, the green glass shade decorated with red, c1900, 17½in (44.5cm) high.
£3,250–3,750 S

A painted spelter table lamp, with original painted glass flambeau shade, c1900, 22in (56cm) high.
£250–300 ML

A Handel copper-patinated bronze and stained-glass Apple Blossom table lamp, c1910, 23¾in (60.5cm) high.
£1,750–2,000 NOA

A brass lamp with a globe shade, early 20thC, 24in (61cm) high.
£100–120 ASA

An Edwardian gas table lamp, with vaseline glass shade, fitted for electricity, 19in (48.5cm) high.
£700–800 CHA

An Art Nouveau brass lamp, the shade inset with coloured glass berries and leaves, on a curved stem and lily pad base set with an illuminated frog, early 20thC, 20in (51cm) high.
£3,000–3,300 DN

An American Art Nouveau spelter and slag glass table lamp, the base with moulded poppies, early 20thC, 23in (58.5cm) high.
£1,300–1,500 DuM

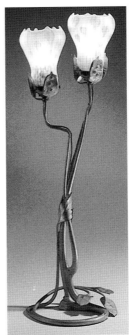

A Gallé chinoiserie-style cameo glass table lamp, internally mottled with lemon and overlaid in red, c1910, 10in (25.5cm) high.
£11,500–12,500 CSK

A brass table lamp, with black ceramic base and glass shade, c1910, 15in (38cm) high.
£100–125 LIB

◀ A silver-plated and glass table lamp, on a silver-plated base signed 'Empire Lamp Mfg Co, Chicago, 6.30.14', early 20thC, 22in (56cm) high.
£380–420 FBG

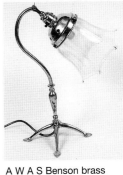

A W A S Benson brass table lamp, with opaline glass shade, c1905, 15in (38cm) high.
£700–800 MoS

◀ A Daum Nancy cameo glass and Majorelle gilt-iron lamp, the shades in grey glass overlaid in lime green and pale peach and cut with a pattern of blossoms, c1903, 27½in (70cm) high.
£6,000–7,000 S(NY)

▶ An Edwardian brass Tilley lamp, c1910, 23in (58.5cm) high.
£80–90 HEM

A Müller Frères cameo glass lamp, c1910, 22½in (57cm) high.
£5,000–6,000 ABS

Table & Standard Lamps • LIGHTING 185

An obverse-painted scenic lamp, the glass shade with textured hand-painted surface, mounted on a gilt-metal base with handles, dated '1913', 13½in (34.5cm) high.
£700–800 SK

A brass table lamp, with Corinthian column stand and decorative glass shade, c1920, 18½in (47cm) high.
£125–145 LIB

A pair of Sabino desk lamps, with glass shades and bronze bases, signed, c1925, 23in (58.5cm) high.
£5,000–5,500 ART

An Art Nouveau brass table lamp, with transfer-printed glass shade, 1910–20, 21in (53.5cm) high.
£120–140 ML

A René Lalique lamp, Gros Poissons Vagues, the bronze base fitted for electricity, engraved mark, after 1922, 15½in (39.5cm) high.
£2,250–2,500 S

A Daum Nancy lamp, the shade and base in grey glass acid-etched with furrows, the iron mount painted silver, signed, c1925, 16¼in (41.5cm) high.
£5,000–5,500 S(NY)

A cut-crystal electric table lamp, with cut-crystal shade, c1920, 22in (56cm) high.
£190–220 LF

An Art Deco glass lamp, decorated with stylized red over black amethyst, the back deeply cut with angular stripes and geometric devices, a matching cone shade and internally-lit shaft mounted on a wrought-iron base with applied flowers, the shade signed 'Degué' in cameo, c1920, 16½in (42cm) high.
£1,650–1,850 SK(B)

An Art Deco opalescent glass lamp, in the shape of an upright seashell, c1925, 10¾in (27.5cm) high.
£500–550 P

A Lalique blue-stained opalescent glass vase, Ceylan, moulded with love birds, with light fitting and contemporary painted shade, etched 'R Lalique, France', c1920, 9½in (24cm) high.
£1,800–2,000 Bea

A Pairpoint moulded glass boudoir lamp, the shade in grey glass moulded with clusters of flowers, painted on the interior with yellow, white, black, purple and crimson, on gilt-metal base, c1920, 14½in (37cm) diam.
£3,500–4,000 S(NY)

A Le Verre Français cameo glass *veilleuse*, the grey glass tinted with yellow and orange, overlaid with red and green and cut with a branch and berry design, inscribed, c1925, 7¼in (18.5cm) high.
£520–620 S(NY)

A brass Pullman lamp, with painted glass shade, 1920s, 16½in (42cm) high.
£100–120 LIB

A brass table lamp, with floral-decorated glass shade, 1920s, 17½in (44.5cm) high.
£80–90 LIB

A pair of glass lamps, each with a globular shade, decorated in relief with geometric panels picked out in soft colours and screwed into a black glass three-legged base, probably American, c1925, 7½in (19cm) high.
£320–400 P

A Daum frosted glass table lamp and shade, acid-etched in high relief, etched marks, small crack to shade, c1925, 15in (38cm) high.
£1,200–1,500 P

A brass table lamp, with a green glass shade, 1920s, 18in (45.5cm) high.
£115–135 LIB

A Louis Poulson brown enamelled metal and Bakelite table lamp, by Poul Henningsen, with opalescent glass shade, Copenhagen, c1927, 16¾in (42.5cm) high.
£10,000–11,000 S
This is an early form of the well-known Poul Henningsen table lamp 'PH'. Several variations on the design were shown in Paris in 1925, each conforming to the principle that lighting fixtures should illuminate without generating glare from the naked bulb.

An Art Deco copper and brass lamp, with glass shade, 1920s, 18in (45.5cm) high.
£110–130 LIB

A brass table lamp, with reeded stem and marbled decorative shade, 1920s, 19in (48.5cm) high.
£130–150 LIB

A table lamp, the brass base modelled as a boy, 1920s, 18in (45.5cm) high.
£180–220 LIB

A G Argy-Rousseau *pâte-de-verre* lamp, the grey glass moulded with stylized flowerheads shaded with blue, green and purple, on an illuminated iron base, c1928, 7in (18cm) high.
£5,700–6,500 S(NY)

A Lalique amber moulded glass table lamp, Languedoc, modelled as a stylized artichoke, engraved in script 'R Lalique, France', after 1929, 9in (23cm) high.
£1,500–1,800 LRG

An André Delatte clear glass lamp and shade, internally-decorated with white streaks, overlaid with pink and etched with flowering branches, the base and shade marked 'A Delatte Nancy', the shade with two cameo marks, 1920s, 22in (56cm) high.
£1,800–2,000 S

A brass table lamp, with white glass shade, 1920s, 13½in (34.5cm) high.
£100–120 LIB

A green pressed glass lamp in the shape of a shell, with a young girl standing with angel fish, aquatic decoration to base, c1930, 8½in (21.5cm) high.
£120–150 BKK

A pair of Italian glass figural table lamps, with rectangular bodies, on domed bases, c1930, 15in (38cm) high, with rectangular lamp shades.
£460–500 P

A Lalique frosted-glass lamp, Six Danseuses, the underside of the base with stencilled mark 'R Lalique France', c1932, 10in (25.5cm) high.
£5,000–6,000 S

A Bagley green glass lamp, 1930s, 8in (20.5cm) high.
£80–95 BEV

A green phenolic table lamp, with glass shade, 1930s, 17in (43cm) high.
£120–140 GFR

A black metal and chrome table lamp, with glass saturn shade, 1930s, 22in (56cm) high.
£125–150 GFR

A pair of Art Deco chrome lamps, with milk glass globes, 1930s, 15in (38cm) high.
£140–160 ML

A green plastic bedside lamp, with white glass shade, c1945, 13in (33cm) high.
£35–45 CAB

A Venini clown lamp, 20thC, 23½in (59.5cm) high.
£100–120 ASA

A Venini hanging lamp, the body in opaque glass with purple, lilac, yellow and green band decoration and brass fixing around the waist, 1954, 26¼in (66.5cm) high.
£1,000–1,200 Bon
This lamp was designed by BBPR Design Group for the new Olivetti showroom in New York.

A Snoopy table light, 1970s, 21in (53.5cm) high.
£20–25 DUD

TIFFANY LAMPS

A Tiffany Favrile Peacock lamp base, the green glass decorated with iridescent feathering and silvery-blue eyes, mounted on a beaded bronze base, c1892, 16¾in (42.5cm) high.
£8,500–9,500 S(NY)

A Tiffany Favrile glass and bronze lamp, with counter-balance weight, c1899, 16in (40.5cm) high.
£2,000–2,200 S(NY)

▶ A Tiffany Favrile glass and bronze lamp, decorated with amber and white leaves, c1899, 21in (53.5cm) high.
£4,500–5,000 S(NY)

A Tiffany Favrile glass and bronze Linenfold lamp, the ten-sided shade with emerald green glass panels, c1899, 19in (48.5cm) high.
£3,200–3,500 S(NY)

> **Cross Reference**
> See Colour Review

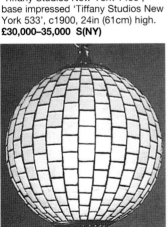

A Tiffany Favrile glass and bronze Dragonfly lamp, shade impressed 'Tiffany Studios New York 1495', base impressed 'Tiffany Studios New York 533', c1900, 24in (61cm) high.
£30,000–35,000 S(NY)

A Tiffany leaded glass and bronze Wisteria table lamp, impressed mark, c1900, 16¾in (42.5cm) high.
£31,000–34,000 FBG

A Tiffany leaded glass and bronze Poppy table lamp, shade and base with impressed marks, c1900, 24¼in (61.5cm) high.
£18,500–21,000 FBG

A Tiffany Favrile glass and bronze hall light fitting, of yellow and white opalescent glass brickwork tiles, c1899, 19in (48.5cm) high.
£6,700–8,000 S(NY)

A Tiffany Favrile glass and gilt-bronze turtleback tile chandelier, composed of iridescent amber glass tiles, c1899, 18½in (47cm) high.
£3,400–4,000 S(NY)

A Tiffany Favrile patinated-bronze and glass three-light lily table lamp, 1899–1920, 8½in (21.5cm) high.
£2,200–2,500 S(NY)
Ex-Leonard Bernstein collection.

A Tiffany Favrile glass and bronze Wisteria lamp, shade impressed '30025/02', base impressed '30250', c1900, 25½in (65cm) high.
£95,000–110,000 S(NY)

A Tiffany Favrile glass and gilt-bronze Parasol lamp, shade impressed 'Tiffany Studios New York', base impressed 'Tiffany Studios New York 1651', c1900, 28in (71cm) high.
£7,500–8,500 S(NY)

▶ A Tiffany Favrile glass and gilt-bronze Bridge lamp, chipped, shade inscribed 'L.C.T. Favrile', base impressed 'Tiffany Studios New York 425', c1900, 55in (139.5cm) high.
£2,000–2,400 S(NY)

A Tiffany Favrile glass and gilt-bronze Linenfold lamp, shade impressed 'Tiffany Studios New York 1950 PAT Applied For', base impressed 'Tiffany Studios 444', c1900, 24½in (62cm) high.
£3,200–3,800 S(NY)

> **Miller's is a price GUIDE not a price LIST**

A Tiffany Favrile glass and bronze Butterfly lamp, shade unsigned, base impressed 'Tiffany Studios 25918', c1900, 23¾in (60.5cm) high.
£60,000–70,000 S(NY)

A Tiffany Favrile glass and Rookwood standard glaze pottery lamp, decorated by Matthew Daly, inscribed, c1900, 20½in (52cm) high.
£8,000–9,500 B&B

A Tiffany Favrile glass and bronze two-arm lamp, each shade inscribed 'L.C.T.', base impressed 'Tiffany Studios New York 316', c1900, 26¼in (66.5cm) high.
£4,600–5,200 S(NY)

A Tiffany Favrile glass and bronze Daffodil lamp, impressed 'Tiffany Studios New York', c1900, 24in (61cm) high.
£31,000–36,000 S(NY)

▶ A pair of Tiffany leaded glass and bronze sconces, one with square tapered shade set with amber glass panels, and another with shade lacking, c1914, 12in (30.5cm) high.
£1,300–1,500 CNY

A Tiffany Favrile glass and bronze Laburnham table lamp, impressed mark 'Tiffany Studios New York No. 368', c1910, 27in (68.5cm) high.
£58,000–68,000 DN

WALL LIGHTS

A brass gimbal spring-loaded candle holder, with glass shade, c1840, 13in (33cm) high.
£150–180 PC

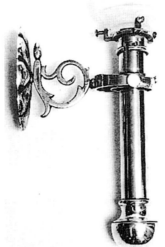

A brass gimbal spring-loaded candle holder, c1860, 12in (30.5cm) high.
£140–170 PC
A gimbal is the term used for a jointed metal lampshade carrier.

A pair of gas wall lights, with a gilt mermaid support and glass shades, fitted for electricity, c1880, 13in (33cm) high.
£1,400–1,600 CHA

A brass wall lamp, with marbled glass shade, c1900, 13in (33cm) wide.
£95–110 LIB

A set of four brass wall lights, with holophane glass shades, originally gas, c1900, 9in (23cm) wide.
£400–440 LIB

A pair of brass wall lights, originally gas, c1900, 9in (23cm) high.
£180–200 LIB

A pair of wall lights, with copper fittings, originally gas, c1900, 12½in (32cm) wide.
£200–220 LIB

◀ A pair of wall lights, with copper and brass fittings, originally gas, c1900, 8½in (21.5cm) high.
£200–230 LIB

A brass wall light, with reeded holophane glass shade, c1900, 9in (23cm) high.
£350–400 CHA
Holophane glass shades were manufactured in large numbers and a variety of shapes. Their prismatic design was intended to redirect the light where it was needed and to minimise the shadows. The name holophane and a pattern number is pressed into the rim of these shades.

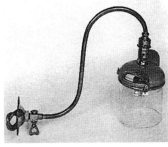

A swan-necked wall lamp, with porcelain burner, originally gas, c1900, 11in (28cm) wide.
£85–100 LIB

◀ A Victorian brass wall light, with original milk glass shade, c1900, 15½in (39.5cm) high.
£140–170 ML

A pair of brass swan-neck gas wall lights, with marbled glass globe shades, converted to electricity, c1900, 10in (25.5cm) wide.
£200–240 LIB

A pair of brass wall lights, with frosted glass shades, 1900–10, 7in (18cm) high.
£125–145 ML
These were original samples from an Edwardian salesman's stock.

◄ A pair of brass wall lights, originally gas, with registration mark for 1908, 10in (25.5cm) wide.
£200–230 LIB

An Edwardian brass wall light, with glass globe, c1910, 11in (28cm) high.
£120–140 ML

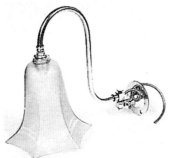

A pair of gas swivelling wall lights, in brass, with etched frosted glass shades, c1910, 12½in (32cm) wide.
£200–240 ML

A set of four iron candle wall lights, with glass crystal drops, 1910–20, 10in (25.5cm) high.
£500–580 ML

A pair of Arts & Crafts embossed copper and glass wall lanterns, the side panels cut and embossed with various scenes of New York city, enclosing striated opalescent glass panels in shades of green, red and white, both suspended from a scrolling bracket with small chains, unsigned, c1915, 9½in (24cm) high.
£1,200–1,400 S(NY)

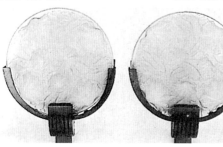

A pair of Art Deco wall lights, the opalescent disc-shaped shades moulded with seashells and aquatic tendrils, partly enclosed by a gilt-metal wall bracket with frosted glass side panels, moulded 'Verlys France', c1920, 12½in (32cm) long.
£800–900 P

A pair of Daum clear glass wall lights, with alternating textured and satin glass bands, each with engraved mark 'Daum Nancy France', with a Cross of Lorraine, c1920, 11½in (29cm) wide.
£1,000–1,200 S

Sets/pairs

Unless otherwise stated, any description which refers to 'a set' or 'a pair' includes a guide price for the entire set or the pair, even though the illustration may show only a single item.

An Art Deco metal wall light, with an opaque white glass shade, designed by Ray Hille, 1935, 22½in (57cm) high.
£350–420 P

◄ A pair of Art Deco glass wall lights, c1924, 11in (28cm) high.
£1,000–1,200 DRU

A Baccarat scrambled paperweight, 1845–60, 3in (7.5cm) diam.
£400–450 SWB

A Baccarat scrambled paperweight, with millefiori and filigree rods, 1845–60, 3in (7.5cm) diam.
£400–450 MLa

A Baccarat close-pack millefiori paperweight, signed and dated '1846', 3in (7.5cm) diam.
£4,000–4,500 STG

Pricing antique close-pack millefiori

The standard Baccarat paperweight would be a three-inch diameter close-pack millefiori with about seven silhouettes and a B1848 date cane. This should cost in the region of £3,000. An 1847 is slightly better; more silhouettes would also improve the price. 1846 and 1849 are rare dates and you would expect to be paying over £4,000. Lower measurements and less silhouettes would be reflected in the price.

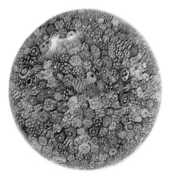

A Baccarat close-pack millefiori paperweight, marked 'B/1847', 3in (7.5cm) diam.
£2,900–3,250 S

A Baccarat paperweight, with spaced millefiori on muslin and silhouettes, dated '1847', 3in (7.5cm) diam.
£3,000–3,500 SWB

A Baccarat faceted camomile paperweight, on a star-cut base, slight chip to footrim, 1845–60, 3in (7.5cm) diam.
£2,200–2,600 C

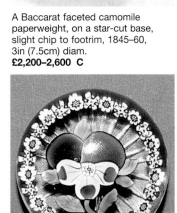

A Baccarat pansy paperweight, 1845–60, 2¼in (5.5cm) diam.
£1,500–1,800 SWB

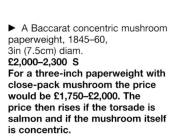

A Baccarat garlanded pompom paperweight, on a star-cut base, bruised, 1845–60, 3in (7.5cm) diam.
£2,250–2,800 C

A Baccarat dog rose paperweight, with six side facets and one top facet, 1845–60, 3in (7.5cm) diam.
£1,400–1,600 SWB

▶ A Baccarat concentric mushroom paperweight, 1845–60, 3in (7.5cm) diam.
£2,000–2,300 S
For a three-inch paperweight with close-pack mushroom the price would be £1,750–£2,000. The price then rises if the torsade is salmon and if the mushroom itself is concentric.

A Baccarat faceted double clematis paperweight, 1845–60, 2in (5cm) diam.
£1,200–1,400 SWB

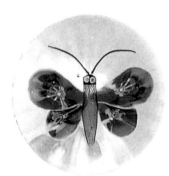

A Baccarat butterfly paperweight, on a star-cut base, 1845–60, 3in (7.5cm) diam.
£2,500–3,000 C

A Baccarat butterfly and garland paperweight, on a star-cut base, 1845–60, 3in (7.5cm) diam.
£3,600–3,900 S

A Baccarat pansy paperweight, on a star-cut base, 1845–60, 2in (5cm) diam.
£450–550 SWB

A Baccarat paperweight, 1845–60, 2¾in (7cm) diam.
£550–650 SWB

A Baccarat 'thousand petalled' rose paperweight, 1845–60, 3in (7.5cm) diam.
£4,000–4,500 C

► A Baccarat paperweight, decorated with a sulphide of Princess Anne, 1977, 3in (7.5cm) diam.
£65–75 SWB

A Baccarat garlanded buttercup paperweight, scratched, 1845–60, 2⅜in (6.5cm) diam.
£3,500–4,000 C

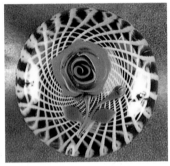

A Baccarat paperweight, with engraved base, signed and date cane, 1976, 3in (7.5cm) diam.
£450–500 STG

A Baccarat paperweight, dated '1984', 3in (7.5cm) diam.
£250–350 MLa

► A Baccarat paperweight, with a scarab beetle, signed and date cane, 1985, 3¼in (8.5cm) diam.
£400–450 STG

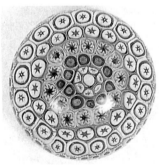

A Bacchus concentric millefiori paperweight, c1848, 3½in (9cm) diam.
£3,500–4,000 S

Canes

A cane is a glass rod made up from concentric layers of coloured glass and fused by heating. They are then cut across the grain to form the flowers in millefiori work.

A set of four Baccarat paperweights, by John Pinches of Canada Ltd, decorated with sulphides of four members of the Royal Family, each base stamped, 1976, 3in (7.5cm) diam.
£250–300 GH
Apart from Princess Diana and the Queen Mother royal paperweights are not popular. At the moment there are many of these sets on the market and prices are therefore falling.

Sweetbriar Gallery
Paperweights Ltd.
International Paperweight Dealers

<u>*Express Mail Order Service*</u>

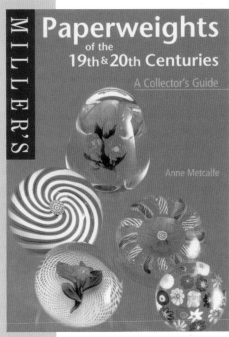

MILLER'S

Paperweights
of the
19th & 20th Centuries
A Collector's Guide

Anne Metcalfe

Anne Metcalfes' New Book
Order your copy now
(£6 Postage Included)

**Gallery Open Daily
By Appointment Only**

**Can't visit us in person?
Why not visit us on the
web!**

**106 Robin Hood Lane
Helsby
Cheshire
WA6 9NH**

**Phone: 01928 723851
Fax: 01928 724153
Mobile: 0860 907532**

■ **Quality Glass Paperweights**

■ **Buy & Sell**

■ **Gallery / Fairs / Internet**

■ **Paperweight Starter Pack
(Phone for details)**

■ **Newsletter Subscriptions
(£8 for 6 issues)**

■ **Paperweight Books**

■ **Valuation Service**

www.sweetbriar.co.uk

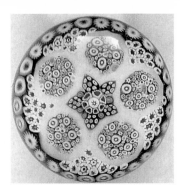

A Bacchus millefiori paperweight,
c1848, 3in (7.5cm) diam.
£4,000–5,000 S

A Caithness paperweight, by William
Manson, limited edition of 50, 1978,
3in (7.5cm) diam.
£625–700 SWB

A Caithness 'Tawny Owl'
paperweight, limited edition of 500,
1989, 3in (7.5cm) diam.
£85–95 SWB

▶ A Clichy millefiori paperweight,
with interlaced garlands, 1845–60,
3in (7.5cm) diam.
£1,100–1,300 C

A Clichy patterned millefiori
paperweight, with six facets
revealing C-scrolls, with central pink
rose and three concentric cane
circles, 1845–60, 3in (7.5cm) diam.
£3,800–4,300 C

A set of four Caithness abstract paperweights, depicting the Elements,
marked 'CT/PH' and '180/1000' and with trade label, 1973, 3in (7.5cm) diam.
£900–1,000 GH

A Caithness 'Atlantis' paperweight,
limited edition of 1,500, 1979,
3in (7.5cm) diam.
£120–135 SWB

A Clichy millefiori paperweight,
with white muslin latticinio,
1845–60, 2¼in (5.5cm) diam.
£1,500–1,600 STG

A Caithness 'Lunar III' paperweight,
designed by Colin Terris,
limited edition of 750, 1981,
3in (7.5cm) diam.
£90–100 Cai

A Clichy patterned millefiori
paperweight, with five facets,
five flutes and five roses, 1845–60,
3in (7.5cm) diam.
£3,800–4,300 SWB

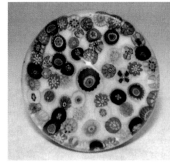

A Clichy paperweight, the scattered
millefiori on a 'sodden snow' ground,
incorporating three 'C' canes,
1845–60, 3in (7.5cm) diam.
£2,250–2,750 SWB

◀ A Clichy faceted double-overlay
close-concentric millefiori mushroom
paperweight, small chips, 1845–60,
3in (7.5cm) diam.
£4,000–4,500 C
**This paperweight is very desirable,
but has no rose. However, double-
overlays are rare, the concentric
circles are perfect and so it will
still fetch a high price.**

A Clichy garland millefiori paperweight, possibly repolished, 1845–60, 3in (7.5cm) high.
£1,200–1,600 STG

A Clichy paperweight, with a pink daisy on a spiral filigree cushion, 1845–60, 3in (7.5cm) diam.
£6,000–7,000 DLP

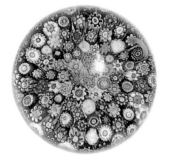

A Clichy close-pack millefiori paperweight, bruised and chipped, 1845–60, 2¾in (7cm) diam.
£2,500–2,800 C

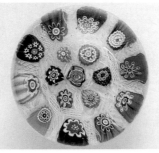

A Clichy double-overlay close-concentric millefiori mushroom paperweight, with five pink roses, 1845–60, 3in (7.5cm) diam.
£5,500–6,500 C

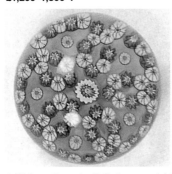

A Clichy millefiori paperweight, 1845–60, 2½in (6.5cm) diam.
£1,200–1,300 P

A Clichy patterned millefiori paperweight, 1845–60, 3½in (9cm) diam.
£1,350–1,600 S

◀ A Clichy spaced millefiori paperweight, with one pink rose, 1845–60, 3in (7.5cm) diam.
£850–950 SWB

A Clichy 'Magnum' chequer paperweight, with two white roses, 1845–60, 4in (10cm) diam.
£4,500–5,000 S

◀ A Clichy flat bouquet paperweight, slight bruise, 1845–60, 3in (7.5cm) diam.
£12,000–15,000 C

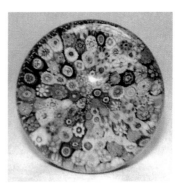

A Clichy paperweight, the tightly packed canes resting on a basket of dark blue and white staves, 1845–60, 3in (7.5cm) diam.
£2,500–2,700 SWB

A Clichy paperweight, with interlaced trefoils centred by a white and green rose, 1845–60, 3in (7.5cm) diam.
£3,200–3,400 SWB

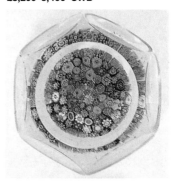

A Clichy 'Magnum' faceted close-pack millefiori mushroom paperweight, with four roses, 1845–60, 3½in (9cm) diam.
£4,500–5,500 C

A John Deacons paperweight, with a pink rose on latticinio, 1993, 2½in (6.5cm) diam.
£65–75 SWB

A John Deacons cartwheel
paperweight, 1990, 2¼in (5.5cm) diam.
£14–16 SWB

A John Deacons swirl pattern
paperweight, 1993, 2½in (6.5cm) diam.
£35–40 SWB

A John Deacons miniature
paperweight, 1993, 2in (5cm) diam.
£10–12 SWB

A Glasform peacock eye
paperweight, signed by John
Ditchfield, 1982, 3½in (9cm) diam.
£90–100 GLA

▶ Four sets of
Glasform apple
paperweights,
by John
Ditchfield, 1995,
largest 6½in
(16.5cm) high.
**£8–28 each set
GLA**

A Glasform paperweight, by John
Ditchfield, with lily decoration and
surmounted by a silver frog, 1995,
4¼in (11cm) diam.
£40–50 GLA

A William Manson 'Secret Garden'
paperweight, 1997, 3¼in (8.5cm) diam.
£175–200 SWB

A William Manson paperweight,
1997, 3¼in (8.5cm) diam.
£100–120 SWB

A Perthshire 'Annual Collection'
paperweight, dated '1976',
3in (7.5cm) diam.
£200–230 STG

A Perthshire 'Annual Collection'
paperweight, 1979, 3¼in (8.5cm) diam.
£250–300 STG

A Perthshire floral overlay
paperweight, signed 'P', 1980,
2¾in (7cm) diam.
£220–250 STG

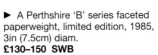

◀ A Perthshire three-colour swirl
paperweight, limited edition of 300,
1980, 3in (7.5cm) diam.
£200–250 MLa

▶ A Perthshire 'B' series faceted
paperweight, limited edition, 1985,
3in (7.5cm) diam.
£130–150 SWB

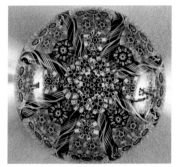

A Perthshire paperweight, marked 'PP84', limited edition, 1986, 3¼in (8.5cm) diam.
£110–120 STG

A Perthshire paperweight, marked 'PP5', 1995, 2½in (6.5cm) diam.
£30–35 SWB

A Ken Rosenfeld lampwork paperweight, signed and dated '1993', 3in (7.5cm) diam.
£300–350 MLa

A Ken Rosenfeld lampwork paperweight, signed and dated '1993', 3in (7.5cm) diam.
£300–350 MLa

A Ken Rosenfeld paperweight, signed and dated '1993', 3in (7.5cm) diam.
£300–350 MLa

◄ A Ken Rosenfeld paperweight, for the 100th anniversary of the Statue of Liberty, 1989, signed, 3in (7.5cm) diam.
£150–200 MLa

A Ken Rosenfeld paperweight, with a bouquet of tulips, signed and dated '1993', 3in (7.5cm) diam.
£300–350 MLa

A Ken Rosenfeld paperweight, with a bouquet of crocuses, signed and dated '1993', 3in (7.5cm) diam.
£300–360 MLa

A St Louis fruit paperweight, 1845–60, 3in (7.5cm) diam.
£900–1,100 S

A St Louis diamond-faceted paperweight, 1845–60, 3in (7.5cm) diam.
£1,000–1,300 SWB

A St Louis fruit paperweight, on a latticinio ground, 1845–60, 2½in (6.5cm) diam.
£850–950 SWB

A St Louis fruit paperweight, 1845–60, 2¾in (7cm) diam.
£950–1,250 C

A St Louis crown paperweight, 1845–60, 3in (7.5cm) diam.
£2,250–2,750 C

◄ A St Louis paperweight, the red and green crown with twisted ribbons, 1845–60, 3in (7.5cm) diam.
£2,500–2,800 DLP

A St Louis millefiori paperweight, with five flowerheads within a circle of canes, on an amber-flashed flat base, 1845–60, 2¾in (7cm) diam.
£750–850 MLa

A St Louis paperweight, with four radiating panels set in a white ground, 1845–60, 3in (7.5cm) diam.
£6,500–8,000 C
This paperweight is rare.

A St Louis red pelargonium paperweight, 1845–60, 2¾in (7cm) diam.
£1,500–1,800 C

A St Louis pink dahlia paperweight, 1845–60, 3in (7.5cm) diam.
£2,300–2,800 C

A St Louis flat bouquet paperweight, 1845–60, 2½in (6.5cm) diam.
£2,500–3,000 S

A St Louis faceted upright bouquet paperweight, cut with a window and three rows of printies, 1845–60, 3in (7.5cm) diam.
£1,800–2,250 C

A St Louis faceted upright bouquet paperweight, with a blue gentian and three florettes and leaves, within a spiralling torsade, 1845–60, 3in (7.5cm) diam.
£2,200–2,600 S

A St Louis faceted upright bouquet paperweight, slight chip to the edge of one printy, 1845–60, 3¼in (8.5cm) diam.
£2,250–2,650 C

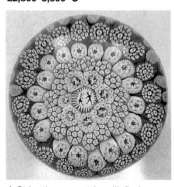

A St Louis concentric millefiori mushroom paperweight, slight bruising, dated '1848', 3in (7.5cm) diam.
£2,800–3,300 C

A St Louis concentric millefiori mushroom paperweight, 1845–60, 3in (7.5cm) diam.
£2,500–3,000 S

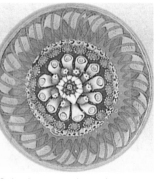

A St Louis concentric mushroom paperweight, with stardust centre cane within four rows of cogged and composite canes, dated '1848', 2¾in (7cm) diam.
£2,800–3,300 P

A St Louis concentric millefiori paperweight, with central dancing figures and a circle of dancing devil canes, 1848, 3in (7.5cm) diam.
£5,000–6,000 S

St Louis concentrics

The existence of a date in a St Louis concentric paperweight is unusual enough to add a hefty premium to its value. However, on the downside, it often pushes the other canes a little awry so that the circles are not truly concentric.

A St Louis close concentric millefiori paperweight, with large central pink cogwheel cane, 1845–60, 3in (7.5cm) diam.
£2,500–2,800 C

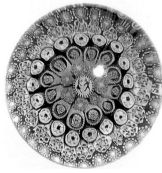

A St Louis close concentric millefiori paperweight, with central silhouette cane, signed, 1845–60, 3in (7.5cm) diam.
£2,800–3,500 C

A St Louis concentric millefiori paperweight, dated 'SL1848', 3in (7.5cm) diam.
£3,000–3,500 S

A St Louis paperweight, limited edition of 250, date cane '1988', 3in (7.5cm) diam.
£500–550 MLa

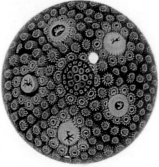

A St Louis concentric millefiori carpet-ground paperweight, inscribed '1848', 2¾in (7cm) diam.
£6,000–7,000 C
Carpet-ground St Louis paperweights are unusual and therefore expensive.

A St Louis carpet-ground patterned millefiori paperweight, 1845–60, 2¾in (7cm) diam.
£5,000–6,000 C

A Wedgwood dolphin paperweight, 1969–74, 8¼in (21cm) long.
£40–50 SWB

A Wedgwood dolphin paperweight, 1969–84, 7in (18cm) long.
£40–50 SWB

A Wedgwood Christmas paperweight, 1983, 4¼in (11cm) high.
£30–35 SWB

A Wedgwood glass elephant paperweight, 1969–84, 4¾in (12cm) long.
£50–55 SWB

A Wedgwood glass stoat paperweight, 1969–84, 6in (15cm) long.
£80–85 SWB
This is a rare paperweight.

A Whitefriars faceted paperweight, 1953, 3in (7.5cm) diam.
£325–365 SWB

◄ A Whitefriars paperweight, c1977, 2¾in (7cm) diam.
£325–360 SWB

A Whitefriars Silver Jubilee paperweight, limited edition of 1,000, 1977, 3in (7.5cm) diam.
£200–250 MLa

A Whitefriars Christmas paperweight, limited edition of 1,000, 1977, 2¾in (7cm) diam.
£350–400 MLa

A Whitefriars telephone commemorative paperweight, limited edition of 500, signed, 1977, 3in (7.5cm) diam.
£200–250 MLa

A Paul Ysart paperweight, 1930s, 3in (7.5cm) diam.
£250–350 SWB

A Paul Ysart paperweight, decorated with a flower and double garland, 1930s, 3in (7.5cm) diam.
£350–400 SWB

A Paul Ysart concentric paperweight, 1930s, 2¾in (7cm) diam.
£450–550 SWB

◄ A Paul Ysart aventurine paperweight, with 'PY' cane, c1970, 3in (7.5cm) diam.
£600–650 SWB

A Paul Ysart inkwell paperweight, c1970, 6in (15cm) high.
£900–1,000 AAV

A Paul Ysart paperweight, c1970, 2½in (6.5cm) diam.
£250–300 STG

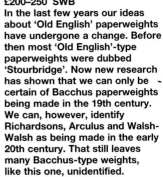

A concentric paperweight, possibly 'Old English', c1850, 3½in (9cm) diam.
£200–250 SWB
In the last few years our ideas about 'Old English' paperweights have undergone a change. Before then most 'Old English'-type paperweights were dubbed 'Stourbridge'. Now new research has shown that we can only be certain of Bacchus paperweights being made in the 19th century. We can, however, identify Richardsons, Arculus and Walsh-Walsh as being made in the early 20th century. That still leaves many Bacchus-type weights, like this one, unidentified.

A Victorian dump, c1850, 3½in (9cm) high.
£60–80 SWB

◄ A Bohemian paperweight, with scattered millefiori on muslin, c1850, 2¾in (7cm) diam.
£350–500 SWB

A Val St Lambert paperweight,
c1880, 4in (10cm) diam.
£250–300 SWB

A Victorian dump, c1890,
4in (10cm) high.
£100–150 CB

A Stourbridge concentric millefiori ink bottle
and paperweight desk set, probably
Richardsons, c1912, bottle 6in (15cm) high.
£1,500–2,000 SWB

A Victorian dump, 19thC,
4in (10cm) high.
£45–55 FD

A Vasart millefiori paperweight,
Scotland, 1946–64, 3in (7.5cm) diam.
£40–60 STG

A Murano paperweight, with 'cog'
canes, post WWII, 2½in (6.5cm) high.
£12–16 SWB

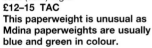

A Mdina mushroom paperweight,
signed, Malta, 1950–2000,
3½in (9cm) high.
£12–15 TAC
**This paperweight is unusual as
Mdina paperweights are usually
blue and green in colour.**

A Strathearn millefiori and
latticinio paperweight, 1964–80,
2¾in (7cm) diam.
£40–50 TAC

A Webb Corbett paperweight,
on a star-cut base, c1970,
3in (7.5cm) diam.
£30–40 SWB

A Lundberg Studios paperweight,
signed and dated '1991',
3¼in (8.5cm) diam.
£250–300 MLa

A Ferro & Lazzarini paperweight,
from a series covering the signs
of the Zodiac, Italy, 1970–2000,
3¼in (8.5cm) diam.
£50–60 SWB

An Okra 'Opal' paperweight, 1997,
3¾in (9.5cm) diam.
£75–85 SWB

▶ A Ferro & Lazzarini paperweight,
Italy, 1992, 3¼in (8.5cm) diam.
£40–50 SWB

A Flemish stained-glass panel, depicting 'Sorgheloos in Poverty', 16thC, 9in (23cm) diam.
£18,000–20,000 P

A German armorial stained-glass panel, damaged and restored, dated '1582', 14in (35.5cm) wide.
£1,500–1,650 S(Z)

An armorial stained-glass panel, by Wittnawer & Mueller, Basle, dated '1670', 13¼in (33.5cm) high.
£2,300–2,500 S(Z)

A German-Swiss stained leaded-glass panel, with double armorial bordered with flowers and heads, dated '1619', 21in (53.5cm) wide.
£4,500–5,000 RAG

◀ A German painting on glass, depicting Frederick the Great on horseback, 18thC, 7¾in (19.5cm) wide.
£750–825 P

▶ A pair of leaded-glass windows, attributed to Donald MacDonald, decorated with stencilled flowerheads and leafage, the central medallions with birds, dragonflies, sunflowers and foliage, c1890, 39½ x 21⅛in (100.5 x 54.5cm), framed.
£3,000–3,500 CNY

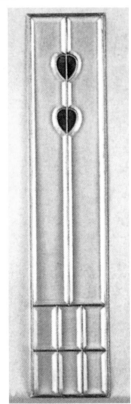

◀ A German three-panel stained-glass window, the upper part painted with foliage and blossoms in brown and beige, the lower part painted with a rural scene, late 19thC, 78in (198cm) wide.
£7,500–9,000 DORO

A pair of stained-glass panels, attributed to Loetz, c1900, 50in (127cm) high.
£3,000–3,300 S

A pair of scent bottles, decorated with enamel and gilt, with gold caps, in original fitted shagreen case, c1760, 1½in (4cm) high.
£3,000–3,500 Som

Two cylindrical scent bottles, one with viniagrette, late 18thC.
l. £450–500
r. £200–250 Som

▶ A blue flat scent bottle, decorated with gilt, c1780, 4½in (11.5cm) high.
£750–800 Som

Three clear glass scent bottles, l-r. c1830, c1780, c1840.
£200–300 each Som

Three scent bottles, c1820,
l. A silver-mounted, dual-purpose bottle, with flip lid to reveal a vinaigrette. **£600–650**
c. A clear glass bottle, with gold mounts. **£450–600**
r. A cut-glass bottle, with gold mounts. **£380–450 Som**

A French turquoise opaline glass scent bottle, with gold top and panel decorated with coloured enamels, c1830.
£1,200–1,400 BHa

l. A splatter-type, clear-cased scent bottle, c1830.
£850–900
r. A double-ended scent bottle, c1880.
£180–200 Som

Two scent bottles, with embossed silver-gilt mounts, c1840, largest 4in (10cm) high.
£200–280 each Som

A French ormolu-mounted glass scent bottle, decorated with brass filigree work, surrounded with enamelled plaques depicting various buildings, mid-19thC, 7½in (19cm) high.
£400–475 ANT

A cut-glass scent bottle, c1850, 5in (12.5cm) high.
£160–180 CB

▶ Three double-ended scent bottles, with hinged silver binocular mounts, c1860–80.
£300–350 each Som

A Clichy scent bottle, with silver top, mid-19thC, 4in (10cm) high.
£350–400 BHa

A scent bottle, with red on white overlay and gilt-decorated panels, c1860, 4¾in (12cm) high.
£720–800 Som

A clear scent bottle, with cut green overlay, with embossed silver mount, c1860.
£275–300 Som

A cut-glass scent bottle,
c1870, 3½in (9cm) high.
£90–140 ABE

A French opaline glass
scent bottle, the brass
cagework with couples
linking hands and dancing,
c1870, 1½in (4cm) high.
£180–240 LBr

A two-compartment
scent bottle, with
silver-gilt mounts, c1880,
3¾in (9.5cm) long.
£800–1,200 Som

Three scent bottles, c1870,
largest 5½in (14cm) long.
£130–200 each Som

A blue glass overlay double scent bottle, with
Continental silver tops, possibly Bohemian,
c1870, 5in (12.5cm) long.
£250–280 THOM

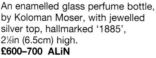

An Oxford lavender gilded scent bottle, c1880.
£100–120 Som

Three double-ended scent bottles,
with silver-gilt mounts, c1880.
£125–180 each Som

An enamelled glass perfume bottle,
by Koloman Moser, with jewelled
silver top, hallmarked '1885',
2½in (6.5cm) high.
£600–700 ALiN

◀ An opaline scent bottle, probably
by Thomas Webb, with silver-gilt
stopper by Hilliard and Thompson,
c1880, 4in (10cm) high.
£800–900 BHa

Three glass scent bottles, with brass and silver-
gilt mounts, c1875, largest 5½in (14cm) long.
£150–400 each Som

Three scent bottles, the
central bottle known as a throwaway,
Oxford lavender or teardrop, in its
original 'Otto of Roses' box, 1880,
largest 4¾in (12cm) long.
£120–280 each Som

Three single-ended scent bottles,
with embossed silver mounts,
c1880, largest 4in (10cm) high.
£150–300 each Som

Three glass scent bottles, each with vinaigrettes:
l & r. by Samson Mordan, with silver-gilt
mounts, c1880, 3¾in (9.5cm) high.
£750–800 each
c. with finger ring and chain, c1800,
2½in (6.5cm) high.
£600–650 Som

A Victorian cameo glass scent bottle,
by Thomas Webb, with silver mounts, c1880,
5in (12.5cm) long.
£1,200–1,500 THOM

A Perthshire millefiori
scent bottle and stopper,
marked 'PP74', signed
with a 'P' cane, 1984,
6½in (16.5cm) high.
£115–125 SWB

A Stourbridge cameo scent bottle, c1885,
5in (12.5cm) high.
£1,200–1,400 BHa

Six Victorian scent bottles, with glass, silver
and brass stoppers, largest 1½in (3.5cm) high.
£35–100 each VB

▶ Four hand-painted French scent bottles,
in an ormolu and cranberry glass globe,
on a marble base, 19thC.
£600–650 WAG

l. A Stourbridge satin glass scent
bottle, with silver mounts, c1887.
£900–1,100
r. An opaque scent bottle, c1880.
£150–200 Som

A hexagonal-cut table
scent bottle, with green
overlay and gilt highlights,
19thC, 7in (18cm) high.
£200–220 AAV

A pair of silver-topped
glass scent bottles,
Birmingham 1896,
6½in (16.5cm) high.
£600–650 THOM

A St Louis cranberry
and green overlay glass
scent bottle, 19thC,
7½in (19cm) high.
£375–425 MAT

A French glass scent
bottle, the stopper in the
shape of a maltese cross,
c1900, 5½in (14cm) high.
£140–160 LBr

An American cylindrical glass
scent bottle, with cork and
brass stopper and hanging
tassel, 'The Ricksecker
Cologne N.Y.' in gilt,
c1910, 9in (23cm) high.
£120–160 LBr

A René Lalique glass scent
bottle, 'Bouchon Fleurs de
Pommier', with a tiara stopper,
c1920, 5½in (14cm) high.
£6,000–7,000 LBr
**This type of scent bottle is
extremely rare and sought
after but it must be in mint
condition. Even a tiny crack
or chip can lower its value.**

▶ A Steuben Aurene glass
scent bottle, by Frederick
Carder, inscribed, c1910,
6¾in (17cm) high.
£13,500–15,000 S(NY)

A René Lalique moulded
glass scent bottle, 1926
model, 3in (7.5cm) high.
£5,500–6,500 S(NY)

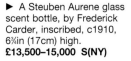

Two wrythen-moulded glass cream jugs, and a sugar
basin, c1800, jugs 2¾in (7cm) high.
£150–200 each Som

A blue glass cream jug and sugar basin, each with a
band of gilt navette decoration, probably by Jacobs,
Bristol, c1810, jug 3in (7.5cm) high.
£1,000–1,200 Som

An amethyst glass cream jug and sugar basin,
probably North Country, c1810,
jug 4½in (11.5cm) high.
£400–440 Som

l & r. Two glass cream jugs, c1830, largest 4in (10cm) high.
c. A circular glass salt, c1840, 2½in (6.5cm) high.
£100–250 each Som

A glass sugar basin, the body cold-
enamelled with a floral band, c1820,
4¼in (11cm) high.
£220–250 Som

A glass cream jug and sugar basin, both with gilt inscription 'A Present from
Newcastle 1845', slight damage, jug 3¼in (8.5cm) high.
£330–360 Som

A blue glass jug and bowl, with fluted edges and applied
white trailed decoration, c1880, jug 5in (12.5cm) high.
£200–220 BELL

A vaseline glass jug and bowl, with applied trailed
decoration and feet, c1880, jug 6in (15cm) high.
£250–300 BELL

A Davidson & Co pearline glass cream jug and sucrier,
c1890, 5½in (14cm) high.
£100–120 GLN

An opalescent wrythen-moulded glass jug and bowl,
c1890, jug 4in (10cm) high.
£140–160 CB

Loetz

When Susanna Gerstner acquired a glassworks in Klostermühle (then in Bohemia, now in the Czechoslovakian Republic), in 1852, she already had several other glass factories, which she had inherited upon the death of her previous husband, and she renamed the new business Loetz.

Under Susanna Gerstner's ownership, the factory made practical and decorative coloured glass wares and glass beads. In 1879, the business was taken over by Susanna's grandson, Max Ritter von Spaun. Toward the end of the 19th century, he became interested in the production of iridescent glass, using a technique developed by Thomas Webb and Sons. The method had been refined by Tiffany in the USA and, in fact, several Loetz pieces were described by the factory as being of Tiffany style. However, von Spaun was to develop the process in his own unique way.

Loetz glass made around the turn of the 20th century is notable for its wide variety of unusual and striking colours. Patterns suggested butterfly wings, peacock feathers, flowers, shells, grasses and leaves together with mottled, crackled and speckled effects. At the time, forms were strongly influenced by Art Nouveau styling. Wares typically displayed dents and multiple handles, while some had close-fitting metal mounts.

Although much Loetz glass was designed in-house, the company also employed outside designers, such as Jutta Sika, Franz Hofstätter and Koloman Moser.

After 1905 the Art Nouveau influence declined, and while iridescent glass continued to be made, wares became much simpler in style, and the colours much more vivid, the factory concentrating on the use of silver lustre. Trailed patterns were common, while some pieces were decorated with silver globules or silver or gold leaf suspended in clear glass over coloured glass and others displayed cracked-ice effects.

Loetz also made iridescent glass under contract for Lobmeyr until the 1920s. Some of these pieces were in their own style, and others were influenced by Tiffany. Another contract customer was the Wiener Werkstätte (Vienna Workshops).

In the 1920s and 1930s, Loetz made a variety of cased glass wares in bold colours and with distinct Art Deco styling. However, the Depression of the early 1930s led to a drop in demand for luxury glass, and in 1939 the company was declared bankrupt. Although the factory continued to produce glass during World War II, it closed for good in 1948.

Loetz glass has been widely copied, which must be borne in mind when faced with pieces displaying the maker's iridescent style.

A Loetz glass vase, internally-decorated with iridescent blue spotting, cased in cranberry-coloured glass, with applied gilt decoration to the rim, c1895, 6¾in (17cm) high.
£400–480 P

A Loetz ruby-red glass vase, decorated with iridescent turquoise and gold streaks, with open-work silvered-metal mount, c1899, 10¼in (26cm) high.
£3,500–4,000 S

A Loetz iridescent glass vase, decorated with silver-blue feathers between swirled borders, inscribed, c1900, 9in (23cm) high.
£12,000–14,000 S(NY)

A Loetz iridescent glass vase, decorated with light peacock blue spotting on a dark blue ground, c1900, 8¼in (21cm) high.
£400–450 RTo

▶ A pink opal iridescent glass vase, probably Loetz, applied with gold trailed decoration, c1900, 6in (15cm) high.
£300–350 MoS

◀ A Loetz iridescent glass vase, decorated with meandering bands of amber, orange and silver-blue feathering, against a golden splashed ground, signed 'Loetz Austria', c1900, 4in (10cm) high.
£500–600 P

A Loetz iridescent glass vase, with pinched rim, decorated with peacock-blue swags on a green ground, overlaid with silver stylized flowers, two pieces of silver lacking, c1900, 7in (18cm) high.
£1,000–1,200 RTo

A Loetz dimpled amber glass vase, decorated with iridescent silvery-blue bands and applied with butterscotch glass drips with iridescent silver-blue streaks, inscribed 'Loetz Austria', c1900, 7in (18cm) high.
£3,000–3,500 S(NY)

A Loetz iridescent glass vase, decorated with swirling iridescent green/blue bands and silver applique of flowers and foliage, inscribed 'Loetz Austria', c1900, 9in (23cm) high.
£1,400–1,600 BIG

A Loetz Art glass vase, the amber cased to luminescent crimson red glass, with lustrous golden combed iridescent surface, recessed pontil, marked 'Loetz Austria', c1900, 12½in (32cm) high.
£2,000–2,500 SK(B)

A Loetz deep blue glass vase, with random bubble pattern, decorated with a band of iridescent combed trails, cased in clear glass, the base drilled, c1900, 14½in (37cm) high.
£450–500 CSK

A Loetz Art Nouveau glass-shaded lamp, c1900, 23in (58.5cm) high.
£7,000–8,000 ART

A Loetz iridescent glass and Gustav Gurschner bronze lamp, impressed marks, c1900, 25in (63.5cm) high.
£8,000–9,500 S(NY)

A Loetz iridescent glass vase, in a pewter mount, c1900, 12in (30.5cm) high.
£300–350 P

A Loetz iridescent glass vase, designed by Franz Hofstätter, c1900, 8¼in (21cm) high.
£8,500–10,000 S(NY)

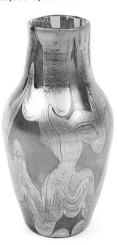

A Loetz iridescent glass vase, etched mark, c1900, 6in (15cm) high.
£620–690 P(B)

A Loetz iridescent glass vase, c1900, 8in (20.5cm) high.
£1,200–1,500 ASA

A Loetz iridescent glass shell-shaped vase, c1900, 10in (25.5cm) wide.
£225–250 MJW

◄ A Loetz milky glass bowl, for J & L Lobmeyr, internally-decorated with bands of green and blue-mauve, washed with purple/gold iridescence, 1900, 4in (10cm) high.
£9,500–11,000 S

A Loetz clear glass vase, the dimpled body washed with golden/pale blue iridescence and applied with five trailing lily pads in red and iridescent stripes, engraved mark 'Loetz Austria', c1900, 8¼in (21cm) high.
£2,000–2,200 S

A Loetz glass vase, the pale yellow glass washed with bands of peach and purple iridescence at the foot and neck, the central section with lustrous ripples of pale green/gold iridescence, the underside with engraved mark 'Loetz Austria', c1900, 7½in (19cm) high.
£4,000–4,500 S

A Loetz yellow iridescent glass vase, inscribed 'Loetz Austria', c1900, 9¾in (25cm) high.
£10,000–11,000 S(NY)

A Loetz shell-shaped yellow/pink glass candleholder, with blue iridescence, the interior with moulded mark 'Regsns 787802 FGC', c1900, 12in (30.5cm) high.
£700–800 S

A Loetz iridescent glass footed bowl, with a twisted stem on a pad foot, c1900, 8½in (21.5cm) high.
£2,000–2,400 P

A Loetz glass vase, with applied handles, c1900, 8in (20.5cm) high.
£600–700 ABS

A Loetz iridescent green glass bowl, c1900, 4½in (11.5cm) high.
£240–270 RUSK

A Loetz red and white glass vase, by Jutta Sika, c1905, 8½in (21.5cm) high.
£9,000–10,000 S
Art glass items by the Bohemian firm of Loetz are always particularly sought-after.

► A Loetz four-handled glass vase, the pale green washed with purple, with blue and green/gold iridescence, engraved mark 'Loetz Austria', c1910, 9¾in (25cm) high.
£3,000–3,500 S

A Loetz glass vase, decorated with yellow, violet, peacock blue/green and gold iridescence, etched mark 'Loetz Austria', c1902, 9in (23cm) high.
£3,500–4,000 S

A Loetz iridescent glass vase, Papillon, with silver deposit overlay, c1905, 4in (10cm) high.
£550–650 MoS

A Loetz cobalt blue glass vase, etched with a lozenge pattern, c1907, 7in (18cm) diam.
£4,000–4,400 DORO

A Loetz iridescent glass and bronze chandelier, the shades decorated with peach oil spots and emerald green stringing, c1900, 24in (61cm) high.
£8,000–8,800 S(NY)

A Loetz glass bowl, the design attributed to Koloman Moser, internally- decorated with bubbles and silver iridescence, c1910, 11in (28cm) diam.
£1,800–2,000 P

Lustres

A pair of table lustres, each with baluster-shaped stems, cut with diamond and faceted bands, hung with two tiers of faceted drops, on stepped square bases, some damage, early 19thC, 11in (28cm) high.
£400–450 DN

A pair of cut lead crystal glass lustre vases, the shaped supports with fan-cut rims, star-cut feet and pillar-cut drops, c1810, 8in (20.5cm) high.
£1,500–1,800 Som

◀ A pair of cut lead crystal glass candle lustres, c1810, 9in (23cm) high.
£1,500–1,800 CB

A lustre, the cut baluster stem on a square-cut pedestal foot, the sconce with crenellated rim, c1820, 10in (25.5cm) high.
£500–550 Som

A pair of lustres, on coloured marble socles, c1830, 12in (30.5cm) high.
£1,600–1,800 GH

A pair of Bohemian green lustres, with opaque white turned-over tops, gilt leaf vines, with feather gilt work, mid-19thC, 10in (25.5cm) high.
£480–550 GAK

A turquoise opaque candlestick, with clear turquoise lustre drops and buttons, on a black base, c1840, 9in (23cm) high.
£350–400 CB

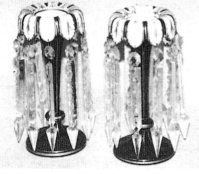

A pair of Victorian blue lustres, 13in (33cm) high.
£1,000–1,200 BRK

▶ A pair of Bohemian lustres, c1890, 15in (38cm) high.
£2,500–3,000 LT

A pair of Victorian cranberry lustre vases, decorated in gilt and enamel colours, with concentric rings of lustre drops, c1890, 15in (38cm) high.
£650–750 Mit

Sets/pairs

Unless otherwise stated, any description which refers to 'a set' or 'a pair' includes a guide price for the entire set or the pair, even though the illustration may show only a single item.

◀ A pair of Bohemian opaque white overlay tulip-shaped lustres, decorated with floral sprays and enriched in gilt, c1860, 10in (25.5cm) high.
£1,600–1,800 L

A green with white overlay lustre, c1880, 12in (30.5cm) high.
£220–250 CB

A pair of cut-glass table lustres, c1880, 10in (25.5cm) high.
£675–800 CB

◀ A garniture of cut-glass lustres, comprising a three-light gilt-metal-mounted candelabrum and a pair of lustres, damaged and repaired, 19thC, tallest 15¾in (40cm) high.
£1,200–1,500 S(S)

A pair of Continental pink satin lustre vases, with gold decoration, each baluster body hung with clear prism drops, c1890, 11in (28cm) high.
£320–380 Bea

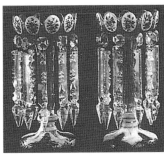

A pair of Richardson & Sons white overlay lustres, with hipped gilt rims, latticed panels with gilt detail, the bowls and domed bases decorated with stylized flowers, hung with clear glass prismatic drops, c1870, 13in (33cm) high.
£1,400–1,600 GAK

A pair of cut-glass and ormolu table lustres, each ormolu support formed as a temple containing an urn and pineapple, surmounted by a sconce and drip pans cut with bands of diamonds, hung with faceted button and icicle drops, some damage, 19thC, 12½in (32cm) high.
£1,200–1,400 P

A pair of English ruby and white overlay lustres, enriched in gilt, slight damage, late 19thC, 10in (25.5cm) high.
£600–700 C

A pair of Bohemian ruby two-tier lustres, decorated with polychrome floral enamelling embellished with gilt, with turned ebonized bases and glass domes, late 19thC, 14½in (37cm) high.
£1,000–1,200 WIL

▶ A pair of Bohemian clear table lustres, each with overlaid enamel oval plaques, alternately painted with portrait busts of ladies and flowers, surrounded by gilt overlaid foliate borders, late 19thC, 14in (35.5cm) high.
£1,800–2,000 RTo

Mugs & Tankards

A south German or Bohemian enamelled blue-tinted mug, painted in opaque white with four panels of dots enclosing applied glass beads, restored, early 17thC, 4in (10cm) high.
£1,600–2,000 S

A coin tankard, with trailed neck and base, gadrooning, plain conical foot, applied loop handle, silver coin in base, c1780, 5½in (13.5cm) high.
£680–750 Som

A Nailsea mug, with opaque white splashes and a band around rim, c1810, 3¾in (9.5cm) high.
£400–450 Som

A Venetian enamelled mug, possibly made for the Turkish market, c1730, 4⅛in (11.5cm) high.
£2,300–2,600 S

A Continental *milchglas* mug, painted in coloured enamels with a young man within a scroll cartouche, flanked by flowers and leaves, late 18thC, 5½in (14cm) high.
£350–400 HOLL

An opaline mug, c1830, 3in (7.5cm) high.
£170–200 CB

◀ A pressed glass mug, by H Greener, depicting oarsman Edward Hanlon seated in his boat, 1880, 4in (10cm) high.
£100–200 Som

▶ A Bohemian cranberry glass tankard, with white overlay and applied handle, c1870, 4¾in (12cm) high.
£250–300 CB

A central European opaque mug, the flared thistle-shaped white body with iron-red pulled decoration, with applied opalescent loop handle and crimped footrim, c1750, 5½in (14cm) high.
£320–380 C

An Irish mug, with a band of small cut diamonds below rim, the base with flute cutting, engraved, c1800, 3½in (9cm) high.
£170–200 Som

Two mercury glass mugs, with inscriptions, c1860, 3½in (9cm) high.
£125–145 each MJW

Paperweights

The most striking thing about the paperweight market over the last five years is the continued upward trend of French antique, English Bacchus, Paul Ysart and Whitefriars weights.

The supply of French antique weights at auction in England is dwindling, as auction houses filter their best examples, and big collections, to New York where the main market seems to be. This is bad news for Europe.

Of the three main French makers, Clichy seem to have the edge over the others, although individual types of all three continue to create excitement when they appear on the market. Any Clichy paperweight with a rose, or better still roses, or even better than that, roses in the rare yellow, green or violet colours will create even more of a stir. Scrambled weights of Clichy and St Louis are suddenly racing ahead in price, leaving Baccarat at a standstill. It is the possible addition of a rose, a C-cane, a silhouette in St Louis or an SL and date cane, which make these weights interesting. At the moment antique millefiori seem to be moving ahead smartly, leaving behind the beautiful flower weights. In particular it is noticeable that Baccarat garlanded flowers seem to have lost their edge. The usual thing in the prices of antique weights is that they will leap-frog each other. Those currently-unpopular Baccarat flowers, St Louis upright bouquets, and St Louis fruits, will suddenly become sought-after and their prices too will rise.

In the modern second-hand market it is mainly American weights that stand out as being on a rising price spiral. Stankard weights are now so expensive, it is difficult to imagine them increasing much more. Anything at all nice will cost over £1,000 and a good bouquet could easily command £2,000, with the botanical varieties rising even higher. Rick Ayotte's birds are creating a lot of interest at auction, and fetching more than his current issues. Chris Buzzini is also a maker to watch. Whitefriars have already been spotted and anything fine or a bit different is going for over £300. Paul Ysart prices are rising fast and are very volatile. As always it is the very best pieces which rocket, £3,000 is quite common now for the better Bacchus weights and interesting examples are easily fetching £4,000. There is beginning to be some interest in unidentified English weights too, some of which are as good as a Bacchus, but they remain at £300 plus.

All in all there is plenty of excitement in the world of paperweights. **Anne Metcalfe**

BACCARAT

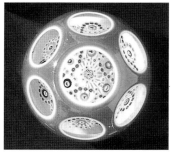

A Baccarat paperweight, with double overlay millefiori garlands and silhouettes, 1845–60, 3¼in (8.5cm) diam.
£4,750–5,250 DLP

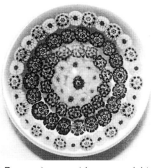

A Baccarat concentric paperweight, with a central white rose, 1845–60, 2½in (6.5cm) diam.
£500–600 SWB

A Bacarrat close-pack mushroom faceted paperweight, on a star-cut base, 1845–60, 2½in (6.5cm) diam.
£1,600–1,800 SWB

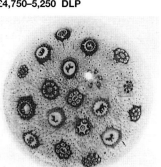

A Baccarat pink and white carpet-ground scattered millefiori paperweight, 1845–60, 3in (7.5cm) diam.
£7,500–8,500 CSK

A Baccarat patterned paperweight, 1845–60, 3in (7.5cm) diam.
£5,000–5,500 P

A Baccarat faceted sulphide paperweight, depicting Louis XIV within a garland of green and white and pink and white canes, on a star-cut base, 1845–60, 3in (7.5cm) diam.
£500–550 C

A Baccarat millefiori paperweight, with coloured canes forming garlands, c1845–60, 3in (7.5cm) diam.
£700–800 MLa

A Baccarat close-pack millefiori paperweight, signed 'B', dated '1847', 2¾in (7cm) diam.
£1,800–2,000 SWB

A Baccarat paperweight, with flower and silhouette canes, on white ribbon latticinio, with 'B' signature, dated '1847', 3in (7.5cm) diam.
£3,000–3,500 STG

A Baccarat scattered millefiori paperweight, with large brightly coloured canes including silhouettes of a monkey, elephant, cockerel, horse, goat, dog and butterflies, with a cane inscribed 'B 1847', very slight surface wear, 3¼in (8.5cm) diam.
£2,500–3,000 C

A Baccarat close-pack millefiori paperweight, with nine silhouettes, dated '1847' in cane, 3in (7.5cm) diam.
£2,000–2,500 SWB

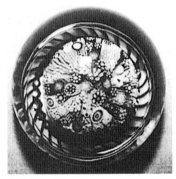

A Baccarat close-pack mushroom paperweight, with blue torsade, 1845–60, 2¾in (7cm) diam.
£1,500–1,850 SWB

A Baccarat scrambled paperweight, the clear glass set with candy stripes and other coloured cut canes and gauzes, chipped, 1845–60, 2½in (6.5cm) diam.
£250–300 HSS

A Baccarat spaced millefiori paperweight, with ten silhouettes, signed 'B', dated 1848, 2½in (6.5cm) diam.
£1,500–1,750 SWB

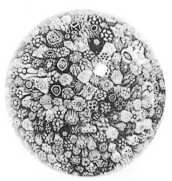

A Baccarat close-pack millefiori paperweight, with brightly coloured canes in shades of blue, lime green, pink and white, with a cane inscribed 'B 1847', 3¼in (8.5cm) diam.
£2,600–3,200 C

> Items in the Paperweight section have been arranged in factory order, with non-specific pieces appearing at the end of each sub-section.

A Baccarat close-pack mushroom paperweight, with blue and white outer torsade, on a star-cut base, 1845–60, 3in (7.5cm) diam.
£1,750–2,000 STG

Baccarat scrambleds

Although Baccarat scrambleds are beautiful paperweights they have not moved up in price like Clichy and St Louis scrambleds, because the supply has remained sufficient to satisfy demand, and they vary so little – unlike the other two factories.

A Baccarat paperweight, the dark red clematis with furrowed pointed petals, honeycomb centre cane and green leaves and stem, 1845–60, 3in (7.5cm) diam.
£850–950 MLa

A Baccarat paperweight, with a
cerise dog rose with white petal
edges, six side facets and one top
facet, stem and 11 leaves, 1845–60,
3in (7.5cm) diam.
£1,400–1,600 SWB

A Baccarat faceted red paperweight,
with a silhouette of Queen Victoria,
inscribed, 1845–60, 3¼in (8.5cm) diam.
£1,150–1,350 SWB
This is a rare paperweight.

A Baccarat garlanded white double
clematis paperweight, the flower
with a red, white and blue centre,
set within a garland of alternate
blue-centred white and claret canes,
on a star-cut base, damaged,
1845–60, 2½in (6.5cm) diam.
£1,000–1,200 C

A Baccarat paperweight, with central
blue and white primrose, 1845–60,
2¾in (7cm) diam.
£1,250–1,500 SWB

A Baccarat paperweight, with a red
and white flower in a garland
surround, 1845–60, 2¾in (7cm) diam.
£2,300–2,500 SWB

A Baccarat pansy paperweight,
Type III, 1845–60, 2in (5cm) diam.
£450–500 SWB

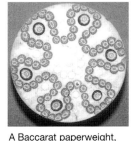

A Baccarat pansy
paperweight, Type III, with
two purple petals and three
smaller yellow petals with
red tips and blue stamens,
around a white stardust
centre, the stem with two
leaf sprigs and a bud,
1845–60, 3in (7.5cm) diam.
£750–850 P

A Baccarat paperweight,
with red, white and blue
millefiori pattern, 1974,
3in (7.5cm) diam.
£300–350 SWB
Baccarat paperweights
c1970–80 sell for less
money than the more
modern ones. Prices are
quite volatile because of
the exorbitant prices of
the new paperweights.

A Baccarat paperweight,
with a snail set in a dark
ground amongst various
leaves and flowers, limited
edition of 300, 1977,
2¾in (7cm) diam.
£275–350 SWB

A Baccarat paperweight,
with a cobra, limited
edition of 300, 1979,
3in (7.5cm) diam.
£380–450 SWB

Sweetbriar Gallery
International Paperweight Dealers

Always wanted to collect

PAPERWEIGHTS?

Here's your chance!

CONTACT US FOR A FREE
COLOUR BROCHURE

Mrs Anne Metcalfe
Sweetbriar House, Robin Hood Lane
Helsby, Cheshire WA6 9NH
Tel 01928 723851 Fax 01928 724153
Mobile 0860 907532
Email: sweetbr@globalnet.co.uk
Internet: http://www.sweetbriar.co.uk

BACCHUS

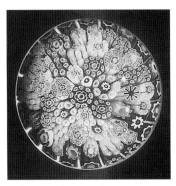

A Bacchus close-pack millefiori paperweight, c1848, 3in (7.5cm) diam.
£2,500–2,800 DLP

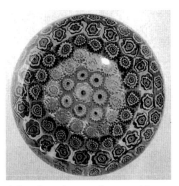

A Bacchus close-pack concentric millefiori paperweight, slight wear, c1848, 3½in (9cm) diam.
£2,200–2,400 C

A Bacchus close-pack millefiori paperweight, with star and open flower canes, within a row of white canes with green centres, some damage, c1848, 3½in (9cm) diam.
£3,500–3,800 S

CAITHNESS

A Caithness Starbase paperweight, designed by Colin Terris, limited edition of 500, issued 1971, 3in (7.5cm) diam.
£300–325 Cai

A Caithness May Dance paperweight, 1972, 3in (7.5cm) diam.
£35–40 SWB
This is one of the first paperweights made by Caithness. They were made in different colours annually from 1972 and are still in production today.

A Caithness engraved paperweight of Silver Jubilee Fleet Review, designed by Colin Terris, limited edition of 100, issued 1977, 3¼in (8.5cm) diam.
£180–200 Cai

A Caithness Jubilee Floating Crown multi-faceted paperweight, designed by Colin Terris, limited edition of 1,000, issued 1977, 3in (7.5cm) diam.
£120–135 Cai

A Caithness black obsidian paperweight, surmounted by a silver lizard, No. 34 from a limited edition of 50, 1978, 3in (7.5cm) diam.
£900–1,000 SWB
This is a very unusual paperweight.

◀ A Caithness Robin multi-faceted lampwork paperweight, designed by Colin Terris and William Manson, limited edition of 500, issued 1981, 3in (7.5cm) diam.
£125–150 Cai

A Caithness Swan faceted lampwork paperweight, by William Manson, limited edition of 100, signed, '79' date cane in base, 3in (7.5cm) diam.
£250–300 MLa

A Caithness Two Salmon paperweight, designed and made by William Manson, limited edition of 100, dated '1984', 3in (7.5cm) diam.
£250–275 MLa

CLICHY

A Clichy spaced millefiori paperweight, with three roses on a turquoise ground, 1845–60, 3in (7.5cm) diam.
£2,400–2,700 STG

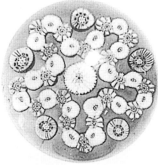

A Clichy patterned millefiori paperweight, on a red ground, 1845–60, 2¾in (7cm) diam.
£1,600–1,800 C

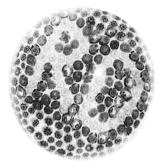

A Clichy carpet-ground initial paperweight, with the letters 'R D', 1845–60, 3½in (9cm) diam.
£4,250–5,000 CSK
This is a very rare and unusual paperweight, probably unique. The fact that it incorporates initials makes it less desirable, but the totally different pattern, including many roses, adds to its value.

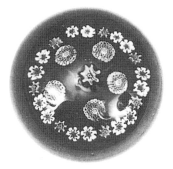

A Clichy paperweight, with coloured 'pastry mould' canes on a turquoise ground, 1845–60, 2½in (6.5cm) diam.
£700–800 MLa

A Clichy patterned millefiori paperweight, the three circles of canes in shades of pink, turquoise and white, surrounded by five large white and blue canes, on a blue ground, slight damage, 1845–60, 3in (7.5cm) diam.
£1,150–1,350 C

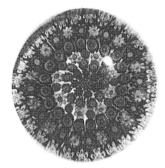

A Clichy close-pack concentric millefiori pedestal paperweight, on a clear circular foot, 1845–60, 3in (7.5cm) diam.
£2,500–3,000 CSK

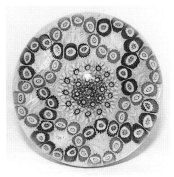

A Clichy paperweight, with interlaced quatrefoils on a muslin ground, 1845–60, 3in (7.5cm) diam.
£1,350–1,550 SWB

A Clichy paperweight, with five C-scrolls in different coloured millefiori, five facets and a central pink rose, on a star-cut base, 1845–60, 2¾in (7cm) diam.
£1,200–1,500 SWB

A Clichy paperweight, with a small central white rose cane, 1845–60, 2½in (6.5cm) diam.
£550–600 STG

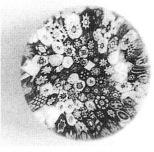

A Clichy close-pack millefiori miniature paperweight, with three roses contained in a basket of blue, white and purple staves, 1845–60, 1½in (4cm) diam.
£2,000–2,300 S(S)

Clichy rose

The Clichy Rose has become highly collectable. The most common being the pink rose with green sepals and, of course, more than one rose will increase the value of the paperweight. In America only Clichy paperweights with roses are sold.

A Clichy paperweight, with spaced concentric garlands and a central pink rose, 1845–60, 2½in (6.5cm) diam.
£650–700 SWB

A Clichy paperweight, with concentric coloured canes on a turquoise ground, 1845–60, 2¼in (5.5cm) diam.
£1,200–1,350 SWB

A Clichy chequer spaced millefiori paperweight, with a central pink and green rose and two rows of colourful pastry-mould canes, on an upset muslin ground, 1845–60, 2in (5cm) diam.
£950–1,050 P

A Clichy chequer paperweight, with a pink rose and a hidden pink rose, 1845–60, 2½in (6.5cm) diam.
£1,800–2,000 SWB

A Clichy paperweight, with a garland of pastry-mould canes, seven canes including pink and green Clichy rose cane, 1845–60, 3in (7.5cm) diam.
£700–800 STG

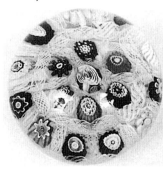

A Clichy chequer paperweight, with a central pink rose, green sepals and various pastry-mould canes, 1845–60, 2¾in (7cm) diam.
£1,350–1,500 SWB

A Clichy garlanded flat bouquet paperweight, with two pink pastry-mould canes and a red and green rose on a bed of leaves, the garland with six large red pastry-mould canes separated by groups of three turquoise canes, on an upset muslin ground, 1845–60, 3in (7.5cm) diam.
£1,300–1,500 P

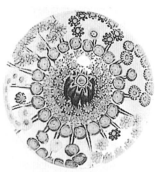

A Clichy patterned millefiori paperweight, the central pink pastry-mould within two circles of green, pink and blue, with an outer circle of pink roses and six C-scrolls in pink, blue, green, purple and white, on a star-cut base, slight chips to foot rim, 1845–60, 3in (7.5cm) diam.
£2,200–2,500 C

A Clichy swirl millefiori paperweight, the four central white and green cut canes surrounded by two concentric circles of coloured canes, 1845–60, 2½in (6.5cm) diam.
£650–750 HSS

A Clichy swirl paperweight, with alternate turquoise and white staves radiating from a central pink and red pastry-mould cane, lined in white with a ring of green and white inner canes, scratched, 1845–60, 3in (7.5cm) diam.
£950–1,050 HSS

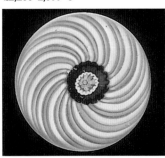

A Clichy swirl paperweight, with alternate turquoise and white staves radiating from a central claret cane, 1845–60, 1¾in (4.5cm) diam.
£450–550 C

A Clichy paperweight, with a purple, black and white spoke design, 1845–60, 3¼in (8.5cm) diam.
£6,500–7,500 DLP

A Clichy paperweight, with a turquoise and white swirl pattern, 1845–60, 3in (7.5cm) diam.
£1,200–1,500 DLP

GLASFORM

◀ Three Glasform paperweights, with trail and feathered patterns, signed, c1994, 3½in (9cm) diam.
£30–40 each GLA

Two Glasform frog paperweights, with green and purple lustre effect, c1995, 4¼in (11cm) high.
£50–60 GLA

WILLIAM MANSON

A William Manson paperweight, with a red rose on a white background, signed, limited edition of 250, c1980, 2½in (6.5cm) diam.
£220–250 MLa

A William Manson paperweight, with aventurine sea horse in amethyst glass, with front facet, c1985, 3in (7.5cm) high.
£185–210 SWB

A William Manson paperweight, with a snake and a ladybird, 1995, 2¾in (7cm) diam.
£250–300 SWB

Cross Reference
See Colour Review

NEW ENGLAND GLASS CO

A New England Glass Co paperweight, with a lampwork cluster of five yellow and red pears, with dark green leaves and white latticinio basket, c1860, 2¼in (5.5cm) diam.
£350–380 MLa

A New England Glass Co paperweight, with a white latticinio ground, slight damage, c1860, 3in (7.5cm) diam.
£1,500–1,700 S(NY)

A New England Glass Co paperweight, with violet-coloured poinsettia on a spiral filigree cushion, c1860, 3in (7.5cm) diam.
£875–1,150 DLP

Lampwork

This term is used for all those paperweights made by melting a rod of coloured glass and shaping it, usually into the form of a flower, which is then encased in clear or coloured glass to make the complete weight.

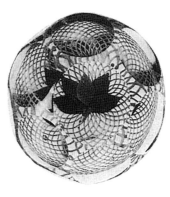

▶ A New England Glass Co faceted leaf spray paperweight, set with a cluster of one pink, two green and two blue leaves above a white latticinio ground, cut with top and two rows of six side windows, c1860, 2½in (6.5cm) diam.
£500–600 P

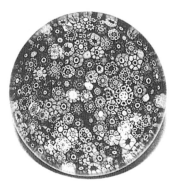

A Perthshire close-pack paperweight, limited edition of 400, dated '1973', 2½in (6.5cm) diam.
£250–300 SWB

► A Perthshire faceted flat bouquet paperweight, with a white double clematis, a red and white wild rose and three blue flowers with stardust centres, cut with nine windows, on a star-cut base, signed 'P' cane, with certificate No. 1 from a limited edition of 450, issued in 1979, 3in (7.5cm) diam, boxed.
£175–225 P

A Perthshire floral spray paperweight, with a central pink flower, 1984, 2½in (6.5cm) diam.
£125–145 SWB

Miller's is a price GUIDE not a price LIST

A Perthshire hollow-blown squirrel paperweight, limited edition of 200, 1984, 3in (7.5cm) diam.
£300–350 SWB
One of an annual series of hollow-blown weights featuring different birds or animals.

A series of ten Perthshire hollow-blown faceted paperweights, enclosing a lampwork swan, seal, squirrel, penguin and bald eagle, with various coloured flashes, limited edition of 250–400, 1973–87, largest 3½in (9cm) diam.
£325–350 each SWB

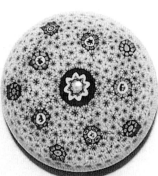

A Perthshire carpet-ground paperweight, No. 40 from a limited edition of 300, 1994, 2½in (6.5cm) diam.
£120–150 SWB

A Perthshire millefiori inkwell paperweight, 1969–94, 5½in (14cm) high.
£200–220 STG

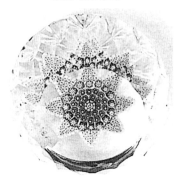

A Perthshire star paperweight, faceted overall and with a star-cut base, limited edition of 300, signed 'P', dated 1982, 2½in (6.5cm) diam.
£130–160 MLa

Contemporary paperweights

Contemporary paperweights are often overshadowed by their 'loftier cousins' the antique weights who, because of their age, lay claim to a superiority which may not be justified by better craftsmanship. Modern weights on the other hand are not only as beautiful but more available and within the reach of the collector's pocket. Thus they are widely collected and very much sought after.

Modern paperweights are produced in many parts of the world. The French Baccarat and St Louis factories produced some of the finest antique specimens and are still producing weights today. In the UK Caithness and Perthshire are probably the best known, although Whitefriars, now a subsidiary of Caithness, still produces a small range and some of the crystal manufacturers also make a few weights. It could be argued that some of the best weights now come from America where the trend is towards small workshops.

The form of modern weights has developed widely since the war. Traditional millefiori designs are still produced, largely by Perthshire and the French factories. Caithness and some of the Continental artists also produce a large range of abstract designs in both limited and unlimited versions. There has also been a substantial move towards lampwork design, led by Paul Ysart, the 'father' of modern Scottish paperweights. Many self-employed glass artists, particularly in the USA, produce wonderful examples of this work.

Contemporary paperweight makers identify their work with an initial cane or an etched logo. Other artists engrave their signature on the weight. However, care should be taken when buying as there are many fakes.

ST LOUIS

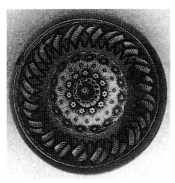

A St Louis concentric millefiori mushroom paperweight, the central florette cane within rows of white, red, blue and green coloured millefiori canes, with an outer row of hollow white cogwheel canes lined in red, divided by a single dark blue cane, with a torsade of white corkscrew cable, within a cobalt blue spiral thread, signed and dated 'S.L. 1848', on a star-cut base, chipped, 3in (7.5cm) diam.
£2,500–3,000 HSS

A St Louis concentric millefiori mushroom paperweight, the tuft with five circles of canes in shades of blue, pink, white and green, around a white centre, bruise to side, 1845–60, 3in (7.5cm) diam.
£1,800–2,200 C

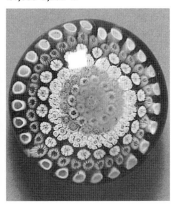

A St Louis millefiori paperweight, with green, red, white and blue canes enclosed by a basket of turquoise canes with white centres, slight damage, 1845–60, 3in (7.5cm) diam.
£1,300–1,600 S

A St Louis paperweight, with a bouquet of flowers and leaves encircled by a blue and opaque white torsade, on a star-cut base, slight wear, 1845–60, 2¾in (7cm) diam.
£1,800–2,000 WW

A St Louis crown paperweight, 1845–60, 2¾in (7cm) diam.
£1,750–2,000 CSK

Modern millefiori

Most modern makers worldwide make more lampwork paperweights than millefiori. Two American makers produce millefiori only: Parabelle and Drew Ebelhare. In Scotland Perthshire are famed for their fine millefiori work. In France both Baccarat and St Louis produce quality millefiori, but they produce far more lampwork.

A St Louis paperweight, with a pink chrysanthemum in clear glass, 1845–60, 3¼in (8.5cm) diam.
£1,500–1,800 DLP

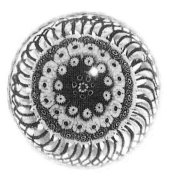

A St Louis concentric millefiori mushroom paperweight, on a star-cut base, 1845–60, 3in (7.5cm) diam.
£2,000–2,300 CSK

A St Louis crown paperweight, the red and green twisted ribbon alternating with white entwined latticinio thread, radiating from a white, green and blue centre, 1845–60, 2½in (6.5cm) diam.
£1,750–2,000 C

A St Louis paperweight, the pattern in the form of an upright bouquet of red flowers, with a blue torsade, 1845–60, 3in (7.5cm) diam.
£2,250–2,500 SWB

A St Louis faceted paperweight, with a white flower on latticinio, 1845–60, 3in (7.5cm) diam.
£2,000–2,300 SWB

A St Louis garlanded flat bouquet paperweight, with blue and red canes, 1845–60, 2½in (6.5cm) diam.
£500–600 P

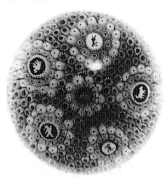

A St Louis green carpet-ground concentric millefiori paperweight, 1845–60, 2½in (6.5cm) diam.
£5,000–6,000 CSK

A St Louis salamander paperweight, with a gilt reptile lying coiled on top of a green-tinted hollow sphere, 1845–60, 3½in (9cm) diam.
£3,000–3,500 C

A St Louis paperweight, with a red rose and green stem, limited edition of 350, signature cane, with a certificate, 1978, 3¼in (8.5cm) diam.
£280–350 STG

A St Louis dahlia paperweight, the flower with overlapping rows of pink striped petals, blue and white cogwheel cane and green leaves, 1845–60, 1¾in (4.5cm) diam.
£1,150–1,300 P

A St Louis faceted paperweight, with a sulphide of Napoleon III in profile, within a torsade of red and white spirals, with three rows of circular printies around a top window, titled 'L 'n bonaparte', 1845–60, 3½in (9cm) diam.
£550–650 P

A St Louis paperweight, set with garlands of clematis flowers, 1845–60, 3in (7.5cm) diam.
£3,000–3,500 STG
An example of this type with a central flower as well as an outer border is rare.

▶ A St Louis bouquet paperweight, with three bundled canes representing flowers and five yellow-green leaves, in clear glass, on a strawberry-cut base, 1845–60, 2½in (6.5cm) diam.
£550–600 SWB

A St Louis faceted paperweight, with three stylized millefiori cane flowerheads on green leaves, within a circle of canes, on a flat base, 1845–60, 2¾in (7cm) diam.
£750–850 MLa

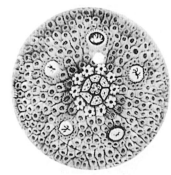

A St Louis green carpet-ground millefiori paperweight, with a central set-up in red and white, surrounded by six silhouette canes, thread of cullet to one side, 1845–60, 2¾in (7cm) diam.
£3,000–3,500 C

A St Louis pelargonium paperweight, the flower with a yellow, brown and green centre, surrounded by five pink heart-shaped petals edged in white and with four green sepals between, 1845–60, 3in (7.5cm) diam.
£1,300–1,500 C

WEDGWOOD

A Wedgwood pink frog paperweight, 1969–84, 4½in (11.5cm) high.
£45–55 SWB

A Wedgwood paperweight, decorated with a bust of Lord Mountbatten of Burma, 1969–84, 3in (7.5cm) diam.
£60–70 SWB

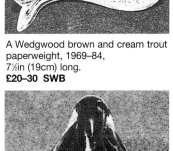

A Wedgwood brown and cream trout paperweight, 1969–84, 7½in (19cm) long.
£20–30 SWB

A Wedgwood panda paperweight, 1969–84, 3½in (9cm) high.
£50–60 SWB

A Wedgwood bird paperweight, marked, 1969–84, 3in (7.5cm) high.
£20–25 SWB

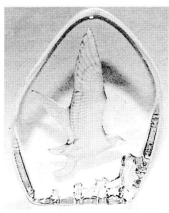

A Wedgwood green penguin paperweight, 1969–84, 4½in (11.5cm) high.
£40–50 SWB

A Wedgwood clear glass polar bear paperweight, 1969–84, 5in (12.5cm) long.
£40–50 SWB

A Wedgwood clear glass paperweight, decorated with a seagull, 1969–84, 4½in (11.5cm) high.
£20–25 SWB

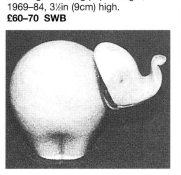

A Wedgwood dog paperweight, 1969–84, 3½in (9cm) high.
£60–70 SWB

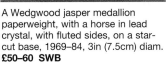

A Wedgwood jasper medallion paperweight, with a horse in lead crystal, with fluted sides, on a star-cut base, 1969–84, 3in (7.5cm) diam.
£50–60 SWB

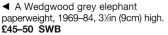

◀ A Wedgwood grey elephant paperweight, 1969–84, 3½in (9cm) high.
£45–50 SWB

A Wedgwood Christmas paperweight, 1984, 4in (10cm) high.
£35–40 SWB

WHITEFRIARS

A Whitefriars amber-bubbled paperweight, 1960–80, 2¾in (7cm) diam.
£30–35 TAC

Whitefriars christmas paperweights

There were five: 1975 The Angels, 1976 Three Wise Men, 1977 The Nativity, 1978 Holy Family and Donkey, 1979 Partridge in a Pear Tree and 1980 The Christmas Bell. The series is uniform 1975–1979. The Christmas Bell is a different style, having to be rushed out at the last minute. The Partridge in the Pear Tree uses 9469 canes and is generally felt to be the most desirable. The number of angels used in the 1975 weight varies from 10–14.

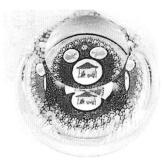

A Whitefriars paperweight, The Crib, 1977, 3in (7.5cm) diam.
£350–400 MLa

◀ A Whitefriars paperweight, with blue and green millefiori canes, Whitefriars signature cane, 1978 date cane, 3in (7.5cm) diam.
£250–280 MLa

A Whitefriars glass paperweight, with Whitefriars signature cane, with certificate, 1977, 3½in (9cm) diam.
£220–250 STG
This is one of four designs produced by Whitefriars Glass for the Queen's Silver Jubilee.

PAUL YSART

A Paul Ysart paperweight, with a bouquet on a red and white cushion, 1960–70, 2¾in (7cm) diam.
£650–750 SWB

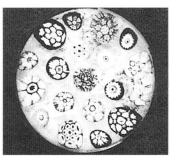

A Scottish paperweight, by Paul Ysart, with spaced millefiori on muslin, with 'PY' cane and circular sticker, c1970, 3in (7.5cm) diam.
£600–650 SWB

A Paul Ysart 'basket' paperweight, with 'PY' cane, c1960, 2¾in (7cm) diam.
£700–800 SWB
Paul Ysart prices have risen dramatically during the last year. The most sought after are good millefiori or lampwork with a PY cane.

MISCELLANEOUS

Venetian weights

These are very rare and always of the scrambled pattern. It would be more typical for them to have a horse silhouette, portrait canes of people such as the Pope, or gondalas and a PB cane or canes. Their surface is decidedly uneven.

◀ An Italian paperweight, by Pietro Bigaglia, the canes depicting animals, birds and lyres, signed 'B', dated '1845', 2in (5cm) diam.
£1,800–2,000 P

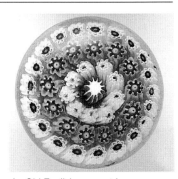

An Old English concentric paperweight, with a red and white central cane within three rows of blue and white canes, c1850, 3¼in (8.5cm) diam.
£300–350 P

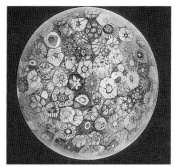

A Continental close-pack millefiori mushroom paperweight, the loosely packed canes in shades of blue, white and pink and including pink Clichy roses contained in a basket of alternate white and pairs of blue staves, probably Bohemian, 1845–60, 5½in (14cm) diam.
£800–900 C
This is likely to have started life surmounting a newel post.

A French sulphide portrait paperweight, with a crystallo ceramic bust of Queen Victoria, set on a blue and white spiral cushion, 1845–60, 3in (7.5cm) diam.
£575–650 Bea

A Boston & Sandwich Glass Co poinsettia miniature paperweight, in the style of Nicholas Lutz, with pointed dark red petals and yellow stamens, on a stem with three serrated leaves set above a white latticinio ground, c1860, 1¾in (4.5cm) diam.
£300–350 P

A Boston & Sandwich Glass Co paperweight, with a red poinsettia, c1860, 3in (7.5cm) diam.
£500–550 DLP

An American blue poinsettia paperweight, the flower with deep blue pointed petals around a central copy of a Clichy rose, on a short stem with two large and three small serrated leaves, probably New England Glass Co, c1860, 2¾in (7cm) diam.
£375–425 P

▶ A magnum or dump paperweight, possibly by Kilner or J Tower, 1860, 4¾in (12cm) diam.
£60–70 TAC

Use of dumps

'Canonballs' were used as doorstops. Tall items were mantel ornaments, since the rough bases would have damaged a gentleman's desk, so it is unlikely they were used as paperweights.

Victorian dumps

The price structure of Victorian dumps is:
a) bubbles
b) bubbles in a good regular pattern
c) flower pot with flower
d) flower pot with increasing number of flowers
e) flower pot design using silverfoil effectively
f) dump with blue glass used in pattern
g) blue dump
The prices rise from a–g depending on condition, shape and size.

A Victorian green dump, c1880, 5in (12.5cm) high.
£75–85 DUN
It is impossible to date dumps accurately except for those stamped Kilner (and the various permutations), since the same patterns were used for half a century or more.

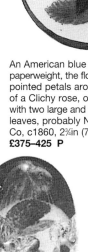

A Victorian green dump, 19thC, 5in (12.5cm) high.
£160–180 ACA
Dumps this shape were displayed as ornaments. They were not heavy enough to be used as door stops.

Dump production

These were made of bottle glass in blue (very rare) or green. The bases are usually knocked in with a ring of wear and are very rough. If they are flat and unpolished then the glass is modern and good quality. They were possibly made by Hartley Wood of Sunderland. Most green dumps, however, are perfectly genuine and often have been roughly treated.

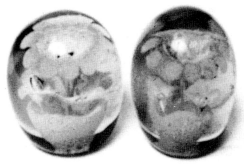

A pair of dumps, c1880, 3½in (9cm) high.
£250–300 DUN

Two Belgian paperweights, by Val St Lambert, flashed in blue and red, faceted and heavily cut, bases also heavily cut, c1880, 4in (10cm) diam.
£200–250 each SWB

Three advertising paperweights, c1920, 4in (10cm) wide.
£20–35 each MRT
These are avidly collected and are therefore increasing in value. Some have a milky white backing, but most are engraved into the glass.

A Bohemian faceted paperweight, with three flowers, 1900–20, 3½in (9cm) high.
£70–80 SWB

An Isle of Wight Glass Co paperweight, post WWII, 3½in (9cm) high.
£15–20 SWB

▶ A Chinese white paperweight, painted with a landscape, 1930, 2in (5cm) diam.
£40–50 SWB

A Kosta paperweight, Sweden, signed, post WWII, 3in (7.5cm) high.
£20–30 SWB

A Chinese paperweight, post WWII, 3in (7.5cm) high.
£10–12 SWB

Collecting paperweights

Glass paperweights are beautiful collectables. Some of the finest contemporary examples are produced by individual paperweight artists in America and Scotland. Check for signatures on the base, side, or on a marked cane within the paperweight itself.

Features to look out for include clarity of glass and quality of the canes or lampwork. Find a specialist dealer and ask questions, even if you are not ready to buy.

Although paperweights can seem expensive, reports suggest they are an investment with prices rising every year, especially for limited editions, and bargains may still be found.

A Murano paperweight, Italy, post WWII, 3in (7.5cm) diam.
£25–35 SWB

A Mdina paperweight, Malta, 1960s, 3in (7.5cm) diam.
£18–20 SWB
This design is said to represent the Mediterranean Sea.

A Webb Corbett faceted paperweight, with an engraving of a ship's wheel and blue overlay, 1960–70, 2¾in (7cm) diam.
£35–45 TAC

◀ An Isle of Wight Glass Co Studio paperweight, 1960–70, 4¾in (12cm) high.
£35–45 TAC

A Chinese paperweight, with a yellow flower, unmarked, 1960–70, 2¼in (5.5cm) diam.
£8–10 MAC

A Strathearn paperweight, with flowers on a green and red background, 1964–80, 2¾in (7cm) diam.
£38–45 CSA

John Deacons

The public have an insatiable appetite for the works of John Deacons, which are attractive and value for money. He worked for Strathearn, then Perthshire Paperweight when they split from Strathearn, then had his own firm 'J Glass', and now trades as John Deacons and works on his own.

A Strathearn concentric millefiori paperweight, 1964–80, 3in (7.5cm) high.
£45–55 SWB

A Strathearn large leaf green millefiori and latticinio star paperweight, 1964–80, 3in (7.5cm) diam.
£38–45 TAC

A Modena paperweight, with a blue and green coloured base, 1970s, 6in (15cm) high.
£14–16 HEI

A Delmo Tarsitano fruit and flower paperweight, set with an open white blossom and a blackberry on a stem with five leaves, on a star-cut base, signed with an indistinct 'DT' cane, USA, 1970–90, 2in (5cm) diam.
£250–300 P

A Paul Joseph Stankard paperweight, with a bee on a branch of pink apple blossom, signed with an 'S' cane, USA, inscribed 'Experimental A317 1980', 3in (7.5cm) diam.
£900–1,000 P

A Lundberg Studios paperweight, Beta Fish, signed 'Daniel Salazar', USA, 1994, 2¼in (5.5cm) diam.
£140–180 MLa

Modern American paperweights

Several American makers use a distinctive paperweight-making style called the California Torchwork technique. This involves drawing with a molten glass and is used by Lundberg Studios, Stephen Lundberg Art Glass and Orient & Flume.

◄ An Orient & Flume egg-shaped paperweight, with a yellow pansy on a black background, dated '1990', 3in (7.5cm) high.
£60–70 MLa

A Correia paperweight, decorated in relief with a snake, USA, 1998, 3¼in (8.5cm) diam.
£135–155 SWB

Pictures

A painting on glass, depicting a young lady in a blue dress holding a basket of flowers, c1750, 15 x 12½in (38 x 32cm).
£2,200–2,500 CAT
This painting is of exceptional quality.

A pair of south German reverse glass paintings, depicting The Virgin Mary and Child, and The Holy Trinity, each in circular panels hung with drapery, one damaged, c1800, 9½ x 7in (24 x 18cm).
£250–275 S(Am)

A picture on glass, depicting Admiral Lord Nelson, c1808, 12 x 10in (30.5 x 25.5cm).
£720–800 TVM

> **Miller's is a price GUIDE not a price LIST**

Plates

A Sowerby opaque blue glass basketwork plate, c1880, 8in (20.5cm) diam.
£30–35 GLN
The Sowerby glasshouse, Gateshead-on-Tyne, specialized in producing inexpensive pressed glassware in the second half of the 19thC.

A blue pearline glass plate, c1890, 8½in (21.5cm) diam.
£38–45 GLN

A Venetian glass plate, with red and yellow decoration, c1900, 7in (18cm) diam.
£120–140 MJW

A Val St Lambert *faux* cameo red and white glass plate, Belgium, c1890, 6in (15cm) diam.
£200–240 MJW

A blue, white and red cut-glass plate, c1900, 8in (20.5cm) diam.
£600–700 MJW

A Lalique stained glass plate, Epis No. 1, the border moulded and stained in blue with a repeated band of wheatears, with a fluted radiating centre, moulded 'R Lalique', engraved 'France', c1922, 12½in (32cm) diam.
£220–240 ASA

◀ A René Lalique opalescent glass plate, Assiette Calypso, stencilled mark, after 1930, 12in (30.5cm) diam.
£2,000–2400 S

Rolling Pins

A Nailsea black and white flecked glass rolling pin, early 19thC, 15¾in (40cm) long.
£85–100 FD

An amethyst glass rolling pin, with remains of gilt decoration, c1820, 13½in (34.5cm) long.
£125–145 JAS

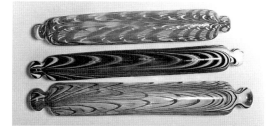

Three Nailsea glass rolling pins, with pulled loop decoration, c1860, longest 15¾in (40cm) long.
£150–170 each Som

Three coloured glass rolling pins, c1860, 15¾in (40cm) long.
£80–100 each Som

A Nailsea green glass rolling pin, with rounded ends, decorated with white trailed looped bands, 19thC, 14½in (37cm) long.
£85–100 DN

A Victorian Kilner-type glass rolling pin, with rounded ends, 16¼in (41.5cm) long.
£85–100 DN

▶ A Victorian glass rolling pin, with rounded ends, decorated with ruby-tinted trailed looped bands, 15in (38cm) long.
£120–140 DN

Salts

An amethyst glass salt, with hollow-blown bowl and deep domed foot, c1760, 3¼in (8.5cm) high.
£350–400 Som

A set of four Irish glass salts, c1790, 3in (7.5cm) high.
£600–700 WGT

A pair of Irish glass salts, c1790, 3in (7.5cm) high.
£250–300 WGT

A pair of cut-glass salts, with slice cutting and crenellated rims, on moulded diamond lemon squeezer feet, c1800, 3in (7.5cm) high
£250–300 Som

Two fan-cut glass salts, c1800, 3½in (9cm) high.
£75–85 each FD

A boat-shaped glass salt, with step cutting on a diamond-cut foot, c1810, 2½in (6.5cm) high.
£75–85 FD

▶ A set of three glass salts, the bodies with cut-leaf and sliced decoration, notched rims and oval-moulded scalloped lemon squeezer feet, probably Irish, c1800, 3in (7.5cm) high.
£400–450 Som

◄ A set of four cut-glass salts, with moulded lemon squeezer diamond feet, c1810, 3in (7.5cm) high.
£1,000–1,200 Som

A pair of moulded and cut-glass salts, with lemon squeezer feet, c1810, 3¼in (8.5cm) high.
£200–£225 BrW

Three cut-glass salts, the oval bodies, on diamond-shaped moulded and cut stems and square-cut bases, c1810, 3¼in (8.5cm) high.
£75–85 each Som

Silvered glass

Silvered glass was made with double walls which were silvered in the middle with mercury and then sealed in the base to prevent oxygen from turning the silvering black. Sometimes the outside was layered with coloured glass which was engraved or cut to reveal the silver underneath.
Because of their bulk it was difficult to produce articles which were elegant in shape, however several important presentation pieces were made. Although silvered glass may have been made as early as the late 18th century, it is often called 'Varnish' glass after Edward Varnish.

A pair of Varnish & Co mercury glass salts, c1845, 3in (7.5cm) high.
£150–180 MJW

A pair of Varnish & Co mercury glass salts, c1850, 3in (7.5cm) high
£200–220 ARE

► A pair of Sowerby opalescent glass salts, c1880, 1¼in (3cm) high.
£160–180 JHa

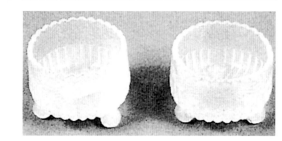

A Stourbridge double-overlay glass cruet, c1880, 2½in (6.5cm) high.
£140–180 WAC

A Davidson blue pearline glass pedestal salt, c1890, 2½in (6.5cm) high.
£42–50 GLN

A pink opaline glass salt, c1890, 1¾in (4.5cm) high.
£100–120 MJW

A Stourbridge blue glass salt, c1890, 2in (5cm) wide.
£60–70 CB

► A pair of cranberry glass salts, c1910, 2½in (6.5cm) diam.
£85–100 CB

Scent Bottles

Only in the 20th century did it become commonplace to buy perfume and bottle together as a complete package. Previously a lady would have her own personal bottles into which the scent she bought from the perfumer, or made for herself, was decanted.

Shapes of bottles have, over the years, been influenced by many different factors. Nineteenth century flacons, for instance, were produced in a wide range of sizes, materials and shapes, for both decorative and practical purposes. Because of their corsets, Victorian women were prone to fainting, and double-ended scent bottles were designed to contain perfume in one half and sponge soaked in aromatic vinegar, ie smelling salts, in the other. Miniature bottles, worn like jewellery, enabled ladies to keep their scent with them at all times. By the early 1900s customers were giving up mixing their own perfume in favour of buying named brands. The 20th century saw the massive commercial expansion of the perfume industry dominated by couturiers such as Chanel and Dior. Whereas for enthusiasts of Victorian bottles, the individual bottle is enough, the collector of 20th century commercial scent bottles wants the whole package – the specific bottle designed for a named scent complete with labels, stickers, box, and ideally still containing at least some of the original perfume.

As examples in the following section show, design of commercial scent bottles became extremely inventive as the great fashion houses competed to gain a share of the luxury market. At the top end of the range, prices for scent bottles can run to thousands of pounds – in 1990 a bottle designed by René Lalique fetched a record £38,000. At the other end of the scale the simpler Victorian, Edwardian and commercial bottles can still be found at reasonable prices, possibly even as little as £10 for a commercial bottle with contents.

Lynda Brine

A German green glass perfume bottle, c1700, 9½in (24cm) long.
£90–115 MJW

A glass scent bottle, engraved with flowers, with monogram on one side, diamond cutting on the reverse, with silver-gilt top, c1780, 4½in (11.5cm) high.
£480–520 Som

An amethyst cut-glass scent bottle, with gold screw top, the flattened sides cut with diamond facets, one side enamelled in colours with doves in a tree, minor damage, c1760, 2¾in (7cm) high.
£1,500–1,800 C

A Bohemian red glass scent bottle, with gold mounts and chain, mid-18thC, 3¾in (9.5cm) high.
£720–800 Som

A blue glass scent bottle, with gilt diaper decoration and wrythen gold screw top, c1760, 2¼in (5.5cm) high.
£800–900 Som

A clear glass scent bottle, with embossed gold top, c1790, 4in (10cm) long, in fitted case.
£600–700 Som

◄ A clear glass scent bottle, with cut decoration, the silver plaque with gilt inscription, with silver top, c1790, 4in (10cm) long.
£850–950 Som

History of British scent bottles

The first British-made scent bottles appeared at the beginning of the 18th century. Early exmples followed European designs and were flat in shape, but had characteristic British features such as heavy, lead crystal bodies with cut decoration. British-style scent bottles began to be manufactured in the mid-18th century in a variety of colours, including blue, white, pale green and occasionally amethyst. Bottles were often made in pairs to go inside a travelling case – one for perfume and one for smelling salts.

A diamond-cut double-ended scent bottle, with gilt-metal tops, c1790, 5½in (14cm) long.
£400–450 Som

▶ An Irish glass double-ended scent bottle, with prism and diamond cutting, with plain silver tops, c1790, 5¼in (13.5cm) long.
£350–400 Som

A Bohemian cut-glass scent bottle, c1800, 3¼in (8.5cm) high.
£200–220 LBr

Items in the Scent bottles section have been arranged in date order

l. A double-ended scent bottle, with diamond and prism cutting, with gold tops, c1800, 5½in (14cm) long.
£450–500

r. A disc-shaped clear glass scent bottle, with diamond-cut panels, silver-gilt top, c1820, 3¼in (8.5cm) high.
£180–220 Som

A clear glass four-compartment scent bottle, cut with strawberry diamonds and star-cut base, with fan-cut stoppers, c1820, 3¾in (9.5cm) high.
£450–500 Som

◀ An Apsley Pellatt commemorative scent bottle, for the coronation of George IV, inset with a central sulphide medallion of the king in the guise of a Roman Emperor, the reverse with a medallion depicting the Coronation and dated 'July 19th 1821', the sides and base with hobnail cutting, with flame stopper, 5½in (14cm) high.
£2,000–2,500 S

A hobnail-cut glass scent bottle, with silver top, c1830, 10in (25.5cm) long.
£200–250 LBr

▶ A cut-glass scent bottle, with gold top, probably Dutch, c1840, 4in (10cm) high.
£200–250 LBr

Two clear glass miniature scent bottles, one with a silver top, c1830, largest 1½in (4cm) high.
£70–80 LBr

Two Apsley Pellatt scent bottles, engraved with portraits of Lord Brougham and Princess Victoria, rim chip, c1835, 4in (10cm) high.
£900–1,100 S
Lord Brougham was Chancellor in the Reform Parliament of 1832, and was a prime figure in the movement to abolish slavery.

Two glass ring-shaped scent bottles, with silver tops, c1840, largest 1½in (4cm) diam.
l. £150–175
r. £200–250 LBr

A Swiss glass scent bottle, with gold top, c1840, 3¼in (8.5cm) high, in original shagreen case.
£700–800 LBr

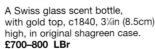

Two white and amber cut-glass attar bottles, mid-19thC, 5in (12.5cm) long.
£35–50 each DAC

◀ A rock crystal scent bottle, c1840, 1½in (4cm) high.
£140–160 LBr

A set of three glass scent bottles, with gilt-metal base and mounts, possibly Swiss or French, c1840, 4½in (11.5cm) high.
£400–450 LBr

A cut-glass scent bottle, with gold top, probably French, c1840, 4in (10cm) high.
£250–300 LBr

A blue glass scent bottle, c1850, 9½in (24cm) high.
£250–300 MJW

A glass scent bottle, by Hale Thompson & Co, with cased silvered interior and cut amethyst exterior, signed, c1850, 8in (20.5cm) high.
£700–800 ALiN
Silvered glass is made with double walls of glass that are silvered in the middle with mercury. Frederick Hale Thompson and Edward Varnish took out the British patent for the technique in 1849, and it is often called Varnish glass.

A glass scent bottle, with red body and cut white overlay decoration, with embossed silver mount, c1860, 3¾in (9.5cm) high.
£280–300 Som

A Bohemian red-flashed glass scent bottle, engraved with deer in landscapes, with embossed silver top, c1860, 6¼in (16cm) high.
£550–600 Som

l. A green overlay glass scent bottle, with embossed silver top, c1860, 3½in (9cm) high.
£230–280
r. A brick-red Lithyalin scent bottle, with silver top, c1850, 2¾in (7cm) high.
£380–430 Som

Prices

The price ranges quoted in this book reflect the average price a purchaser might expect to pay for a similar item. The price will vary according to the condition, rarity, size, popularity, provenance, colour and restoration of the item. If you are selling it is quite likely that you will be offered less than the price range.

► A clear glass double-ended scent bottle, with plain silver-gilt tops, c1860, 5in (12.5cm) long.
£110–130 Som

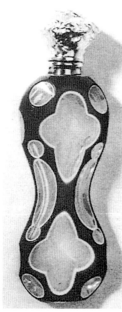

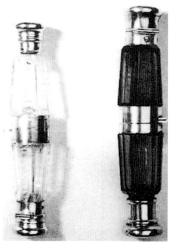

A blue glass faceted barrel-shaped double-ended scent bottle, with embossed silver tops, c1860, 3¼in (8.5cm) long.
£250–300 Som

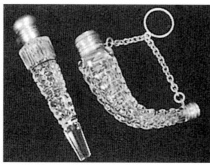

A glass scent bottle, with blue and white double overlay, with embossed silver top, c1860, 4in (10cm) high.
£260–310 Som

l. A double-ended scent bottle, the clear tapered body with diamond-cut panels, with hinged vinaigrette compartment in centre, with silver-gilt mounts, c1860, 5¼in (13.5cm) long.
r. A double-ended flute-cut red scent bottle, with picture frame inside hinged compartment, plain silver-gilt mounts, c1880, 5¼in (13.5cm) long.
£250–300 each Som
The vinaigrette compartment in the clear glass bottle would have contained a sponge soaked in either liquid ammonia or aromatic vinegars, and would be secured by a pierced grille.

l. A tear-shaped cut-glass scent bottle, with silver-gilt top, c1880, 3½in (9cm) long.
£70–90
r. A horn-shaped cut-glass scent bottle, with silver-gilt mounts and finger chain, c1860, 3½in (9cm) long.
£170–220 Som

A Clichy scent bottle, with silver top and inner stopper, c1870, 3in (7.5cm) high.
£300–350 BHa

► A bloodstone circular scent bottle, the gold mount set with gems and engraved with acanthus leaves and scrolling foliage, c1870, 2in (5cm) diam.
£1,200–1,500 C

l. A dark blue double-ended flute-cut glass scent bottle, with plain silver tops, c1870, 5¼in (13.5cm) long.
c. An opaque pea-green flute-cut glass double-ended scent bottle, with gilt-brass tops, c1860, 5¼in (13.5cm) long.
r. An amber double-ended flute-cut glass scent bottle, with gilt-brass mounts, c1860, 5¾in (14.5cm) long.
£100–150 each Som
Double-ended scent bottles were designed to hold scent at one end and smelling salts at the other. The scent end usually has a screw top whilst the other end often has a hinged lid with a spring-loaded fastener.

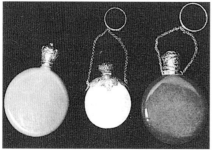

l. A blue opaline flat disc scent bottle, with silver-gilt top, c1870, 2¼in (5.5cm) diam.
c. An opaque white flat disc scent bottle, with embossed silver mount and chain, c1870, 1¾in (4.5cm) diam.
r. A green opaline flat disc scent bottle, with silver-gilt mount and chain, c1870, 2½in (6.5cm) diam.
£200–230 each Som

◄ A blue moulded glass scent bottle, c1870, 8in (20.5cm) high.
£150–220 CB

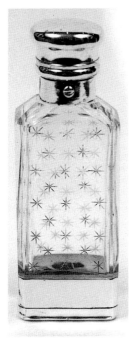

An S Mordan & Co red glass scent bottle, with two compartments, the silver-gilt tops with diamond registration mark, the base with a silver-gilt vinaigrette, marked, c1870, 4in (10cm) high.
£900–1,000 Som

An S Mordan & Co star-cut glass scent bottle and vinaigrette, with silver mounts, 1879, 4in (10cm) high.
£650–720 THOM

An S Mordan & Co cranberry glass scent bottle, decorated with gilt, with silver top, c1880, 3½in (9cm) high.
£650–720 THOM

A Thomas Webb cameo glass scent bottle, decorated with violets, with silver top, c1880, 3½in (9cm) high.
£1,250–1,500 BHa

top. An amethyst-tinted glass double-ended scent bottle, with chased gilt tops, marked 'Samson and Mordan', c1880, 5½in (14cm) long.
bottom. A vaseline glass double-ended scent bottle, with wrythen-moulded body, with chased white-metal tops, c1880, 5½in (14cm) long.
£340–380 each Som

A blue glass scent bottle, with silver top, c1880, 3¼in (8.5cm) high.
£170–200 LBr

> **Cross Reference**
> See Colour Review

▶ A Venetian glass scent bottle, with brass mounts and finger chain, c1880, 2¼in (5.5cm) high.
£180–220 LBr

An S Mordan & Co red glass double-ended scent bottle and vinaigrette, modelled as opera glasses, with silver-gilt mounts, c1880, 5½in (14cm) long, with fitted case marked 'Face, Keen & Face, Plymouth'.
£820–920 Som

A clear glass double-ended scent bottle, with silver tops, c1880, 5in (12.5cm) long.
£100–120 LBr

A cut-glass double-ended scent bottle, with plain silver-gilt tops, c1880, 4¾in (12cm) long, in fitted case.
£130–150 Som

A glass scent bottle, modelled as a champagne bottle, with hallmarked silver-gilt top, c1880, 2½in (6.5cm) high.
£280–350 ALiN

◄ An amethyst-shaded glass toilet water bottle, with diamond and fan-cut decoration, with silver top marked Birmingham, c1880, 6¾in (17cm) high.
£400–450 Som

A novelty glass scent bottle, modelled as a lemon, with silver top, maker's mark 'C.M.', top damaged, 19thC, 2¾in (7cm) high.
£320–350 GH

A cameo glass scent bottle, decorated with leaves, probably French, c1880, 3in (7.5cm) high.
£200–240 LBr

A horn-shaped novelty scent bottle, with a whistle at one end, with silver-gilt mounts and glass inner stopper, c1880, 3in (7.5cm) long.
£250–280 LBr

A novelty cut-glass scent bottle, with hinged silver-gilt lid modelled as a fish head, with cut-glass stopper, c1880, 6½in (16.5cm) long.
£450–500 WeH

A double-ended scent bottle, with clear wrythen-moulded body, wrythen-cast silver tops, marked 'Samson Mordan 1883', 4½in (11.5cm) long.
£340–380 Som

A clear glass two-compartment scent bottle, with silver-gilt mounts, c1882, 3¼in (8.5cm) high.
£700–750 Som

A silver-topped scent bottle, Birmingham 1882, 2in (5cm) high.
£70–90 DAC

A Webb citron-coloured icicle scent bottle, with opaque-white cameo decoration, with silver top marked 'London 1884', 6in (15cm) long.
£900–1,000 Som

A Thomas Webb cameo glass scent bottle, the top with embossed silver outer cover, moulded mark, marked for Birmingham 1888, 6in (15cm) high.
£800–950 Bea

A Royal Worcester scent bottle, commemorating Queen Victoria's Golden Jubilee, the metal top modelled as the Imperial State Crown, the bottle with a portrait of the Queen within a garland of roses, shamrocks and thistles entwined with a dated and inscribed banner, the reverse inscribed with the principal overseas possessions, the blush ivory ground enriched in pale blue and gilt, printed marks, c1887, 3½in (9cm) high.
£1,800–2,000 CSK

◄ A double-ended scent bottle, with cranberry overlay, with silver tops, c1885, 4in (10cm) long.
£250–300 THOM

A pair of Victorian cut-glass scent bottles, decorated with birds, flowers and foliage, the hinged silver tops by William Comyns, London, c1888–1900, 5¼in (13.5cm) high.
£500–600 Bea

A latticinio green and white glass scent bottle, with brass hinged cover, late 19thC, 3½in (9cm) high.
£150–200 GH

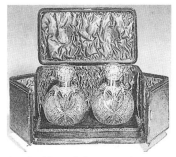

A pair of Drew & Sons cut-glass cologne bottles, with silver tops, in a plush and quilted satin-lined tooled leather case, London 1892, 6in (15cm) high.
£1,300–1,500 CSK

Four Venetian glass miniature scent bottles, c1890, 1¼in (3cm) high.
£80–120 each LBr

A ruby glass scent bottle, the hinged gold cover finely engraved with scrolling against a diaper ground, late 19thC, 3¼in (8.5cm) high.
£250–300 P

A pair of Art Nouveau glass scent bottles, decorated in gilt with fuchsias, c1900, 6½in (16.5cm) high.
£150–200 LBr

A ruby red overlay glass scent bottle, with lozenge decoration, the hinged silver cover embossed with foliate scrolls, maker's mark of Hilliard & Thomason, Birmingham 1897, 6in (15cm) high.
£280–320 Bon

A Daum etched, gilt and enamelled glass perfume bottle and stopper, decorated with purple and green layers, branches and berries, printed mark, 1890–96, 3¾in (9.5cm) high.
£700–850 S(Am)

▶ A cut-glass cylindrical scent bottle, with silver top, Birmingham 1902, 3in (7.5cm) high.
£75–90 PSA

A glass scent bottle, with silver top, c1900, 3½in (9cm) high.
£70–80 WN

A French cut-glass teardrop-shaped scent bottle, with silver screw top, c1900, 5in (12.5cm) long.
£140–160 LBr

SCENT BOTTLES 239

A pair of William Comyns scent bottles, engraved with anthemion shells and daisies, the hinged silver tops with similar decoration and glass stoppers, London 1907, 7in (18cm) high.
£500–600 Bea

A cut-glass scent bottle and stopper, with silver neck ring, Birmingham 1907, 5½in (14cm) high.
£70–80 DAC

A pair of cut-glass scent bottles and stoppers, with silver neck rings, c1910, 7¼in (18.5cm) high.
£150–170 LBr

Two perfume bottles, modelled as a White Hart Scotch Whisky bottle and a Guiness Extra Stout bottle, c1910, 3in (7.5cm) high.
£40–50 each LBr

A glass scent bottle, with gilt overlay, top and chain, c1910, ¾in (2cm) high.
£70–90 LBr

A bottle of perfume, 'Maharajah de Kapurthaj' by Lenthéric, boxed, c1920, 4in (10cm) long.
£140–150 LBr

A basket-weave design cut-glass scent bottle, with plain silver top, by Joseph Gloster & Sons, Birmingham 1919, 10in (25.5cm) long.
£300–350 HofB

A Lalique perfume bottle, made for Worth, c1920, 4in (10cm) high, in original box.
£80–90 RAC
René Lalique, 1860–1945, designed many perfume presentations. The shape of this bottle was inspired by the Empire State Building.

A Lalique blue-enamelled scent bottle, 'Dans la Nuit' by Worth, decorated with stars, c1924, 4in (10cm) high.
£500–600 RIT

A cut-glass scent bottle, with silver top, Birmingham 1919, 6in (15cm) high.
£70–80 WN

A Lalique scent bottle, 'Pan', decorated with swags and classical masks, c1920, 5in (12.5cm) high.
£2,500–3,000 ABS

Lalique scent bottles

- Lalique's earliest scent bottles were commissioned by François Côty.
- The most inventive forms are in greatest demand.
- Sealed bottles with original contents are always at a premium.
- More than one stopper was designed for some bottles.
- The underside of the stopper should carry a number corresponding to that on the bottle base.
- Some small scent bottles carry the initials 'R L' instead of a full signature.

A Lalique moulded glass scent bottle, 'Origan' by D'Héraud, one side moulded with the face of a girl with the horns of a goat, the reverse with a label, with a brown patina top, in original box, 1925, 2½in (6.5cm) high.
£500–600 P

A Lalique frosted glass scent bottle and stopper, 'Perles', decorated with swags of pearls, c1926, 6¾in (17cm) high.
£500–550 LBr

An etched glass scent bottle and stopper, with silver neck ring, London 1927, 8in (20.5cm) high.
£130–150 DAC

◄ A glass scent bottle, 'Maderas de Oriente' by Myrurgia, in a wooden case with a tassel, c1930, 6in (15cm) high.
£40–50 LBe

Scent and smelling salt bottles are almost impossible to tell apart, but in terms of value this is not important.
For more information on scent bottles see Miller's *Perfume Bottles A Collector's Guide*

A Lalique frosted glass scent bottle, 'Skyscraper' by Lucien Lelong, in enamelled chrome case, with four tiers of black enamel swags, with complementary stopper, c1929, 4½in (11.5cm) high.
£4,250–4,750 B&B

▶ A Lanvin glass scent bottle, in original box, 1930s, 3in (7.5cm) high.
£25–30 RAC
The value of commercial scent bottles is increased by the presence of the original contents and the box.

A Lalique glass scent bottle, 'L'Aimant' by Coty, with briar design on stopper, c1930, 3¼in (8.5cm) high.
£340–400 LBr

A Czechoslovakian silver and glass scent bottle brooch, c1930, 1½in (4cm) high.
£100–120 LBr

◄ A pair of American glass scent bottles, modelled as binoculars, with metal tops, c1930, 2½in (6.5cm) wide.
£30–40 LBr

▶ Four glass scent bottles, with glass stoppers, c1930, largest 3½in (9cm) high.
£20–30 each LBr

A clear glass scent atomizer, with glass dauber, c1930, 3½in (9cm) high.
£35–40 DAC

A Lalique glass eau de cologne bottle, 'Je Reviens' by Worth, with original box, c1955, 3in (7.5cm) high.
£20–30 Rac

► A glass scent bottle, 'Evening in Paris' by Bourjois, in a horshoe-shaped container, with original box, 1930s, 4in (10cm) long.
£140–160 LBr

A glass scent bottle, 'Saison' by Muriel, Paris, modelled as the Eiffel Tower and with a Stanhope in the plastic top showing scenes of Paris, c1960, 3¼in (8.5cm) high.
£45–55 PC

◄ An Avon glass perfume bottle, modelled as a rabbit, 1970s, 3in (7.5cm) high.
£12–15 RAC

A glass scent bottle, 'Carnet de Bal' by Ravillon, Paris, 1930–40, 2¼in (5.5cm) high.
£85–95 LBe
When turned upside down this bottle looks like a glass of brandy.

A glass scent bottle, 'Evening in Paris' by Bourjois, in shell-shaped plastic container, with original box, c1930, 4in (10cm) long.
£140–160 LBr

A Vasart green glass scent bottle, with cut-cane pink millefiori decoration, 1950s, 4½in (11.5cm) high.
£145–165 SWB

A 'Fiorinelli' limited edition glass scent bottle, by Saint Louis, France, c1995, 8½in (21.5cm) high, with box and certificate.
£1,500–1,800 STG

Two glass scent atomizers, signed 'J Ditchfield', 1995:
l. pearl decoration with feathering,
r. blue with pearl lily trail, largest 4¼in (11cm) diam.
£40–50 each GLA

Two Glasform mottled glass scent atomizers, coral and green, 1995, largest 4½in (11.5cm) diam.
£30–50 each GLA

Smoking Accessories

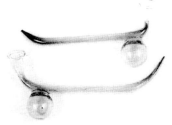

Two Georgian glass tobacco pipes, the bubbles used for cooling with water, 9½in (24cm) long.
£35–45 each FD

A green, blue and white glass pipe, possibly Nailsea, mid-19thC, 21in (55cm) long.
£180–200 FD

A Nailsea orange glass pipe, c1860, 21½in (54.5cm) long.
£400–450 MJW

A Victorian blue-tinted glass pipe, with tapering stem and rounded bowl, trailed overall with white bands, 17in (43cm) long.
£150–170 DN

A Davidson jet glass match striker, late 19thC, 3in (7.5cm) high.
£24–30 TS

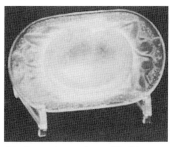

A Lalique glass ashtray, Medicis, with two pairs of naked female figures amongst flowers, moulded mark 'R Lalique', engraved 'R Lalique, France, No. 280', after 1924, 6in (15cm) long.
£350–400 S(S)

A Lalique opalescent glass ashtray, Jamaique, with beetle design, after 1928, 5½in (14cm) diam.
£180–200 ASA

A Lalique blue stained glass ashtray, after 1928, 5½in (14cm) diam.
£150–180 ASA

A Lalique frosted opalescent glass ashtray, Louise, in the form of a flowerhead, with black enamelled stamens and traces of blue staining, slight damage, moulded 'R Lalique', after 1929, 3in (7.5cm) diam.
£250–300 CSK

A glass ashtray, hand-painted with a hunting scene, 1930s.
£40–45 HEW

A green glass ashtray, in a decorative silver-plated mount, c1930, 1½in (4cm) high.
£38–45 MON

A Glasform ashtray, No. 4422, signed, 1995, 7in (18cm) diam.
£45–55 GLA

Sucrier & Cream Jug Sets

l. An amethyst glass cream jug, with overall honeycomb moulding, foot ring and loop handle, c1700, 3¼in (8.5cm) high.
£380–420
r. A blue wrythen-moulded glass sugar basin, with folded rim, c1800, 2½in (6.5cm) high.
£100–120 Som

◀ A clear glass cream jug and sugar basin, with translucent blue rims, c1800, jug 4in (10cm) high.
£380–450 Som

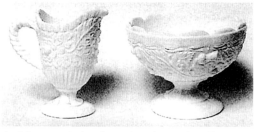

A white pressed-glass jug and sucrier, marked 'Greener', c1876, jug 4in (10cm) high.
£85–95 GLN

◀ A purple slag pressed-glass sucrier and cream jug, decorated with ivy leaf design, c1890, jug 3in (7.5cm) high.
£60–70 GLN

▶ A Hepple white pressed-glass jug and bowl, on shell-form bases, late 19thC, 3½in (9cm) high.
£100–115 GLN

An amethyst cream jug and sugar basin, inscribed in gold enamel, c1800, jug 4½in (11.5cm) high.
£350–400 Som

l. An opaque white glass cream jug, c1810, 5in (12.5cm) high.
£125–150
r. An opaque white glass sugar basin, with opalescent glow, c1820, 3in (7.5cm) high.
£35–40 Som

A purple slag pressed-glass jug and bowl, decorated with faggot and rope design, marked 'Greener', c1880, jug 4½in (11.5cm) high.
£95–115 GLN

◀ An opaque blue pressed-glass creamer and sucrier, c1890, jug 3½in (9cm) high.
£85–95 GLN

A Bristol blue glass jug and bowl, 1960s, jug 9in (23cm) high.
£85–100 LF

Sweetmeat & Jelly Glasses

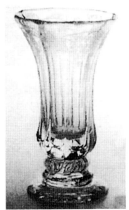

A baluster goblet or sweetmeat glass, the double ogee bowl supported on a collar above a ball knop and true baluster section enclosing an elongated tear, on a domed and folded foot, c1720, 6in (15cm) high.
£750–850 C

A sweetmeat glass, with double ogee bowl and dentilated rim, on a Silesian-moulded stem with star-studded shoulders with coiled collars at each end, on a domed folded foot, c1730, 5½in (14cm) high.
£600–700 Som

A sweetmeat bowl and cover, moulded with eight panels, the cover with an acorn finial, on a domed and folded foot with similar panel moulding, early 18thC, 8¾in (22cm) high.
£4,600–5,200 P
This is possibly a world record price for a sweetmeat bowl. It is an extremely rare item, especially since it retains its original cover.

A jelly glass, the eight-sided panel-moulded flared bowl engraved with a vine band, on beaded knopped stem and domed foot, c1730, 4¼in (11cm) high.
£170–200 DN

A sweetmeat stand, with saucer platform, the gadroon-moulded stem with two ball knops and folded conical foot, c1740, 3in (7.5cm) high.
£380–420 Som

A sweetmeat glass, with ogee-shaped bowl, on collared stem and domed and folded foot, c1740–50, 3¼in (8.5cm) high.
£230–260 DN

A baluster sweetmeat glass, the vertically ribbed ogee bowl with everted rim supported on an inverted baluster stem enclosing an elongated tear, terminating on a basal knop, on a radially-ribbed domed and folded foot, c1740, 6in (15cm) high.
£500–600 C

A moulded light baluster sweetmeat glass, the double ogee bowl and everted rim with all-over honeycomb moulding, the stem with a beaded knop between two plain sections above a honeycomb-moulded domed and folded foot, c1745, 5½in (14cm) high.
£1,000–1,200 C

A ribbed glass sweetmeat, with double ogee bowl, on teared knop pedestal and domed foot, c1745, 6¼in (16cm) high.
£600–680 FD

A sweetmeat glass, the flared bowl with star-cut rim and facet-cut bands, c1750, 6¼in (16cm) high.
£300–350 DN

A sweetmeat glass, the double ogee bowl with a dentillated rim, on a stem with centre ball knop, on a plain domed foot, c1750, 3½in (9cm) high.
£350–400 Som

Miller's is a price GUIDE not a price LIST

▶ A sweetmeat glass, the double ogee bowl on a moulded Silesian stem with base collar and domed folded foot, c1750, 3¼in (8.5cm) high.
£250–300 Som
This glass has trapped air threads in the folded foot.

l. A jelly glass, c1800, 4½in (11.5cm) high.
£60–75
c. A bonnet glass, c1750, 3in (7.5cm) high.
£40–50
r. A rib-moulded jelly glass, c1750, 3¾in (9.5cm) high.
£75–90 Som

l. A jelly glass, with double ogee rib-moulded bowl and collar, on a rib-moulded domed folded foot, c1760, 4¼in (11cm) high.
£130–150
r. A jelly glass, with hexagonal bowl and air-beaded plain domed foot, c1760, 4in (10cm) high.
£190–220 Som

A set of eight jelly glasses, with hexagonal moulded bowls and plain conical feet, c1760, tallest 4½in (11.5cm) high.
£850–1,000 Som

A jelly glass, with hexagonal bowl and plain domed foot, c1760, 4in (10cm) high.
£140–160 Som

A facet-cut sweetmeat glass, on a domed scalloped foot, c1770, 7in (18cm) high.
£320–380 CB

A sweetmeat glass, on a moulded pedestal stem, on a plain domed foot, c1750, 5½in (14cm) high.
£350–390 Som

A sweetmeat glass, the double ogee bowl with moulded panels and a dentated rim, supported on a multi-spiral opaque-twist stem and radially grooved foot, c1760, 4in (10cm) high.
£300–350 GS

A jelly glass, with bell-shaped bowl, on opaque spiral-twist knop and domed foot, c1760, 4in (10cm) high.
£300–350 DN

▶ A jelly glass, with beaded knop and domed foot, c1770, 4¼in (11cm) high.
£300–350 GS

A sweetmeat glass, with notched rim, centre knop stem and domed foot, c1755, 7in (18cm) high.
£300–350 GS

An early George III sweetmeat tree, with a panel-moulded ogee-shaped bowl, the tapering stem with three tiers of four scroll branches, on a domed and folded foot, repaired, one basket missing and two replaced, c1760, 16¼in (41.5cm) high.
£7,500–9,000 DN
This item realized a considerable sum at auction despite the damage, as it is extremely rare. Only a few have survived, and almost all have 'mix and match' baskets.

Sweetmeat glasses

Sweetmeat glasses were used to serve dry sweetmeats (chocolates, dried fruits etc), as opposed to desserts such as trifle and jelly, which were eaten from jelly glasses.

A blue bonnet glass, with diamond-moulded double ogee bowl, c1780, 3in (7.5cm) high.
£250–280 Som
Bonnet glasses were used for sweetmeats. In the USA they are known as 'salts'.

► A pair of bonnet glasses, with serrated rims and segmented bowls, on square lemon squeezer feet, c1800, 3¾in (9.5cm) high.
£140–170 GS
A lemon squeezer foot is dome-shaped with moulded ribs, usually on a solid square base, but occasionally diamond or oval-shaped.

Three jelly glasses, with trumpet bowls and plain conical feet, 1780–1800, tallest 4¼in (11cm) high.
£75–90 each Som

◄ A cut-glass sweetmeat dish, the ogee bowl diamond-cut with scalloped rim, facet-cut stem with centre knop and scalloped-cut foot, c1780, 6½in (16.5cm) high.
£360–420 Som

A Lobmeyr Persian-style enamelled sweetmeat dish, painted in turquoise and gilt with a rosette within a scroll pattern, gilt line rim, on a spreading foot, marked 'JLL', c1800, 8¾in (22cm) high.
£1,600–1,800 S

l & r. A pair of cut jelly glasses, the trumpet bowls with flute- and diamond-cut notched rims, c1820, 4in (10cm) high.
£120–145
c. A syllabub glass, with pan top and notched rim, with facet-cut foot, c1820, 4in (10cm) high.
£65–75 Som

A set of eight jelly glasses, with wide-fluted trumpet bowls and plain conical feet, c1840, 4½in (11.5cm) high.
£160–170 Som

Tazzas

A Venetian filigree glass tazza, the wide shallow bowl inset with swirling bands of lacework alternating with opaque threads, set above a latticinio inverted baluster stem flanked by clear glass mereses and knops, the folded conical foot with filigree decoration, c1600, 4½in (11.5cm) high.
£5,500–6,500 S

A Venetian diamond-point engraved glass tazza, with panels of stylized foliate scroll within a leaf border, c1600, 4½in (11.5cm) diam.
£20,000–22,000 S

A *façon de Venise* diamond-point engraved glass tazza, Low Countries, 17thC, 14½in (37cm) high.
£5,500–6,500 S

A Bohemian glass tazza, engraved with leaves and flowers, c1740, 5in (12.5cm) high.
£300–345 MJW

▶ Two glass patch stands:
l. c1740, 3½in (9cm) high.
£250–275
r. c1750, 3in (7.5cm) high.
£300–345 MJW

A glass patch stand, the flat platform with everted rim, bobbin-knopped stem and folded conical foot, c1740, 2in (5cm) diam.
£350–400 Som

A Silesian stemmed glass tazza, the eight-sided stem on a collared and high-domed fold-over foot, c1740, 13½in (34.5cm) diam.
£500–600 WW

A selection of glass patch stands, 1740–50, tallest 5in (12.5cm) diam.
£300–480 each MJW
Patch stands were used by ladies to hold their patches, or beauty spots.

A glass tazza, the rimmed flat platform on a stem with pedestal-moulded stalk and three neck rings below, on a domed folded foot, c1740, 10¼in (26cm) diam.
£250–300
A set of six jelly glasses, with flared trumpet bowls, on plain conical feet, c1830, 4¼in (11cm) high.
£150–170 Som

A glass tazza, with upturned rim, on moulded Silesian stem and domed folded foot, c1750, 9in (23cm) diam.
£325–375 Som

A Silesian stemmed glass salver, with domed and folded foot, c1750, 9in (23cm) diam.
£350–400 BrW

A glass tazza with an everted rim, on pillar-moulded basal-knopped stem and domed and folded base, 1760–80, 16in (40.5cm) diam.
£725–850 CSK

A glass tazza, with galleried rim, on a turned knop stem and spreading circular base, 1760–80, 9in (23cm) diam.
£750–850 C(S)

An opaque pink glass campana-shaped tazza, with ormolu mounts and birds perched on the rim, 19thC, 4½in (11.5cm) high.
£6,000–7,000 TMA

◀ A French *Gorge de Pigeon* ormolu-mounted glass tazza, c1835, 8½in (21.5cm) wide.
£1,700–2,000 C

A graduated tier of three glass tazzas, each with Silesian stem and domed folded foot, 18thC, largest 12¼in (31cm) high.
£725–850 FW&C

LOCATE THE SOURCE
The source of each illustration in Miller's can be found by checking the code letters below each caption with the Key to Illustrations, pages 305–307.

A pair of Henry Walker mercury glass tazzas, American, c1869, 6½in (16.5cm) high.
£650–700 MJW

A French white opaline glass tazza, with gilt wavy rim and enamelled with orange flowers, c1870, 6¾in (17cm) diam.
£250–275 CB

A glass tazza, decorated in gold with Greek key pattern, c1890, 5¾in (14.5cm) high.
£300–350 MJW

A Whitefriars green crackleglass tazza, on a chrome-plated stand, c1930, 6in (15cm) high.
£30–35 BKK

A pair of French opaline glass stands, c1870, 3½in (9cm) high.
£275–300 CB

A Lobmeyr enamelled gilt-metal-mounted glass tazza, engraved with fruit and foliage, c1880, 7¾in (19.5cm) diam.
£1,800–2,000 C

A yellow vaseline glass tazza, c1890, 5in (12.5cm) high.
£280–320 MJW

A Bagley clear flint glass salver, pattern No. 2, 1922, 6in (15cm) high.
£15–20 PC

A Thomas Webb glass tazza, designed by Daniel Pearce, with cranberry overlay, c1880, 6in (15cm) high.
£800–900 MJW

A pair of glass tazzas, c1900, 5in (12.5cm) high.
£400–440 CB

A glass tazza, on a chrome base, c1930, 9in (23cm) high.
£75–80 TS

Auction or dealer?

All the pictures in our price guides originate from auction houses and dealers. When buying at auction, prices can be lower than those of a dealer, but a buyer's premium and VAT will be added to the hammer price. Equally, when selling at auction, commission, tax and photography charges must be taken into account. Dealers will often restore pieces before putting them back on the market.

Both dealers and auctioneers will provide professional advice, so it is worth researching both sources before buying or selling your antiques.

Vases

An Islamic glass vase, chipped, 6thC AD, 2½in (6.5cm) high.
£750–900 JFG

> Items in the Vases section have been arranged in date order.

A *façon de Venise* crizzled two-handled vase, applied with large strawberry prunts, the reeded scroll handles applied with pincered ornament, slight damage, possibly Venice, early 18thC, 11¾in (30cm) high.
£5,000–6,000 C

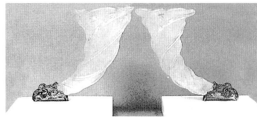

A pair of Regency glass cornucopia, on gilt-metal rams' mask mounts and white marble bases, 1811–20, 8in (20.5cm) high.
£360–400 HYD

◀ A pair of cut-glass oviform vases and covers, the bowls with a band of diamonds, on fluted stems and square bases, the domed covers with bands of diamonds and flutes and with fluted mushroom finials, damaged, possibly Irish, early 19thC, 7½in (19cm) high.
£500–600 C

A glass celery vase, cut with alternating strawberries, diamonds and stars between slice cutting, pedestal stem, star-cut foot, c1820, 8¾in (22cm) high.
£180–220 JHa

A trumpet-shaped glass celery vase, cut with plain and strawberry diamond pattern, scalloped rim, on a plain foot, c1825, 7½in (19cm) high.
£300–350 Som

A glass hyacinth vase, 19thC, 7½in (19cm) high.
£85–100 DUN

A three-branch glass épergne, the central trumpet vase cut with diamonds and raised on a gilt-metal stem, flanked by two tusk-shaped vases, above a star-cut petal base, minor chips, central vase possibly matched, 19thC, 15½in (39.5cm) high.
£230–280 S(S)

Cut glass

The technique for cutting glass for decorative purposes began as early as the 1st century BC. Today there are basically four processes involved:
• The piece is marked by drawing the required pattern onto the blank glass body with a felt-tip pen.
• The item is then roughed by cutting the main lines of the pattern into the glass using a power-driven iron wheel, which has a steady stream of fine wet sand running over it to act as an abrasive on the surface of the item. These cuts are dull and coarse and do not cover the whole of the pattern. The wheel used can either be flat, curved or V-shaped, depending on the type of cut required.
• The glass is then smoothed using a variety of sandstone wheels, with a continuous flow of water running over the cutting surface for cooling and lubrication. The wheels have a similar-shaped cutting edge to those used in the roughing process, but many different-sized wheels are used to cut the detail of the pattern onto the glass, with the smaller lines being cut at this stage, without previous roughing. The accuracy of the cutting relies solely on the skill of the craftsman. One of the most obvious signs of poorly-cut glass is small inaccuracies, particularly on the base, where all the points have to meet precisely in the centre.
• Polishing the item is the final and most time-consuming process. A wooden wheel with a fine abrasive surface is worked by hand over all the cut lines, and a felt wheel is often used for finishing to give a final shine to the piece. Polishing by acid-dipping leaves a bright finish but the uniformity of the surface, with no wheelmarks, can leave a flat, bland appearance that lacks some of the sharpness of hand-finished glass.

Three coloured glass hyacinth vases:
l. green, c1820, 7in (18cm) high.
£100–125
c. blue, c1860, 5½in (14cm) high.
£90–110
r. blue, c1870, 7½in (19cm) high.
£70–90 MJW

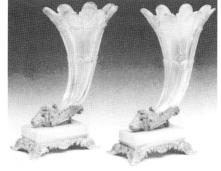

A pair of glass cornucopia vases, with gilt-bronze mounts, white marble on bases, each in the form of a fluted vase supported by a ram's mask, 1830, 11in (28cm) high.
£6,800–8,000 S(S)

A black pressed glass vase, c1848, 3½in (9cm) high.
£20–25 GLN

A Bohemian baluster glass vase, with white overlay and a ruby-flash shaped panel engraved with a recumbent stag in a wooded landscape, cut with lenses and arcaded sections, slight wear, 19thC, 13in (33cm) high.
£350–450 C

A pair of vaseline glass posy vases, 19thC, 4½in (11.5cm) high.
£65–80 DUN

Three glass celery vases:
l. engraved with ferns, c1870, 9¼in (23.5cm) high.
£110–135
c. cut-glass, c1830, 10in (25.5cm) high.
£240–280.
r. moulded-blown, c1840, 9in (23cm) high.
£130–160 MJW

◄ A pair of cranberry glass vases, 19thC, 5½in (14cm) high.
£200–250 PSA

A pair of Bohemian ruby-tinted glass vases, with white overlay, flared rims, chased gilt-metal scrolled handles, on circular feet, 19thC, 13½in (34.5cm) high.
£750–850 AH

Bohemian coloured glass

One of the most famous colours to be developed was ruby glass, created by the addition of gold chloride. The use of ultramarine in glassmaking during the early 19th century produced shades from very pale blue to almost black. Many different colours were discovered during the 1820s and 1830s including violet, pink and new shades of green and blue. Unusual new colours were transparent yellow-green and green-yellow produced by adding small quantities of uranium to the batch. Uranium was also used to produce an opaque apple-green glass known as chrysoprase. Silver chloride was used to produce a yellow stain and an agate-like effect called Lithyalin.

The techniques used in the 19th century by Bohemian glassmakers to colour glass were:
• the addition of a metal oxide to a batch of glass
• casing or overlay, where a clear body was covered with a coloured outer layer, giving a good double surface for cutting
• covering the clear body with a thin layer of colour

When identifying Bohemian coloured glass several points need to be considered:
• the quality of the colour and overall condition are the main determinants of the value of 19th century Bohemian glassware
• feel the item carefully to detect any damage: chips are less obvious on coloured glass
• look for damage to feet; ornate feet can easily be re-cut, but they will be smaller and may look out of proportion
• blue-stained Bohemian glass often fades; this can seriously affect value

A Bohemian Lithyalin sealing-wax red glass vase, possibly from Friedrich Egermann workshop, incised on the base 'Alexander Cunningham July 1842', 9½in (24cm) high.
£900–1,200 S
Lithyalin is a polished opaque glass resembling hardstones, patented by Friedrich Egermann in 1829 at his factory in Haida, northern Bohemia.

Cameo glass

Cameo glass was first produced in Roman times, but the technique fell into disuse until the beginning of the 19th century. It is produced from two or more layers of different coloured glass, which are cut away from the base vessel leaving the subject standing out in relief. Most cameo glass comprises a body with a white overlay, although up to four layers of different colours may occur. The major British manufacturers of cameo in the 19th century were Thomas Webb, W H, B & J Richardson, and Stevens & Williams, who were all based in the Midlands.

A Bohemian glass vase, the blue ground with white overlay and painted in colours, with scrolling gilt foliage, damaged and repaired, 19thC, 18½in (47cm) high.
£320–380 CSK

A cameo glass vase, overlaid in white with stylized leaves and ribbons, with stiff-leaf and geometric bands, on a brown ground, 19thC, 4½in (11.5cm) high.
£550–650 DN

A pair of blue glass bud vases, with baluster bodies and flared rims, c1840, 7in (18cm) high.
£300–350 JHa

A burgundy glass bulb vase, c1840, 7¼in (18.5cm) high.
£100–120 MJW

A pair of Bristol blue glass vases, c1840, 7in (18cm) high.
£450–500 MJW

A Victorian glass épergne, with a silver-plated stand, 16in (40.5cm) high.
£240–290 SUL

A Victorian glass flower vase épergne, on original mirror back, 12in (30.5cm) high.
£250–300 AA

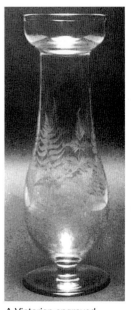

A Victorian engraved glass hyacinth vase, 8½in (21.5cm) high.
£145–170 CB

A Victorian hand-painted opaline glass vase, 10½in (26.5cm) high.
£100–120 ING

A pressed glass posy vase, 19thC, 3½in (9cm) high.
£25–30 DUN

◄ A Victorian glass vase, applied with a flower, small chips, 3½in (9cm) high.
£120–150 WAC

An opaque white glass vase, polychrome-painted with birds in a flower garland, with gilt line rims, probably by Richardson, slight rubbing, mid-19thC, 15½in (39.5cm) high.
£600–700 WW
Originally probably one of a pair. These vases are often converted to lamps because of their good size and lovely painting.

A Bohemian trumpet-shaped glass vase, ruby-flashed and overlaid in white with six diamond-cut panels above a flattened faceted knop, on a circular base, decorated with gilt borders and vermiculation, slight rubbing, mid-19thC, 15½in (39.5cm) high.
£500–600 WW

◄ A pair of Bohemian green-tinted glass vases, each overlaid in white with two panels, one finely decorated in coloured enamels with a young girl, the other with flowers and leaves, on a gilt leaf-scroll ground, on white overlaid base, mid-19thC, 13in (33cm) high.
£1,200–1,500 DN

An opaque white glass bulb vase, the brown base decorated with Greek key pattern, with gilding on the neck, c1850, 5in (12.5cm) high.
£100–120 MJW

A pair of French lavender blue glass vases, each decorated with a partial cobalt blue overlay on the lower body and overall gilt tracery, mid-19thC, 10¼in (26cm) high.
£500–550 B&B

A pair of Bohemian cranberry glass vases, with white enamel overlay, the enamel panels decorated with floral and gilt sprays and heightened with gilding, c1860, 13in (33cm) high.
£950–1,100 Mit
Although contemporary, these vases did not necessarily start life together.

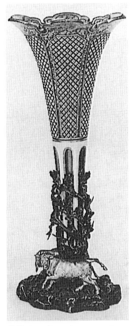

A Bohemian glass overlay trumpet-shaped vase, in an English silver-plated and gilt stand, marked 'Published by Elkington Mason & Co, April 1851', 18½in (47cm) high.
£500–600 P

A cut-glass celery vase, c1860, 10½in (26.5cm) high.
£120–150 CB

An opaline glass vase, painted with flowers, c1860, 20in (51cm) high.
£1,000–1,200 CB

► A pair of vaseline glass vases, c1860, 10in (25.5cm) high.
£400–450 ARE

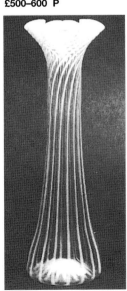

A pair of French turquoise overlay opaque glass vases, the turquoise grounds decorated with gilt anthemion and stylized foliage, the circular feet and rims heightened with gilding, slight wear, possibly St. Louis, c1860, 15¾in (40cm) high.
£4,000–4,500 C

A green glass hyacinth vase, with rough pontil, c1860, 6in (15cm) high.
£85–100 CB

A Molineux Webb glass celery vase, c1865, 10¼in (26cm) high.
£140–160 GLN

A pair of Varnish glass vases, with mercury discs sealed into their bases, c1870, 9in (23cm) high.
£700–800 ARE

An opaline glass vase, enamelled with flowers, c1860, 12in (30.5cm) high.
£270–320 CB

A Continental glass hyacinth vase, with enamel decoration, c1870, 5½in (14cm) high.
£65–80 WGT

A Continental glass vase and cover, cut with stylized flowers and diamond panels, minor rim chips, 1880–1900, 21in (53.5cm) high.
£500–550 S

Three coloured glass hyacinth vases:
l. amethyst, c1860, 5¾in (14.5cm) high.
£60–70
c. vaseline, c1870, 7¼in (18.5cm) high.
£120–140
r. amber, 5¾in (14.5cm) high.
£50–60 MJW

A garniture of four Bohemian gilt and overlay glass vases, each overlaid in white and cut with stiff leaves, with tall waisted neck and overturned rim, cased in blue and cut with printies, overall gilded with stars and scrolls, c1870, largest 14½in (37cm) high.
£2,750–3,500 S

A vaseline glass three-branch crib vase, c1880, 7½in (19cm) high.
£140–160 CB
It is difficult to identify the specific glasshouses where these items were made, as the glassworkers moved from one factory to another.

A clear glass lily vase, c1870, 41in (104cm) high.
£300–400 DUN

A Bohemian cut-glass and enamelled bud vase, c1870, 10¼in (26cm) high.
£200–240 CB

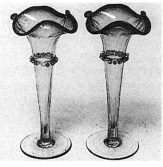

Two glass celery vases:
r. gadrooned and scalloped,
1870, 10in (25.5cm) high.
£120–150
l. with moulded pedestal,
1880, 10in (25.5cm), high.
£120–150 CB

A pair of Victorian cranberry glass
épergne vases, c1880,
8in (20.5cm) high.
£220–250 DUN

A cranberry glass vase, c1880,
5½in (14cm) high.
£125–145 AnS

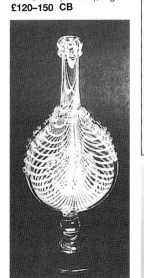

A Nailsea glass vase,
in the shape of a pair
of bellows, c1880,
14in (35.5cm) high.
£300–345 ARE

Nailsea glass

The group of glass articles known as 'Nailsea' gain their name from the glass
company started in 1788 by John Robert Lucas, in Nailsea near Bristol. Until its
closure in 1869 this glasshouse produced green-tinted bottle or window glass
which was used to make a variety of domestic and garden articles, as well as
novelty items in the shape of walking sticks, pipes and hats.
Much of the output was plain glass but some had coloured glass worked into it.
Looped white, blue, red or pink designs are traditionally known as Nailsea.
The name is often applied to any article with splashes of colour marvered into its
surface. In fact, there is strong evidence to show that a great deal of Nailsea was
made elsewhere in the country and was probably more likely to have come from
the north of England. Similar wares were also made in New England, USA.

A pair of cranberry
glass vases, c1880,
7¾in (19.5cm) high.
£165–185 AMH

A clear glass vase,
c1880, 6½in (16.5cm) high.
£100–120 DUN

A cranberry glass vase,
with clear foot, c1880,
12in (30.5cm) high.
£110–130 CB

A Bohemian cranberry
glass vase, hand-painted
with flowers, c1880,
8½in (21.5cm) high.
£55–65 AnS

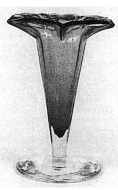

A cranberry glass vase,
c1880, 5½in (14cm) high.
£100–120 AMH

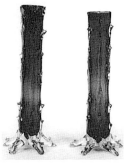

A pair of Bohemian gilt-
overlaid cranberry glass
portrait vases, the flared
rims and narrow necks
above slender bodies,
painted with panels of
busts of maidens and
flowers, on circular feet,
c1880, 12½in (32cm) high.
£1,000–1,200 RTo

A Victorian cranberry glass
vase, with long fluted stem,
on green-tinted base,
c1880, 12in (30.5cm) high.
£120–150 PCh

A Bohemian cylindrical crackled cranberry glass vase, painted in coloured enamels and gilt, heron, insects and lakeside flowers on a pedestal base, c1880, 14in (35.5cm) high.
£420–500 RBB

A pair of Bohemian glass vases, with knopped stems, flared feet, overlaid with alternating panels in gilt and white on a cranberry glass ground, the gilt panels painted with flowers, c1880, 11in (28cm) high.
£1,200–1,400 WL

A Peloton pink glass posy vase, c1880, 3½in (9cm) high.
£100–120 CB
Patented on 25th October 1880 by Wilhelm Kralik of Neuwelt Bohemia, Peloton glass was produced in various other glasshouses.

A glass celery vase, cut and engraved with birds and flowers, c1880, 8in (20.5cm) high.
£180–200 CB

A Bohemian Jugendstil glass vase, c1880, 10¼in (26cm) high.
£250–300 MJW

A coralene-type glass vase, the body shading from pink to yellow, applied with yellow coral fronds, c1880, 10in (25.5cm) high.
£180–200 Som

A vaseline glass vase, c1880, 8in (20.5cm) high.
£120–150 DUN

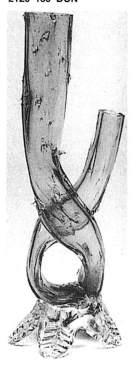

An opalescent glass vase, c1880, 9in (23cm) high.
£60–70 CB

Cross Reference
See Colour Review

A spiral vaseline glass specimen vase, c1880, 7½in (19cm) high.
£85–100 WAC

A ruby and white cameo glass vase, carved with bees flying amongst foxgloves, the neck with zig–zag border, c1880, 8½in (21.5cm) high.
£2,750–3,250 P(S)

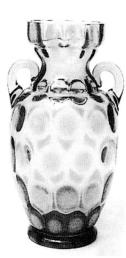

A blue opalescent glass bulb vase, c1880, 6½in (16.5cm) high.
£85–100 AnS

A pair of Swedish neo-classical ormolu-mounted cobalt blue glass vases, late 18thC, 10¼in (26cm) high.
£25,000–28,000 S(NY)

A Bohemian blue-flashed glass vase, 19thC, 12½in (32cm) high.
£1,000–1,100 HOK

A French opaline glass vase, c1850, 20in (51cm) high.
£1,400–1,600 CB

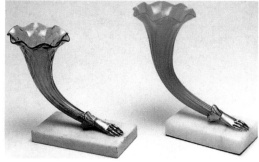

Two pairs of English citrine cornucopia, mounted on white marble bases, c1820.
£950–1,150 each pair CB

Two cornucopia vases, on marble and alabaster bases, c1840.
£900–1,000 CB

► A pair of enamelled Etruscan-style baluster glass vases, possibly c1850, 15in (38cm) high.
£200–250 FD

A Bohemian ruby overlay centre vase and cover, probably by Harrach Glasshouse, c1850, 25in (63.5cm) high.
£4,500–5,500 S

A pair of Stourbridge vases, with cut panels and gilt decoration, c1850, 11½in (29cm) high.
£900–1,100 Som

► A pair of Baccarat enamelled double-overlay glass vases, by Jean-François Robert, slight damage, c1855, 11¾in (30cm) high.
£4,500–5,000 S

Sets and pairs

Unless otherwise stated, any description which refers to 'a set' or 'a pair' includes a guide price for the entire set or the pair, even though the illustration may show only a single item.

A pair of French hand-painted opaline vases, c1840, 9in (23cm) high.
£1,000–1,200 MJW

A Bohemian cameo green glass vase, overlaid with white and heavily gilded, c1845.
£950–1,150 CB

A Peking glass vase,
c1860, 10in (25.5cm) high.
£500–650 CB

A pair of Bohemian overlay
glass bottle vases and
covers, possibly Neuwelt
or Adolfhütte bei
Winterberg, slight damage,
c1860, 25¼in (64cm) high.
£20,000–25,000 S

A pair of French opaline
vases, with flared
crenellated rims on knopped
stems and splayed feet,
c1860, 20in (51cm) high.
£4,000–4,800 S

A mercury glass double-
walled vase, marked
Varnish & Co, c1860,
9in (23cm) high.
£950–1,150 ARE
**This technique was
patented in 1849. Always
ensure that the seal is
intact on these vases or
atmospheric conditions
will cause the 'silver'
to deteriorate.**

A Baccarat cased
glass vase, c1860,
11½in (29cm) high.
£800–900 MJW

A Richardson opaline
glass vase, c1860,
10in (25.5cm) high.
£650–800 CB

Items in the Vases
section have been
arranged in date order.

A mercury glass vase,
c1860, 11½in (29cm) high.
£950–1,150 DUN

A green mercury
glass vase, c1860,
9½in (24cm) high.
£700–850 DUN

A selection of Victorian hyacinth vases,
1860–1920, tallest 9in (23cm) high.
£40–110 each CB

A pair of Baccarat vases, c1868,
19½in (49.5cm) high.
£2,000–2,400 S

A Russian vase, originally
one of a pair, dated '1869',
23¼in (59cm) high.
£3,000–3,600 S

A pair of Victorian vaseline glass vases, with pincer work collar and 'leaf' feet, 8½in (21.5cm) high.
£185–220 CB

◄ A selection of hyacinth vases, c1870, largest 8½in (21.5cm) high.
£70–120 CB

A Victorian vaseline glass vase, 10in (25.5cm) high.
£150–180 CB

A pair of French opaline glass vases, by Jean-François Robert, painted with flowers, c1870, 14in (35.5cm) high.
£1,100–1,300 CB

A flask-shaped glass vase, c1870, 13¾in (35cm) high.
£350–400 MJW

A French hyacinth vase, c1870, 8in (20.5cm) high.
£90–100 MJW

An opaline glass vase, with enamel decoration, c1870, 11in (28cm) high.
£220–260 CB

A Lobmeyr Persian-style enamelled and gilt two-handled vase, with painted 'JLL' grid mark in white, c1875, 6¾in (17cm) high.
£8,500–9,500 S

A pair of Bohemian enamelled and gilt glass vases, c1875, 13in (33cm) high.
£3,400–4,000 ALiN

A pair of Northwood glass vases, with intaglio cut decoration, c1880, 9in (23cm) high.
£2,400–2,800 MJW

An Emile Gallé two-piece praying mantis vase, c1880, 11¾in (30cm) high.
£10,500–11,500 S

A ruby glass vase, with acid-etched body, c1880, 6½in (16.5cm) high.
£475–600 MJW

A pair of Stourbridge glass vases, decorated with white 'pull-up' pattern, c1880, 4½in (11.5cm) diam.
£150–200 JHa

A pair of Bohemian glass tulip vases, c1880, 12in (30.5cm) high.
£1,000–1,200 P(B)

A vaseline opalescent vase, c1880, 8in (20.5cm) high.
£180–220 CB

A Eugène Rousseau 'Japonisant' vase, moulded with stylized flowerheads, c1880, 9in (23cm) high.
£2,000–2,200 S

A Lobmeyr Persian-style glass vase, marked 'JLL', c1880, 17in (43cm) high.
£10,500–12,500 S

A cranberry glass celery vase, c1880, 9½in (24cm) high.
£140–160 AMH

◀ A pair of Bohemian ruby glass and 'jewelled' baluster-shaped vases, each decorated with trails of foliage, on a cylindrical base, probably by Moser, c1880, 37in (94cm) high.
£11,000–12,000 S

A pair of Stourbridge yellow glass and gilt enamel vases, c1880, 5in (12.5cm) high.
£330–370 MJW

◀ A cranberry glass vase, c1880, 8in (20.5cm) high.
£180–200 AMH

A Webb three-coloured cameo vase, attributed to William Fritsche, c1880, 18½in (47cm) high.
£10,500–12,500 S

A cased glass vase, decorated with gilt, c1880, 14in (35.5cm) high.
£500–600 CB

◀ A Stevens & Williams Mat-Su-Noke cased and applied glass vase, designed by Northwood, c1884, 6½in (16.5cm) high.
£900–1,100 ALiN

A pressed glass vase, decorated with swans, c1880, 6½in (16.5cm) high.
£100–120 GLN

A Victorian splashed and spiralled vase, 10¾in (27.5cm) high.
£250–300 PGA

A Thomas Webb cameo vase, decorated in white over blue satin glass, c1890, 6in (15cm) high.
£850–1,050 CB

A pair of Lobmeyr opalescent glass vases, c1885, 9½in (24cm) high.
£4,000–4,500 S

A Thomas Webb cameo glass vase, depicting Ceramia, signed 'G. Woodall', c1889, 6¼in (16cm) high.
£18,500–22,000 P

A Thomas Webb & Sons double-cameo glass vase, decorated with a spray of budding and leafy branches on a Burmese ground, late 19thC, 10in (25.5cm) high.
£5,000–6,000 P

◄ A glass lily stem vase, of bifurcated form, with an applied green stem and opalescent flowerhead, c1890, 13½in (34.5cm) high.
£250–300 P(B)

A Thomas Webb & Sons Chinese-style cameo glass vase, carved with a frog and leafy branches, c1885, 7¾in (19.5cm) high.
£4,500–5,000 P

An amethyst glass hyacinth vase, c1890, 6in (15cm) high.
£50–60 CB

A pink and green vaseline glass 'Jack-in-the-Pulpit' vase, c1890, 10in (25.5cm) high.
£250–300 MJW

► A cranberry glass vase, c1890, 6in (15cm) high.
£140–160 BELL

A Webb cameo glass vase, c1885, 5½in (14cm) high.
£950–1,000 MJW

A vaseline opalescent glass vase, on green leaf-moulded foot, c1890, 5in (12.5cm) high.
£85–100 CB

A James Couper Clutha vase, 'Liberty' and 'Dresser' marks on base, c1890, 7in (18cm) high.
£2,000–2,250 NCA

A cranberry glass vase,
with applied leaves,
c1890, 8in (20.5cm) high.
£160–200 ARE

A crystal posy vase, in
gilded metal frame, c1890,
8¼in (21cm) high.
£185–225 MJW

A glass lily vase, c1890,
23in (58.5cm) high.
£1,300–1,450 ARE

A blue-over-ivory cased
glass vase, in the style
of Jules Barbe, c1890,
9¾in (25cm) high.
£275–325 JHa

A rainbow spangle
glass vase, c1890,
11in (28cm) high.
£290–340 CB

A Tiffany Favrile glass
vase, decorated with links,
c1895, 11½in (29cm) high.
£2,800–3,200 S(NY)

A French enamelled
opaline glass vase, late
19thC, 7¼in (18.5cm) high.
£200–240 GH

A Tiffany Favrile glass
vase, inscribed 'L.C.T.'
and 'H1754', c1897,
5in (12.5cm) high.
£1,000–1,200 S(NY)

A pair of American
glass vases, with silver
overlay, marked 'Quezal'
on base, c1900,
15¼in (38.5cm) high.
£12,500–14,000 SFL

A Eugène Feuillâtre silver-
mounted enamelled vase,
on a three-footed base,
c1900, 9½in (24cm) high.
£7,500–8,500 S(NY)

A Eugène Michel glass
vase, decorated with stag
beetles, engraved mark,
c1900, 8in (20.5cm) high.
£12,000–13,500 S

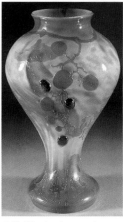

A Gallé wheel-carved,
applied and fire-polished
glass vase, with grape
and vine decoration,
signature in relief, c1900,
12in (30.5cm) high.
£2,000–2,200 FBG

Prices

The price ranges quoted in this book reflect the
average price a purchaser might expect to pay for
a similar item. The price will vary according to the
condition, rarity, size, popularity, provenance, colour
and restoration of the item. If you are selling it is quite
likely that you will be offered less than the price range.

A St Louis Art Nouveau amethyst glass vase, with flame enamelling, c1900, 8in (20.5cm) high.
£100–120 MON

A Daum wheel-carved cameo glass vase, inscribed 'Daum Nancy', c1900, 10½in (26.5cm) high.
£5,000–6,000 S(NY)

An Emile Gallé Lotus flower vase, decorated with applied scarab beetles, c1900, 11in (28cm) high.
£8,000–9,000 S

An Emile Gallé overlaid and etched glass vase, with cameo signature, c1900, 22in (56cm) high.
£20,000–22,000 CNY

A Gallé glass vase, with floral design in three layers, signed in cameo 'Gallé', c1900, 6½in (16.5cm) high.
£2,500–3,000 PSG

► A Tiffany Favrile bronze-mounted glass vase, c1900, 21¼in (54cm) high.
£17,000–20,000 S(NY)

An Art Nouveau cameo glass vase, by Mountjoy, decorated with a blue flower design with gilded stars, c1900, 8in (20.5cm) high.
£650–750 ANO

A glass vase, c1900, 5in (12.5cm) high.
£12–25 COL

A Daum wheel-carved cameo glass Crocus vase, signed 'Daum Nancy', c1900, 11¾in (30cm) high.
£6,000–7,000 S(NY)

► A Gallé cameo glass vase, c1900, 3¾in (9.5cm) high.
£450–500 MON

A Daum *intercalaire* internally-decorated, etched, enamelled and gilded vase, depicting aquatic plants and animals, marked 'Daum Nancy', c1900, 16in (40.5cm) high.
£14,500–16,000 S

A Daum maize vase, of opalescent dichroic glass, overlaid and etched, engraved mark, c1900, 11½in (29cm) high.
£3,200–3,600 S

A Daum landscape 'blow-out' vase, mould-blown with trees and a village, c1900, 11½in (29cm) high.
£5,500–6,000 S

A Daum cameo glass vase, overlaid and etched with sunflowers, with tapered rim, marked, c1900, 23¼in (59cm) high.
£6,000–7,000 C

A Gallé narcissus vase, decorated in *marquetrie-sur-verre* technique, engraved mark, c1900, 8¼in (21cm) high.
£16,000–17,000 S

A Daum wheel-carved cameo glass vase, decorated with magnolias, signed 'Daum/Nancy', c1900, 19½in (49.5cm) high.
£7,000–8,000 S(NY)

◀ A Gallé cameo etched and carved mushroom and web vase, c1900, 12¼in (31cm) high.
£2,200–2,400 S

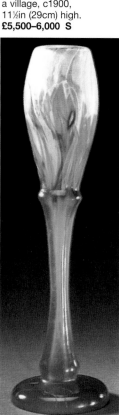

A Gallé vase, of clear glass, decorated in *marquetrie-sur-verre* technique with crocus, engraved mark, c1900, 15in (38cm) high.
£25,000–27,000 S

▶ A Gallé cameo glass vase, red and brown overlaid on amber, signed, c1900, 7⅛in (19cm) high.
£2,000–2,200 PSG

A Daum glass vase, marked 'Daum Nancy', c1900, 13in (33cm) high.
£12,000–14,000 C

A Daum Nancy enamel vase, acid-etched with blue lilies, painted in naturalistic colours and gilt, c1900, 9in (23cm) high.
£2,600–2,800 ART

◀ A Daum Nancy cameo glass vase, acid-etched and painted with poppies, c1900, 24¾in (63cm) high.
£3,800–4,200 S(NY)

A Daum Nancy enamelled 'Solifleur' vase, painted with violets, c1900, 5in (12.5cm) high.
£1,300–1,500 ART

Three glass hyacinth vases:
l & r. enamelled with flora and gilt highlights, c1900.
c. mottled in amethyst and ochre, c1900.
£60–80 each CB

A Daum internally-decorated and acid-cut vase, cameo mark 'Daum Nancy' and Cross of Lorraine, c1900, 21in (53.5cm) high.
£4,500–5,000 Bon

An Emile Gallé cameo glass vase, c1900, 7in (18cm) high.
£1,200–1,500 ASA

A Daum internally-decorated glass vase, signed and marked, c1900, 11¾in (30cm) high.
£4,800–5,000 DORO

A Daum purple-tinted cameo glass vase, decorated with iris, on round base, signed 'Daum Nancy', c1900, 16in (40.5cm) high.
£3,000–3,500 E

◄ A Gallé cameo glass vase, overlaid in blue and green with flowering plants, c1900, 7in (18cm) high.
£2,500–2,800 ART

A Gallé cameo glass vase, with long slender neck, decorated with a leaf, c1900, 7in (18cm) high.
£650–750 ANO

A pair of ormolu-mounted vases, deeply engraved, impressed Baccarat mark, c1900, 13½in (34.5cm) high.
£3,000–3,500 S

A Gallé glass vase, with floral decoration, c1900, 5¾in (14.5cm) high.
£500–550 PC

A Tiffany Favrile 'Jack-in-the-Pulpit' vase, marked '2466H', c1900, 20in (51cm) high.
£7,000–8,000 CNY

◄ A Bohemian iridescent glass vase, c1900, 8in (20.5cm) high.
£90–100 MiA

An Emile Gallé chrysanthemum vase, c1900, 23in (58.5cm) high.
£10,000–11,000 S

A Gallé cameo glass pilgrim vase, signed in cameo, c1900, 17in (43cm) high.
£6,750–8,000 S(NY)

An American opaline glass vase, embossed with silver, c1900, 6¼in (16cm) high.
£75–85 MON

A Gallé cameo glass vase, minor fleck at base, c1900, 13½in (34.5cm) high.
£3,000–3,500 S(NY)

▶ A Daum acid-cut and enamelled glass vase, c1905, 4in (10cm) diam.
£2,000–2,200 ART

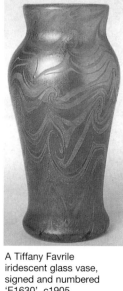

A Tiffany Favrile iridescent glass vase, signed and numbered 'E1630', c1905, 9in (23cm) high.
£1,000–1,200 P

An Emile Gallé carved vase, c1902, 11in (28cm) high.
£20,000–22,000 S

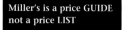

Miller's is a price GUIDE not a price LIST

A Daum wistaria vase, in opalescent glass, overlaid and etched, engraved mark, c1905, 20in (51cm) high.
£3,800–4,200 S

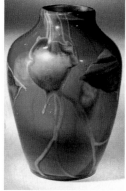

◀ A Tiffany Favrile reactive paperweight glass vase, inscribed 'L.C.T. Y3030', c1905, 7¼in (18.5cm) high.
£9,500–10,000 S(NY)

A Tiffany Favrile flowerform glass vase, engraved 'L.C.T.' and numbered, c1905, 18in (45.5cm) high.
£8,500–9,500 CNY

A Daum internally decorated and acid-cut trumpet vase, engraved 'Daum Nancy' and Cross of Lorraine, c1905, 13½in (34.5cm) high.
£9,000–10,500 Bon

A Daum internally-decorated, acid-cut enamelled and applied vase, signed in cameo and Cross of Lorraine, c1905, 21½in (54.5cm) high.
£4,600–5,400 Bon

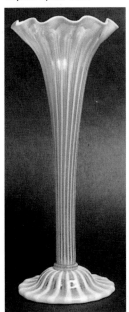

An opalescent striped glass trumpet-shaped lily vase, c1910, 15½in (39.5cm) high.
£500–550 ARE

A Tiffany Favrile yellow glass 'Jack-in-the-Pulpit' vase, 1905, 18¼in (46.5cm) high.
£5,000–5,500 S

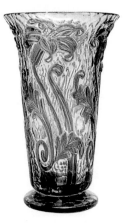

A Webb *faux* cameo vase, with amethyst decoration, c1930, 9½in (24cm) high.
£600–700 MJW

A Continental iridescent glass vase, with pressed leaf design, in rainbow colours, 20thC, 9in (23cm) high.
£190–220 SUC

◄ A Gallé cameo glass vase, overlaid with blue and amethyst glass acid-etched with anemones, c1910, 8in (20.5cm) high.
£4,000–4,500 ART

A Daum internally-decorated, carved and acid-etched vase, engraved mark and Cross of Lorraine, c1905, 18in (45.5cm) high.
£6,000–7,000 Bon

A pair of Bohemian overlay glass and enamel-decorated vases, 20thC, 14in (35.5cm) high.
£1,500–2,000 B&B

A overlaid, engraved and cut vase, c1910, 6in (15cm) high.
£400–450 MJW

A Daum applied wheel-carved cameo glass vase, marked, slight damage and restoration, c1909, 10¾in (27.5cm) high.
£40,000–50,000 S(NY)

A Steuben Aurene blue iridescent glass vase, inscribed 'Steuben Aurene 2479', c1910, 12½in (32cm) high.
£1,000–1,200 S(NY)

A Daum acid-cut and enamelled glass vase, c1910, 9¾in (25cm) high.
£700–800 AH

A Tiffany Favrile glass 'Gooseneck' vase, 1912, 12¼in (31cm) high.
£8,000–9,000 S

A Lalique moulded and frosted glass vase, 'Monnaie du Pape', moulded and inscribed, after 1914.
£1,600–2,000 S(NY)

An Artisti Barovier murrhines glass vase, decorated with roses, c1920, 9in (23cm) high.
£4,500–5,000 S(NY)

A Daum internally-decorated acid-cut and enamelled glass vase, c1920, 18in (45.5cm) high.
£6,500–7,500 ART

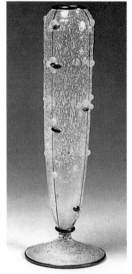

A Daum internally-decorated vase, with applied decoration, engraved mark 'Daum Nancy', 1920–30, 10½in (26.6cm) high.
£6,000–7,000 Bon

◄ A WMF Myra Cristal glass vase, with golden iridescence, c1925, 5½in (14cm) high.
£100–125 MON

A Tiffany Favrile paperweight glass vase, decorated with Morning Glory blossoms, c1915, 7½in (19cm) high.
£20,000–22,000 S(NY)

A Quezal iridescent glass vase, signed 'Quezal 937', c1920, 11in (28cm) high.
£1,500–1,800 S(NY)

An Emile Gallé mould-blown glass vase, overlaid and etched with elephants, c1925, 15in (38cm) high.
£23,000–25,000 CNY

A Tiffany Favrile glass vase, with thick rolled rim, inscribed 'Louis C. Tiffany 865N', c1919, 13in (33cm) high.
£10,000–12,000 S(NY)

A Gallé cameo glass Polar Bear vase, intaglio carved mark 'Gallé', c1920, 11in (28cm) high.
£30,000–35,000 C

A René Lalique glass vase, 'Aras', moulded mark 'R. Lalique', after 1924, 9in (23cm) high.
£3,000–3,500 S

A Tiffany Favrile lava glass vase, decorated in amber coated with blue, dripping golden-amber around the rim, inscribed, c1921, 4½in (11.5cm) high.
£15,500–17,500 S(NY)

◄ A Daum acid- and wheel-cut glass vase, c1925, 5in (12.5cm) diam.
£400–450 SUC

A Rosenthal studio glass vase, c1925, 9¼in (23.5cm) high.
£100–120 DSG

A Gabriel Argy-Rousseau *pâte-de-verre* glass vase, entitled 'Le Jardin des Hesperides', impressed mark, 1926, 9½in (24cm) high.
£22,000–24,000 S

A Murano glass vase, 20thC, 8in (20.5cm) high.
£30–35 ROW

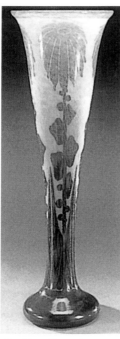

A Le Verre Français dahlia vase, c1925, 29in (73.5cm) high.
£2,000–2,200 S

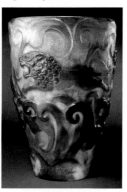

A Gabriel Argy-Rousseau *pâte-de-verre* vase, 'Lions', moulded marks, c1926, 8¾in (22cm) high.
£22,000–24,000 S(NY)

A Bohemian hand-blown Flames glass vase, 20thC, 17in (43cm) high.
£85–100 BKK

A Gabriel Argy-Rousseau *pâte-de-verre* vase, entitled 'Les Loups dans la Neige', c1926, 9½in (24cm) high.
£10,000–12,000 CNY

A René Lalique black-enamelled clear glass vase, 'Inimroud', wheel-cut 'R. Lalique' and engraved 'France No. 970', after 1926, 8in (20.5cm) high.
£3,000–3,500 CNY

A Thomas Webb 'wavy' vase, 1930s, 7in (18cm) high.
£50–70 JHa

◄ A Gray-Stan vase, with red swirls, fully marked, c1930, 10in (25.5cm) high.
£350–400 JHa

A Lalique moulded, frosted and enamelled glass vase, 'La Gamar', model introduced 1926, inscribed 'R. Lalique', 7in (18cm) high.
£3,000–3,500 S(NY)

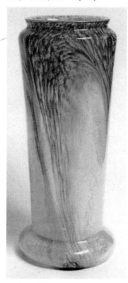

A Gray-Stan glass vase, with engraved signature, 1930s, 10¼in (26cm) high.
£350–450 CMO

A Gray-Stan ovoid glass vase, with white and blue swirls, 1930s, 12in (30.5cm) high.
£450–500 CMO

A Stevens & Williams
'Rainbow' vase, c1930,
6in (15cm) high.
£80–90 JHa

A Davidson glass vase, of
globular shape with flared
neck and broadly-ribbed
lower body, c1930,
8in (20.5cm) high.
£70–80 JHa

An Art Deco vase, with
a flecked base, 1930s,
7in (18cm) high.
£100–110 PSA

A blue glass double
overlay vase, 20thC,
10in (25.5cm) high.
£60–70 MJW

A Gray-Stan blue glass
vase, streaked with
white festoons, 1930s,
13in (33cm) diam.
£350–400 CMO

◄ A blue-and-
black swirls
cloud glass
vase, with frog,
1930s, 13½in
(34.5cm) diam.
£60–70 BEV

A cloud glass vase, 1930s,
6in (15cm) high.
£60–90 BEV

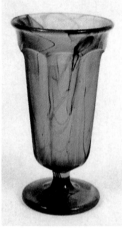

A Davidson blue and
amethyst cloud glass vase,
1930s, 6in (15cm) high.
£20–25 COL

A Lamoirtine acid-etched
vase, enamelled on
mottled white and amber,
1930s, 11in (28cm) high.
£150–200 HEM

A Bagley clear glass three-piece flower set, 'Wyndham'
1333/D, c1934, 11in (28cm) wide.
£50–60 PC

▶ A René Lalique
opalescent glass
vase, 'Orléans',
marked, after 1930,
8in (20.5cm) high.
£1,600–1,800 S

A Stevens & Williams
glass vase, 1930s,
11in (28cm) high.
£100–120 JHa

A Bagley clear glass four-
piece flower set, 'Queen's
Choice' No. 1122, c1936,
9¼in (25.5cm) diam.
£70–80 PC

Three bulb vases, 1950s, 7½in (19cm) high.
£6–8 each AL

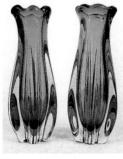

A pair of glass vases, 1950s, 9¾in (25cm) high.
£25–36 CaL

A cameo glass vase, marked 'Misale', 20thC, 4½in (11.5cm) high.
£200–250 ASA

A glass vase, 1960s, 13in (33cm) wide.
£25–35 CaL

▶ A Maltese emerald-and-clear cased glass vase, signed, late 20thC, 6in (15cm) high.
£35–40 SER

A Bohemian etched glass vase, mid-20thC, 7½in (19cm) high.
£80–90 FMN

A Chance Bros glass vase, 1970s, 4in (10cm) high.
£7–10 FD
Chance Bros were bought by Pilkington in 1945.

A Whitefriars Studio Art glass vase, c1969, 10in (25.5cm) high.
£250–300 JHa

A Glasform glass vase, 1994, 5¼in (13.5cm) high.
£50–65 GLA

A Glasform glass vase, 1994, 7in (18cm) high.
£40–50 GLA

◀ A Glasform glass vase, c1991, 5in (12.5cm) high.
£20–30 GLA

A Glasform glass vase, c1990, 9in (23cm) high.
£50–65 GLA

◀ Two Glasform vases, Nos. 4486 & 4485, signed, 1995, 4in (10cm) high.
£20–30 each GLA

A Siddy Langley Navajo vase, 1997, 10½in (26.5cm) high.
£120–140 NF

A pair of Murano-style glass clowns, late 20thC, 9in (23cm) high.
£25–30 each HEI

A Nailsea crown glass inkwell, c1820, 2½in (6.5cm) high.
£60–70 Som

► An enamelled *Kurfurstenhumpen*, possibly Francoma, late 17thC, 8in (20.5cm) high.
£9,000–10,000 S

A Stourbridge night light, c1900.
£120–140 CB

A set of wax still life ornaments under glass, c1870.
£50–150 each CB

A Nailsea glass ornament, c1860, 13in (33cm) high.
£160–180 Som

A glass pen stand, decorated with hounds, c1880, 5¾in (14.5cm) high.
£300–350 MJW
Usually called Nailsea but normally made around Stourbridge.

A double-overlay armorial part dessert service, with the crest of John Campbell, 5th Marquess of Breadalbane, French or Bohemian, c1840, carafe 6½in (16.5cm) high.
£2,000–2,500 S

Condition

The condition is absolutely vital when assessing the value of an antique. Damaged pieces on the whole appreciate much less than perfect examples. However, a rare desirable piece may command a high price even when damaged.

A German glass snuff bottle, c1860, 4in (10cm) high.
£225–245 MJW

► An amethyst glass trumpet, with wrythen-moulded tube, c1860, 7¾in (19.5cm) long.
£400–420 Som

◄ A cranberry glass smoke bell, c1860–70, 12½in (32cm) diam.
£100–125 WAB

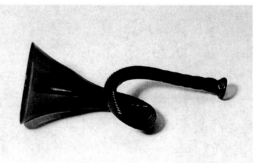

A Victorian pink cased glass posy vase, with butterfly decoration, c1880, 8¾in (22cm) high.
£275–325 MJW

An opaque glass vase, with tortoiseshell pattern, c1880, 6in (15cm) high.
£65–80 WAC

An amethyst glass bulb vase, c1880, 5in (12.5cm) high.
£65–80 CB

> Items in the Vases section have been arranged in date order.

A Sowerby opaque blue glass three-footed vase, c1880, 3¼in (8.5cm) high.
£35–40 GLN

A cross-patch amethyst malachite pressed glass vase, c1880, 3½in (9cm) high.
£100–120 JHa

◄ A Queen's ivory pressed glass double-ended swan vase, after a design by Walter Crane, c1880, 5¼in (13.5cm) wide.
£160–180 JHa

A Queen's ivory pressed glass posy vase, c1880, 2¼in (5.5cm) high.
£160–180 JHa

► A pressed glass vase, decorated with a design of Old King Cole, after a Walter Crane design, c1880, 3¼in, (8.5cm) high.
£180–220 JHa

A Persian-style iridescent glass vase, decorated with a band of gilt calligraphy on a vermiculé ground, divided by three lugs, the short trumpet neck with gilt scrolls, painted mark '515/2', probably Austrian, late 19thC, 6in (15cm) high.
£350–400 S(S)

A pair of James Powell, Whitefriars, Venetian-style glass vases, with hollow twisted stems, late 19thC, 6½in (16.5cm) high.
£350–400 JHa

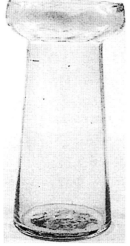

An opalescent vaseline glass bulb vase, possibly Powell, late 19thC, 6in (15cm) high.
£100–120 JHa

► A turquoise opaque glass vase, decorated with cameo portrait, late 19thC, 10¼in (26cm) high.
£70–80 PCh

A pair of opaque green glass vases, on veined marble bases, late 19thC, 7½in (19cm) high.
£700–800 S(S)

A cut-glass and gilt-metal-mounted vase, the crenellated horn rising from a ram's head terminal resting on a marble slab base, late 19thC, 8in (20.5cm) high.
£500–600 S(S)

An opaque white glass vase, with blue trailed rim, commemorating Queen Victoria's Jubilee, c1887, 5½in (14cm) high.
£85–100 JMC

An A J Couper & Sons Clutha glass vase, designed by Dr Christopher Dresser, the bulbous body with tall flared cylindrical neck and inverted rim, the green-tinted glass with milky white striations and with foil and air bubble inclusions, late 19thC 19½in (49.5cm) high.
£1,800–2,000 C

A pair of Bohemian engraved blue-stained glass vases, the rims cut with flutes, late 19thC, 13in (33cm) high.
£1,600–1,800 S

An Arsall French cameo glass vase, c1890, 5in (12.5cm) high.
£600–700 ASA

A Gallé faceted and enamelled glass dragonfly vase, heightened with gilding, the underside with engraved mark 'Cristallerie d'Emile Gallé Nancy Modèle et décor déposés', c1890, 11½in (29cm) high.
£1,600–1,800 S

A Gallé smoked glass vase, decorated in raised gilt with pendant sprays of apple blossom, carved 'Gallé 1884', 16in (40.5cm) high.
£800–900 CSK

▶ An Eugène Rousseau and E Leveille, French glass vase, c1890, 7¾in (19.5cm) high.
£600–650 SUC

An Ernest Leveille cameo glass vase, internally-decorated with lemon and coral-red patches, overlaid with a deep reddish-brown glass, acid-etched and wheel-carved with fish swimming, signed, dated '1890', 7in (18cm) high.
£12,000–14,000 P

Gallé cameo glass

Within the last five years a significant number of fake Gallé cameo glass vases have appeared on the market. Most have come from eastern Europe; they are signed in cameo 'Gallé Tip' (for Tip read 'Type'). It does not take too much imagination on the part of the unscrupulous to arrange the removal of the word 'Tip' by means of grinding and polishing, and many examples have had this treatment. Careful examination of the surface often reveals a depression near the signature which should raise suspicion. The bases of most of these recent imports are moulded and lack evidence of the polished and ground pontil mark found on many of the originals.

A Bohemian Mary Gregory-style cranberry glass vase, c1890, 4in (10cm) high.
£95–110 FMN

◀ A cranberry glass vase, c1890, 10in (25.5cm) high.
£100–125 COL

A Gallé enamelled glass dragonfly vase, the underside with engraved mark, 'Emile Gallé', c1890, 4½in (11.5cm) high.
£1,000–1,200 S

A pair of vaseline glass vases, applied with spiral citrus decoration, c1890, 8in (20.5cm) high.
£185–220 ARE

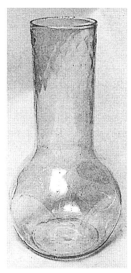

A clear glass vase, c1890, 16in (40.5cm) high.
£150–180 DUN

A cranberry glass bud vase, with clear foot, c1890, 6½in (16.5cm) high.
£85–100 CB

A Bohemian amber and red-flashed glass vase, engraved with flowers and gilded, c1890, 11½in (29cm) high.
£400–480 CB

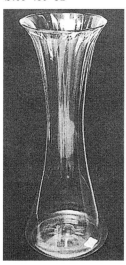

◀ A clear glass waisted vase, c1890, 18in (45.5cm) high.
£150–180 DUN

A cranberry glass vase, c1890, 6½in (16.5cm) high.
£85–100 CB

A vaseline glass vase, with moulded decoration, c1890, 7½in (19cm) high.
£250–300 MJW

A pair of George Bacchus transfer-printed glass vases, c1890, 12in (30.5cm) high.
£325–375 ARE
Based in Birmingham, George Bacchus & Sons was one of the first firms to use transfer-printing on glass.

A cranberry ribbed-glass vase, with turnover rim, c1890, 6in (15cm) high.
£110–130 CB

A Stuart & Co green glass lily vase, with thrown top and domed and folded foot, c1890, 6½in (16.5cm) high.
£60–70 JHa

A white-trailed vaseline glass vase, c1890, 12in (30.5cm) high.
£200–220 ARE

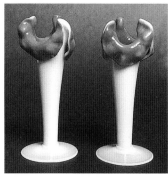

A pair of opaline glass vases, with ruby foldover tops, c1890, 6in (15cm) high.
£200–240 ARE

A pair of Victorian vaseline glass *solifleur* vases, c1890, 6in (15cm) high.
£130–150 BELL

A pink vaseline glass posy bowl, c1890, 4in (10cm) high.
£100–120 MJW

A Victorian opalescent blue and yellow striped glass vase, c1890, 4¼in (11cm) high.
£100–120 ARE

A Jack-in-the-Pulpit green vaseline glass vase, c1890, 7in (18cm) high.
£150–180 ARE
Jack-in-the-Pulpit vases were shaped and named after the American flower of the same name.

A pair of blue and yellow vaseline glass posy holders, c1890, 4¼in (11cm) high.
£170–190 ARE

A glass posy holder, c1890, 8in (20.5cm) high.
£130–150 ARE

A pair of glass posy vases, decorated with blue glass ribbons, c1890, 2in (5cm) high.
£250–280 MJW

A pair of late Victorian opalescent glass vases, with twist stems and five-leaf feet, 8½in (21.5cm) high.
£200–240 CB

A stag's horn vaseline glass vase, c1890, 8in (20.5cm) high.
£100–120 DUN

A Victorian cut and etched glass celery vase, c1890, 9½in (24cm) high.
£120–145 DUN

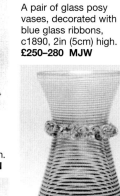

A turquoise trailed glass posy vase, with clear collar, c1890, 4in (10cm) high.
£75–90 CB

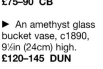

► An amethyst glass bucket vase, c1890, 9½in (24cm) high.
£120–145 DUN

Three glass celery vases, c1890, largest 8½in (21.5cm) high.
£100–160 each AL

A clear glass vase, c1890, 11in (28cm) high.
£100–120 DUN

A millefiori and latticinio glass vase, late 19thC, 5in (12.5cm) high.
£50–60 FD

A Daum Nerine vase, in colourless glass overlaid with pink and green, etched with flowering sprays against a textured ground, the underside with gilded inscription 'Daum Nancy fecit d'après E Lachenal 1896', 10in (25.5cm) high.
£1,700–2,000 S

A Harrach'sche Glasfabrik vase, the violet-tinted glass with a spray of flowers enamelled in gold, the lower rim decorated with a gold band, gold slightly rubbed, c1900, 9½in (24cm) high.
£850–950 DORO

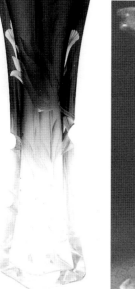

A Moser clear glass vase, the top with amethyst tint and deeply wheel-carved with tulips, c1900, 8in (20.5cm) high.
£85–100 MON

A Tiffany Favrile glass vase, in the shape of a flower, with a gold and white iridescent centre, the bowl finely feathered in green with streaks of opaque white, c1900, 12in (30.5cm) high.
£2,200–2,500 C

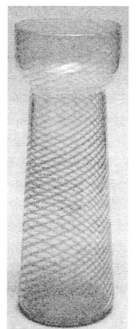

A glass celery vase, c1900, 9½in (24cm) high.
£40–50 DUN

◄ A glass hyacinth vase, with combed decoration, c1900, 7¾in (19.5cm) high.
£60–70 MJW

Insurance values

Always insure your valuable antiques for the cost of replacing them with similar items, regardless of the original price paid. Both dealers and auctioneers will provide a valuation service for a fee.

A clear glass vase, c1900, 10in (25.5cm) high.
£70–80 DUN

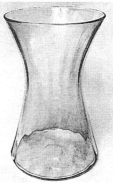

A clear glass waisted vase, c1900, 16in (40.5cm) high.
£100–120 DUN

▶ A Moser enamelled blue glass vase, decorated with leaves and branches, painted in colours and applied with metal acorns, signed, c1900, 3½in (9cm) high.
£350–420 P(B)

VASES 277

A Harrach'sche Glasfabrik vase, the green-flashed clear glass wheel-carved with geometric banding, foliage, fruit and flowers, heightened with gilding, c1900, 8¾in (22cm) wide.
£230–250 P

A James Powell lustre glass vase, c1900, 4in (10cm) high.
£85–100 MON

A Powell glass vase, c1900, 12in (30.5cm) high.
£60–70 DUN

◄ A Daum grey and blue glass vase, by Majorelle, internally streaked with amber and infused with gold foil inclusions, within a wrought-iron mount, inscribed marks, c1900, 10in (25.5cm) high.
£3,500–4,000 S(NY)

A pair of Art Nouveau blue glass spill vases, with WMF metal mounts, 1900–10, 3in (7.5cm) high.
£180–200 RAC
The value of these vases is in the metal mounts rather than the glass liners. They would typically be either green or clear glass, not blue.

A Gallé cameo glass landscape vase, with blue mountains and lake, c1900, 13in (33cm) high.
£7,500–8,500 ART

A Tiffany Favrile glass floriform vase, the golden-yellow iridescent glass decorated with fine-lined feathering in white and orange, 1894–1918, 5½in (14cm) high.
£2,200–2,500 S(NY)

A WMF metal-mounted glass vase, c1900, 7in (18cm) high.
£75–95 DUN

A pair of James Powell vaseline glass iris vases, c1900, 10in (25.5cm) high.
£160–180 MON

▶ A trailed glass vase, possibly James Powell, c1900, 12in (30.5cm) high.
£120–140 DUN

A satin glass lustre vase, with decorative metal top, c1900, 9½in (24cm) high.
£50–60 DKH

A Gallé grey glass vase, internally decorated with pink, overlaid with lilac and olive-green and etched with flowering sprays, cameo mark 'Gallé', c1900, 10in (25.5cm) high.
£1,000–1,200 S

A Gallé cameo glass vase, overlaid, acid-etched and carved with pendant stems of flowering wisteria, c1900, 13½in (34.5cm) high.
£1,000–1,200 DaD

A Daum etched and enamelled glass vase, with inclusions of vitrified powdered glass, c1900, 9½in (24cm) high.
£1,800–2,000 PSG

A Gallé cameo glass vase, the yellow glass overlaid in brown, acid-etched and carved with trees overlooking a river, cameo signature 'Gallé', c1900, 6½in (16.5cm) high.
£1,000–1,200 CSK

◄ A hand-painted cream glass vase, c1900, 14in (35.5cm) high.
£80–90 TS

A Daum rose-tinted glass vase, acid-etched with poppies and foliage, heightened with gilding and applied with a flower and foliage embellished foot, maker's mark 'LP', c1900, 5in (12.5cm) high.
£250–300 P

A Gallé glass vase, with lemon ground and brown cameo decoration, c1900, 4½in (11.5cm) high.
£300–350 PC

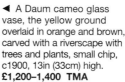

A blue glass vase, with raised decoration, slight damage, c1900, 10¾in (27.5cm) high.
£55–65 TS

◄ A Daum cameo glass vase, the yellow ground overlaid in orange and brown, carved with a riverscape with trees and plants, small chip, c1900, 13in (33cm) high.
£1,200–1,400 TMA

► A Gallé triple overlay cameo glass vase, acid-etched and carved, c1900, 4¾in (12cm) high.
£1,800–2,000 ABS

A Daum carved cameo and martelé glass anemone vase, internally streaked with light blue at the top and rust towards the base, decorated in *marqueterie-sur-verre* technique with three carved anemones and etched stems on a carved ground, engraved mark, c1900, 7in (18cm) high.
£3,000–3,500 S(Am)

A Gallé cameo glass vase, overlaid with purple glass, acid-etched with marsh plants against a pink ground, signed 'Gallé', c1900, 4½in (11.5cm) high.
£600–700 P

A pair of gilded glass vases, c1900, 6in (15cm) high.
£80–95 DUN

A Stourbridge aquamarine cameo glass vase, overlaid in opaque white and carved with poppies to either side, above a banded dentil base, c1900, 9½in (24cm) high.
£650–750 Bon

A Gallé enamelled smoky-grey glass vase, with trefoil neck, decorated with pink, green, yellow and blue dragonflies and flowering waterlilies, signed, c1900, 8¾in (22cm) high.
£1,800–2,000 P

A Gallé glass vase, with red ground and brown cameo decoration, c1900, 5¾in (14.5cm) high.
£600–700 PC

A Daum cameo and enamelled miniature vase, c1900, 3¼in (8.5cm) high.
£900–1,000 ABS

A Daum etched and enamelled glass vase, depicting a winter landscape, with enamelled signature, c1900, 4¾in (12cm) high.
£2,000–2,200 PSG

A Daum enamelled cameo glass vase, Summer, the mottled yellow-green and blue frosted glass body etched and enamel-painted with sunny waterfront riverscape with trees and purple mountains beyond, inscribed in black on base 'Daum Nancy HF', c1900, 9½in (24cm) high.
£4,000–4,500 SK(B)

A Daum etched and enamelled square glass vase, depicting sailing boats in orange, yellow, blue and green, engraved mark 'Daum Nancy', c1900, 4⅛in (11.5cm) high.
£1,000–1,200 AH

An iridescent deep purple glass vase, decorated with overall spider-web threading, early 20thC, 11¾in (30cm) high.
£65–75 RIT

Daum Frères

The Daum brothers, Auguste (1835–1909) and Antonin (1864–1930) worked together with Emile Gallé before establishing their own glassworks in Nancy. No distinction has so far been made between their work. The firm, now operating as Cristallerie Daum, is still in business today. Although Daum Frères produced some carved and enamelled pieces, most of their Art Nouveau wares are cameo glass or acid cut and colour-enamelled. Early Daum pieces tend to be enamelled.

A Daum cameo and enamelled miniature vase, c1900, 2¾in (7cm) high.
£1,200–1,400 ABS

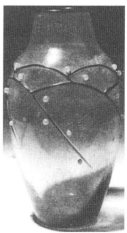

A Daum vase, the clear glass with air inclusions and areas of mottled grey towards the base, applied with trailed purple glass and small yellow globules in the form of stylized thorns and berries, with wheel-carved signature 'Daum Nancy' with the Cross of Lorraine, c1900, 11½in (29cm) high.
£2,000–2,400 C

A pair of Art Nouveau green and pink iridescent glass vases, with crimped bulbous necks and slender tapering stems, c1900, 13in (33cm) high.
£200–220 AP

◀ A French cameo glass vase, with a lustrous pink and green ground, overlaid and etched in green with pendant fuchsias and foliage, indecipherable incised mark, c1900, 16in (40.5cm) high.
£300–350 S(S)

A Gallé cameo glass *solifleur* vase, decorated with red overlaid on amber, acid-etched with berries and leaves, signed in cameo, c1900, 8¼in (21cm) high.
£1,000–1,200 PSG

A Gallé colourless glass vase, overlaid in pink and purple and etched with prunus blossom, fire-polished, c1900, 11¾in (30cm) high.
£2,200–2,500 S(Am)

A Burgun Schverer & Co glass vase, with a hammered silver mount, the grey glass enclosing deep reddish-brown swirling decoration and cut with three curving martelé swirls, early 20thC, 6¾in (17cm) high.
£600–700 S(NY)

A Gallé cameo glass vase, amber-tinted and overlaid with blue and amethyst glass, acid-etched with marguerites, signed, c1900, 9in (23cm) diam.
£2,500–3,000 PSG

A Gallé cameo glass vase, in brown and green overlaid on pink, c1900, 4⅜in (12cm) high.
£1,500–1,700 PSG

Miller's is a price GUIDE not a price LIST

A Gallé cameo glass vase, etched with blossoms and leaves, enamelled in pink, green, grey and orange, heightened with gilding, c1900, 9in (23cm) high.
£1,100–1,300 S(NY)

A Gallé glass vase, decorated with flowers and leaves, c1900, 4¼in (11cm) high.
£800–900 SHa

A pair of Baccarat gilt-decorated blue and green glass vases, moulded with daisies, supported by a grasshopper on a wheat-moulded mound, early 20thC, 8¼in (21cm) high.
£1,000–1,200 S(NY)

◀ A Gallé glass vase, decorated in brown with trees in a landscape, c1900, 6½in (16.5cm) high.
£1,000–1,100 SUC

A Gallé mould-blown glass vase, decorated with a clematis design in yellow, red, blue and green, c1900, 6¾in (17cm) high.
£3,000–3,500 PSG

A pair of Edwardian cut-glass and gilt-bronze-mounted vases, with pierced collars and cameo ceramic plaques, raised on white stone bases, 1901–10, 10½in (26.5cm) high.
£1,200–1,500 P

A Gallé vase, overlaid in green and brown and etched with seed pods and leaves, cameo signature, c1900, 5in (13cm) high.
£375–450 S(S)

◀ A Gallé cameo glass vase, in grey and pink glass overlaid in green and etched with sycamore seeds and foliage, minor chips, cameo mark 'Gallé', c1900, 8in (20.5cm) high.
£450–500 S(S)

A Gallé yellow glass aquatic vase, cameo mark 'Gallé', c1900, 9¾in (25cm) high.
£2,400–2,800 S

A Gallé cameo glass vase, overlaid in yellow, lilac and mauve, etched with a lakeside landscape, incised signature, c1900, 7in (18cm) high.
£1,000–1,200 S(S)

A Walsh vaseline glass vase, with opalescent brocade design, c1900, 6½in (16.5cm) high.
£180–200 JHa

A Gallé grey glass vase, internally decorated with pink at the neck and base, overlaid with purple and brown and etched with flowering branches, cameo mark 'Gallé' with star, after 1904, 23in (58.5cm) high.
£1,400–1,600 S

A Palme-König & Habler Art glass vase, in iridescent red with bronze mount, c1905, 15¼in (38.5cm) high.
£700–800 ANO
Palme-König, established in 1786, were Bohemian glassmakers who produced fine quality Art Nouveau iridescent glass wares and table glass in forms popularized by Loetz.

An H Copillet et Cie iridescent glass vase, the milky amber-green glass overlaid with lustrous copper-pink and etched with sprays of creeper, c1905, 16in (40.5cm) high.
£3,400–3,800 C

▶ A Daum enamelled glass vase, acid-etched in relief with poppies on leafy stems, painted in pink, yellow, white, green, brown and gilding, supported in a gilt-bronze leaf-form armature and base, signed 'Daum, Nancy' with Cross of Lorraine, c1905, 10in (25.5cm) high.
£1,200–1,400 P

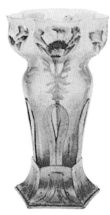

A Lobmeyr Wiener Werkstätte silver-mounted glass vase, attributed to Josef Hoffmann, the flat flange mounts pierced with formalized geometric design, remains of manufacturer's paper label, mounts stamped 'Austria 925', c1905, 5in (12.5cm) high.
£2,000–2,400 C

Lobmeyr

The Lobmeyr glassworks was founded in Vienna in 1822 by Josef Lobmeyr. Later he was joined in the company by his sons Louis and Josef Jr. By the late 19th century, under the leadership of Josef Jr, the factory had become internationally famous for the design and beauty of their products.
Lobmeyr brought together the best Bohemian and Austrian craftsmen and designers to create glassware which reflected the contemporary mood, but used earlier techniques such as enamelling, gilding and engraving. Much of their work was influenced by Islamic art or the intricate rococo designs of the 17th and 18th century.
Lobmeyr's introduction of iridescent glass to the 1873 International Exhibition in Vienna led to its use by Thomas Webb in England and Tiffany in the USA. Pieces by Lobmeyr were sometimes signed, but signatures may be hard to find as they are often worked into the pattern.

A Tiffany Favrile iridescent miniature glass vase, the pale amber glass decorated with millefiori cane flowers among green lily pads and trails, on a gilt ground, engraved 'L.C.T. 8429A', c1906, 1½in (4cm) high.
£600–700 S(S)

A Tiffany Favrile paperweight glass vase, the pale amber glass decorated with foliage and trailings in brick-red and ochre, the interior with amber iridescence, inscribed mark, c1909, 4¾in (12cm) high.
£4,000–4,500 S(NY)

A vaseline glass vase, with frilled top, c1906, 14in (35.5cm) high.
£200–220 ARE

A Gallé yellow and white glass vase, decorated with red flowers, c1907, 7in (18cm) high.
£1,250–1,500 ASA

A Tiffany Favrile amber-over-white glass vase, decorated with rows of iridescent green peacock feathers in iridescent blue, brown and grey-green, inscribed 'Louis C Tiffany-Favrile 1997 C', c1908, 10in (25.5cm) high.
£2,800–3,200 S(NY)

A Steuben Jack-in-the-Pulpit glass vase, the iridescent amber glass decorated with silvery-blue feathering, inscribed 'aurene', c1910, 8½in (21.5cm) high.
£2,700–3,000 S(NY)

An amber glass hyacinth vase, c1910, 5in (12.5cm) high.
£14–16 CaL

◄ A Steuben Jack-in-the-Pulpit glass vase, the iridescent amber glass decorated with silvery-blue feathering, inscribed 'aurene', c1910, 8½in (21.5cm) high.
£2,700–3,000 S(NY)

A Frederick Carder Steuben intarsia glass vase, the crystal stemmed bowl internally-decorated with blue repeating leaf and vine design, with blue lip wrap and six-sided blue base below colourless stem, inscribed 'Fredek Carder' at base, c1910, 7in (18cm) diam.
£6,000–7,000 SK(B)

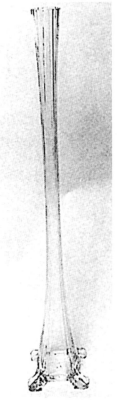

A glass lily vase, c1910, 36in (91.5cm) high.
£80–100 DUN

Three pressed glass celery vases, c1910, tallest 8in (20.5cm) high.
£10–12 each AL

A Daum glass vase, internally mottled with yellow, orange and green, etched and enamelled with a distant riverbank and flowering alliums, marked 'Daum Nancy' with a Cross of Lorraine, c1910, 10¾in (27.5cm) high.
£4,000–4,500 S

A Daum etched and enamelled white mottled glass sweet pea vase, with orange foot, etched mark, c1910, 9in (23cm) high.
£1,400–1,600 S(Am)

A Gallé cameo glass vase, the amber-tinted body overlaid with amethyst and pale blue, acid-etched with marsh plants and grasses, c1910, 5½in (14cm) high.
£1,800–2,000 ART

A Daum cameo grey glass vase, overlaid in orange and brown, acid-etched and carved with pendant sprays of catkins, cameo factory marks, c1910, 19½in (49.5cm) high.
£1,600–1,800 CSK

A Powell's Whitefriars sea-green glass vase, applied with a serpent c1910, 9¼in (23.5cm) high.
£250–300 JHa

A Daum mottled yellow and aubergine glass vase, etched and enamelled with cornflowers, c1910, 3in (7.5cm) high.
£1,200–1,350 ART

A Tiffany Favrile glass crocus vase, decorated in yellow with green and amber foliage, the interior with subtle iridescence, inscribed 'L C Tiffany-Favrile 3357 G', c1912, 4½in (11.5cm) high.
£4,000–4,200 S(NY)

A Moser and Shone amethyst glass vase, c1910, 10in (25.5cm) high.
£200–240 ZEI

A pair of Leune orange and grey glass vases, enamelled with a riverscape and trees, painted mark, c1910, 16in (40.5cm) high.
£520–580 S(Am)

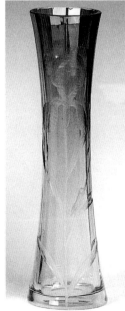

A Ludwig Moser & Söhne clear glass vase, graduating to purple and decorated with a carved iris stem, c1914, 15¾in (40cm) high.
£650–700 DORO

A Lalique polished and frosted glass vase, Sauterelles, moulded with grasshoppers perched on curving stems, heightened with green and blue staining, etched 'R Lalique France', 10½in (26.5cm) high.
£2,000–2,200 P

A glass celery vase, early 20thC, 6½in (16.5cm) high.
£18–20 TS

A Lalique opalescent glass vase, Monnaie du Pape, moulded with stems of honesty, heightened with blue staining on a wooden stand, etched 'R Lalique France', after 1914, 9in (23cm) high.
£1,300–1,500 P

A Tiffany Favrile brick red glass vase, the foot and rim wrapped with black, the neck and shoulder decorated with silvery-grey stringing, inscribed 'L C Tiffany-Inc Favrile 5020 N', c1918, 9¼in (23.5cm) high.
£7,000–8,000 S(NY)

◀ A Moser Animor series etched and gilded cameo glass vase, signed, c1920, 12in (30.5cm) high.
£700–800 GRI

A Walsh green glass vase, with iridescent finish and thrown top, c1920, 7¾in (19.5cm) high.
£180–200 JHa

An Orrefors vase, designed by Vicke Lindstrand, engraved with a bird and standing on a black foot, marked 'Orrefors', c1930s, 7in (18cm) high.
£250–300 RUSK

A pair of green glass bulb vases, early 20thC, 8in (20.5cm) high.
£70–80 PCh

A René Lalique green glass vase, Perruches, moulded with lovebirds and prunus blossom, after 1919, 10in (25.5cm) high.
£4,500–5,000 P

A Moser Bohemian turquoise glass vase, engraved with pheasants, c1920, 6½in (16.5cm) high.
£120–140 Mon

◀ A Le Verre Français glass vase, with narrow neck and everted rim, the mottled pink and yellow glass overlaid with mottled brown fading to orange, with pendant sprays of columbine, on domed foot, incised factory mark, c1920, 18½in (47cm) high.
£1,200–1,500 CSK

A Fachschule Steinschönau clear glass vase, decorated with yellow-tinted oval medallions surrounded by black, enamel and gold leaves in spirals, c1915, 6in (15cm) high.
£550–600 DORO

A blue glass hyacinth vase, c1920, 6in (15cm) high.
£25–30 DUN

A Daum acid-etched glass vase, enamelled in green, with silver mounts on rim and base, c1920, 8in (20.5cm) high.
£2,400–£2,800 ART

An American Art Deco iridescent gold glass vase, with crackled finish, c1920, 7in (18cm) high.
£320–380 ANO

A Lalique red glass vase, Ronces, after 1921, 9in (23cm) high.
£4,500–5,000 ART

◀ A Lalique frosted glass vase, Archers, moulded in relief with a frieze of naked male archers, with birds in flight above, heightened with a greyish staining, signed 'R Lalique, France No. 893', after 1921, 10½in (26.5cm) high.
£2,400–2,600 P

A Lalique smokey grey glass vase, Archers, moulded with naked male archers aiming their bows at birds overhead, moulded 'R Lalique', after 1921, 10½in (26.5cm) high.
£1,800–2,200 P

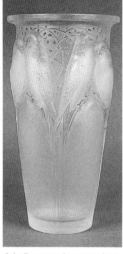

A Lalique opalescent glass vase, Ceylan, moulded in relief with pairs of lovebirds perched amidst boughs of prunus blossom, engraved 'R Lalique, France', after 1924, 10in (25.5cm) high.
£1,800–2,000 P

▶ A pale yellow glass vase, horizontally-ribbed with acid-textured ground, etched mark 'Daum Nancy France' with a Cross of Lorraine, 1920s, 8in (20.5cm) high.
£800–1,000 S

◀ A Lalique frosted glass vase, Nefliers, moulded in relief with leaves and blossom, with pale mauve staining, signed on base 'R Lalique', 1923, 5½in (14cm) high.
£450–500 P

A Lalique opalescent glass vase, Laurier, moulded in bold relief with berries and leaves, etched mark, 'No. 947', after 1922, 7½in (19cm) high.
£500–600 DN

A Lalique frosted glass vase, Formose, moulded with swimming fish, heightened with blue staining, the underside with engraved mark 'R Lalique, France, No. 934', after 1924, 6½in (16.5cm) high.
£750–850 S

A Lalique enamelled globular glass vase, Baies, moulded overall in shallow relief with thorny branches and berries interwoven and heightened with black enamel, moulded on base 'R Lalique', after 1924, 10½in (26.5cm) high.
£4,500–5,000 P

A Lalique opalescent glass vase, Béliers, with beast-shaped handles, on a circular foot, etched mark, after 1925, 7½in (19cm) high.
£800–900 DN

A gilt-decorated red glass vase, c1925, 6½in (16.5cm) high.
£45-50 FMN

A French pale brown moulded glass vase, c1925, 9in (23cm) high.
£60-70 CSA

A Steuben yellow and jade green acid-cut glass vase, designed by Frederick Carder, decorated with Acanthus pattern, c1925, 9¼in (23.5cm) high.
£4,000-4,400 S(NY)

A Daum Nancy smokey topaz glass vase, deeply acid-etched with geometric design, signed in intaglio, c1925, 20in (51cm) high.
£2,200-2,500 S(NY)

Steuben Glass Works (American, 1903–present)

The company was founded in 1903 by an Englishman, Frederick Carder, and became a division of Corning in 1918. In the United States its work is regarded as the epitome of elegance in Art Deco glass . Before 1930 Carder designed many items himself, but from 1930 onwards the company employed a number of leading designers such as Signey Waugh and Walter Dorwin Teague.

A Schneider clear glass vase, internally-decorated with air bubbles, applied with a band of clear glass discs with olive-green spirals, each centring a red cabochon glass sphere, inscribed c1925, 8¼in (21cm) high.
£10,000-12,000 S(NY)

A Lalique opalescent jade green glass vase, Ormeaux, with spherical body, narrow neck and everted rim, moulded in relief with overlapping leaves, chips to rim and pontil, etched 'R Lalique, No. 985', after 1926, 6½in (16.5cm) high.
£1,400-1,600 CSK

An Argy Rousseau *pâte-de-verre* glass vase, Vagues et Poissons, decorated with mauve and purple and moulded with a frieze of green fish swimming through stylized waves, intaglio-moulded mark, c1925, 6¼in (16cm) high.
£18,000-20,000 S

A Lalique baluster-shaped vase, Domrémy, moulded in high relief, etched 'R Lalique, France', after 1926, 8½in (21.5cm) high.
£400-450 L

A Lalique opalescent and blue-stained globular glass vase, Ormeaux, moulded with overlapping leaves, etched mark and number '984', reduced in height, after 1926, 6in (15cm) high.
£500-600 DN

A Lalique frosted glass vase, Aigrettes, moulded on the upper section with the interwoven bodies and long tail feathers of exotic birds in flight, heightened with some blue staining, signed on base 'R Lalique, France', after 1926, 10in (25.5cm) high.
£2,800-3,200 P

A Lalique opalescent glass vase, Bacchantes, moulded in high relief with a frieze of naked bacchantes, signed on the base in block letters 'R Lalique France', after 1927, 9¾in (25cm) high.
£8,500-10,000 P

◄ A Lalique opalescent glass vase, Espalion, moulded overall with formalized ferns, signed 'R Lalique, France, No. 996', after 1927, 7in (18cm) high.
£700-800 P

A Lalique glass vase, moulded with birds perched among berry-laden branches, incised 'R Lalique, France, No. 986', after 1927, 5½in (14cm) high.
£1,000–1,100 C(S)

An André Hunebelle glass vase, the compressed globular shape moulded with densely-packed stylized sunflowers and foliage, heightened with green-blue staining, 1928, 4¼in (11cm) high.
£450–550 BKK

A Lalique blue glass vase, Penthièvres, with everted neck rim, moulded in polished relief with stylized tropical fish swimming in alternate directions, the neck applied with white metal fish, signed on base 'R Lalique', after 1928, 10in (25.5cm) high.
£2,500–3,000 P

A Müller Frères commemorative glass vase, the yellow cased glass flecked with pink and blue around the rim, intaglio-etched with a bi-plane flying over Strasbourg, with indistinct inscription '5 May 1928', etched factory mark, 6½in (16.5cm) high.
£600–700 CSK

A Lalique smoked glass two-handled vase, Caudebec, the handle moulded with flowerheads and foliage, moulded mark, after 1929, 5½in (14cm) high.
£750–850 C(S)

A Czechoslovakian clear glass vase, the fins acid-etched and moulded in relief, c1930, 12in (30.5cm) high.
£25–30 BKK

A Monart glass vase, c1930, 9in (23cm) high.
£700–800 TWr

A Monart glass vase, c1930, 7½in (19cm) high.
£700–800 TWr

A pair of cranberry glass vases, enamelled with scenes depicting children in a garden, raised on circular base, heightened with gilt, 1930s, 8in (20.5cm) high.
£180–200 AH

A pair of Mary Gregory-style cranberry glass vases, the hollow stems raised on domed circular bases, 1930s, 10¼in (26cm) high.
£100–120 CGC

▶ A Bohemian ruby glass hand-painted vase, 1930s, 16in (40.5cm) high.
£650–700 RIA

A Monart pink and blue glass vase, with combing, c1930, 7½in (19cm) high.
£180–220 TCG

A pair of Whitefriars glass vases, c1930, 5in (12.5cm) high.
£20–25 HEM

An Art Deco blue glass vase, c1930, 6in (15cm) high.
£20–25 PC

A brown cloud glass vase-on-stand, possibly Davidson, c1930, 5in (12.5cm) high.
£35–40 TS

An Orrefors Graal glass vase, designed by Edward Hald, decorated with seaweed and fish, etched to base 'Orrefors Graal No. 403K' signed 'E D W Hald', c1930, 4½in (11.5cm) high.
£300–350 Mit

A Daum acid-etched granite-coloured glass vase, c1930, 6in (15cm) high.
£1,100–1,200 ART

A Whitefriars bull's-eye glass vase, c1930, 6½in(16.5cm) high.
£50–80 JHa

A Powell green glass square vase, c1930, 9in (23cm) high.
£75–90 TCG

A Stevens & Williams green glass globular vase, designed by Keith Murray, with a cylindrical neck applied with two fluted handles, on a spreading circular foot, signed 'S & W', 1930s, 9in (23cm) high.
£350–400 ADE
Stevens & Williams changed its name to Royal Brierley Crystal in 1931, New Zealand born Keith Murray was engaged as a designer at the factory in 1932.

A Lalique opalescent glass vase, Saint Francois moulded with birds perched in leafy branches, damaged, stencilled mark 'R Lalique, France', after 1930, 7in (18cm) high.
£1,000–1,100 S(S)

A Lalique glass vase, Prunes, moulded in high relief with an opalescent band of rounded fruits on leafy branches, damaged, wheel-engraved 'R Lalique, France', after 1930, 7in (18cm) high.
£2,600–3,000 S(S)

A Monart green and blue glass vase, with bubble inclusions, 1930s, 7½in (19cm) high.
£100–120 TCG

An Orrefors glass vase, engraved with a young mother holding a baby, c1930, 6½in 16.5cm) high.
£600–700 SHa

A Davidson brown cloud glass vase, by 1930s, 8in (20.5cm) high.
£30–35 BEV

A Jobling pale green glass vase, 1930s, 7¾in (19.5cm) high.
£85–95 BEV

A Walsh Walsh amethyst glass vase, engraved with a water lily and an iris, c1930, 10in (25.5cm) high.
£250–300 JHa

▶ A Whitefriars trail-ribbed amethyst glass vase, 1930s, 5½in (14cm) high.
£60–70 JHa

A Sabino blue glass vase, moulded with overlapping peacock feather motifs in low relief with slight frosting, incised 'Sabino, France', c1930, 8in (20.5cm) high.
£350–400 S(S)

A Bagley amber glass vase, with plinth and insert, 1932, 5in (12.5cm) high.
£15–20 BKK

A Lalique opalescent glass vase, Chamonix, signed, after 1933, 6in (15cm) high.
£600–700 PSG

A pair of Bagley amber satin glass bamboo vases, c1935, 4in (10cm) high.
£30–40 each BKK

A Daum acid-etched yellow glass vase, signed c1930, 4in (10cm) high.
£1,100–1,200 ART

A Sowerby pink glass stylized vase, c1932, 6½in (16.5cm) high.
£20–25 BKK

A Bagley frosted blue glass épergne, Grantham 334, posy Peg version, 1934, 5½in (14cm) high.
£35–40 PC

A Bagley frosted pink glass three-piece flower set, Wyndham, pattern No. 1333/0, 1934, 7in (18cm) high.
£80–95 PC

A Lalique glass vase, Beauvais, with frosted curved horn-shaped handles, etched script signature 'Lalique, France', after 1931, 7½in (19cm) high.
£1,200–1,400 JL

A Bagley green pressed-glass bamboo-shaped vase, c1933, 8½in (21.5cm) high.
£35–40 BKK

A Bagley green glass leaf vase with centre, designed by Alexander H Williamson, pattern No. 3001, RD 798844, 1934, 7½in (19cm) high.
£90–110 PC

LOCATE THE SOURCE

The source of each illustration in Miller's can be found by checking the code letters below each caption with the Key to Illustrations, pages 305–307.

◀ A Powell's Whitefriars amethyst ribbon-trailed glass vase, c1935, 9in (23cm) high.
£70–80 JHa

A Lalique frosted glass vase, Oursin, with blue staining, after 1935, 7in (18cm) high.
£500–600 AAV

A Lalique opalescent glass vase, Terpsichore, moulded on each broad side with two naked maidens, linked by highly stylized folds of drapes, signed in block letters on base 'R Lalique France', after 1937, 8in (20.5cm) high.
£8,000–9,000 P

A Bagley blue frosted glass two-piece flower set, Queen's Choice 1122, decorated with painted leather flowers, 1937, 4½in (11.5cm) diam.
£42–50 PC

A Bagley amber glass vase, with flower holder, decorated with koala bears, 1937, 8in (20.5cm) high.
£180–220 PC

A Stevens & Williams globular light blue glass vase, designed by Keith Murray, with sand-blasted surface texture, decorated with vertical ribbing, signed, 1932–39, 9¾in (25cm) high.
£450–500 ADE

▶ A Whitefriars smoky-amber optic-moulded glass vase, 1930s, 9¾in (25cm) high.
£40–50 P(B)

A Sowerby amber-coloured pressed glass vase, with textured panels and stylized floral motifs in relief, on separate black glass base, c1938, 8½in (21.5cm) high.
£90–100 BKK

A Lalique clear glass cylinder-shaped vase for washing grapes, Ricquewihr, decorated with horizontal banding moulded with grapes and vines, heightened with brown staining, marked 'Lalique' in block letters, after 1938, 5in (12.5cm) high.
£350–400 P

A cut and etched glass vase, supported in a stylistic WMF electro-plated frame, on four splayed feet, arched and flanked by two handles, with matching shallow square cover, 1930s, 8½in (21.5cm) high.
£250–300 CGC

A cameo glass oval trumpet-shaped vase, the rim and sides in raised amber colour and with flowering stems against a cut mottled ground, etched signature, 'Richardson' on underisde of foot, 1930s, 10in (25.5cm) high.
£250–300 HCC

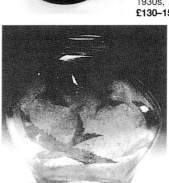

A Powell white glass vase, decorated with combed herringbone pattern, 1930s, 7½in (19cm) high.
£130–150 TCG

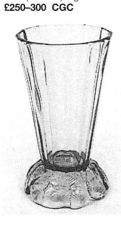

◀ A Jobling amber glass vase, with butterfly design on base, 1930s, 9in (23cm) high.
£40–45 HEW

◀ A Continental glass vase, internally-decorated in blue with birds in flight, on a speckled white ground graduating to red at the neck, 20thC, 7in (18cm) high.
£120–150 S(S)

A Lalique thistle-shaped clear glass vase, moulded with a band of birds perched among ivy, on a waisted circular foot, engraved 'Lalique, France', after 1945, 5in (12.5cm) high.
£250–300 WeH

A Flavio Poli cased-glass vase, with red interior, 1950s, 9in (23cm) high.
£225–250 Gar

A red glass cornucopia, heightened with gilding, c1950, 7in (18cm) high.
£55–65 TS

A Stromberg glass vase, c1954, 10in (25.5cm) high.
£20–25 BEN

▶ A Bagley Jetique Polka Dot glass handkerchief vase, c1957, 6in (15cm) high.
£10–15 JMC

A Venini handkerchief glass vase, with pale blue and white latticinio decoration, etched 'Venini Murano Italia', small chip, c1955, 6in (15cm) high.
£150–180 S(S)

An Orrefors clear glass vase, designed by Sven Palmqvist, the thick-walled glass engraved with geese in flight, engraved factory marks and monogram, 'No. 3724', c1950, 7¼in (18.5cm) high.
£100–120 WeH

◀ A Vasart Harlequin glass vase, 1956–68, 7½in (19cm) high.
£60–70 TCG

A Bagley Jetique Polka Dot wall vase, pattern 3193, 1957, 5in (12.5cm) wide.
£15–18 PC

An Art glass vase, 1950s, 8in (20.5cm) high.
£20–25 AA

◀ A pair of green and multi-coloured glass vases, with brass covers, 20thC, 6in (15cm) high.
£50–60 ROW

A Kosta glass vase, designed by Vicke Lindstrand, c1959, 4½in (11.5cm) high.
£150–170 KAC

◀ A Vicke Lindstrand clear glass vase, inscribed mark on base, 1950–60, 6in (15cm) high.
£70–80 TCG

An Orrefors smoky grey glass vase, by Nils Landberg, c1960, 9in (23cm) high.
£60–70 TCG

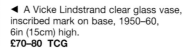

An Italian glass vase, 1960s, 6½in (16.5cm) high.
£25–30 ASA

An Orrefors glass vase, engraved with a child and flowers, c1970, 6in (15cm) high.
£40–50 BEN

A Glasform gold glass vase, with black iridescent trails, signed, marked 'No. 4496', c1995, 7in (18cm) high.
£180–200 GLA

A coral and clear glass bottle vase, No. 4420, c1995, 5¼in (13.5cm) high.
£35–40 GLA

A Whitefriars amethyst glass vase, 1960s, 6in (15cm) high.
£20–25 JHa

A Whitefriars green glass vase, by Geoffrey Baxter, c1974, 9in (23cm) high.
£80–100 TCG

A Malcolm Sutcliffe glass vase, decorated with dolphins, 20thC, 8in (20.5cm) high.
£100–130 DUN

▶ A garniture of three engraved glass vases, with applied label 'Harrach. Novy Svet. Czechoslovakia', 20thC, vases 16in (40.5cm) high.
£5,000–6,000 S

A Vasart red and blue mottled glass vase, c1960, 11in (28cm) high.
£70–80 CSA

A Whitefriars kingfisher-blue glass vase, with green spots, designed by Geoffrey Baxter, 1969–71, 6in (15cm) high.
£50–60 TCG

A blue overlaid cut-glass vase, 20thC, 11in (28cm) high.
£50–60 LF

A Dartington glass vase, 1960s, 5½in (14cm) high.
£10–15 TCG

A Glasform glass vase, gold with black feathering, signed, marked 'No. 3158', 1986, 12in (30.5cm) high.
£70–80 GLA

A Loetz-style iridescent glass vase, applied with a dot and thin line pattern in a deep blue on a mottled green ground, slight rubbing to neck, unmarked, 20thC, 5in (12.5cm) high.
£200–240 S(S)

Webb

Thomas Webb inherited the White House Glass Works near Stourbridge in 1833. In 1855 he moved to the Dennis Glass Works and, in 1859, the name was changed to Thomas Webb & Sons when Thomas was joined by his sons Thomas Wilkes Webb and Charles Webb. Up to that time the company had made cut lead crystal tableware, chandeliers and ornamental glass. The sons were to change that by introducing new techniques such as staining and casing.

In the late 19th century Webb was noted for cameo glass, although the factory made a variety of decorative glass including satin glass, which featured air patterns trapped between coloured and opal glass. Two Bohemian craftsmen employed by the factory, Frederick Kny and William Fritsche, developed rock crystal by combining deep relief-cutting with polished copper-wheel engraving.

After World War I the company merged with the Edinburgh & Leith Flint Glass Co to form Webb's Crystal Glass Co, and during the 1930s they introduced the Cameo Fleur range, which involved a technique whereby clear glass was cased with transparent coloured glass which was then etched, leaving a raised coloured cameo on a clear textured ground. The Connoisseur stemware range won a Design Centre award in 1957. The company produced some innovative designs during this period, although it continued with more traditional styles in cut lead crystal.

Webb's Crystal Glass Co was taken over by Crown House in 1964, and in 1978 was acquired by the Coloroll Group, but was closed in 1990 when the parent company failed.

That is not the entire Webb story, however, for Thomas Wilkes Webb's sons, Herbert and another Thomas, went into partnership with George Harry Corbett in 1897, under the name Thomas Webb and Corbett. Early work included notable examples of rock crystal and intaglio engraving, some forms displaying distinct Art Nouveau influence. Alongside these luxury wares the company produced less expensive machine-etched and dip-moulded tableware and, just prior to World War I, introduced enamelled glass, painted in translucent colours.

In the period leading up to World War II, cut-glass formed the bulk of production, and continued to do so after the war. In 1953, the company became Webb Corbett Ltd. The 1950s also saw the advent of the Pearlstone range. This design combined raised polished cut circles with a sandblasted matt ground.

Royal Doulton acquired Webb Corbett in 1969 and, subsequently, the company's output became even more traditional in style. During the 1980s the glass was marketed as Royal Doulton Crystal by Webb Corbett. In 1986 the Webb Corbett name was dropped altogether.

A pair of Stourbridge glass vases, with pale blue bodies, applied with pale amber rims, branch handles and feet, applied all-over in colours with fruiting branches, probably Thomas Webb, slight damage, c1880, 9½in (24cm) high.
£700–800 CSK

A Thomas Webb Queen's Burmese ware glass centrepiece, the central trumpet vase with crimped end tapering to a tripod brass fitting, each brass tripod arm holding a crimped bowl to enclose the Clarke's Patent Fairy Light fittings and support the enamelled shades, some wear to enamels, c1886, 11in (28cm) high.
£2,500–3,000 CSK

◀ A blue-tinted glass vase, attributed to Jules Barbe, gilded and silvered with a large carp on one side, the other with a frog leaping among lily pads, within stylized scroll borders, possibly Thomas Webb, c1890, 10in (25.5cm) high.
£3,200–3,700 S
The decoration on this vase bears a strong resemblance to the work of Jules Barbe, particularly the characteristic tooled gilding.

A Thomas Webb cameo glass vase, by George Woodall, the dark brown ground overlaid in white and carved with a figure of Psyche holding a box issuing smoke, the neck and foot with leaf motifs, damaged and repaired, signed, c1889, 7in (18cm) high.
£3,200–3,600 P
This piece was severely damaged but still sold for double its pre-sale estimate. A similar example in excellent condition in the same sale realized in the region of £18,500.

A Thomas Webb gem cameo glass bowl, the pale blue ground decorated in white with birds and trees, signed, c1880, 9in (23cm) diam.
£17,000–18,500 JAA

A Webb cameo glass claret jug, with silver-plated mounts, the body of pale yellow glass overlaid in opaque white, etched and carved with arum lilies, the engraved mount repeating the design, remounted, late 19thC, 8¾in (22cm) high.
£1,200–1,350 S(S)

A Thomas Webb amber glass vase, engraved with water lilies, c1920, 8¼in (21cm) high.
£70–80 MON

◄ A Webb pseudo-cameo glass vase, c1930, 9in (23cm) high.
£300–350 TCG

Four Thomas Webb Queen's Burmese ware items, with orange rims fading to yellow, 1890–1900:
l. a night-light, acid-stamped mark, 4in (10cm) high.
£120–135
c. a vase, 6¼in (16cm) high.
£200–250
r. a pair of vases, 3¼in (8.5cm) high.
£300–350 MJW

A Thomas Webb bronze glass two-handled vase, made as an experimental piece, c1890, 9¼in 23.5cm) high.
£320–400 MJW

A pair of Thomas Webb engraved glass vases, on star-cut bases, chipped, signed 'W Fritsche', 1924, 16in (40.5cm) high.
£1,500–1,800 S

A Thomas Webb Queen's Burmese ware glass vase, with rolled-over rim, decorated with garlands of green ivy, signed, c1890, 7in (18cm) high.
£300–350 JL

A Webb glass decanter, with amethyst stopper and foot, 1930s, 10½in (26.5cm) high.
£60–70 JHa

Insurance values

Always insure your valuable antiques for the cost of replacing them with similar items, regardless of the original price paid. Both dealers and auctioneers will provide a valuation service for a fee.

Walking Sticks

A Victorian glass walking cane, applied with red, white and blue spiral twist canes, 37in (94cm) long.
£180–200 DN

A Victorian glass shepherd's crook, containing blue, pink and green-tinted canes, 38in (96.5cm) long.
£140–160 DN

A Victorian blue-tinted glass walking stick, with corkscrew stem, 36½in (92.5cm) long.
£130–150 DN

A Victorian spirally-moulded blue-tinted glass walking stick, 52in (132cm) long.
£95–110 DN

Wine Glass Coolers

An Irish ribbed glass rinser, c1790, 4½in (11.5cm) diam.
£100–120 WGT

An Irish glass single-lipped wine glass cooler, the plain body faintly marked under the base with 'Penrose Waterford', c1800, 3½in (9cm) high.
£600–700 Som

A pillar-cut wine glass rinser, c1820, 4in (10cm) high.
£42–50 JHa

A set of six cut-glass wine glass rinsers, c1840, 5in (12.5cm) wide.
£220–250 DUN

Wine Glass Coolers

Wine glass coolers, or rinsers, as they are known in the USA, are an unusual item of the late 18th and 19thC. They are approximately the same size as a finger bowl with pouring lips on either side of the rim, and were used to rinse or cool wine glasses between each course of a meal.

A red glass rinser, c1860, 3½in (9cm) high.
£150–170 MJW

Witches' Balls

A green glass witch's ball, c1860, 12in (30.5cm) diam.
£220–250 DUN

A dark blue glass witch's ball, c1880, 5in (12.5cm) diam.
£100–120 DUN

A blue glass witch's ball, 19thC, 16¼in (41.5cm) diam.
£220–250 LF

Miscellaneous

A crystal ball, c1910, 4½in (11.5cm) high.
£45–50 TER

A vaseline glass bell, the clapper missing, 19thC, 10¼in (26cm) high.
£125–150 TAC

A glass biscuit barrel, with silver lid, decorated with ferns, c1880, 6½in (16.5cm) high.
£150–180 MJW

A pale green glass bell, with dark and clear glass handle, c1860, 9in (23cm) high.
£180–200 CB

A pale green cased glass biscuit barrel, with silver-plated cover, c1900, 8½in (21.5cm) high.
£250–300 ARE

◄ An Art Deco blue pressed glass biscuit barrel and cover, 20thC, 8in (20.5cm) high.
£12–15 BKK

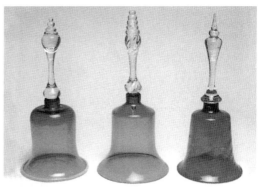

Three coloured glass bells, c1890, cranberry c1880, largest 13½in (34.5cm) high.
£150–200 each CB

Five Continental glass hand bells, with spirally-moulded bodies, below clear handles with multi-knopped terminals, damaged, late 19thC, largest 14in (35.5cm) high.
£600–700 C

◄ A pair of white combed-glass bellows on a stand, mid-19thC, 13¾in (35cm) high.
£180–220 FD

Two miniature clear glass bellows, with ribbed notched edges, c1860, largest 6in (15cm) long.
£45–50 each Som

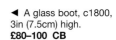

◄ A glass boot, c1800, 3in (7.5cm) high.
£80–100 CB

A wrythen glass bugle, c1900, 8in (20.5cm) high.
£40–45 TS

A wrythen glass
bugle, early 19thC,
9¼in (23.5cm) high.
£55–65 FD

A Sowerby blue malachite
pressed glass cauldron,
c1880, 2½in (6.5cm) high.
£50–60 JHa

◄ A frosted glass bust of
Napoleon III, inscribed on
base 'Chislehurst 1873',
8in (20.5cm) high.
£400–450 BrW

A Bagley frosted glass cake
stand, Fish Scale 3067,
c1938, 9½in (24cm) diam.
£30–35 PC

A Roman glass cosmetic
pot, 1st–2ndC AD,
2½in (6.5cm) high.
£240–260 MJW

A glass chamber pot, with fold-over rim
and simple scrolled handle, 18thC,
8in (20.5cm) diam.
£350–400 MCA
**Believed, by family tradition, to have
been used by one of Queen Anne's
ladies-in-waiting.**

A Venetian calcedonio glass
trembleuse cup and saucer, the
marbled brown and green glass
with aventurine inclusions,
late 17thC, 3½in (9cm) high.
£2,750–3,500 S

An Antonio Salviati glass cup and
saucer, c1880, 2in (5cm) high.
£600–680 MJW

A semi-opaque pale blue glass part dessert service, each piece silvered
to the centre, with concentric lines below turnover castellated rims,
including a shallow bowl, two comports supported on baluster stems,
six plates, slight wear, and a similar fluted baluster vase, silvered with
scrolling foliage, 19thC.
£1,250–1,500 CSK

A green glass dessert service, comprising 16 pieces, each piece
decorated with a gilt Greek key pattern border, centred by a gilt
foliate medallion, possibly Bohemian, some damage, c1870.
£450–500 S(S)

A Bristol blue egg
cup, with opaline
rim, c1790,
3in (7.5cm) high.
£130–140 FD

A Bohemian cased glass
egg cup set, c1900,
6½in (16.5cm) diam.
£65–80 WAC

Miller's is a price GUIDE
not a price LIST

A hand-blown blue eye glass, c1840, 2¾in (7cm) high.
£85–100 CB

A pair of John Derbyshire & Co pressed glass figures of Mr & Mrs Punch, c1880, 6¾in (17cm) high.
£175–200 PC

A Lalique opalescent glass figure of Thais, signed 'R Lalique', after 1925, 8½in (21.5cm) high.
£5,500–6,500 SLN

A Murano glass figure, with lilac and clear glass body, 1950s, 14in (35.5cm) high.
£250–300 TCG

A René Lalique glass figure, Suzanne, engraved and moulded mark, after 1925, 9in (23cm) high.
£5,000–6,000 S

A free-blown glass fly trap, on three blob feet, early 19thC, 7in (18cm) high.
£55–65 FD

▶ A glass fly trap, early 19thC, 7¾in (19.5cm) high.
£55–65 FD

A blown glass friggar of a crown, mid-19thC, 9in (23cm) diam.
£95–110 FD

A glass fly trap, on three feet, 19thC, 6½in (16.5cm) high.
£55–65 FD

A gilded glass friggar, 'I Love A Sailor', mid-19thC, 14in (35.5cm) long.
£160–180 CB

A Waterford crystal globe, 1970s, 12½in (32cm) high.
£700–800 WeH

A glass hammer and axe, both with hollow handles, mid-19thC, 9¾in (25cm) long.
£120–125 each FD

A glass hat, early 19thC,
2½in (6.5cm) high.
£60–70 JHa

A Greener & Co malachite pressed
glass hat, c1880, 3½in (9cm) high.
£100–120 JHa

Two glass top hats, with
folded brims, late 19thC,
largest 7in (18cm) wide.
£55–65 each FD

A pressed amber glass hat,
possibly by Greener & Co,
c1890, 3½in (9cm) high.
£25–30 JHa

► Two Austrian
iridescent glass
inkwells, the
lids with
brass stylized
decoration, c1900,
2in (5cm) high.
**£100–120 each
ASA**

◄ A Jobling green
glass jardinière,
decorated with
birds, 1930s,
15in (38cm) wide.
£180–200 BEV

A Tiffany Studios bronze-
mounted glass inkstand,
c1900, 3½in (9cm) diam.
£125–150 ZEI

A set of three Bagley clear flint glass
jelly moulds, in the shape of rabbits,
1934, largest 6in (15cm) wide.
£35–40 PC

A Lalique glass hand mirror, Narcisse
Couché, moulded with a panel
depicting Narcissus gazing into
a pool, later signed 'R Lalique',
after 1912, 11½in (29cm) long.
£1,400–1,600 P

A Continental ice glass ice
pail, 1930s, 6in (15cm) high.
£30–35 JHa

A piece of Sam Herman Studio
glass, 1980s, 7½in (19cm) high.
£400–450 JHa
**Sam Herman was given
permission to set up a glass
studio in the Royal College
of Art in 1968.**

l. A glass dry mustard pot, with loose hollow
lid, c1800, 6in (15cm) high.
£120–140
c. A glass toddy lifter, c1830, 7in (18cm) high.
£100–120
r. A glass pepper, on square lemon squeezer
foot, brass cap, c1810, 4in (10cm) high.
£120–140 Som

► A pair of Victorian blue marbled pressed
glass obelisks, on square stepped bases,
some damage, 11in (28cm) high.
£130–150 DN

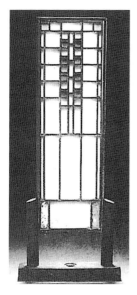

An Arts and Crafts stained glass panel, painted with birds, animals and mythical beasts, c1900, 16½ x 21¼in (42 x 54cm).
£350–400 CSK

◄ A Frank Lloyd Wright leaded glass panel, decorated with opaque white and iridescent glass segments, and a single yellow glass segment, c1902, 12¾in (32.5cm) high.
£3,000–3,300 CNY

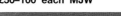

Three glass patty pans, 1770–1800, largest 3in (7.5cm) high.
£50–100 each MJW

Six glass patty pans, with folded rims, c1780, largest 4¾in (12cm) high.
£300–340 Som

A Lalique glass pendant, Feuilles, moulded with leaves, signed 'R Lalique', after 1920, 2in (5cm) diam.
£250–300 P

A Sowerby pressed glass pin tray, with peacock trademark, c1880, 3in (7.5cm) diam.
£50–60 JHa

A glass sulphide plaque, depicting George III in old age, minor manufacturing flaw, c1820, 4¼in (11cm) diam.
£230–260 BrW

A René Lalique glass and nickel-plated-metal plaque, moulded mark, slightly polished, c1925, 16in (40.5cm) high.
£5,000–6,000 S

A Baccarat engraved glass plaque, c1930, 5½in (14cm) high.
£100–120 BrW

A pair of Webb pinched glass posy holders, engraved with flower sprays and foliage, flanked by diaper-pattern panels, on everted feet with star-cut bases, one marked, 20thC, 3in (7.5cm) high.
£250–300 CSK

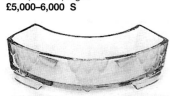

A Czechoslovakian amber pressed glass posy vase, c1931, 8in (20.5cm) wide.
£10–15 BKK

► A collection of Bagley glass posy vases, 1930s, largest 11in (28cm) wide.
£5–20 each PC

A Bohemian or Venetian cranberry-tinted glass punch bowl, cover, stand and twelve beakers, of globular quatrefoil form with foot ring, the stand with raised centre, the domed cover with raspberry prunt finial and shell handles, gilt rims, the globular beakers with gilt rims, traces of burnished gilding, one beaker damaged, late 19thC, stand 18in (45.5cm) diam.
£700–800 S

A Bohemian Art glass engraved punch set, the bowl and undertray of frosted colourless glass with red glass jewels centring gold enamelled swags and medallions, dated 1875, 11in (28cm) high.
£180–200 SK

A Lalique black glass ring, Fleurs, with solid domed top and intaglio-moulded with florets and stems picked out with white enamelling, unsigned, after 1931.
£850–1,000 P

A Lalique black glass seal, Bleuet, on solid base and moulded with cornflowers, heightened with green staining, with metal base engraved with monogram, signed on edge 'R Lalique', 2in (5cm) high.
£150–170 P

A part Sunderland cut-glass armorial service, comprising 26 pieces, each piece heavily cut with large diamonds, fan shapes and horizontal step-cutting, star-cut bases, the decanters and rinsers engraved with a lozenge cartouche enclosing a crest of a cubit arm holding in the hand a dagger upwards, some damage, probably Wear Flint Glass Co, c1820.
£4,200–5,000 S

▶ A Vereinigte Lausitzer Glaswerke set of glass storage containers, with two-handled tray, Kubus-Geschirr by Wilhelm Wagenfeld, marked, 1938, tray 16½in (42cm) wide.
£2,000–2,250 S

A glass three-masted ship and cutter, with glass dome, on round ebonized base, 19thC, 7¾in (19.5cm) high.
£165–185 FD

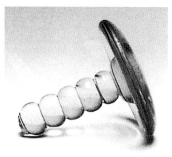

A heavy glass mushroom-top slicker stone, with five-knop handle, early 19thC, 3½in (9cm) high.
£180–200 CB
A slicker stone, or linen smoother, was used to iron and glaze the linen with a circular sweeping movement, and was made of glass, marble or lignum.

◀ Two glass swizzle sticks, in the form of golf clubs, c1900, 5¼in (13.5cm) high.
£8–10 each AMH

▶ A silver-mounted cut-glass tea caddy, c1800, 4½in (11.5cm) high.
£900–1,100 CB

A pair of glass tea caddies, engraved with the owner's initials 'M.R.', 'Bohea' and 'Green', with original stoppers, 1750, 5½in (14cm) high.
£600–700 QSA

A glass toothpick holder, hand-painted with a snipe, 1930s, 3½in (9cm) high.
£18–20 AMH

An oval cut-glass tea caddy, the body cut with a band of flutes below a band of diamonds, with flute-cut neck and rim, diamond-cut mushroom stopper, c1810, 6in (15cm) high.
£330–380 Som

A pair of engraved glass caddies and stoppers, with star-cut bases, slight damage, 19thC, 5in (12.5cm) high.
£450–500 CSK

A pair of round glass urns, cut with diamond- and lozenge-shaped bands, early 19thC, 5in (12.5cm) high.
£250–300 DN

A Persian Sasanid cut-glass vessel, used for cosmetics, 4thC AD, 1in (2.5cm) high.
£75–100 JFG

◄ A hand-blown glass specimen vase, c1910, 3in (7.5cm) high.
£10–15 TS

Join The Miller's Club

M I L L E R ' S CLUB

Send in your name and address to the Miller's Club and we will send you a copy of the latest *Miller's Club News*, which includes illustrated articles about the antiques and collectables market, information about our authors, plus a wealth of hints and tips for the collector. You will also have the opportunity to send your questions to Miller's experts who will answer a selection in each issue.

ALL ABSOLUTELY FREE OF CHARGE!

MILLER'S CLUB
2–4 Heron Quays, Docklands, London E14 4JP
www.millers.uk.com

Directory of Specialists

20th Century Glass Nigel Benson, Kensington Church Street Antique Centre, 58–60 Kensington Church Street, London W8 4DB Tel: 020 7938 1137

F. W. Aldridge Ltd 28 Mead Park Industrial Estate, River Way, Harlow, Essex CM20 2SE Tel: 01279 442876

Artemis 36 Kensington Church Street, London W8 4BX Tel: 020 7937 9900
Email: Artemis.W8@btinternet.com
Website: artemisdecorativearts.com
Lighting, glass by Daum, Gallé, Lalique

Christine Bridge 78 Castelnau, London SW13 9EX
Tel: 07000 445277
Email: christine@bridge-antiques.com
Websites: www.bridge-antiques.com
www.antiqueglass.co.uk
Fine 18th century collectors' glass, 19th century coloured glass and small decorative antiques

Lynda Brine Assembly Antique Centre, 5–8 Saville Row, Bath, Somerset BA1 2QP Tel: 01225 448488
Perfume bottles

W. G. T. Burne (Antique Glass) Ltd PO Box 9565, London SW20 9ZD Tel: 020 8543 6319

Caithness Glass Ltd Inveralmond, Perth, Scotland PH1 3TZ Tel: 01738 637373
Website: www.caithnessglass.co.uk

Jasmin Cameron Antiquarius, 131–141 King's Road, London SW3 4PW Tel: 020 7351 4154
Specializing in drinking glasses and decanters 1750–1910. Early 20th century Art Deco glass, René Lalique and Monart

The Cedars Antiques
Website: www.csonline.com.cedars
American dealer with extensive online inventory of glass of all kinds

Chislehurst Antiques 7 Royal Parade, Chislehurst, Kent BR7 6NR Tel: 020 8467 1530
Lighting

Clancy Chandaliers 'Villanova', Ballywaltrim, Bray, Co Wicklow, Republic of Ireland Tel: 00 353 286 3460
strictly by appointment only

Delomosne & Son Ltd Court Close, North Wraxall, Chippenham, Wiltshire SN14 7AD Tel: 01225 891505

Frank Dux Antiques 33 Belvedere, Bath, Somerset BA1 5HR Tel: 01225 312367
Email: antique.glass@which.net
Website: www.antique-glass.co.uk

Friends of Broadfield House Glass Museum
Compton Drive, Kingswinford, West Midlands DY6 9NS
Tel: 01384 273011

Glasform Ltd 123 Talbot Road, Blackpool, Lancashire FY1 3QY Tel: 01253 626410
Email: Glasform@btinternet.com
Website: www.btinternet.com/-glasform

Glass Collector's Fair 155 St John's Road, Congleton, Cheshire CW12 2EH Tel: 01260 271975
Email: hier@talk21.com

Grimes House Antiques High Street, Moreton-in-Marsh, Gloucestershire GL56 0AT Tel: 01608 651029
Email: grimes_house@cix.co.uk
Websites: grimeshouse.co.uk
cranberryglass.co.uk
Cranberry glass, plus other Victorian coloured glass

Jeanette Hayhurst Fine Glass
32a Kensington Church Street, London W8 4HA
Tel: 020 7938 1539

Lin Holroyd Antique Glass 11a Hardcastle Lane, Flockton, Wakefield, Yorkshire WF4 4AR Tel: 01924 848780

Just Glass Cross House, Market Place, Alston, Cumbria Tel: 01434 381263
Antique glass, Victorian decorative glass

Carol Ketley Antiques PO Box 16199, London NW1 7WD Tel: 020 7359 5529
Glassware, mirrors and decorative antiques

Marion Langham Claranagh, Tempo, Co Fermanagh, N Ireland BT94 3FJ
Tel: 028895 41247/020 7730 1002
Email: paperweights@ladymarion.co.uk
Websites: www.ladymarion.co.uk
www.ladymarion.co.uk/treasure
Paperweights

Andrew Lineham Fine Glass The Mall, Camden Passage, London N1 8ED
Tel: 01243 576241/020 7704 0195
Email: Andrew@AndrewLineham.co.uk
Website: www.AndrewLineham.co.uk
Continental and English coloured glass

Lillian Nassau 220 East 57th Street, New York City, NY USA

Passion for Glass Tel: 01745 888107

Ruskin Decorative Arts 5 Talbot Court, Stow-on-the-Wold, Cheltenham, Gloucestershire GL54 1DP Tel: 01451 832254
Specializing in the Decorative Arts 1860–1930. Arts & Crafts, Art Nouveau and Art Deco items. Cotswold School Movement including Guild of Handicraft, Gordon Russell and Gimson and The Barnsleys etc

Sarah Scott Antiques Court House Antiques Centre, 2–6 Town End Road, Ecclesfield, Sheffield, Yorkshire S35 9YY Tel: 0114 257 0641
Mirrors and lighting

Alan Sedgwick
E-mail: Alan.Sedgwick@BTInternet.com
Glass

Kevin A. Sives Antiques
Website: www.antiquez.com
US-based dealer specializing in American blown glass

Somervale Antiques 6 Radstock Road, Midsomer Norton, Bath, Somerset BA3 2AJ
Tel: 01761 412686 Open by appointment only
Email: ronthomas@somervaleantiquesglass.co.uk
Website: www.somervaleantiquesglass.co.uk
18th and early 19th century English drinking glasses, decanters, cut and coloured, 'Bristol' and 'Nailsea' glass. Also bijouterie, scent bottles etc

Sweetbriar Gallery Robin Hood Lane, Helsby, Cheshire WA6 9NH Tel: 01928 723851
Email: sweetbr@globalnet.co.uk
Website: www.sweetbriar.co.uk
Paperweights

Templar Antiques
Website: www.templar-antiques.co.uk
18th and 19th century English, Irish and Bohemian glass

Joscelyn Vereker Arbras Gallery, 292 Westbourne Grove, Portobello Market, London W11
Tel: 020 7237 9030

Brian Watson Antique Glass Foxwarren Cottage, High Street, Marsham, Norwich, Norfolk NR10 5QA
Tel: 01263 732519

Mark J. West Cobb Antiques Ltd, 39b High Street, Wimbledon Village, London SW19 5BY
Tel: 020 8946 2811

Key to Illustrations

Each illustration and descriptive caption is accompanied by a letter code. By referring to the following list of contributors, auctioneers (denoted by *) and dealers (•), the source of any item may be immediately determined. In no way does this constitute or imply a contract or binding offer on the part of any of our contributors to supply or sell the goods illustrated, or similar articles, at the prices stated. Advertisers are denoted by †.

A&A • Antiques & Art, 116 State Street, Portsmouth, USA NH 03802 Tel: 603–431–3931

AA • Ambeline Antiques, By George Antique Centre, St Albans, Hertfordshire AL3 4ES Tel: 01727 853032/020 8449 8307

AAV * Academy Auctioneers & Valuers, Northcote House, Northcote Avenue, Ealing, London W5 3UR Tel: 020 8579 7466 Website: www.thesaurus.co.uk/academy/

ABS • Abstract, 58–60 Kensington Church Street, London W8 4DB Tel: 020 7376 2652

ACA • Acorn Antiques, Sheep Street, Stow-on-the-Wold, Gloucestershire GL54 1AA Tel: 01451 831519

ADE • Art Deco Etc, 73 Upper Gloucester Road, Brighton, East Sussex BN1 3LQ Tel: 01273 329268 Email: poolepottery@artdeco.co.uk

AH * Andrew Hartley, Victoria Hall Salerooms, Little Lane, Ilkley, Yorkshire LS29 8EA Tel: 01943 816363 Email: ahartley.finearts@talk21.com

AHL • Adrian Hornsey Ltd, Langdons, Sidmouth Road, Clyst St Mary, Exeter EX5 1DR Tel: 01392 877395

AL • Ann Lingard, Ropewalk Antiques, Ropewalk, Rye, East Sussex TN31 7NA Tel: 01797 223486

ALiN •† Andrew Lineham Fine Glass, The Mall, Camden Passage, London N1 8ED Tel/Fax: 01243 576241/020 7704 0195 wed & sat Email: Andrew@AndrewLineham.co.uk Website: www.AndrewLineham.co.uk

AMH • Amherst Antiques, Monomark House, 27 Old Gloucester Street, London WC1N 3XX Tel/Fax: 01892 725552 Mobile 07850 350212 Email: amherstantiques@monomark.co.uk

ANO • Art Nouveau Originals, Stamford Antiques Centre, The Exchange Hall, Broad Street, Stamford, Lincolnshire PE9 1PX Tel: 01780 762605

AnS • The Antique Shop, 30 Henley Street, Stratford-Upon-Avon, Warwickshire CV37 6QW Tel: 01789 292485

ANT • Anthemion, Bridge Street, Cartmel, Grange Over Sands, Cumbria LA11 7SH Tel: 015395 36295 Mobile 0468 443757

ARE • Arenski, 185 Westbourne Grove, London W11 2SB Tel: 020 7727 8599

ART • Artemis Decorative Arts Ltd, 36 Kensington Church Street, London W8 4BX Tel: 020 7376 0377/ 020 7937 9900 Email: Artemis.w8@btinternet.com

ASA • A. S. Antiques, 26 Broad Street, Pendleton, Salford, Greater Manchester M6 5BY Tel: 0161 737 5938

ASe • Alan Sedgwick E-mail: Alan.Sedgwick@BTInternet.com

ASM • Art Smith Antiques at Wells Union, Route 1, 1755 Post Road, Wells ME 04090, USA 207 646 6996

B * Boardman Fine Art Auctioneers, Station Road Corner, Haverhill, Suffolk CB9 0EY Tel: 01440 730414

B&B * Butterfield & Butterfield, 220 San Bruno Avenue, San Francisco CA 94103, USA Tel: 00 1 415 861 7500

BBR * BBR, Elsecar Heritage Centre, Wath Road, Elsecar, Barnsley, Yorkshire S74 8HJ Tel: 01226 745156

Bea * Bearnes, Avenue Road, Torquay, Devon TQ2 5TG Tel: 01803 296277

BELL • Bell Antiques Tel: 0121 745 9034

BEN See TCG

BEV • Beverley, 30 Church Street, Marylebone, London NW8 8EP Tel: 020 7262 1576

BHa • Judy & Brian Harden Antiques, PO Box 14, Bourton on the Water, Cheltenham, Gloucestershire GL54 2YR Tel: 01451 810684

BIG * Bigwood Auctioneers Ltd, The Old School, Tiddington, Stratford-upon-Avon, Warwickshire CV37 7AW Tel: 01789 269415

BKK • Bona Art Deco Store, The Hart Shopping Centre, Fleet, Hampshire GU13 8AZ Tel: 01252 372188/616666 Website: www.bona.co.uk Email: rda@bona.co.uk

BKS * Bonhams & Brooks, Montpelier Street, Knightsbridge, London SW7 1HH Tel: 020 7393 3900 Website: www.bonhams.com

Bon * Bonhams & Brooks, Montpelier Street, Knightsbridge, London SW7 1HH Tel: 020 7393 3900

BON(C) * Bonhams & Brooks, 65–69 Lots Road, Chelsea, London SW10 0RN Tel: 020 7393 3900

BrW •† Brian Watson Antique Glass, Foxwarren Cottage, High Street, Marsham, Norwich NR10 5QA Tel/Fax: 01263 732519

BWA • Bow Well Antiques, 103 West Bow, Edinburgh, Scotland EH1 2JP Tel: 0131 225 3335

C * Christie, Manson & Wood Ltd, 8 King Street, St James's, London SW1Y 6QT Tel: 020 7839 9060

C(S) * Christie's Scotland Ltd, 164–166 Bath Street, Glasgow, Scotland G2 4TG Tel: 0141 332 8134

CAB • Candlestick & Bakelite, PO Box 308, Orpington, Kent BR5 1TB Tel: 020 8467 3743

CAG * The Canterbury Auction Galleries, 40 Station Road West, Canterbury, Kent CT2 8AN Tel: 01227 763337

Cai • Caithness Glass Ltd, Inveralmond, Perth, Scotland PH1 3TZ Tel: 01738 637373 Website: www.caithnessglass.co.uk

CaL • Warr & Pearce Antiques, No 6 First Floor, Georgian Village, Camden Passage, London N1 8DU Tel: 01206 212183

CAT • Lennox Cato, 1 The Square, Church Street, Edenbridge, Kent TN8 5BD Tel: 01732 865988 Mobile: 07836 233473

CB •† Christine Bridge, 78 Castelnau, London SW13 9EX Tel: 07000 445277 Email: christine@bridge-antiques.com Website: www.bridge-antiques.com www.antiqueglass.co.uk

CGC * Cheffins Grain & Comins, 2 Clifton Road, Cambridge CB2 4BW Tel: 01223 358731

CHA * Chislehurst Antiques, 7 Royal Parade, Chislehurst, Kent BR7 6NR Tel: 020 8467 1530

CMO • Brian Cargin & Chris Morley, Ginnell Antiques Gallery, 18–22 Lloyd Street, Greater Manchester M2 5WA Tel: 0161 833 9037

CNY * Christie Manson & Woods International Inc., 502 Park Avenue, (including Christie's East), New York, U.S.A. NY 10022 Tel: 01 212 546 1000

COL • Collectables, PO Box 130, Chatham, Kent ME5 0DZ Tel: 01634 828767

CSA • Church Street Antiques, 10 Church Street, Godalming, Surrey GU7 1EH Tel: 01483 860894

CSK * Christie's South Kensington Ltd, 85 Old Brompton Road, London SW7 3LD Tel: 020 7581 7611

DaD See DOC

DA * Dee, Atkinson & Harrison, The Exchange Saleroom, Driffield, Yorkshire YO25 7LJ Tel: 01377 253151 Email: exchange@dee-atkinson-harrison Website: www.dee-atkinson-harrison.co.uk

DAC • Didcot Antiques Centre, now Trading as Yetta Decorative Arts, Oxfordshire

DAF • Moderne, 14 Widcombe Parade, Bath, Somerset BA2 4JT Tel: 01225 465000

DBo • Dorothy Bowler, Ely Street Antique Centre, Stratford-on-Avon, Warwickshire CV37 6LN Tel: 01789 204180

DD * David Duggleby, The Vine St Salerooms, Scarborough, Yorkshire YO11 1XN Tel: 01723 507111 Email: auctions@davidduggleby.freeserve.co.uk Website: www.thesaurus.co.uk/david-duggleby

Del • Delomosne & Son Ltd, Court Close, North Wraxall, Chippenham, Wiltshire SN14 7AD Tel: 01225 891505

DKH • David K. Hakeney, PO Box 65, Hull, Humberside HU10 7XT Tel: 01482 651177

DLP • The Dunlop Collection, P. Box 6269, Statesville, NC 28687 USA Tel: (704) 871 2626 or Toll Free Telephone (800) 227 1996

DN * Dreweatt Neate, Donnington Priory, Donnington, Newbury, Berkshire RG13 2JE Tel: 01635 553553

DOC * Dockree's, Cheadle Hulme Centre, Clemence House, Mellor Road, Cheadle Hulme, Cheshire SK8 5AT Tel: 0161 485 1258

DOL • Dollectable, 53 Lower Bridge Street, Chester
CH1 1RS Tel: 01244 344888/679195

DORO * Dorotheum, Palais Dorotheum, A-1010 Wien
Dorotheegasse, 17 1010 Austria Tel: 0043 1 515 600

DQ • Dolphin Quay Antique Centre, Queen Street,
Emsworth, Hampshire PO10 7BU
Tel: 01243 379994/379994

DRU • Drummond's Architectural Antiques, The Kirk Patrick
Buildings, 25 London Road (A3), Hindhead,
Surrey GU26 6AB Tel: 01428 609444

DSG • Delf Stream Gallery, 14 New Street, Sandwich,
Kent CT13 9AB Tel: 01304 617684

DUD • Dudley Howe, SO55/56/57 Alfies Antique Market,
13–25 Church Street, London NW8 8DT
Tel: 020 7723 6066

DuM * Du Mouchelles, 409 East Jefferson, Detroit, Michigan
48226 USA Tel: 001 313 963 0248

DUN • Richard Dunton, 920 Christchurch Road, Boscombe,
Bournemouth, Dorset BH7 6DL Tel: 01202 425963

E * Ewbank, Burnt Common Auction Rooms, London
Road, Send, Woking, Surrey GU23 7LN
Tel: 01483 223101

FBG * Frank H. Boos Gallery, 420 Enterprise Court,
Bloomfield Hills, Michigan 48302 USA
Tel: 001 248 332 1500

FD • Frank Dux Antiques, 33 Belvedere, Bath, Somerset
BA1 5HR Tel: 01225 312367

FMN • Forget Me Not Antiques, Over the Moon,
27 High Street, St Albans, Hertfordshire AL3 4EH
Tel: 01727 53032/01923 261172

FW&C • Finan & Co, The Square, Mere, Wiltshire BA12 6DJ
Tel: 01747 861411

GAK * G A Key, Aylsham Salerooms, 8 Market Place,
Aylsham, Norfolk NR11 6EH Tel: 01263 733195

Gam * Clarke Gammon, The Guildford Auction Rooms,
Bedford Road, Guildford, Surrey GU1 4SJ
Tel: 01483 880915

Gar • Garry, Alfies Antique Market, 13–25 Church Street,
Marylebone, London NW8 8DT Tel: 020 7723 6066

GAZ * Thomas Wm Gaze & Son, Diss Auction Rooms,
Roydon Road, Diss, Norfolk IP22 3LN
Tel: 01379 650306 Website: www.twgaze.com

GFR • Geoffrey Robinson, G077–78 (Ground floor) Alfies
Antique Market, 13–25 Church Street, Marylebone,
London NW8 8DT Tel: 020 7723 0449

GH * Gardiner Houlgate, The Bath Auction Rooms,
9 Leafield Way, Corsham, Nr Bath,
Somerset SN13 9SW Tel: 01225 812912
Email: gardiner-houlgate.co.uk
Website: www.invaluable.com/gardiner-houlgate

GIN • The Ginnell Gallery Antique Centre,
18–22 Lloyd Street, Greater Manchester M2 5WA
Tel: 0161 833 9037

GLA • Glasform Ltd, 123 Talbot Road, Blackpool,
Lancashire FY1 3QY Tel: 01253 626410
Email: Glasform@btinternet.com
Website: www.btinternet.com/-glasform

GLN • Glenville Antiques, 120 High Street, Yatton,
Avon BS19 4DH Tel: 01934 832284

GRI •† Grimes House Antiques, High Street, Moreton-in-
Marsh, Gloucestershire GL56 0AT
Tel/Fax: 01608 651029 Email: grimes_house@cix.co.uk
Websites: www.cranberryglass.co.uk
www.collectglass.com

GS • Ged Selby. By appointment Tel: 01756 799673

Hal * Halls Fine Art Auctions, Welsh Bridge, Shrewsbury,
Shropshire SY3 8LA Tel: 01743 231212

HAM * Hamptons International, Baverstock House,
93 High Street, Godalming, Surrey GU7 1AL
Tel: 01483 423567 Email: fineart@hamptons-int.com
Website: www.hamptons.co.uk

Har • Hardy's Collectables/Hardy's Clobber,
862 & 874 Christchurch Road, Boscombe,
Bournemouth, Dorset BH7 6DQ
Tel: 01202 422407/473744 Mobile 07970 613077

HCC * H C Chapman & Son, The Auction Mart, North Street,
Scarborough, Yorkshire YO11 1DL Tel: 01723 372424

HEI • Heirloom Antiques, 68 High Street, Tenterden,
Kent TN30 6AU Tel: 01580 765535

HEM • Hemswell Antique Centre, Caenby Corner Estate,
Hemswell Cliff, Gainsborough, Lincolnshire DN21 5TJ
Tel: 01427 668389

HEW • Muir Hewitt, Halifax Antiques Centre, Queens Road,
Gibbet Street, Halifax, Yorkshire HX1 4LR
Tel: 01422 347377

HofB • Howards of Broadway, 27A High Street, Broadway,
Worcestershire WR12 7DP Tel: 01386 858924

HOK * Hamilton Osborne King, 4 Main Street, Blackrock,
Co. Dublin, Republic of Ireland Tel: 353 1 288 5011
Email: blackrock@hok.ie Website: www.hok.ie

HOLL * Dreweatt Neate Holloways, 49 Parsons Street,
Banbury, Oxfordshire OX16 8PF Tel: 01295 253197

HSS * Phillips, 20 The Square, Retford, Nottinghamshire
DN22 6BX Tel: 01777 708633

HUX • David Huxtable, Stand S03/05 (Top Floor),
Alfies Antique Market, 13–25 Church Street,
Marylebone, London NW8 8DT Tel: 020 7724 2200

HYD * Hy Duke & Son, Dorchester Fine Art Salerooms,
Dorchester, Dorset DT1 1QS Tel: 01305 265080

INC • The Incurable Collector Tel: 01932 860800

ING • Inglewood Antiques, Ely St Antique Centre,
Stratford-upon-Avon, Warwickshire CV37 6LN
Tel: 01789 297496

JAA * Jackson's Auctioneers & Appraisers,
2229 Lincoln Street, Cedar Falls, USA IA 50613
Tel: 00 1 319 277 2256

JAd * James Adam & Sons, 26 St Stephen's Green,
Dublin 2, Republic of Ireland Tel: 00 3531 676 0261

JAS • Jasmin Cameron, Antiquarius, 131–141 King's Road,
London SW3 4PW Tel/Fax: 020 7351 4154
Mobile 077 74 871257

JFG • Jafar Gallery Tel: 020 8300 2727

JHa •† Jeanette Hayhurst Fine Glass, 32a Kensington Church
Street, London W8 4HA Tel/Fax: 020 7938 1539

JL • Joy Luke, The Gallery, 300E Grove Street,
Bloomington, USA IL 61701 Tel: 001 309 828 5533

JMC • J & M Collectables Tel: 01580 891657

JPr • Joanna Proops Antique Textiles, 34 Belvedere,
Lansdown Hill, Bath, Somerset BA1 5HR
Tel: 01225 310795

JUN • Junktion, The Old Railway Station, New Bolingbroke,
Boston, Lincolnshire PE22 7LB Tel: 01205 480068

KAC • Kensington Antique Centre, 58–60 Kensington Church
Street, London W8 4DB Tel: 020 7376 0425

L * Lawrence Fine Art Auctioneers, South Street,
Crewkerne, Somerset TA18 8AB Tel: 01460 73041

L&E * BBG Locke & England, 18 Guy Street, Leamington
Spa, Warwickshire CV32 4RT Tel: 01926 889100
Website: http://www.auctions-online.com/locke

LBr • Lynda Brine, Assembly Antique Centre, 5–8 Saville
Row, Bath, Somerset BA1 2QP Tel: 01225 448488

LEN See CAT

LF * Lambert & Foster, 102 High Street, Tenterden,
Kent TN30 6HT Tel: 01580 763233

LIB • Libra Antiques 01580 860569

LIO • Lions Den, 11 St Mary's Crescent, Leamington Spa,
Warwickshire CV31 1JL Tel: 01926 339498

LRG * Lots Road Galleries, 71–73 Lots Road, Chelsea,
London SW10 0RN Tel: 020 7351 7771

LT * Louis Taylor Auctioneers & Valuers, Britannia House,
10 Town Road, Hanley, Stoke-on-Trent, Staffordshire
ST1 2QG Tel: 01782 214111

MAC • The Mall Antique Centre, 400 Wincolmlee, Hull,
Humberside HU2 0QL Tel: 01482 327858

MARK • 20th Century Marks, 12 Market Square, Westerham,
Kent TN16 1AW Tel: 01959 562221
Email: lambarda@msn.com

MAT * Christopher Matthews, 23 Mount Street, Harrogate,
Yorkshire HG2 8DQ Tel: 01423 871756

MCA * Mervyn Carey, Twysden Cottage, Benenden,
Cranbrook, Kent TN17 4LD Tel: 01580 240283

McC * McCartneys, Ox Pasture, Overture Road, Ludlow,
Shropshire SY8 4AA Tel: 01584 872251

MEA * Mealy's, Chatsworth Street, Castle Comer, Co
Kilkenny, Republic of Ireland Tel: 00 353 56 41229

MEG • Megarry's and Forever Summer, Jericho Cottage,
The Duckpond Green, Blackmore, Essex CM4 0RR
Tel: 01277 821031 and 01277 822170

Mit * Mitchells, Fairfield House, Station Road,
Cockermouth, Cumbria CA13 9PY Tel: 01900 827800

MJW • Mark J West, Cobb Antiques Ltd, 39b High Street,
Wimbledon Village, London SW19 5BY
Tel: 020 8946 2811

ML • Magic Lantern (Josie Marsden), By George Antique
Centre, 23 George Street, St Albans, Hertfordshire
AL3 4ES Tel: 01727 853032

MLa •† Marion Langham Tel: 020 7730 1002
Email: paperweights@ladymarion.co.uk
Website: www.ladymarion.co.uk
www.ladymarion.co.uk/treasure

MON • Monty Lo, Stand 369, Grays Antique Market,
58 Davies Street, London W1Y 1AR Tel: 020 7493 9457

MoS • Morgan Stobbs. By appointment Mobile 0402 206817

MRT • Mark Rees Tools Tel: 01225 837031

MRW • Malcolm Russ-Welch, PO Box 1122, Rugby,
Warwickshire CV23 9YD Tel: 01788 810 616

MSh • Manfred Schotten, The Crypt Antiques,
109 High Street, Burford, Oxfordshire OX18 4RG
Tel: 01993 822302

N * Neales, 192–194 Mansfield Road,
Nottingham NG1 3HU Tel: 0115 962 4141

N(A) * Amersham Auction Rooms, 125 Station Road,
Amersham, Buckinghamshire HP7 0AH Tel: 01494
729292 Website: www.thesaurus.co.uk/amersham

NCA • New Century, 69 Kensington Church Street, London
W8 4BG Tel: 020 7376 2810/020 7937 2410

NF • Nick Fletcher, PO Box 411, Longton, Stoke-on-Trent,
Staffordshire ST3 4SS

NOA * New Orleans Auction Galleries, Inc., 801 Magazine
Street, AT 510 Julia, New Orleans, Louisiana 70130
USA Tel: 00 1 504 566 1849

NWi • Neil Wilcox, 113 Strawberry Vale, Twickenham,
Middlesex TW1 4SJ Tel: 020 8892 5858

OBS • The Old Button Shop, Lytchett Minster, Poole,
Dorset BH16 6JF Tel: 01202 622169

OCA • The Old Cinema, 160 Chiswick High Road,
London W4 1PR Tel: 020 8995 4166

OD • Offa's Dyke Antique Centre, 4 High Street, Knighton,
Powys, Wales LD7 1AT Tel: 01547 528635/528940

OO • Pieter Oosthuizen, Unit 4 Bourbon Hanby Antiques
Centre, 151 Sydney Street, London SW3 6NT
Tel: 020 7460 3078

OOLA • Oola Boola, 166 Tower Bridge Road, London
SE1 3LS Tel: 020 7403 0794/020 8693 5050
Mobile 0956 261252

P * Phillips, 101 New Bond Street, London W1Y 0AS
Tel: 020 7629 6602

P(B) * Phillips, 1 Old King Street, Bath, Somerset BA1 2JT
Tel: 01225 310609

P(E) * Phillips, Alphin Brook Road, Alphington, Exeter,
Devon EX2 8TH Tel: 01392 439025

P(F) * Phillips, Folkestone

P(NE) * Phillips North East, 30/32 Grey Street, Newcastle
Upon Tyne, Tyne & Wear NE1 6AE Tel: 0191 233 9930

P(O) * Phillips, 39 Park End Street, Oxford OX1 1JD
Tel: 01865 723524

P(S) * Phillips, 49 London Road, Sevenoaks,
Kent TN13 1AR Tel: 01732 740310

PC Private Collection

PCh * Peter Cheney, Western Road Auction Rooms,
Western Road, Littlehampton, West Sussex
BN17 5NP Tel: 01903 722264/713418

PGA • Paul Gibbs Antiques, 25 Castle Street, Conwy,
Gwynedd, Wales LL32 8AY Tel: 01492 593429
Email: teapot@marketsite.co.uk

PSA • Pantiles Spa Antiques, 4, 5, 6 Union House, The Pantiles,
Tunbridge Wells, Kent TN4 8HE Tel: 01892 541377

PSG • Patrick & Susan Gould Tel/Fax: 020 8993 5879

Rac/
RAC • Field, Staff & Woods, 93 High Street, Rochester, Kent
ME1 1LX Tel: 01634 846144

RAG * Rye Auction Galleries, Rock Channel, Rye,
East Sussex TN31 7HL Tel: 01797 222124

RBB • Brightwells Ltd, Ryelands Road, Leominster,
Herefordshire HR6 8NZ Tel: 01568 611122
Email: fineart@rbbm.co.uk Website: www.rbbm.co.uk

RCh • Rayner & Chamberlain Tel: 020 8293 9439

RID * Riddetts of Bournemouth, 177 Holden Hurst Road,
Bournemouth, Dorset BH8 8DQ Tel: 01202 555686

RIT * Ritchie Inc., D & J Auctioneers & Appraisers of
Antiques & Fine Arts, 288 King Street East, Toronto,
Ontario, Canada M5A 1K4 Tel: (416) 364 1864

RTo * Rupert Toovey & Co Ltd, Star Road, Partridge Green,
West Sussex RH13 8RA Tel: 01403 711744
Website: www.rupert-toovey.com

RUL • Rules Antiques, 62 St Leonards Road, Windsor,
Berkshire SL4 3BY Tel: 01753 833210/01491 642062

RUSK • Ruskin Decorative Arts, 5 Talbot Court, Stow-on-the-
Wold, Cheltenham, Gloucestershire GL54 1DP
Tel: 01451 832254

S * Sotheby's, 34–35 New Bond Street,
London W1A 2AA Tel: 020 7293 5000

S(Am) * Sotheby's Amsterdam, De Boelelaan 30, 1083 HJ
Amsterdam, Netherlands Tel: 00 31 20 550 22 00

S(NY) * Sotheby's, 1334 York Avenue, New York, USA
NY 10021 Tel: 00 1 212 606 7000

S(S) * Sotheby's Sussex, Summers Place, Billingshurst,
West Sussex RH14 9AD Tel: 01403 833500

S(Z) * Sotheby's Zurich, Gessneralee 1, CH-8021 Zurich,
Switzerland Tel: 00 41 1 226 2200

SER • Serendipity, 125 High Street, Deal, Kent CT14 6BQ
Tel: 01304 369165/366536

SFL • The Silver Fund Ltd, 40 Bury Street, St James's,
London SW1Y 6AU Tel: 020 7839 7664

SHa • Shapiro & Co, Stand 380, Gray's Antique Market,
58 Davies Street, London W1Y 1LB Tel: 020 7491 2710

SK * Skinner Inc, The Heritage On The Garden, 63 Park Plaza,
Boston, USA MA 02116 Tel: 001 617 350 5400

SK(B) * Skinner Inc, 357 Main Street, Bolton, USA
MA 01740 Tel: 00 1 978 779 6241

SLN * Sloan's, C G Sloan & Company Inc, 4920 Wyaconda
Road, North Bethesda, USA MD 20852
Tel: 00 1 301 468 4911/669 5066

Som •† Somervale Antiques, 6 Radstock Road, Midsomer
Norton, Bath, Somerset BA3 2AJ
Tel/Fax: 01761 412686 Mobile 07885 088022
Email: ronthomas@somervaleantiquesglass.co.uk
Website: www.somervaleantiquesglass.co.uk

STG • Stone Gallery, 93 The High Street, Burford,
Oxfordshire OX18 4QA Tel/Fax: 01993 823302

SUC • Succession, 18 Richmond Hill, Richmond, Surrey
TW10 6QX Tel: 020 8940 6774

SUL • Sullivan Antiques (Chantal O'Sullivan),
43–44 Francis Street, Dublin 8, Republic of Ireland
Tel: 00 3531 4541143/4539659

SUS • Susannah, 142/144 Walcot Street, Bath,
Somerset BA1 5BL Tel: 01225 445069

SWB •† Sweetbriar Gallery, Robin Hood Lane, Helsby,
Cheshire WA6 9NH Tel: 01928 723851
Email: sweetbr@globalnet.co.uk
Website: www.sweetbriar.co.uk

TAC • Tenterden Antiques Centre, 66–66A High Street,
Tenterden, Kent TN30 6AU Tel: 01580 765655/765885

TAR • Lorraine Tarrant Antiques, 23 Market Place,
Ringwood, Hampshire BH24 1AN Tel: 01425 461123

TC • Timothy Coward Tel: 01271 890466

TCG • 20th Century Glass, Nigel Benson, Kensington
Church Street Antique Centre, 58–60 Kensington
Church Street, London W8 4DB Tel: 020 7938 1137
Tel/Fax: 020 7729 9875 Mobile 07971 859848

TEN * Tennants, The Auction Centre, Harmby Road,
Leyburn, Yorkshire DL8 5SG Tel: 01969 623780

TER • Terrace Antiques, 10 & 12 South Ealing Road, London
W5 4QA Tel: 020 8567 5194/8567 1223

THOM • S & A Thompson Tel/Fax: 01306 711970
Mobile 0370 882846

TMA * Brown & Merry, Tring Market Auctions, Brook Street,
Tring, Hertfordshire HP23 5EF Tel: 01442 826446
Email: sales@tringmarketauctions.co.uk
Website: www.tringmarketauctions.co.uk

TRU • The Trumpet, West End, Minchinhampton,
Gloucestershire GL6 9JA Tel: 01453 883027

TS • Tim's Spot, Ely Street Antique Centre,
Stratford-upon-Avon, Warwickshire CV37 6LN
Tel: 01789 297496/204182

TVM • Teresa Vanneck-Murray, Vanneck House,
22 Richmond Hill, Richmond Upon Thames,
Surrey TW10 6QX Tel: 020 8940 2035

TWa • Time Warp, c/o Curioser & Curioser, Sydney Street,
Brighton, East Sussex BN1 Tel: 01273 821243

TWr • Tim Wright Antiques, Richmond Chambers,
147 Bath Street, Glasgow G2 4SQ Tel: 0141 221 0364

VB • Variety Box, 16 Chapel Place, Tunbridge Wells,
Kent TN1 1YQ Tel: 01892 531868

WAB • Warboys Antiques, Old Church School, High Street,
Warboys, Cambridge PE17 2SX Tel: 01487 823686

WAC • Worcester Antiques Centre, Reindeer Court,
Mealcheapen Street, Worcester WR1 4DF
Tel: 01905 610680

WAG • The Weald Antiques Gallery, 106 High Street,
Tenterden, Kent TN30 6HT Tel: 01580 762939

WBH * Walker, Barnett & Hill, Waterloo Road Salerooms,
Clarence Street, Wolverhampton,
West Midlands WV1 4JE Tel: 01902 773531

WeH • Westerham House Antiques, The Green, Westerham,
Kent TN16 1AY Tel: 01959 561622/562200

WIL * Peter Wilson, Victoria Gallery, Market Street,
Nantwich, Cheshire CW5 5DG Tel: 01270 623878

WL * Wintertons Ltd, Lichfield Auction Centre, Wood End
Lane, Fradley, Lichfield, Staffordshire WS13 8NF
Tel: 01543 263256

WN • What Now, Cavendish Arcade, The Crescent, Buxton,
Derbyshire SK17 6BQ Tel: 01298 27178/23417

WTA Witney and Airault 20th Century Decorative Arts

WW * Woolley & Wallis, Salisbury Salerooms,
51–61 Castle Street, Salisbury, Wiltshire SP1 3SU
Tel: 01722 424500

ZEI • Zeitgeist Antiques, 58 Kensington Church Street,
London W8 4DB Tel/Fax:Q 020 7938 4817

Glossary

acid etching cold decoration technique in which the surface of the glass is partially covered with a wax or resin then submerged in acid, which bites into the exposed areas.

air-twist a stem in which fine, spiralling channels of air are trapped, created by piercing a **gather** of molten glass with a ring of needles, then drawing it out lengthwise while twisting it.

Ariel technique of creating air-bubble designs in glass by sandblasting a pattern in deep relief on to a clear or multicoloured **blank**, then reheating and casing the blank in a layer of clear glass so that the design is captured in trails of air. Developed by Orrefors in 1937.

aventurine from the Italian for 'chance', a decoration of flecked metallic particles.

baluster glass drinking glass with a swelling at the base of the stem, rising in a concave curve to a narrow stem or neck.

balustroid a taller, lighter form of **baluster**.

blank a partially formed vessel or sculpture which has been allowed to cool so that it can be treated to various cold decoration techniques, such as cutting, acid-etching, or sandblasting. With **Ariel** and **Graal**, the blank is then reheated and cased with another layer of glass.

blazes fine flutes cut in glass, with the tallest in the centre. They can also be slanting.

blowing a technique of producing glass vessels by blowing a molten mass of glass, or **gather**, through a blowpipe, either freehand or into a mould.

Burmese glass an opaque, heat-sensitive glass.

cameo glass two or more layers of coloured glass in which the top layer/s are then cut or etched away to create a multi-coloured design in relief. An ancient technique popular with Art Nouveau glassmakers in the early 20thC.

canes rods of glass drawn by the glass-blower to required thickness for use as decoration.

cased glass one layer of glass, often coloured, sandwiched between two plain glass layers or vice versa, the outer layer engraved to create a decorative effect. An ancient technique revived in the 19thC. See **cameo glass** and **overlay**.

cordial a small drinking glass for liqueurs.

core-forming a technique of producing a glass vessel by shaping **trails** of molten glass over a core usually made from mud or clay, and fusing them together in a furnace; the core is carved or acid-etched out when cool.

cranberry glass transparent, reddish-pink glass, in America named after the fruit. Originally known as **ruby glass**.

cristallo type of **soda glass** developed in 15thC Venice, made with soda derived from the ashes of the barilla plant.

crizzling where an imbalance in the glass batch has caused the surface of the glass to become fogged by a network of tiny cracks.

diamond-point engraving minutely detailed, fine line decoration using a stiletto-type tool with a sharp diamond point.

engraving lightly-abraded matt surface decoration created with a fine copper wheel.

faceting technique used to decorate curved glass surfaces by grinding to create flat, geometric sections.

façon de Venise French, meaning 'in the Venetian style', used to describe high quality, Venetian-influenced glassware made in Europe during the 16th–17thC.

faïence a substance made from finely-ground quartz (a form of silica) covered with a glass-like vitreous glaze.

firing glass a low drinking glass, with a short, thick stem and a thick foot, used on ceremonial occasions when, after toasting, the glass would be rapped on the table. Also known as a 'bumping glass'.

flashed a method of colouring glass that involves applying a thin layer of coloured glass to a vessel, either by painting it or dipping it into a pot of colourant; flashed glass can be carved to produce a less expensive version of overlay glass.

flint glass alternative name for **lead glass**.

flux an alkaline substance added to the glass batch to aid fusion of ingredients.

folded foot the foot of a glass with its rim turned slightly under to provide a more solid, stable base.

gather ball of molten glass collected from the furnace on the end of an iron rod before a vessel is formed.

gilding a technique of glass decoration that involves painting the glass surface with gold leaf, gold dust or gold paint and then firing to fix the design.

Graal technique of creating a coloured pattern within the wall of a vessel, developed by Orrefors in 1916. The process involves making a small, cased **blank**, which is then cut, engraved, or acid-etched with a pattern. The **blank** is then reheated, cased with clear glass, and blown into its final form, leaving the expanded pattern suspended inside the wall.

holophane glass prismatic pressed glass, very popular for lampshades because of its refractive qualities which maximized and evenly distributed the light without glare.

Humpen tall, cylindrical German beer glass made from the mid-16thC to the 18thC.

intaglio incised decoration, the opposite of carving in relief.

intercalaire a technique whereby pieces would be **cameo**-carved – usually by laminating two layers of glass together – and then covered with a layer of carved or etched semi-transparent glass.

iridescence rainbow-like surface effect created with lustre colours, or by exposing the piece to hot vapours of metal oxides.

Jacobite glass 18thC glassware celebrating Bonnie Prince Charlie and his descendants and decorated with Jacobite symbols, motifs and mottoes.

kick indentation in the base of a glass vessel where the **pontil** rod is attached.

knop a swelling, which can be solid or hollow, on the stem of a glass.

lampwork glass that is blown or manipulated from clear or coloured glass rods over a blow lamp or torch.

latticinio lace glass. Fine threads of white or clear glass in filigree mesh effects enclosed in clear glass. Ancient technique perfected by Venetians and found, for example, in some **millefiori** paperweights and Nailsea glass.

lattimo from the Italian *latte* meaning 'milk'; an opaque white glass made by adding bone ash or tin oxide to the glass batch.

lead glass formerly known as **flint** glass, has a high lead content, suitable for cutting and faceting.

Lithyalin polished, opaque glass resembling hardstones, patented by Friedrich Egermann in 1829 at his factory in Haida, northern Bohemia.

'lost-wax' casting a technique in which a wax model is cased in plaster and the wax is then steamed out (lost) to make a mould for *pâte-de-cristal* and *pâte-de-verre*.

lustres metal oxides suspended in an oily material and used for painting onto hot glass.

malachite a marble-effect opaque pressed glass.

marqueterie-sur-verre a technique developed by Émille Gallé, in which localized blobs, or 'pads', of coloured glass were **marvered** into the gather, often part of the **cameo glass** process.

marver hard, flat surface made of metal or stone, used by the glassmaker for rolling and smoothing the gather and picking up decorative materials such as ground enamels or gold leaf.

merese a flat disk of glass which links the bowl and stem, and sometimes the stem and foot, on a drinking glass.

metal term used to describe hot or cold glass.

milchglas milk glass or *lattimo*, an opaque white glass made by adding bone ash or tin oxide to the glass batch, to look like white porcelain.

millefiori Italian, meaning 'a thousand flowers', multi-coloured, or mosaic, glass made by fusing a number of coloured glass rods into a cane, and cutting off thin sections; much used in paperweights.

murrhines slices of decorative glass canes, sometimes described as mosaic sections, made of transparent or opaque coloured glass. They include the rosette-shaped **millefiori**, as well as others decorated with more abstract patterns.

ogee bowl cylindrical bowl with a concave curve where it joins the stem.

opalescent glass a type of glass that appears to have fiery internal highlights.

opaque-twist a stem enclosing fine, spiralling threads of opaque glass, which can be white or coloured.

overlay in cased glass, the top layer, usually engraved to reveal a different-coloured layer beneath.

pâte-de-cristal a French term meaning 'crystal paste'; translucent glassware made from very finely powdered glass made into a paste and shaped using the '**lost-wax**' method.

pâte-de-verre translucent glass created by melting and applying powdered glass in layers or by casting it in a mould.

pontil mark a mark in the centre of the base of a blown glass object, made when the pontil, or iron rod, used during glass manufacture, is broken off.

pot a crucible in which glass is melted.

pressed glass glass made by the technique of pouring molten glass into a metal mould and pressing it to the sides using a metal plunger.

Primrose the name of Davidson's yellow opalescent glass.

printies impressions in the glass, similar to thumbprints.

prunts blobs of glass applied to the stem of a drinking vessel both as decoration and to stop the glass from slipping in the hand.

Queensware opaque, warm-cream vitro-porcelain glass that imitated later 18thC creamware. The name was borrowed from Wedgwood by Sowerby glassmakers.

roemer traditional German low drinking vessel with an ovoid bowl and a cylindrical stem with applied **prunts** and a spreading foot.

ruby glass a richly-coloured red glass created by adding copper or gold oxide to the glass mix, also known as **cranberry glass**.

rummer a 19thC English low drinking goblet, traditionally used for drinking rum and water. (German **roemer**).

satin glass glass with a satin finish.

slag glass glass with a marbled or malachite effect resulting from waste slag from metal being included in the glass.

soda glass light, malleable glass with a slightly brownish or greenish tinge, has no lead content and does not ring when struck. Made by using sodium carbonate as a flux; sodium carbonate can be derived from various sources. See *cristallo*.

staining a method of colouring glass by painting the surface with metal oxide, and reheating to fix the colour.

star-cutting multiple cuts meeting at a central point to create a star effect.

stipple engraving see **diamond-point engraving**.

studio glass one-off pieces designed and produced by artist-craftsmen.

syllabub glass a vessel for drinking syllabub, a popular drink in the 17th and 18thC, made from cream whipped to a froth with sherry ratafia and spices.

tazza wide but shallow bowl on a stem with a foot; ceramic and metal tazzas were made in antiquity and the shape was revived by Venetian glassmakers in the 15thC.

tear air bubble, in the shape of a tear, encased in the stem of a glass.

tesserae thin slices of circular, square, or rectangular coloured glass, often patterned, used to decorate the surface of blown glass vessels. Tesserae are created by slicing vertically or horizontally through pre-formed coloured canes. See **murrhines**.

thistle glass a drinking glass in the form of a thistle.

torsade an ornamental twist.

trails or trailing, a decorative technique where strands of glass are drawn out from a gather and trailed over a glass surface.

transfer-printing design printed on paper from an engraved copper plate and applied to the surface of a piece.

twists decorations in drinking glass stems produced by twisting one or several rods of glass. There are said to be over 150 varieties of twists, ranging from **air-twists**, using embedded columns of air, to **opaque-twists**, decorated with threads of opaque glass.

uranium glass an acid-green or yellow radio-active glass that contains **uranium oxide**, also known as **vaseline glass**.

uranium oxide a powder added to the **batch** to produce sharp yellows or greens.

vaseline glass glass containing **uranium oxide**, giving a yellowish 'vaseline' effect.

vetro a reticello a criss-cross or network pattern.

vitro-porcelain a glass that looks like ceramic.

Waldglas ('Forest glass') type of greenish-yellow glass originally produced in Germany in the Middle Ages.

wheel-engraved a form of decoration achieved by abrading the surface with a rotating copper wheel.

wheel-carved a technique of abrading **cameo glass** using a rotating stone or copper wheel.

wrythen twisted or plaited.

Index to Advertisers

Index

Italic page numbers denote colour pages; **bold** numbers refer to introductions and information boxes.